Women, Horse Sports, and Liberation

This book is the first full-length scholarly examination of British women's involvement in equestrianism from the eighteenth through the twentieth centuries, as well as the corresponding transformations of gender, class, sport, and national identity in Britain and its Empire.

It argues that women's participation in horse sports transcended limitations of class and gender in Britain and highlights the democratic ethos that allowed anyone skilled enough to ride and hunt – from chimney-sweep to courtesan. Furthermore, women's involvement in equestrianism reshaped ideals of race and reinforced imperial ideology at the zenith of the British Empire. Here, British women abandoned the sidesaddle – which they had been riding in for almost half a millennium – to ride astride like men, thus gaining complete equality on horseback. Yet female equestrians did not seek further emancipation in the form of political rights. This paradox – of achieving equality through sport but not through politics – shows how liberating sport was for women into the twentieth century. It also brings into question what "emancipation" meant in practice to women in Britain from the eighteenth through twentieth centuries.

This is fascinating reading for scholars of sports history, women's history, British history, and imperial history, as well as those interested in the broader social, gendered, and political histories of the nineteenth and twentieth centuries, and for all equestrian enthusiasts.

Erica Munkwitz is Professorial Lecturer in Modern British and European history at American University in Washington, D.C., U.S.A. Her research focuses on gender, sport, and empire in modern Britain, and specifically on women's involvement in equestrianism. In 2016, she received the Junior/Early Career Scholar Award from the European Committee for Sports History, and, in 2018, she received the Solidarity Prize for Excellence in Early Career Equine Research.

Routledge Research in Sports History

The *Routledge Research in Sports History* series presents leading research in the development and historical significance of modern sport through a collection of historiographical, regional, and thematic studies that span a variety of periods, sports, and geographical areas. Showcasing ground-breaking, cross-disciplinary work from established and emerging sport historians, the series provides a crucial contribution to the wider study of sport and society.
Available in this series:

A History of Chinese Martial Arts
Edited by Fan Hong and Fuhua Huang

The Early Development of Football
Contemporary Debates
Edited by Graham Curry

Sport, War, and the British
1850 to the Present
Peter Donaldson

The Emergence of Football
Sport, Culture, and Society in the Nineteenth Century
Peter Swain

Britain's Olympic Women
A History
Jean Williams

Women, Horse Sports, and Liberation
Equestrianism and Britain from the 18th to the 20th Centuries
Erica Munkwitz

For more information about this series, please visit: www.routledge.com/sport/series/RRSH

Women, Horse Sports, and Liberation

Equestrianism and Britain from the 18th to the 20th Centuries

Erica Munkwitz

LONDON AND NEW YORK

First published 2021
by Routledge
2 Park Square, Milton Park, Abingdon, Oxon OX14 4RN

and by Routledge
52 Vanderbilt Avenue, New York, NY 10017

Routledge is an imprint of the Taylor & Francis Group, an informa business

© 2021 Erica Munkwitz

The right of Erica Munkwitz to be identified as author of this work has been asserted by her in accordance with sections 77 and 78 of the Copyright, Designs and Patents Act 1988.

All rights reserved. No part of this book may be reprinted or reproduced or utilized in any form or by any electronic, mechanical, or other means, now known or hereafter invented, including photocopying and recording, or in any information storage or retrieval system, without permission in writing from the publishers.

Trademark notice: Product or corporate names may be trademarks or registered trademarks, and are used only for identification and explanation without intent to infringe.

British Library Cataloguing-in-Publication Data
A catalogue record for this book is available from the British Library

Library of Congress Cataloging-in-Publication Data
Names: Munkwitz, Erica, author.
Title: Women, horse sports and liberation : equestrianism and Britain from the 18th to the 20th centuries / Erica Munkwitz.
Description: Abingdon, Oxon ; New York, NY : Routledge, 2021. | Series: Routledge research in sports history | Includes bibliographical references and index. | Identifiers: LCCN 2020051427 | ISBN 9780367209506 (hardback) | ISBN 9780429264351 (ebook)
Subjects: LCSH: Women in horse sports--Great Britain--History--18th century. | Women in horse sports--Great Britain--History--19th century. | Women in horse sports--Great Britain--History--20th century.
Classification: LCC SF294.27.G7 M86 2021 | DDC 798.20820941--dc23
LC record available at https://lccn.loc.gov/2020051427

ISBN: 978-0-367-20950-6 (hbk)
ISBN: 978-0-367-76957-4 (pbk)
ISBN: 978-0-429-26435-1 (ebk)

Typeset in Goudy
by MPS Limited, Dehradun

For my family – for everything.

Table of Contents

Acknowledgments		viii
Introduction: The Development of Horsemanship, Gender Construction, and National Identity in Britain		1
1	Ladies, Hunting, and the Sporting Revolution in Britain, 1772–1825	44
2	Horseback Riding as Exercise and Female Accomplishment, 1805–1857	88
3	Fox Hunting and Sporting Emancipation for Women, 1857–1913	136
4	Horse Sports, Imperial Ideology, and Gender Construction in British India, 1850–1913	181
5	Femininity, Sporting Equality, and Riding Astride in Britain Before and After the First World War, 1894–1932	228
	Conclusion: Equestrianism, Feminism, and the Olympic Games, 1932–1956	283
	Index	301

Acknowledgments

This book encompasses over 13 years of sustained academic research as well as a lifetime of practical experience and equestrian expertise. Because of this, I fear that I have inadvertently forgotten many of the people and institutions who have so graciously supported me along the way. In fact, there are so many to thank that it might be easier to list those places I *haven't* been, and scholars and practitioners I *haven't* met. The complete list would extend into multiple volumes. So, please know that *you* – yes, *you* reading this – are thanked.

First, thank you to Routledge, editor Simon Whitmore, and editorial assistant Rebecca Connor for publishing this book as part of the Routledge Research in Sports History list. I am grateful for their advice, assistance, and especially patience.

I also owe many thanks to American University and A.U.'s History Department, as well as American University's Library – especially the Inter-Library Loan Department (Shane and Andrea). Many of the details in this book would not have been included without their assistance. I also thank the National Sporting Library and Museum, the Alfred Munnings Museum, the Virginia Museum of Fine Arts, and the British Library, particularly the lovely staff in the Rare Books & Music Reading Room.

I also thank those wonderful friends who have given so freely of their time and expertise to make this project a reality. Heartfelt appreciation to Sally Goodsir, Mike Huggins, Sally Mitchell, and Lindsay Smith. Furthermore, words do not exist to thank two incredible mentors – April Shelford and Sara Helmer – for their confidence, optimism, and continual encouragement.

But, in the end, this book is for my family – for everything. Without them, I would not have ridden horses, become passionate about hippology, or always found encouragement and inspiration in the darkest moments of school, study, and writing. Without them, this book – as a labor of love – would not exist.

Introduction
The Development of Horsemanship, Gender Construction, and National Identity in Britain

Amazons and Angels

"That's the consequence of letting a girl follow the hounds," Mary Elizabeth Braddon wrote in 1862, "she learns to look at everything in life as she does at six feet of timber or a sunk fence; she goes through the world as she goes across country – straight ahead, and over everything."[1] Today, the importance and prominence of the horse in society has waned, but horses once offered the first mobility, purpose, and freedom for humans, especially for women.[2] Horses have always been especially important to Britons. The first Queen Elizabeth remarked that the British people "possessed a remarkable love for the horse that was found in no other country."[3] Thus, this book examines British women's participation in horse sports and how such involvement shaped – and was shaped by – gender, social, cultural, and sporting ideals.

The special relationship between women and horses goes beyond recorded time. Horses were first domesticated around 4000 BC for sustenance (meat and milk) and work (horsepower) in the lands around the Black Sea. Herodotus and the Greeks labeled the female warriors of the Scythian tribes as "Amazons," and these women gained a vaunted reputation for their equestrian prowess. According the Greek author Lysias (395 BC), these Amazons were the first to ride horses.[4] On the steppes, the horse was a great equalizer of the sexes. The earliest artifacts depicting Amazons date to 575-550 BC, but the plethora of existing items from this period show how important female riders were in the popular imagination.[5] In fact, "the Greek source which described the original Amazons did not imply that they rode in any way other than men did except rather better."[6]

For centuries, female horseback riders have formed extraordinary bonds with animal companions (Figure 0.1). Women's ability to tame, control, and ride horses was as mythical as it was real. Legend holds that the bridle was invented by Athena to aid Bellerophon in controlling Pegasus, while later lore attested to the unique female ability to tame a unicorn.[7] In Greek mythology, Artemis, goddess of the hunt and open places, was one of the twelve major deities, while

Figure 0.1 Sir Francis Grant, P.R.A., "The Hon. Mrs. J. Wortley on Horseback" (1845–1846): This stunning portrait of The Hon. Mrs. J. Wortley (née Miss Jane Lawley) was exhibited at the Royal Academy in 1847 (no. 177), but sittings began in 1845 upon the announcement of her engagement. She rides a half-bred mare named Lily and displays all the qualities of an accomplished horsewoman in a two-pommel sidesaddle. This painting is similar to Grant's 1845 equestrian painting of Queen Victoria.
Credit: Image Courtesy of Patrick Bourne & Co., London

Diana, her Roman counterpart, was venerated throughout Roman Britain.[8] These figures clearly linked venery and veneration, and while there were also connections between the chase and chastity, hunting was associated with wild eroticism, of chasing an elusive and perhaps unattainable prey.

The cult of the Huntress, representing female independence and spatial freedom, remained strong in popular British imagination. Well through the twentieth century and even today, skilled horsewomen were called "Dianas of the Chase," and Sir Walter Scott's famed female character from *Rob Roy* was named "Diana Vernon."[9] This age-old recognition of women's unique equestrian abilities has resulted in a centuries-long fascination with Amazons, hunting goddesses, and subsequent generations of female equestrians – all of whom have gone "straight ahead and over everything."

Ladies Aside

Initially, women in England either traveled in carriages, or simply rode astride like men, as Gerald of Wales confirmed in the late twelfth century (Figure 0.2).[10] A Book of Hours, known as "The Taymouth Hours" and probably created for a noble lady (or even a queen) in London during the second quarter of the fourteenth century (1325–1350), shows two ladies riding astride in high-cantled knight's saddles and hunting with bows.[11] Tradition holds that Anne of Bohemia introduced the sidesaddle to England when she arrived for her marriage to King Richard II in 1382. According to chronicler John Stow, "Anne, daughter to the King of Bohemia, that first brought hither the riding upon sidesaddles; and so was

Figure 0.2 Detail of a *bas-de-page* scene of two women with lances and shields, jousting on horseback, from the Queen Mary Psalter (c. 1310–1320). A fanciful but accurate depiction of women riding in medieval saddles with a high cantle and pommel, similar to the two female riders in The Taymouth Hours. Women were an important part of a vibrant and flourishing equestrianism during the Middle Ages.
Credit: © The British Library Board Royal 2 B VII f. 197v.

the riding in whirlicotes and chariots forsaken ..."[12] The sidesaddle had come northward from Persia to continental Europe by the twelfth century, eventually spreading to England.[13] This single act – Anne's importation from Europe of sporting equipment and gendered ideologies – irreversibly transformed gender, social, and sporting ideals in England (and later Britain and its Empire) for centuries.

By the beginning of the fifteenth century, female riders were expected to ride on a sidesaddle and were now depicted in this demure fashion in contemporary manuscripts.[14] By this time, the straddle position was no longer deemed proper for women. Riding astride was considered indecent and even immoral, according to the decrees of the Catholic Church, which viewed any pleasurable activity like hunting with suspicion.[15] Riding astride was taboo for another reason: it might cause genital stimulation for women. Unbridled sexual desire would thus lead to a loss of self-control and the cardinal sin of lust. Thus, only one woman was illustrated still riding astride in the Ellesmere Manuscript of Chaucer's *The Canterbury Tales*, produced around 1400: the Wife of Bath with her hat, foot-mantel, and "spurs sharp."[16] The ancient freedom of movement glimpsed fleetingly in the Wife of Bath's independent equestrianism was soon curtailed by new gendered ideals of proper femininity and sexuality. In the Ellesmere Manuscript, both the Prioress and the Second Nun are depicted riding sideways, visual indications that women were expected to keep their legs respectably "closed."[17]

Ladies on horseback now rode completely sideways. The first "sidesaddles" were little more than pack saddles or padded platforms strapped to a horse's back. Most were molded like chair seats and included side rails around the seat and cantle, so that a woman had to sit with her shoulders parallel to the horse's spine.[18] A *planchette*, or foot-rest, was added to one side – there was no stirrup until later. Without having a view forward or a way to control the reins, a female rider required a groom to lead and control her horse. A second option was to ride "pillion," or on an oversized pillow pad cinched to a horse's back behind a man's saddle, sometimes with a handle for grip.[19] Again the lady sat sideways and only steadied herself by holding her attendant's belt.[20] Both methods of riding meant that women were unable to command the horses they rode. Due to the unsteadiness of their seats, they could not ride faster than a walk or gentle amble for fear of falling off. Even though new ideals of demure femininity and more closely fitted clothes limited athletic movement and mobility, women were still – paradoxically – an important part of a vibrant and flourishing equestrianism during the Middle Ages.[21]

During the sixteenth century, elite women adopted a new, more forward-looking position on horseback. By the 1500s, the lady's sidesaddle had evolved into a regular saddle seat with flap, or the large piece of leather between the rider's leg and the girth trappings beneath. A single raised horn was added at the front center of ladies' saddles, similar to that on men's saddles.[22] This horn may initially have been used as a decorative handle, but it evolved into a pommel over which women hooked their right leg. A woman's shoulders were now parallel to her horse's shoulders; this position enabled her to hold her own reins and command her mount. It allowed women to take back equestrian authority, to become powerful rather than powerless. This innovation in riding style and saddles is usually attributed (perhaps falsely) to the French Queen Catherine de Medici in the middle of the sixteenth century, an enthusiastic huntress who wished to flaunt her shapely legs more effectively when on horseback.[23]

The new fashion appeared in Britain by at least the mid-sixteenth century, as shown by sidesaddles in the collections of the Colchester Museums and the Shakespeare Birthplace Trust (Figure 0.3).[24] Given the backward curve of the horn and the padded flap on the Shakespeare saddle, it is likely that a woman would have hooked her right leg around this horn, rather than sit sideways as on a pillion pad and use this horn as a hand-hold.[25] This new seat made

Figure 0.3 Saddle, c. 1525–1575: This early sidesaddle, constructed of green silk velvet with silk and metal fringe decoration, is built on a wood frame, with a tall center horn, cushioned circular seat (padded with wool), and decorative skirts on either side, to protect a rider's fine clothes. Given the backward curve of the horn and the padded flap, it is likely that a woman would have hooked her right leg around this horn, rather than sit sideways as on a pillion pad with this horn as a hand-hold. This was the first step to achieving female equestrian independence.
Credit: CC-BY-NC-ND Image Courtesy of the Shakespeare Birthplace Trust

women's position on horseback more secure and stable, and allowed them to do more than just appear ceremonially or travel on horseback. Elizabeth I's Ambassador from Spain, Álvaro de la Quadra, wrote in 1560 that the Queen was training for war every day "on one of the saddles they use here," thus indicating that she was using a more secure sidesaddle, and that the new saddle was unique to England and differed from the typical platforms used in Europe.[26] Without such a saddle, it is unlikely that the Earl of Leicester could have nervously written later that year that the Queen had demanded "strong good gallopers," "whom she spareth not to tire [try] as fast as they can go," or that she would have been able to hunt on horseback every other day during the year before her death at the age of 69 years.[27]

By the seventeenth century, these single-pommel sidesaddles were elaborately decorated and crafted of expensive textiles. The gold and velvet "Kington Saddle," reportedly used by Queen Elizabeth I during her visit to Bristol in 1574, features a small, single, padded pommel, with a cushioned rest for the back part of the knee.[28] Paul van Somer's life-size portrait of Anne of Denmark from 1617 shows the queen's horse bedecked in a red velvet saddle, with a single horn, and saddle skirt or cloth (to protect the rider's expensive garments from mud splashing up from the horse's hooves, similar to fenders on bicycles) that falls below the horse's knee. This saddle would not have enabled her to ride at speed, but as the motto depicted over her head ("My greatness is from on high") shows, riding did literally elevate equestrians into positions of power.[29] Just over a decade later, Daniel Mytens painted King Charles I and Henrietta Maria ready to hunt; the queen's horse wears a padded pillow-type saddle with a single horn and long, decorated saddle skirt.[30]

Equestrianism was a perfect vehicle for conspicuous consumption. Such gorgeous embellishment was a visual representation of wealth and prestige as much as the act of riding and owning a horse. In 1664 the Duchess of Cleveland rode "on a white palfrey, with a red velvet saddle and bridle covered with gold lace."[31] In 1739, Thomas, the fourth Lord Leigh, purchased a "leopard skin side saddle and housing trimmed with gold fringe and lace."[32] Decades later, an Arabian horse given by Sir Sidney Smith to Lady Spencer was lavishly bedecked with coverings of precious metals and fabrics: "The saddle cloths are of crimson satin, embroidered with gold and silver, and trimmed with gold fringe; the stirrups and the bits of the bridle are of solid gold."[33] These luxurious trappings were ornamental rather than practical. Although cloth provided a cushion when riding, it also caused chafing, as well as indecorously rucking up women's skirts. Embroidered velvet, the most common choice for ladies' saddles, was notorious for doing so. An indecent moment could nullify the conspicuous display of equestrian presence: a woman was still little more than a stuffed doll on horseback.

Female riders needed a more secure seat if they were to do anything more than appear on horseback. By the early 1700s, Britain had become an equestrian "influencer" in riding styles and originated sidesaddle improvements.[34] A vital invention was a second pommel which formed a "fork" at the front of the saddle.[35] This addition created a u-shaped hook through which a lady could wedge her right leg, while leaving her left to balance in a stirrup. The term "crutch" denoted the right, or off-side, horn when in the saddle, while "pommel" referred to the horn to the left, or near-side.[36] French authors acknowledged the English origin of the two-pommel sidesaddle; in 1852, French equestrian author Alfred Roger credited it as *"la selle anglaise avec ses deux fourches"* [the English saddle with its two forks].[37]

By the mid-eighteenth century, sidesaddles had evolved further. They were now constructed of leather, and the elaborate saddle cloths had shrunk considerably into small, rectangular saddle pads usually plain or edged.[38] A sidesaddle from Chirk Castle shows a transition from a padded saddle seat and accompanying cloth blanket to an early modern sidesaddle.[39] It retains a quilted and padded seat and the skirts are decorated with bullion braid and spotted fur trim, but the two fixed horns at the front of the leather saddle reveal a new interest in riding, rather than sitting passively and decoratively on a horse. John Wootton's "A Hunting Party," featuring Charles Spencer, third Duke of Marlborough, also depicts his wife Elizabeth and two ladies ready to go hunting.[40] Other Wootton paintings from the mid-1700s, including his portraits of Lady Henrietta Harley and Lady Mary Churchill, show female riders in similar mounted positions, denoting a new body posture made possible by the new seat and saddle.[41] Several of Wootton's paintings depict female riders galloping and hunting, thus showing new mobility at previously impossible speeds.[42] James Seymour likewise depicted female equestrians in such saddles, including Princess Amelia, daughter of King George II, and many others (Figure 0.4).[43] George Stubbs also painted similar portraits, thus giving a new visual prominence to female equestrians.[44] After hundreds of years of sitting sideways, this new innovation, a sidesaddle with two pommels, transformed female equitation, or the practice and performance of riding effectively (Figure 0.5).

From *Haute École* to Hunting and Horsewomen in Britain

Equestrian practices and riding styles have long influenced perceptions of national as well as personal identity. Participants in horse sports coalesced into "imagined communities" of equine interests unified via shared styles of riding. By the time of the European Renaissance, changes in mounted combat and horse breeding led to a transformation of equestrian practices. The invention of gunpowder made heavy horse and armor obsolete and led to the slow decline in knightly horsemanship and mounted sports like the tournament and the joust. Jousting declined in favor in England after Henry VIII suffered a hard fall during a joust and received a concussion that resulted in several hours of unconsciousness; he never jousted again.[45] By the seventeenth century, the military use of the horse in Europe – as cavalry – had been reinvented as part of a wider "military revolution"; the power of firearms was now combined with a charge of lighter *"reiters."*[46]

Figure 0.4 James Seymour (English, c. 1702–1752), "Woman Wearing a Round Hat, Riding to Right:" James Seymour's sketch of a woman riding sidesaddle before the mid-eighteenth century indicates a two-pommel saddle based on the elevated position of her right knee. Seymour sketched and painted many women riding sidesaddle, indicating the ubiquity and acceptance of female riders and the English invention and origin of the two-pommel sidesaddle – "the English saddle with its two forks."

Credit: © Virginia Museum of Fine Arts, Richmond (Paul Mellon Collection), Photo: Troy Wilkinson

Figure 0.5 "A Dun Horse, with Its Groom by Thomas Stringer (1722–1790):" This beautiful painting from the late eighteenth century shows a two-pommel sidesaddle, cinched with an over-girth. The slipper stirrup (with open toe) is attached via a stirrup leather that is only looped over the pommels. This practice was dangerous; if the leather broke or came unlooped, a woman only had her balance to remain in the seat.
Credit: Digital Image ©National Trust Images, Painting © The Property of a Private Collection

Because England was an island with natural defenses – and with the exception of Cromwell's New Model horsemen – keeping and training cavalry for war was less important in England than in Europe, where the importance of cavalry was proven in the Napoleonic Wars as blunt force "shock troops."[47] In Europe, military schools taught classical equitation, or *haute école*, which dominated the practice of horsemanship. Britain did not have similar military horsemanship schools, so when Britons focused on horse breeding, it was for horses for sport rather than for war.[48] Nor did the English government subsidize horse breeding, as was the practice in France and Germany.[49] Horses were bred for sale, rather than quota, encouraging popular rather than military horsemanship.[50]

Haute école declined in Britain following the Civil Wars, in which so many specially trained horses (and their aristocratic owner-riders) had perished. The style was temporarily kept alive by William Cavendish, Marquess and from 1665, first Duke of Newcastle, who taught Charles II to ride. However, even his methods were recognized as an archaic exception following his return to Britain after the Restoration.[51]

This clear rejection of the *haute école* style popular in Europe, and particularly in France, was seen as a British sporting revolution. A different kind of riding, based on free movement of the horse for racing and hunting, had been encouraged and promoted in England at least since agricultural author Gervase Markham's voluminous publications in the late 1500s. In fact, Markham was so prolific in promoting this new style of riding that, in 1617, he had five volumes on horsemanship on the market at once. As a result, London booksellers made him promise not to produce any further volumes.[52] Markham's publications – even if repackaged from old material, as it was claimed – were inexpensive by contemporary standards; they could be purchased by those with incomes either small or large.[53] These shared equine interests bound his audience of readers and riders together, to share in the same, national horse culture. That "imagined community" of equestrianism focused not on military horsemanship but on recreation. Not only did Markham print his own material, he also edited in 1595 a new version of *The Book of St. Albans* by Juliana Berners because hunting was "so necessarie and behouefull to the accomplishment of the Gentlemen of this flourishing Ile."[54]

Beyond military applications, another reason for the decline of *haute école* in England was its association with the circus. Both male and female circus riders performed traditional *haute école* movements like the piaffe, pirouettes, and tempi changes, but also added new "tricks" such as trotting and cantering backward. The purpose of such performances was not to defend against military attack, but to provide entertainment and please a paying audience – the more unique and outlandish the tricks, the better. Philip Astley became famous for his exhibitions of this type of horsemanship, establishing Astley's Amphitheatre near Westminster Bridge in 1769.[55] But England was not fertile ground for such performances; it was more hospitable and profitable to perform across the Channel. So, from 1772 onward, Astley and his company traveled to Paris every year, excepting the years of 1778–1783 during the Anglo-French War.[56] The Napoleonic Wars prevented performances from 1792 forward, and Astley himself died in 1814, followed by his son and protégé only seven years later.[57] By the late eighteenth century, then, *haute école* had become both "neglected and despised" in England, and was even labeled "improper."[58] In 1821, the style even resulted in public humiliation. As Marius Kwint relates: "at George IV's coronation, the Duke of Wellington was commissioned to lead the procession on a horse specially trained at Astley's, but unfortunately the horse, mistaking the cheers of the crowd for a cue, reversed into the face of the new king."[59] Such training certainly did not endear the style of riding to king or country.

Riding styles thus developed differently in Britain than in the rest of Europe. Equestrianism therefore influenced – and was influenced by – complicit and contested constructions of national identity as well as by gender and class. After the French Revolution (and arguably even before), the French were seen as everything Britain and Britons were not, in politics, culture, and sport – and especially in equestrianism.[60] The British considered the French – both men and women – to be woefully inadequate riders. They despised the Continental focus on unnatural and unseemly *haute école* movements and trick-riding acrobatics performed in the artificial conditions of the indoor riding school, or hippodrome. The same was held to be true for Germans.[61] By contrast, the English focus on hunting and racing in open country showcased both skill and virility. English riders trained their horses to be strong and useful, possessing both the speed and stamina needed to cross a demanding landscape, while performing the useful and necessary functions of the hunt – providing food and eliminating vermin. As "Nimrod," the pen name for sporting author Charles James Apperley, noted,

> That any advantage could be gained by teaching a horse, by severe and painful discipline, to dance a Capriole, or a Cornetti, I never could bring myself to imagine, unless the object were to fit him for the stage or the circus. As for the lessons of a riding master, they may be essential to a good military seat, or to teach an Englishman to ride like a Frenchman; but they never will teach a man how to ride, and make the most of his horse, over a country.[62]

These changes revealed the special construction of a national identity based on sport. It was not considered "English" to make one's horse mince about and perform like a trained monkey. Thus, the English consciously used horse sports to differentiate themselves from the French specifically and Continental neighbors more generally.

Female equestrianism was at the heart of such constructions and public performances. By the 1840s, Paris was the center of the circus world, although performances took place all across Europe.[63] The first female *écuyères*, or circus riders – Caroline Loyo and Angelica Chiarini – rose to prominence in Paris during the 1830s – at the same time that British horsewomen swept into fox hunting fields.[64] But there were significant class and gender implications of public equestrianism in France, not least of which was that performers were lowly laborers paid for their appearances. European *écuyères* usually descended from generations of circus artists, beginning their training while young and appearing in public by their teenage years. These closed family businesses limited the ability of others to join and participate in a small, specialist, and usually socially outcast community. *Écuyères* also had to provide their own specially trained horses – at least three, two for *haute école* and one for jumping – which further limited participation to those who could afford such expenses.[65] Thus, equestrianism in France trapped female riders between two binaries, either as professional circus stars or titled ladies who rode for leisure.

European equestrianism, focused as it was on *haute école*, also exposed significant gendered complications and incited debates about proper masculinity and femininity. As Pia Cuneo has shown, early modern horsemanship manuals published in German lands point exclusively toward *haute école* practices and breeding, and all horsemanship terms appear to be in the masculine gender.[66] Kari Weil has further argued that equestrianism was promoted in France for improving and sustaining masculinity through the restoration of an earlier ideal of classical horsemanship and manhood as "thoroughbred" (*pur-sang*, or pureblood).[67] As she writes, "a flaccid aristocracy and flagging bourgeoisie both called upon the horse as a symbol of and means for virilizing and rejuvenating French manhood."[68] This appropriation was not a rejection of *haute école* but a further affirmation of it. Except it was an affirmation for one sex only.

Riding sidesaddle, ordinary women could hardly be expected to master the intricate aids required to perform the complicated maneuvers of *haute école*. Armed with spurs and whip, which served as prosthetic extensions of their repressed bodies, women riding in France were considered unnatural grotesqueries and, more importantly, a threat (rather than complement) to male supremacy. As the French Revolution had shown, Frenchwomen had the wrong kind of power – on horseback, they were, at one extreme, out of control and untamed (per circus performers), and at the other artificial and severely repressed (per *haute école*). As Vicomte d'Hédouville reminded, French women – unless performers or patricians – had no business riding horses: "*la femme n'est pas faite comme l'homme pour monter à cheval*" [woman is not made like man to ride a horse].[69] As French dramatic critic Jules Janin asked in 1841, "*Mais aussi, quel savant et terrible écuyer! Est-ce une femme?*" [What a skilled and terrifying rider! Is it a woman?], using the masculine term for rider.[70] Thus, these public displays of equestrian skills increasingly challenged French notions of respectable femininity and sexuality.

There were further linguistic complications regarding equestrianism. In France, unlike Britain, there were two terms for female riders: *amazones* and *écuyères*. As French circus pioneer Ernest Molier described, the former "*celle qui monte à cheval par pur goût sportif et fait de l'équitation extérieure, c'est-à-dire se promène au Bois, suit une chasse à courre,*" and the latter, "*L'Écuyère qui se spécialise dans le travail en haute école*" [The Amazon, one who rides a horse for pure sporting taste and does outdoor horseback riding, that is, rides on the Bois de Boulogne or follows a hunt with hounds [versus] The rider who specializes in classical equitation].[71] The *amazone* was titled and respectable, a woman who rode or hunted to demonstrate class and her own thoroughbred breeding, while the disreputable professional *écuyère* performed (in the saddle or otherwise) as circus celebrity or courtesan.[72]

In Britain, there was no such etymological division between proper and improper riders; the term adopted for any rider – male or female – was the masculine "equestrian." The feminine "equestrienne" was a "pseudo-French feminine" term and largely out of popular use.[73] British women were called "amazons" like their ancient Scythian forebears, but it was a mark of pride and admiration for equestrian prowess. There was no equivalent term to *écuyère* in English parlance even for an equestrian who was a courtesan like Catherine Walters ("Skittles"). Samuel Sidney found the Scythian moniker perfectly apt: "curiously enough in England, where horsewomen are more numerous and more skilful than in any other country in Europe, there is no such convenient word as *Amazone* for describing a lady who rides – a word so descriptive and compact, that it may certainly be used in the pages devoted to an explanation of the equestrian art without subjecting the writer to the charge of affectation."[74] In Britain, all female equestrians were termed "amazons" or "equestrians," and the appellation was positive.

The move away from *haute école* in England thus opened new opportunities for female riders. While the French aristocracy cloistered itself at Versailles, distanced from rural affairs, the English by contrast grew ever closer to the land at their country houses in agrarian communities. The bonds between city and country, high and low politics, grew stronger as classes mixed in sporting settings, and so did the strength and physical vitality of the English people who pursued sports in the countryside. As equine historian W. Sidney Felton argued, "the last significant English book which sought to present a scientific approach to classical horsemanship" was Richard Berenger's *The History and Art of Horsemanship* in 1771, while just one year later, in 1772, the first formalized instructions for female riders were published in Charles Hughes' *The Compleat Horseman*.[75] Just a few years later, Peter Beckford's influential treatise on fox hunting appeared in 1781; the text was reprinted three more times before the turn of the century.[76] These books – focusing on fox hunting and female equestrianism – showed an important link between the new British riding style and the involvement of female equestrians.

Hunting on horseback also differed on the Continent, especially in France. Here, the art of venery – or hunting with hounds – had changed little since the Middle Ages. Unlike in England, the French pursued two kinds of hunting: for large game (*la Grande Vénerie*, for stag, boar, and wolf) and for smaller game (*la Petite Vénerie*, for hare and fox).[77] Hunts were far more socially exclusive than in Britain, and the chase usually took place on privately owned land. The terrain consisted of wooded parkland or forests, without property lines marked by fences, so the speeds remained slower and the jumping minimal.[78] Although these circumstances would seem to encourage female involvement, this was not the case. Early on the Catholic Church had engineered the replacement of female hunting patrons Artemis and Diana with the males St. Eustace and St. Hubert.[79] In France, Diana was vilified as a "midday demon,"[80] and, as Richard Almond shows, replacing female huntresses with male hunters not only denied "the authenticity of women as hunters[;] it was also a stern reminder to both sexes of women's domesticity and docility, roles approved and continually reinforced and imposed by the Western Church."[81] In Catholic countries, hunting and equestrianism thus remained a sacred space, but in an Anglican nation, it was secularized and participation was not sinful nor forbidden.[82] Thus, in Catholic Europe (and even in many Protestant areas), religion was tied into horse sport, hunting, and female participation.

Social and cultural mores therefore discouraged female participation in France for all but the most enthusiastic of titled ladies, whose status enabled them to ignore public opinion. Prominent French instructors and authors such as François Baucher and Jules Pellier discouraged women from imitating their British sisters in equestrian pursuits.[83] As Pellier admonished in 1861,

> On voit, il est vrai, en Angleterre, des dames suivre les chasses au renard, et s'exposer ux mêmes périls que les hommes; mais les moeurs françaises condamnent absolument cette usurpation du rôle masculin, et n'admettent pas qu'un mari expose sa femme à rouler à terre avec son cheval; comme un jockey de steeplechase; ce fait n'est pas rare, dit-on, chez nos voisins, mais j'avoue qu'il n'excite en moi aucun enthousiasme. [We see, it is true, in England, ladies following the fox hunts, and exposing themselves to the same dangers as men; but French customs absolutely condemn this usurpation of the masculine role, and do not allow a husband to expose his wife to rolling on the ground with his horse like a steeplechase jockey; this fact is not uncommon, it is said, among our neighbors, but I admit that it does not excite in me any enthusiasm.][84]

Whereas the British encouraged female equestrians, the French saw them as hyper-masculine freaks overthrowing the social order (which was somewhat ironic coming from the nation of Madame Defarge). Thus, this French atmosphere was not only inhospitable to female equestrianism, but practically prohibited it from the get-go.

Women in Britain therefore possessed valuable equestrian opportunities to hunt on horseback that their Continental sisters were denied. The reason women in Britain could participate so well in these mounted activities was due to both practical and physical considerations, as well as more flexible social and gender paradigms. Hunting in the early 1700s focused predominantly on stag and carted deer for the royal family, the court, and noble aristocrats, while country gentlemen chased the common brown hare within the limits of the Game Laws. Hunts were drawn-out affairs, with little galloping. Women could participate even on their unwieldy sidesaddles because speeds remained slow and fences and obstacles to jump were practically non-existent in a country that was not yet enclosed. More importantly, there was little social stigma against women's participation if they so chose. After all, why shouldn't the wives and daughters of the upper classes ride over their lands as they wished and visibly demonstrate their rank and status? Their mounted appearance confirmed their rightful places in the social hierarchy and demanded a public acknowledgment of, and deference to, these female riders. Queen Anne was a great lover of the chase (second only to her passion for horse racing), and began a pack of hounds at Ascot, while Lady Mary Wortley Montagu enthusiastically went stag hunting and was "well pleased with it."[85]

The British embrace of female sporting participation, at least in terms of equestrianism, was seen to be a stark contrast to the situation in Europe, and especially in France. Hunting as a sport was felt to be an especially British pursuit. It was also a way to differentiate the physically strong British nation against the effeminate French in a post-Napoleonic world. In fact, following the British victory over France in 1815, women's participation in horse sports was viewed as strengthening on three levels: for themselves, for their sex, and for their country. The equal participation of women in these activities encouraged a strong, healthy, and independent ideal of both womanhood and nation-state. Long after British women took to riding astride and "wearing the breeches," French women were bound by law not to. In France, women were required to obtain legal permission to wear breeches or trousers for riding horses or bicycles, a law which was not reversed until 2013.[86]

Gender at the Gallop

Women's equestrianism in Britain shaped ideas and ideals of gender, sport, class, and national identity from the late eighteenth to mid-twentieth centuries. An examination of equestrianism contributes not only to studies of women's and gender history, but also how sport interacts with class, Empire, and the creation of a specific British vision. Thus, this book integrates centuries of horse history – with a specific focus on early modern and modern Britain – with gender, class, imperial, and sporting historiographies.

This book is not just about the inclusion of women in sport, but about the gendered constructions and shifting ideals of femininity related to athletic pursuits, specifically equestrianism. As Joan Scott (followed by others) argued, gender is "a social category imposed on a sexed body."[87] Gender consists of the social values of what is proper (or not) for a man or woman as imposed on bodies and behaviors – it is not just the binary biological determinism of sexual difference. Differences between men and woman as male and female – appropriate and not – are therefore not natural or normal but rather constructed and contested. As Jeanne Boydston has emphasized, "gender is a language about power in a given society."[88] The power that women had – or had not – was usually controlled by the dictates of what men thought women should be. But, through their own agency and actions, women could revise and rectify those standards.

By the eighteenth century, developments in Britain resulted in rapidly changing gender norms. The decline of the power of the monarchy and the beginning of popular politics, the spread of industrialization and the emergence of a new class society, for example, led to new thinking about the proper role of women in society and their behaviors.[89] By the early 1800s, the long reign of George III had shifted into the lavish Regency era of George IV. While initially there were many opportunities for women in this racy atmosphere, social permissiveness declined by the turn of the century, based on recent events of the French Revolution. Many believed that the breakdown in traditional gender roles had turned the world upside down.[90] Furthermore, the impact of the Industrial Revolution led to many women of the middling and aspiring classes moving out of city homes and businesses and into country or suburban dwellings, where new settings demanded and encouraged new behaviors.

All together these developments resulted in furious debate over proper masculinities and femininities during Queen Victoria's lengthy reign from 1837 to 1901. As Jane Hamlett and Sarah Wiggins argue, "The experience of being a woman, and cultural understandings of femininity, were thus different to any period before or since."[91] Domesticity was an important factor in the creation of Victorian femininity and a crucial component of the separate spheres ideology and the idealization of public man and private woman.[92] In contrast to the masculine characteristics of physical strength, courage, boldness, and rational intelligence, a woman's winning "softness" was based on her tractable subservience. Yet such ideals were not as clear-cut in practice as in theory, and women constantly challenged this prescriptive passivity and expected domesticity.

In fact, the ideology of separate spheres may have developed most intensely at the point when women increased, rather than decreased, their public participation. As Linda Colley argues, "anxiety about keeping British women fertile, busy and contented within the domestic sphere only deepened as more and more of them appeared to be active outside it."[93] Amanda Vickery added, "the broadcasting of the language of separate spheres looks like a conservative response to an unprecedented expansion in the opportunities, ambitions and experience of late Georgian and Victorian women."[94] At the same time, the importance of gendered spaces increased during the early Victorian era, especially the segregation of the middle class home into feminine and masculine rooms.[95] Sporting women increasingly deserted these private places.[96] In fact, more masculinized spaces developed within the home at the same time that women successfully moved into formerly masculine public spheres like sport. These increasingly gendered spaces of the Victorian home contradicted and conflicted with the more open and gender-neutral sporting spheres in Britain and the Empire. Such transitions demonstrated the limits of patriarchy in Victorian Britain and the permeability of gendered spaces.

One of the so-far unexplored facets of this new female behavior was participation in equestrian sport. Linda Colley asserts that fox hunting was "another expression of the new patriotic, patrician machismo," but it was more than that.[97] Riding and hunting also catalyzed a new confident, independent femininity. The boldness, strength, and self-possession of female equestrians directly contradicted the submissive, domestic image of the "angel in the house." As Norbert Elias argued in *The Civilizing Process*, changing attitudes about violence, sex, and manners resulted in new feelings about public behaviors.[98] Displays of barbarity and brutality, as well as coarseness and recklessness, were increasingly castigated, and such changes were actualized in fox hunting through the increasing involvement of women.[99] Female participation was a rebuke to the drunken hooliganism and breakneck riotousness symptomatic of the degeneration of hunting in the late eighteenth and early nineteenth centuries. Female decorum – sober, quiet, and composed – motivated changes in male behavior so that hunting once again focused on sport, rather than shenanigans. Thus, as Eric Dunning has argued, sport is part of a civilizing process, and women, with a "civilizing intent," played important roles.[100] Thus, riding and hunting were not just expressions of "machismo," contributing to sporting masculinities, but they were also fundamental to strong, respectable, and fulfilling femininities.

Leisure, Class, and Horse Sports

Status in society has traditionally been determined by men (through rank, occupation, or income), and, as the many equestrian statues of kings, rulers, and conquerors remind us, there is no clearer display of power than appearing mounted on a horse.[101] Riding was not just about transport but was tangible evidence of "human triumph" in taming and civilizing beasts of nature – not only horses but unmounted humans as well.[102] Riding the great horse was an analogy for ruling the state, and mastery of the horse, as Walter Liedtke argues, legitimized the rider's abilities as "courtier, commander, or king."[103] One of the reasons the British polity survived the transition from divine to constitutional monarchy (and through the disruption of Cromwell's Protectorate) was the ability of rulers to master the state like mastering a horse. The French lacked this competence: as Albert Cler noted, "*Après la révolution de 89, les classes populaires saisirent les rênes de l'État d'une main habile, mais elles ne savaient pas même tenir les rênes d'un cheval*" [After the revolution of '89, the popular classes seized the reins of the state with a strong hand, but they didn't even know how to hold the reins of a horse].[104] The social hierarchy was a public assertion of gradiated power, and it was attained most clearly on horseback – for both men and women.

Horse sports were traditionally limited to those who could afford them, in terms of both money and time, which usually meant the nobility and upper class.[105] Owning, keeping, and riding horses was public evidence of wealth and status. As Thorstein Veblen disparaged, "saddle horses ... at their best serve the purpose of wasteful display", or conspicuous consumption.[106] In the early modern era, owning and keeping a horse could cost more than the yearly wages of a human servant (and horses were often treated better).[107] But horses were not all uniformly expensive luxuries. By the seventeenth century, Joan Thirsk confirms that there was "a highly differentiated demand for highly differentiated animals at a wide range of prices."[108] A plough horse cost less than a riding horse which cost less than a race horse, which enabled horse ownership to spread down the social scale. The new wealth of the Industrial Revolution created an aspiring class of the *nouveau riche*, who demonstrated their profits and prosperity in visible ways: moving from city to country, furnishing a house with a plethora of possessions, installing female family members in enforced idleness, and pursuing activities that indicated their status, from purchasing a piano to buying a horse.[109] After all, during the second half of the nineteenth century, average income per head doubled in real terms, while the cost of food and necessities had declined.[110] This new money could now be used for pleasure: as J.H. Plumb has argued, "one of the incontestable signs of growing affluence in eighteenth-century British society [was] the commercialization of leisure."[111] As one of the most visual and prominent forms of leisure, equestrianism became a preferred method for the aspiring classes to emulate their social betters. Riding was a public marker of social ascent, and new texts, schools, and products all assisted in this transition – for a price, of course.

Mounted hunting had traditionally been limited to the aristocracy and the rural gentry. Game laws had long protected animals like deer by classifying them as private property. The Game Act of 1671 further limited hunting to those with a property qualification of a freehold worth at least £100. Previously, sportsmen had only been able to hunt on their own lands; this new Act allowed qualified sportsmen to pursue game on any land, subject only to (the usually unenforced) laws of trespass.[112] This Act enabled new participation in rural sports and a new conception of the countryside as a place, but it also raised new debates about who belonged there, and why.[113] Like class itself, the British landscape was both open and closed, permeable for common rights but sometimes limited as private property. Hunting – by way of common passage – enabled participants to cross land on horseback that they might not otherwise have been able to; it was both inclusive and exclusive, a rural place and national space.[114] One animal classified as vermin and therefore not protected by the game laws was the fox. Reynard's unprotected status allowed a mixed-class pursuit, although the role of the aspiring classes has often been ignored in historical study. As Richard Holt has noted, "It is odd how often hunting is excluded from accounts of sport despite the huge investment made in it by the landed and the 'nouveaux riches.'"[115] Hunting was never just an elitist hobby, and the Game Reform Act of 1831 further enabled participation from a wider slice of English society.

Fox hunting was, by the eighteenth century, a socially inclusive – if not fully democratic – activity. Provided one had a horse and could ride, one could follow the hounds; all sportsmen gathered and pursued the same aim and vulpine object. As John Hawkes asserted in 1802, fox hunting "links all classes together, from the Peer to the Peasant. It is the English man's peculiar privilege. It is not to be found in any other part of the globe but in England's true land of liberty" – in other words, not in France or Europe, where liberty had become confused with revolution.[116] Today the stereotype exists of fox hunting limited to toffs in red coats but participants came from a surprisingly wide social array. As novelist Anthony Trollope, a follower of hounds himself for many decades, described in 1867:

> The non-hunting world is apt to think that hunting is confined to country gentlemen, farmers, and rich strangers; but anyone who will make himself acquainted with the business and position in life of the men whom he sees around him in an average hunting-field, will find that there are in the crowd attorneys, country bankers, doctors, apothecaries, the profession of medicine has a special aptitude for fox-hunting, – maltsters, millers, butchers, bakers, innkeepers, auctioneers, graziers, builders, retired officers, judges home from India, barristers who take weekly holidays, stock-brokers, newspaper editors, artists, and sailors.[117]

Beyond riding to hounds, the keeping of hunting dogs was also not limited to aristocratic private packs. Farmers and even urban tradesmen kept their own packs; a solicitor's clerk in Finchley taught himself to ride, stabled his horses in a cellar, and fed his hounds on butcher's scraps – all for the opportunity to hunt twice a week when his yearly salary from the City of London was just £60.[118] By the nineteenth century, the rise of subscription packs – whereby members paid small sums to support the pack and thus received the right to ride with them – enabled even more people to join hunting fields.

But if hunting was "the English man's peculiar privilege," what about women? Women were also part of the complex triangle between social class, sport, and sex. As Leonore Davidoff and Catherine Hall have argued, "gender and class always operate together [and] consciousness of class always takes a gendered form."[119] Equestrianism was a demonstration of class; female equestrians demonstrated their elite femininity by having the money, leisure, and skills to ride horses. For the aspiring classes, riding for ladies indicated the possession both wealth and leisure time. Its practice in public, in parks or on roads, legitimated women's presence outside of the home, as a demonstration of moral and social superiority (against the undisciplined and unmounted working classes) and respectable physical robustness (against the debauched and sickly upper classes).[120] By the mid-nineteenth century, participation in horse sports had trickled well down the social ladder. Horses became more affordable for purchase, and mounts were available to rent by the hour, day, or season to ride and hunt. Equestrian equipment also became cheaper: saddles and clothing declined in price, and second-hand riding habits found a ready market in sporting and fashion magazines. These measures went a long way to further enabling more women to ride and hunt, while the availability of horses around the Empire stimulated participation beyond Britain's shores. This new female involvement challenged the elitist nature of equestrianism, as well as the social qualifications of sporting femininity.

Equestrians and Empire

Studies of the British Empire have traditionally focused on the male domains of politics, foreign policy, and economics. These surveys often reduced history to the white settler man, without reading for subaltern voices or recognizing agency of the submissive and oppressed.[121] By the late twentieth century, the cultural turn and "new imperial histories" encouraged research into the wider "imperial experience" and how Empire was lived at home and abroad.[122] These histories highlighted the importance of gender, sexuality, and race in understanding the larger imperial project and its aftermath.[123] The British Empire has long been credited with producing and enhancing new ideas about masculinity, but as William Thackeray pointed out (in 1854), "Besides the lives of myriads of British men, conquering on a hundred fields, from Plassey to Meanee, and bathing them *cruore nostro*: think of the women, and the tribute which they perforce must pay to those victorious achievements."[124] Ronald Hyam may have quipped that the Empire was formed due to an "absence of wives," but British women were crucial to defining – and defending – both home and Empire. Gender and racial dynamics and ideologies buttressed imperial power, and vice versa.[125]

British women challenged imperial practices and their own subordinate positions in the Empire through a myriad of activities from philanthropy to sport. Rather than weak, defenseless, and ultimately marginalized as they had sometimes been depicted, British women around the Empire, and especially in India, created strong, independent identities that were pivotal to supporting and sustaining the imperial project.[126] Women's engagement with imperialism was therefore far more important than passive physical presence; rather, they took an active role in reconfiguring ideals of gender and power by declaring themselves part of a genderless and largely egalitarian imperial ruling class. Per Edward Said's theory of orientalism, a dark, native, and colonized "other" was created – in some ways, just as British women had been subjugated to being a domestic "other."[127] In British India, for example, British women were no longer in the position of a second-class submissive. As Anne McClintock has argued, British "women had positions of decided – if borrowed – power, not only over colonized women, but also colonized men."[128] British women were thus necessary and visible partners in the imperial project, and they influenced – and were influenced by – social, sexual, and racial ideologies within the British Empire.

One place where imperial ideology affected constructions of gender – and vice versa – was hunting and sport. Hunting – for both big and small game – provided a visual illustration not only of a superior sportsman but also of the colonizer and ruler. As J.A. Mangan and Callum McKenzie argued, militarism, hunting, and imperialism all contributed to the "blooding" of a martial male, a white leader with a specifically masculinized identity.[129] Officer hunters represented a "'British' identity which had a proper and legitimate claim to imperial dominance" – as did British women who joined them.[130] Hunting practices around the Empire did create new masculinities, with an emphasis on rugged adventure and rejection of domesticity, but so too was a new femininity formed, accepted, and even admired. A new ideal of capable womanhood, incorporating masculine traits and qualities, like command, authority, and courage, while retaining a respectable femininity, was developed in British India.[131]

British hunting practices were adapted to new surroundings in the Empire, albeit with new strategies and for new game. "In England, hunting has been derided as the unspeakable in full pursuit of the uneatable," proclaimed BBC journalist Rahul Bedi, paraphrasing Oscar Wilde, "But in India it is more a case of the unconventional in full pursuit of the unavailable."[132] Here jackals were hunted rather than foxes. Resurrected from medieval hunting practices, hog hunting, or "pig sticking," for wild boars became extremely popular. Such imported hunting practices expanded and solidified imperial rule through exploration and conquest over ever-larger swathes of territory, while depleting natives of their traditional food and protein supplies.[133] There were no game laws to limit hunting to the elites in India, and in some ways hunting on horseback demonstrated more skill than shooting a gun.[134] Thus, British women's success in fox hunting made it impossible to prevent women from hunting more dangerous game in India; they had already coolly demonstrated their skill and courage. These mounted activities blurred the lines between hunting, sport, and imperial rule.

Imperial scholarship has consistently focused on the significance of big game hunting, but the prominence of mounted sports is also important.[135] Indeed, Britain's imperial project was arguably at its zenith at the same time as the internal expansion of British sport. Yet, as late as 2012, sport was not even mentioned in the Oxford companion on *Gender and Empire*, and the only sport mentioned in the Oxford companion, *Britain's Experience of Empire in the Twentieth Century*, is cricket.[136] Britons brought horse sports with them across the Empire, and British India is especially important in the studies of equestrianism because it was one location where horses did not die *en masse* from disease, as in Africa.[137]

Many horse sports, such as polo, are only now receiving more attention from historians. Horace Laffaye has produced excellent work on polo and its history, but as he and others admit, the work on women's involvement in polo and other imperial equestrian sports is virtually a blank slate.[138] British women's active participation in gymkhanas and mounted competitions such as paper chasing and tilting "astonished the natives," according to a contemporary newspaper (Figure 4.6).[139] One reason they had such astonishment is that British women were "wearing the breeches" and riding astride like men. They did so for varied reasons: for practicality including safety when traveling; for comfort like wearing more practical clothing; and to fulfill their aspirations to better participate in horse sports like hunting and mounted games like polo and gymkhanas. In doing so they became a visual and public representation of British authority; these sportswomen were thus complicit supporters of the dominant imperial ideology. Their sporting actions reshaped ideas about proper femininity as reigning – and reining – rulers.

Sister Suffragists in Sport?

The advances made by women around the Empire were not limited to these far-flung locations because their innovations, both real and ideological, "bounced back" to Britain. So, what was the significance, then, of women achieving sporting equality? Did such advances bleed into the late Victorian and Edwardian political campaigns for female rights? Women had become successful equestrians in Britain before they were able to pursue careers in higher education, medicine, or law, or to widely pursue philanthropy and charity efforts such as anti-slavery or missionary work.[140] Women had gained renown as skilled riders well before the term "suffragette" was coined to describe females campaigning for the vote (1906); before women gained the right to vote (1918 and 1928); and before the Sex Discrimination Removal Act (1919). Female equestrians were some of first feminist forerunners and pioneers, whether they intended to be or not. Although ideals of gender were certainly shaped by the experience and memory of the First World War, important aspects of modern femininity regarding behavior, sport, and clothing had already been established well before the conflict.[141] Many of the advances in opportunities and social standards for women had been made – if not confirmed – before 1914, as illustrated by female participation in various equestrian activities and the switch from riding sidesaddle to riding cross-saddle.

Sports and especially equestrianism offered new avenues of social and athletic opportunity.[142] In fact, the post-Great War years saw a dramatic increase in the number of female riders, an increase made possible by the new affordability of horses and horse sport. Rising wages enabled many lower-class women to pursue sports like riding and hunting which had previously been out of financial reach for many.[143] This female athleticism assisted in the development of a more assertive femininity, a hallmark of modernity and liberation, as Ina Zweiniger-Bargielowska has shown.[144] However, female equestrians began such sporting advances nearly a century earlier.

After 1918, women used sporting opportunities to build on social and cultural advances. It has been traditionally asserted that the war made possible the political and legal emancipation that culminated in women receiving the vote in 1918 and 1928, but that women reverted back to inner lives of domesticity characterized by their roles as housewives and mothers. But, as Adrian Bingham and others have argued, the interwar years were not an era of domesticity and retreat.[145] Though the vote may not have changed lives as dramatically as did other social and cultural shifts, at Pat Thane has confirmed, advances continued – and were continually made – by women, especially in leisure activities like horse sports.[146]

Thus, the credit for achieving women's equality in 1928 does not belong solely to the suffragettes and members of women's political groups. It also belongs to sportswomen who instigated this transformation decades earlier. Yes, suffragists played sports, but sport was not important in their programs for emancipation, which achieved little in practice until after the First World War.[147] In contrast, although female riders did not consciously work to advance the feminist cause in the late nineteenth and early twentieth centuries by protesting for the vote or publicly campaigning for political rights, they achieved some of the most dramatic and successful advancements toward equality in their sport well before 1914. To these pioneering horsewomen, equality by vote was secondary to equality in the field.

Sporting Histories

Sport was an important avenue of personal and public emancipation for women in Britain, although sports history as a field was only born in the 1980s and is arguably just hitting its stride now.[148] Early research focused on physical education and training, while popular sports such as football, rugby, and cricket received the most attention in the following decades.[149] Sports histories explored participation by class, and how sports were a contested social arena, both inclusive by merit and exclusive by cost.[150] Most of all, however, sports histories examined men's participation. Richard Holt claimed in his seminal 1988 work, *Sport and the British*, that "the history of sport in modern Britain is the history of men."[151] Sport was supposedly a male domain and created a special "manliness."[152] Athleticism was drilled into the muscular bodies of generations of public schoolboys, and learning to "play the game" was an essential part of a man's upbringing and eventual destiny as a cog in the machine of the British Empire.[153]

But women in Britain also participated in a variety of sporting pursuits. Croquet was introduced from France in 1852 and became a common ladies' sport after the 1860s, while lawn tennis grew in popularity through the 1870s. By the 1880s, coinciding with the advent of the "New Woman," physical education became an important part of the curriculum in public schools.[154] By the 1890s, golf and bicycling for women increased, while rougher competitive games such as cricket and hockey were adopted in girls' schools.[155] Yet many of these activities served to more sharply define and reinforce sexual and gendered differences rather than to foment female inclusion into a sporting sphere.[156] Women were separated and segregated into female-only games and physically limited by "proper" clothing, modified rules and regulations, social expectations, and gendered ideologies. In this way, female sporting participation was not truly emancipatory but further underlined women's supposedly weak and subordinate status.[157]

Yet there were more positive consequences of female sporting participation. Sportswomen advanced the broader cause for others by creating a strong, independent female image that was both respectable and acceptable. Women's sports not only reflected these changes, but were the "constitutive element" of them.[158] The lack of scholarly attention to sportswomen in light of important social, sporting, and gendered ideals is therefore surprising. As Carol Osborne and Fiona Skillen pointed out in 2010, "dedicated study of women in sport history remains a peculiarly neglected area of academic research in Britain."[159] In the 1980s and 1990s, scholars such as Catriona Parratt, Jennifer Hargreaves, and Kathleen McCrone pioneered research in British women's sporting participation, especially within schools or institutions.[160] Recent work has explored British women's sporting participation more broadly,[161] as well as their contributions to individual sports such as football and cricket.[162] Studies of sport have now highlighted women's roles and involvement, but further examinations are critical to understanding constructions of gender, class, leisure, and national identity.

Victorian women had been pursuing equestrian sports long before these other games and activities. They had entered these new athletic publics before the mid-nineteenth century, visibly demonstrating that sport and exercise were compatible with respectable femininity and female bodies. Unlike other sports and games, equestrianism and hunting did not contribute to continued sex segregation. The hunt field was not divided into teams according to sex. Although it could be argued that riding sidesaddle sustained gender divisions, it also broke them down completely when women rode astride and thus became the equals of male sportsmen. As Kathleen McCrone concluded, British women's participation in sports contributed to feminine self-esteem and self-possession, for "the significance of women's sport lay not in what university men or even public opinion thought of it, but in what it meant to the women themselves. This, in one word, was freedom."[163]

Horse Histories

The literature on horse sports and equine history has until recently remained the domain of practitioners and enthusiasts, rather than scholars.[164] The horse is a special – and specialist – animal; study of equines and equestrian history requires both practical knowledge and technical expertise. In 1983, Keith Thomas, in *Man and the Natural World*, pointed out that horses were a "privileged species," different from other animals and arguably more important.[165] Thus, there are two main ways of looking at the role of the horse in history: through the horse's eyes (animal studies) and through the equestrian's (cultural and sporting history). This book focuses on horse-human interactions from the side of the latter, although it has been influenced by the burgeoning field of animal studies[166] and by increasing research on the horse in society.[167]

Even by the late twentieth century, there were few scholarly works on equestrian history. As J.H. Plumb despaired in 1972, there was "no work by a professional historian on horse-racing, or indeed on horses, vitally important as they are to the economic and social life of the time."[168] As if in response to this clarion call, two types of equine activities began to be explored in academic publications: horse racing and fox hunting. Both were involved in contemporary debates about culture, politics, and Britishness. Early works, such as Roger Longrigg's *The History of Horse Racing* (1972) and Wray Vamplew's *The Turf* (1976), laid scholarly groundwork for future study.[169] That mantle was taken up by Mike Huggins, who single-handedly produced a splendid trilogy of monographs examining British racing culture from the eighteenth through twentieth centuries.[170] More recent work has examined the specific places of British horse racing, such as Newmarket, as well as disreputable aspects such as gambling and betting, as related to sporting culture and class.[171]

Given the peculiar nature of the sport and its intricate but unwritten social and cultural codes, the subject of fox hunting has rarely been examined except by those in the know. Histories of hunting tend to be written by fox hunters themselves, offering keen insights based on personal experience but with little scholarly context. As hunting became more politically charged, a scholarly renaissance occurred in the 1970s with the publication of three popular histories: Roger Longrigg's *The History of Foxhunting* (1975); Raymond Carr's *English Fox Hunting* (1976); and David Itzkowitz's *Peculiar Privilege: A Social History of English Foxhunting, 1753–1885* (1977).[172] In the 1990s, the subject again experienced a historical resurrection as the debate on hunting with dogs raged in Parliament and public.[173] Such study might only be expected after Tony Blair's New Labour Government spent over 700 hours debating the future of fox hunting, but invested only seven on whether to invade Iraq.[174] After the ban on hunting with dogs went into effect in 2005, Emma Griffin detailed the activity's long and contentious past in her 2007 book, *Blood Sport: Hunting in Britain since 1066*, although did not focus exclusively on fox hunting.[175] More recent works have focused on hunting, land use, and landscape transformation,[176] as well as modern opposition to blood sports.[177]

Other works on the role of the horse in history have focused on various aspects of "horse history" in Britain and Europe. Richard Almond, John Cummings, and others have explored the role of the horse and significance of medieval hunting,[178] while Peter Edwards provided a wide-scale historical overview of this interspecies relationship in *Horse and Man in Early Modern England*.[179] In 2005 Karen Raber and Treva Tucker produced an edited collection, *The Culture of the Horse: Status, Discipline, and Identity in the Early Modern World*, but there was little overarching conclusion except to acknowledge the importance of horses to early modern life.[180] Donna Landry has shown the importance of equine "orientalism" in the import of Eastern bloodstock to create the Thoroughbred breed, while examining the impact of horse breeds on the development of British riding styles.[181] Additional research has also added to a nuanced understanding of equine genetics and the shift from "type" to scientific "breed."[182] Further work has expanded on equine iconography and symbolism, medicine and veterinary care, and literary and cultural studies.[183] Pia Cuneo persuasively demonstrates how *haute école* horsemanship was at the heart of a (masculine) Protestant Germany identity,[184] while Treva Tucker, Daniel Roche, and Kari Weil have all explored the role of the horse in defining and debating French identity and nationality from the medieval to modern eras.[185]

But what about female participation in equestrian sports and the contested gender issues of such sporting participation? No full-length scholarly book exists on this subject, and the comparative history of female equestrians in countries beyond Britain also remains understudied.[186] Most books on sidesaddle riding were eminently practical how-to guides for a fast disappearing riding style, although two works stand out for their historical content: Lida Fleitmann Bloodgood's *The Saddle of Queens: The Story of the Side-Saddle* (1959) and Rosamund Owen's *The Art of Sidesaddle: History, Etiquette, Showing* (1984).[187] Early studies on British women's equestrianism included Meriel Buxton's *Ladies of the Chase* (1987) and Caroline Ramsden's *Ladies in Racing: Sixteenth Century to the Present Day* (1973).[188] Fashion historians have addressed riding clothing and changing sartorial norms; whether as "dashing," "walking," or "elegant" Amazons, women ensured that riding habits were always at the cutting edge of fashion and design, well ahead of other sports and games.[189] In terms of gender studies, Monica Mattfield argues that horses and skilled horsemanship enabled the conscious performance of an idealized masculinity,[190] but femininity, with the exception of chapter-length studies, remains unexplored. Miriam Adelman's and Jorge Knijnik's *Gender and Equestrian Sport: Riding Around the World* begins to fill this scholarly vacuum but examines these issues through contemporary sports psychology and gender theory rather than history. Thus, more research on these topics would expand our understanding not just of equestrianism and sport, but of larger social and cultural issues in modern history.

Horse/Sport?

So, how do horseback riding and equestrian activities fit into the definition of – and our ideas about – sport? After all, what is "sport"? There are many meanings: the *Oxford English Dictionary* defines sport as "diversion, entertainment, or fun," and alternately as "competitive activities regulated by set rules or customs."[191] Thus, the definition of sport contains many, sometimes conflicting, components – bodily practice versus physical competitions, individual versus collective participation, amateur versus professional athletes, organized versus spontaneous play, written versus unwritten rules and regulations. The meaning of sport has continuously changed over time, in conjunction with synonyms such as leisure and recreation.[192]

As Dennis Brailsford pointed out, "definitions of sport are never easy and seldom stable."[193]

How equestrianism fits into sport is equally complicated. Is riding merely animal transport, leisured hobby, or competitive sport – or all of the above? Like other sports, riding demands physical fitness, muscle control, and mental strength. In fact, of the 32 Olympic sports, equestrianism ranked as the hardest of all, with the comment: "Can you ride a horse? Me neither."[194] Participation can be casual or organized; some equestrian activities have written rules and regulations, while others have unwritten codes of conduct. What is unique about equestrianism is that it is one of the few sports that take place with a non-human partner. Riding is not just a competition, but a partnership between human and animal. It goes beyond simple hobby, athletic exercise, or competition. Horse and rider enter time and space together; each is transformed by the other.[195]

Equestrianism thus develops special qualities in its human participants. Riding a horse demands bravery and authority, but riding is not about domination; the horse is not a slave. Horses are large, fast, and unpredictable animals; they weigh up to 1500 pounds, reach speeds of 40 miles per hour, have jumped clear over eight-foot obstacles, and can deliver over one ton of force in a single kick.[196] The ability to manage an animal up to ten times larger than humans requires expert skill. A human cannot force a horse to do anything.

Thus, the partnership between human and horse operates on trust and communication. Humans may control and command a horse, but only with equine permission. The powerlessness of a human compared to the strength of a horse demands *sang-froid* in such interactions. As John Butler confirmed in 1861, it was "fearless confidence, coolness, and courage, that make a man a good rider" – and woman too.[197] Fear has no place in equestrian pursuits, and calmness and inner serenity must master human emotions and doubts, especially in moments of chaos or panic. Thus, the teamwork between horse and human is based on mutual respect and the comprehension and acceptance of different perspectives, qualities which color all social attitudes and interactions.

Riding thus instills confidence in equestrians. Handling a horse on the ground or from the saddle requires more audacity and fortitude than other public or social situations. Managing the etiquette of private spaces (the drawing room) or public places (ballrooms or events) pales in comparison to reining in a runaway or negotiating a five-foot fence. Equestrianism presented very real dangers above and beyond the normal circumstances for women before the twentieth century. Even other sporting occupations such as croquet, tennis, golf, and bicycling did not present the same hazards as horseback riding. After all, a tennis racquet or golf club could not buck, gallop, or throw off its handler.

The grit and pluck of riders has always been commented upon, and few activities test one's mettle more than riding. At some point, all riders will be thrown or fall off a horse. Horseback riding has a rate of serious injury of 1 per every 350–2000 hours in the saddle, far higher than the rate of injury for motorcycle riding, for example, which occurs once every 7000 hours,[198] and "horse riders suffer higher rates of severe brain and body injuries than skiers, automobile racers and rugby and football players combined."[199] When mounted, a rider's head might be 13 feet from the ground, and the force of impact to the body in the event of a fall ranges from 100–300 g of deceleration.[200] Even in the most gentle of circumstances, the act of re-mounting and riding again after a fall requires extraordinary fortitude. Thus, the phrase "get back on the horse" has become a metaphor for resuming or completing an activity that has caused pyschological setbacks or physical harm.

Horses thus teach perseverance and a strong work ethic. Riders possess a special inner drive and discipline to keep learning and doing better. The measurements of success and failure are different in equestrian sports; it may not be a failure to fall off, but it is a success to get back on. When faced with obstacles, riders figure out how to negotiate them – keep your head up, your heels down, and throw your heart over the fence first. Thus, riding develops a special humility and capacity for understanding.

Riding also develops a keen sense of patience and compassion. Horses are large animals with small brains and a well-honed flight instinct. These four-legged animals prefer to run away rather than face conflict. Working with horses requires composure and tact. Riders must possess a sympathetic sensitivity to gauge and respond to a horse's actions and reactions. Riders must be slow to anger and cannot rush to judgment. The odds in a fight between horse and human skew in favor of the larger animal. Thus, problems cannot be solved nor battles won by physical strength, but rather communication. One of the most important qualities developed through equestrianism is empathy, or the ability to feel for another being and see the world through their eyes. Without being able to speak, horses must connect with humans in unspoken ways, and humans must be able to decipher and understand those interactions.

Equestrianism thus cultivates an unusual sense of "self-possession," as the Victorians called it. This self-awareness is a highly-developed personal sovereignty or independence and candid assessment of one's own strengths and weaknesses. Such autonomy was virtually unheard-of for Victorian women, faced with prescriptive literature limiting them to home and hearth, warning them from the simplest of public appearances (like shopping) or unaccompanied travel. Yet, once mounted on horseback, a female rider was in charge of herself, her mount, and her surrounding world. The power was hers to command and control; she decided her destiny and direction in life. She could go anywhere, and often did. The purview of such authority was not only offensive (protecting the outside world from oneself) but defensive (protecting oneself from the outside world). A runaway horse could injure not only the rider, but others as well. Thus, horseback riding gave women a new flexibility and power to make decisions. This prerogative was made especially clear when fox hunting, as a woman had to choose where to go, what to jump, and how to follow the hounds – all on her own. A rider had to think ahead, not just to the next fence or field, but to well beyond – to determine her own future. This self-evaluation and self-determination affected a woman's life whether she was mounted on a horse, or not.

Chapters

To demonstrate the importance of horse sports in catalyzing and furthering social, sporting, and gender changes in Britain, this work is divided into five chronologically overlapping chapters: historical change does not occur precisely or uniformly. The first chapter examines women's enthusiastic involvement in horse sports over the late eighteenth century and the publication of the first riding manuals targeted specifically for female riders. This section spans from the publication of Charles Hughes' *The Compleat Horseman* in 1772, the first riding manual to feature instructions for lady riders, to John Allen's *Principles of Modern Riding for Ladies* in 1825, when aspirational equestrianism and park riding had been well established. These texts were aimed at a new mass reading audience interested in educating themselves on sporting subjects, including the new sport of fox hunting. Following the French Revolution and the Napoleonic Wars, British interests turned inwards, leading to a focus on field sports in opposition to the disparaged riding practices of *haute école* on the Continent. A new sporting lifestyle developed in Britain, creating a specialized national culture of leisure of which women were initially a part. With the development of the second pommel on sidesaddles, women gained a new stability on horseback, though this was soon challenged by the changing nature of hunting. By the mid-eighteenth century, the culture of fox hunting had changed and the sport had become ever more masculinized and therefore less compatible with respectable femininity.

The second chapter focuses on the development of urban riding for women and eventually their return to fox hunting. It highlights the years between the publication of John Adams' *An Analysis of Horsemanship* in 1805, with a significant section on ladies' riding that encouraged jumping, to the appearance of Mrs. J. Stirling Clarke's *The Ladies' Equestrian Guide; or, The Habit and the Horse: A Treatise on Female Equitation* in 1857, the first equestrian manual for women written by a woman. At the beginning of this period, female involvement in fox hunting had decreased, though participation in park riding had surged. Despite qualms about over-exertion and reproductive damage caused by riding, equestrianism was deemed both a healthful exercise and social accomplishment, leading more women to learn how to ride and causing major sartorial changes in female clothes for riding. The physical liberty women gained through these specialized sporting garments was enhanced by the most important innovation in women's riding, the invention of the "leaping head," or a third pommel on the sidesaddle. This new addition, as well as their now well-developed horsemanship skills, enabled women to challenge their exclusion from fox hunting and rejoin fields before midcentury. Women's opportunities for public involvement, such as riding and hunting, increased during this time, despite the prescriptive ideology of separate spheres. In part, women had justified their involvement in sports and other activities such as philanthropy and nursing based on their feminine qualities. Their return to fox hunting was similarly defended on the basis of their "civilizing influence," whereby they rid the sport of its excessive rowdiness and improved the manners and behavior of all involved. In doing so, women contributed to the acceptance of equestrianism and fox hunting as Britain's national sport, supported equally by both sexes.

Building on this foundation, the third chapter looks at women's involvement in fox hunting from 1857 to 1913, or from the publication of Clarke's riding manual in 1857, that encouraged women to hunt (sidesaddle), to the release of Mrs. Stuart Menzies' *Women in the Hunting Field* in 1913, that urged women to hunt and ride astride – like men. More women than ever before were able to partake in the sport due to the railway revolution, which enabled affordable transport across the countryside. As fields increased in size, and fences grew bigger and horses faster, a new kind of riding manual was published for women that focused specifically on hunting. In directing women how to become huntresses, these volumes specifically instructed the cultivation of qualities formerly labeled as masculine. In order to ride well and safely, women were to develop confidence, authority, and self-possession, thus challenging the traditional domestic ideal of submissive femininity for a new model of strength and independence. Yet for all they gained through horse sports, such activities still retained elements of danger and many were injured and even killed. This led to the reform of riding clothes for women, including the creation of the "safety habit" and "apron skirt," in which women merely wore an apron-like covering over masculine breeches to prevent being dragged when falling off. However, women were still limited to riding sidesaddle, although even this would soon be challenged through the benefits of riding astride like men as learned via imperial experience.

The fourth chapter focuses on the influence of the Empire in transforming horse sports for women between the years 1850 and 1913, specifically focusing on British India. This section spans from the publication of Augustus Frederick Oakes' *The Young Lady's Equestrian Assistant*, published in Madras in 1850 and the first manual published on ladies' riding in India, to Mrs. Stuart Menzies' *Women in the Hunting Field* in 1913, which highlighted that her own imperial experience was the reason for her abandonment of the sidesaddle for the cross-saddle. Women challenged the Empire as a solely masculine preserve through their presence and involvement in activities like polo and pig sticking. To participate better in these events, as well as hunting (for jackals rather than foxes) and gymkhanas, women abandoned the bulky sidesaddle for the more practical astride saddle, called a cross-saddle. These saddles fit the narrow colonial horses much better and enabled easier, more comfortable travel and sport. The clothing for riding astride was also much more practical for these tropical locations: lightweight breeches, shirts, and short jackets, compared to the traditional heavy wool layers of a skirt and habit. Women therefore transformed accepted sporting and gender ideals, not by abandoning traditional ideas about femininity, but by adapting them to new conditions. Through riding astride and participating in horse sports on equal terms with men, British women visually assimilated themselves into the imperial ideology as part of the ruling class. These practices encouraged new identities and behaviors based on the conquest of both horse and human in the British Empire.

These momentous changes naturally bounced back to affect social, gender, and sporting norms at home in Britain. It is usually argued that the First World War was the transformative event that changed social and cultural life for women, but, as seen through the lens of horse sport, many of these changes had already occurred before 1914. In this way, the fifth chapter on the years between 1894 and 1932 illustrates how imperial influence affected equestrianism and society in Britain. Women were riding astride before the war, and this new style of riding enabled them to aid the war efforts so significantly. This chapter spans from the publication of Lady Greville's *Ladies in the Field: Sketches of Sport* in 1894, acknowledging the importance of imperial experience in transforming equestrian sports, to Eva Christy's *Cross-Saddle and Side-Saddle: Modern Riding for Men and Women* in 1932, by which point the astride style had long been the preferred choice of female riders. By training remount horses, leading horse breeding efforts, and taking over leadership positions in hunts, women saved equestrianism for Britain in a way that would not have been possible, had so many not already adopted riding cross-saddle. The new affordability of horses and sport in the post-war years saw an increase of women riding, especially as riding astride was far cheaper than riding sidesaddle.

After half a millenium of riding aside, British women rejected the sidesaddle for the more comfortable and practical cross-saddle. The concluding chapter ends the book by examining this full and final evolution to women riding astride in Britain. It spans from 1932 and the publication of Lady Diana Shedden's and Lady Viola Apsley's *"To whom the goddess ...": Hunting and Riding for Women*, which encouraged riding astride but lamented the decline of the sidesaddle, to 1956, when British rider Patricia "Pat" Smythe won a bronze medal in show-jumping at the Olympic Games – the first year the event was opened to women. Sport was thus part of a larger movement toward women's rights, as sportswomen and female equestrians contributed to new ideas about femininity and opportunities for female liberation. Female riders proved that equality could be obtained, and that it was right to pursue and achieve it. Women as well as men could "turn and wind a fiery Pegasus/ And witch the world with noble horsemanship" – and this book tells their story.[201]

Notes

1 M.E. Braddon, *Lady Audley's Secret, Volume 1* (London: Tinsley Brothers, 1862), 236.
2 Max E. Ammann, *Equestrian Sport at the Olympic Games, 1912–2008* (Lausanne, Switzerland: Fédération Équestre Internationale, 2012); Jennifer O. Bryant, *Olympic Equestrian: The Sports and the Stories from Stockholm to Sydney* (Canada: The Blood Horse, Inc., 2000).
3 E.M. Kellock, *The Story of Riding* (London: David and Charles, 1974), 56.
4 Adrienne Mayor, *The Amazons: Lives and Legends of Warrior Women Across the Ancient World* (Princeton: Princeton University Press, 2014), 170–171.
5 Mayor, 199.
6 Anthony Dent, *The Horse Through Fifty Centuries of Civilization* (New York: Holt, Rinehart, and Winston, 1974), 152.
7 Richard Almond, *Daughters of Artemis: The Huntress in the Middle Ages and Renaissance* (Cambridge: D. S. Brewer, 2009), 39–48.
8 Almond (2009), 18.
9 "Martingale," "Fox Hunting: The Cover Side: Female Equestrians," *The Knapsack*, 1.1 (November 1859), 318.
10 Richard Almond, "The Way the Ladies Ride," *History Today*, 62.2 (February 2012), 36.
11 Almond (2012), 37; Kathryn A. Smith, *The Taymouth Hours: Stories and the Construction of the Self in Late Medieval England* (London: The British Library, 2012), 145–158; Book of Hours, Use of Sarum/Yates Thompson MS 13 ("The Taymouth Hours"), see f.76v; Bas-de-page scene of two ladies riding out of a castle gate, followed by another horse; f.78v: Bas-de-page scene of a hunting lady whipping her horse, urging it onwards; f.79r: Bas-de-page scene of a hunting lady mounted, stringing her bow as she rides; f.79v: Bas-de-page scene of a hunting lady shooting an arrow from horseback: https://www.bl.uk/catalogues/illuminatedmanuscripts/record.asp?MSID=8148&CollID=58&NStart=13
12 John Stow, *A Survey of London* (London: Whitaker and Co., 1842), 32. Stow's *Survey* was first printed in 1598.
13 Lindsay Smith, "The History and Development of the Side-saddle," in Lauren Adams Gilmour (ed.), *In the Saddle: An Exploration of the Saddle through History* (London: Archetype, 2004), 84.
14 Richard Almond, *Daughters of Artemis: The Huntress in the Middle Ages and Renaissance* (Cambridge: D.S. Brewer, 2009), 77–78.
15 Almond (2009), 119.
16 The Ellesmere Manuscript (*The Canterbury Tales*), c. 1400–1410, see f.72r, for the Wife of Bath; f.148v, for the Prioress; and f. 187r, for the Second Nun: https://hdl.huntington.org/digital/collection/p15150coll7/id/2359
17 Almond (2009), 75–79; Almond (2012), 36–39, 77.
18 Lida Fleitmann Bloodgood, *The Saddle of Queens: The Story of the Side-Saddle* (London: J.A. Allen and Co., 1959).
19 Sally Mitchell and Nick Creaton, *A Brief History of the Side Saddle* (Palette Press, 2019), 8–12.
20 "Saddles," *Baily's Magazine of Sports and Pastimes*, Volume 70, (November 1898), 346.
21 Almond (2009), 156.
22 Bloodgood, 9–10.
23 Bloodgood, 15–16. Jules Pellier gave credit to Catherine de Medici in *La Selle et le Costume de l'Amazone: Étude Historique et Pratique de l'Équitation des Dames* (Paris: J. Rothschild, 1897), 49–51. Challenges to the Medici legend include Isabelle Veauvy, Adélaïde de Savray, Isabelle de Ponton d'Amécourt, *Cavalières Amazones: Une*

Histoire Singulière (Paris: Swan, 2016), 58–64; and Dr. Ulrike Elisabeth Weiss and Claudia P. Pfeiffer, *Sidesaddle, 1690–1935* (Middleburg, VA: National Sporting Library and Museum, 2018), 6–8.
24 Victoria Jackson, "Shakespeare in 100 Objects: Side Saddle," September 10, 2012: https://www.shakespeare.org.uk/explore-shakespeare/blogs/shakespeare-100-objects-side-saddle/. For the Colchester saddle, see Patricia Connor, *All the Queen's Horses: The Role of the Horse in British History* (Lexington: Kentucky Horse Park, 2003), 26.2, 137.
25 Mitchell and Creaton, 14.
26 Simon Adams, "'The Queenes Majestie… is now become a great huntress': Elizabeth I and the Chase," *The Court Historian*, 18 (2013), 152.
27 Adams, 143.
28 Simon de Bruxelles, "Buyer of 'cursed' royal saddle may have the last laugh," *The Times* (London), September 25, 2012, https://www.thetimes.co.uk/article/buyer-of-cursed-royal-saddle-may-have-the-last-laugh-hkvn9qqhl8c
29 Paul Van Somer, "Anne of Denmark (1574–1619)" (1617), *The Royal Collection Trust* (RCIN 405887), https://www.rct.uk/collection/405887/anne-of-denmark-1574-1619
30 Daniel Mytens, "Charles I and Henrietta Maria Departing for the Chase c. 1630-2," *The Royal Collection Trust* (RCIN 404771), https://www.rct.uk/collection/404771/charles-i-and-henrietta-maria-departing-for-the-chase; Anthony Dent, *Horses in Shakespeare's England* (London: J.A. Allen, 1987), 112.
31 "Jacob Larwood" [L. R. Sadler], *The Story of the London Parks* (London: Chatto and Windus, 1881), 57.
32 Jon Stobart and Mark Rothery, *Consumption and the Country House* (Oxford: Oxford University Press, 2016), 123.
33 *The Sporting Magazine*, Volume 15 (October 1799), 47.
34 Weiss and Pfeiffer, 14.
35 In addition to Seymour's paintings, see Thomas Gooch, "Marcia Pitt and Her Brother George Pitt, Later second Baron Rivers, Riding in the Park at Stratfield Saye House, Hampshire" (1782), *Yale Center for British Art, Paul Mellon Collection*: https://collections.britishart.yale.edu/catalog/tms:41827
36 Mr. Carter [Charles Carter], *Instructions for Ladies in Riding, by Mr. Carter* (London, 1783), 27–28.
37 Alfred Roger, *Livre de l'équitation des dames et de la gymnastique* (Paris: Ch. Ploche, 1852), 7; Veauvy, de Savray, and d'Amécourt, 100.
38 For example, see Thomas Butler, "Emma, A Hunter belonging to Lady Mary Carr" (1755); James Seymour, "Princess Amelia" (1755); George Stubbs, "The Duchess of Richmond" (c. 1760); Robert Healy, "Lady Louisa Conolly," (1768), and Francis Stringer, "Sprightly, A Lady's Hack" (1768).
39 "An English Side-saddle Made of Soft Leather," Lot 37, Christie's, *Chirk Castle*, June 21, 2004, https://www.christies.com/lotfinder/Lot/an-english-side-saddle-of-soft-leather-4320881-details.aspx
40 John Wootton, "A Hunting Party; Possibly Depicting Charles Spencer, 3rd Duke of Marlborough (1706-1758) and his Wife Elizabeth, Countess of Marlborough (d. 1761)," Lot 38, Sotheby's, *Old Master and British Paintings Evening Sale*, July 4, 2012, https://www.sothebys.com/en/auctions/ecatalogue/lot.38.html/2012/old-master-british-paintings-evening-sale
41 See John Wootton, "Equestrian Portrait of Lady Henrietta Harley, Countess of Oxford and Countess Mortimer (1694–1755), Led by a Groom with a Hunt Attendant, in a Landscape (1716)"; many versions exist, including one sold at Sotheby's in 2016 for over £80,000: https://www.sothebys.com/en/auctions/ecatalogue/2016/old-masters-day-sale-l16037/lot.192.html; and John Wootton,

"Lady Mary Churchill at the Death of the Hare" (1748), who was Sir Robert Walpole's illegitimate daughter and enthusiastic equestrian; Tate Gallery: https://www.tate.org.uk/art/artworks/wootton-lady-mary-churchill-at-the-death-of-the-hare-t02378

42 John Wootton, "Lady Henrietta Harley Hunting with her Harriers," shows the subject galloping with the field, in a blue habit; the red and gold trimmed saddle cover (and matching breastplate) is just visible, as shown in David Coombs, *Sport and the Countryside in English Paintings, Watercolours, and Prints* (Oxford: Phaidon, 1978), 32–33. Another painting by John Wootton, "Lady Henrietta Harley Hunting the Hare on Orwell Hill" (1716), similarly shows the subject galloping, but this time from the off side, with a long, rectangular saddle skirt visible, in Walter Shaw Sparrow, *British Sporting Artists from Barlow to Herring* (London: Spring Books, 1922), plate 38 before page 99. A further artwork by John Wootton (possibly), "A Hunting Party" ("Fox Hunters at Full Gallop"), shows an unidentified woman speeding after the hounds with two male companions and huntsman, from Sparrow, *British Sporting Artists from Barlow to Herring*, plate 31 after page 98.

43 James Seymour, "A Lady and a Gentleman Riding Out" (undated), *Yale Center for British Art*: https://collections.britishart.yale.edu/catalog/tms:46204; James Seymour, "A Lady Riding Side-Saddle, Turns to Look at a Dismounted Rider" (undated), *Yale Center for British Art*: https://collections.britishart.yale.edu/catalog/tms:46435; James Seymour, "An Elegant Couple on Horseback," *Christie's*, https://www.christies.com/lotfinder/Lot/james-seymour-1702-1752-an-elegant-couple-on-5743360-details.aspx; James Seymour, "Woman Wearing a Tricorne Hat, Riding to Right" (undated), *Yale Center for British Art*: https://collections.britishart.yale.edu/catalog/tms:47065; James Seymour, "Princess Amelia on Horseback" (c. 1755), *The Royal Collection Trust* (RCIN 407453), https://www.rct.uk/collection/search#/2/collection/407453/princess-amelia-on-horseback; James Seymour, "Stag Hunting" (private collection), features two women galloping in the center foreground of the painting, depicted in Coombs, *Sport and the Countryside in English Paintings, Watercolours, and Prints*, cover page and 39.

44 Between 1759 and 1779, George Stubbs completed six paintings featuring horses and riders in the sidesaddle fashion: see Judy Egerton, *George Stubbs, Painter: Catalogue Raisonné* (New Haven: Yale University Press, 2007): "Sketch of Mrs. Angelo Riding a Grey Horse" (c. 1760), 132; "A Young Lady in White Mounted on a Dark Bay Horse" (c. 1759–1760), 138; "The Duchess of Richmond and Lady Louisa Lennox Watching Racehorses in Training at Goodwood" (c. 1760), 142–143; "John and Sophia Musters Riding Past the South Front of Colwick Hall" (c. 1777), 390–391; "Two of Peter Beckford's Hunters with Groom and Dog" (1779), 416; George Stubbs, "The Countess of Coningsby in the Costume of the Charlton Hunt" (c. 1760), *Yale Center for British Art*, https://collections.britishart.yale.edu/catalog/tms:1084

45 Adams, 148.

46 Treva J. Tucker, "Eminence over Efficacy: Social Status and Cavalry Service in Sixteenth-Century France," *The Sixteenth Century Journal*, 32.4 (Winter 2001), 1057–1095; Peter Edwards, "The Influence of Eastern blood on English Cavalry Horses during the Course of the 17th Century," https://www.soas.ac.uk/history/conferences/war-horses-conference-2014/file94821.pdf

47 John Ellis, *Cavalry: A History of Mounted Warfare* (Barnsley, England: Pen and Sword, 2004), 140.

48 R.H.C. Davis, "The Medieval Warhorse," in F.M.L. Thompson (ed.), *Horses in European Economic History: A Preliminary Canter* (Reading: The British Agricultural History Society, 1983), 20.

49 Samuel Sidney, *The Book of the Horse* (London: Cassell and Company, Limited, 1893), 124–125.
50 Keith Chivers, "The Supply of Horses in Great Britain in the Nineteenth Century," in F.M.L. Thompson, (ed.), *Horses in European Economic History: A Preliminary Canter* (Reading: The British Agricultural History Society, 1983), 39–40.
51 Lucy Worsley, *Cavalier: The Story of a 17th Century Playboy* (London: Faber & Faber, 2007), especially pages 209–210; Peter Edwards, *Horses and the Aristocratic Lifestyle in Early Modern England: William Cavendish, First Earl of Devonshire (1551–1626), and his Horses* (Woodbridge: Boydell Press, 2018).
52 Wendy Walls, "Renaissance National Husbandry: Gervase Markham and Publication of England," *The Sixteenth Century Journal*, 27.3 (Autumn 1996), 767–785; and Elspeth Graham, "Reading, Writing, and Riding Horses in Early Modern England: James Shirley's *Hyde Park* (1632) and Gervase Markham's *Cavelarice* (1607)," in Erica Fudge (ed.), *Renaissance Beasts: Of Animals, Humans, and Other Wonderful Creatures* (Urbana, IL: University of Illinois Press, 2004). For more on Markham and his expansive work, see F.N. Poynter, *Bibliography of Gervase Markham, 1568?–1637* (Oxford: Oxford Bibliographical Society, 1962).
53 Allison Kavey, "Secrets Bridled, Gentlemen Trained," in *Books of Secrets: Natural Philosophy in England, 1550–1600* (Chicago: University of Illinois Press, 2007), 130–133.
54 Gervase Markham, *The Gentlemans Academie; or, The Booke of S. Albans* (London: Humfrey Lownes, 1595), image 2 (unnumbered page).
55 Rupert Croft-Cooke and Peter Cotes, *Circus: A World History* (New York: Macmillan Publishing Co., Inc., 1976), 7; Joan Selby-Lowndes, *The First Circus, the Story of Philip Astley* (London: Lutterworth Press, 1957); Karl Shaw, *The First Showman: The Extraordinary Mr. Astley, The Englishman Who Invented the Modern Circus* (Stroud, Gloucestershire: Amberley Publishing, 2019).
56 Kwint, 72–115.
57 Croft-Cooke and Cotes, 46–47.
58 "Origin and Progress of Horses and Horse-racing in this Island," *The Sporting Magazine*, Volume 1 (December 1792), 122–123.
59 Marius Kwint, "The Legitimization of the Circus in Late Georgian England," *Past and Present*, 174.1 (2002), 89.
60 Linda Colley, *Britons: Forging a Nation, 1707–1837* (New Haven: Yale University Press, 2005), 250–254.
61 Anne Topham, "The Riding Stables of the German Emperor," *The Badminton Magazine of Sports and Pastimes*, Volume 24 (January 1907), 66–78.
62 "Continuation of the Essay on Riding to Hounds," *The Sporting Magazine*, Volume 61 (March 1823), 331.
63 Hilda Nelson, *The Great Horsewomen of the 19th Century Circus* (Franktown, VA: Xenophon Press, 2015), 10.
64 Nelson, 4.
65 Nelson, 29.
66 Pia F. Cuneo, "(Un)Stable Identities: Hippology and the Professionalization of Scholarship and Horsemanship in Early Modern Germany," in Karl A.E. Enenkel and Paul J. Smith (eds.), *Early Modern Zoology: The Construction of Animals in Science, Literature and the Visual Arts* (Leiden: Brill, 2007), 347–368. See also Almond (2009), 39.
67 Kari Weil, "Men and Horses: Circus Studs, Sporting Males, and the Performance of Purity in Fin-de-Siècle France," *French Cultural Studies*, 17.1 (2006), 87–105.
68 Weil (2006), 89.

69 Vicomte d'Hédouville, *La Femme à cheval, théorie, pratique, anecdotes* (Paris: Paul Ollendorff, 1884), 13.
70 Baron de Vaux, *Écuyers et écuyères, histoire des cirques d'Europe (1680–1891)* (Paris: J. Rothschild, 1893), 108–109.
71 E. Molier, *L'Équitation et le cheval* (Paris: Pierre Lafitte & Cie, no date [1911]), 287.
72 Kari Weil, *Precarious Partners: Horses and Their Humans in Nineteenth-Century France* (Chicago: The University of Chicago Press, 2020), 9, 104–105, 128.
73 "Equestrienne, n." *OED Online*. Oxford University Press, September 2020.
74 Sidney (1893), 253.
75 W. Sidney Felton, *Masters of Equitation* (London: J.A. Allen and Co., 1962), 48.
76 M. L. Biscotti, *Six Centuries of Foxhunting: An Annotated Bibliography* (London: Rowman & Littlefield, 2017), xiv, 40–41.
77 Jean de Kermaingant, "Venery in France," in Jean Froissard and Lily Powell Froissard (eds.), *The Horseman's International Book of Reference* (London: Stanley Paul, 1980), 273.
78 Kermaingant, 277.
79 Almond (2009), 23–24, 149.
80 James MacKillop, *Dictionary of Celtic Mythology* (Oxford: Oxford University Press, 1998), 122.
81 Almond (2009), 24.
82 Pia Cuneo, "The Reformation of Riding: Protestant Identity and Horsemanship at North German Courts," *The Court Historian*, 24.3 (2019), 235–249.
83 Weil (2020), 8.
84 J. Pellier fils, *L'Équitation pratique* (Paris: La Hachette & Cie, 1861), 127–128.
85 Meriel Buxton, *Ladies of the Chase* (London: The Sportsman's Press, 1987), 28; Letter to the Countess of Mar (1725), *The Letters and Works of Lady Mary Wortley Montagu, Volume 2* (London: Richard Bentley, 1837), 189.
86 Devorah Lauter, "Women in Paris Finally Allowed to Wear Trousers," *The Daily Telegraph* (London), February 3, 2013, https://www.telegraph.co.uk/news/worldnews/europe/france/9845545/Women-in-Paris-finally-allowed-to-wear-trousers.html
87 Joan W. Scott, "Gender: A Useful Category of Historical Analysis," *The American Historical Review*, 91.5 (1986), 1056.
88 Jeanne Boydston, "Gender as a Question of Historical Analysis," *Gender and History*, 20.3 (November 2008), 576.
89 Robert B. Shoemaker, *Gender in English Society, 1650–1850: The Emergence of Separate Spheres?* (London: Longman, 1998); Leonore Davidoff and Catherine Hall, *Family Fortunes: Men and Women of the English Middle Class, 1780–1850* (London: Routledge, 2002).
90 Hannah Barker and Elaine Chalus, eds., *Gender in 18th Century England* (London: Longman, 1997).
91 Jane Hamlett and Sarah Wiggins, "Victorian Women in Britain and the United States: New Perspectives," *Women's History Review*, 18.5 (November 2009), 707.
92 Catherine Hall, *White, Male and Middle Class: Explorations in Feminism and History* (New York: Routledge, 1992), 386–387.
93 Colley, 240.
94 Amanda Vickery, "Golden Age to Separate Spheres? A Review of the Categories and Chronology of English Women's History," *The Historical Journal*, 36.2 (June 1993), 400.
95 Jane Hamlett, "'The Dining Room Should be the Man's Paradise, as the Drawing Room is the Woman's': Gender and Middle-Class Domestic Space in England, 1850–1910," *Gender & History*, 21.3 (November 2009), 576–591.

96 John Tosh, *A Man's Place: Masculinity and the Middle-Class Home in Victorian England* (New Haven: Yale University Press, 1999).
97 Colley, 172.
98 Norbert Elias, *The Civilizing Process* (New York: Urizen Books, 1978).
99 Norbert Elias and Eric Dunning, *Quest for Excitement: Sport and Leisure in the Civilizing Process* (Oxford: Basil Blackwell, 1986), 161–162.
100 Eric Dunning, "Sport in the Western Civilizing Process," in Eric Dunning (ed.), *Sport Matters: Sociological Studies of Sport, Violence, and Civilization* (London: Routledge, 1999), 50, 53, 58, 60–61.
101 Walter Liedtke, *The Royal Horse and Rider: Painting, Sculpture, and Horsemanship, 1500–1800* (New York: Abaris Books, 1989).
102 Keith Thomas, *Man and the Natural World: Changing Attitudes in England 1500–1800* (Oxford: Oxford University Press, 1983), 29.
103 Liedtke, 37.
104 Albert Cler, *La comédie à cheval, ou Manies et travers du monde équestre* (Paris: Ernest Boudin, 1842), 56, cited in Weil (2020), 7.
105 Davidoff and Hall, 403–404.
106 Thorstein Veblen, *The Theory of the Leisure Class* (New York: The MacMillan Company, 1912), 144.
107 Joan Thirsk, "Horses in Early Modern England: for service, for pleasure, for power," in *The Rural Economy of England: Collected Essays* (London: Hambledon Press, 1984), 377.
108 Thirsk, 397.
109 Susie Steinbach, *Understanding the Victorians: Politics, Culture, and Society in Nineteenth-century Britain* (London: Routledge, 2012).
110 Deborah Cohen, *Household Gods: The British and Their Possessions* (New Haven: Yale University Press, 2006), 13, 33.
111 Neil McKendrick, John Brewer, J.H. Plumb, eds., *The Birth of a Consumer Society: The Commercialization of Eighteenth-Century England* (Bloomington: Indiana University Press, 1982), 265; see also Peter Bailey, *Leisure and Class in Victorian Britain* (London: Routledge and Kegan Paul, 1978).
112 William A. Thomas, "Review Essay: Pursuing Wild Symbols of Privilege: Munsche's *Gentlemen and Poachers: The English Game Laws 1671–1831*," *American Bar Foundation Research Journal*, 8.2 (Spring, 1983), 481–482.
113 Donna Landry, *The Invention of the Countryside: Hunting, Walking and Ecology in English Literature, 1671–1831* (New York: Palgrave, 2001).
114 Landry (2001), 65.
115 Richard Holt, "*Sport and the British*: Its Origins, Ideas, and Composition," *Sport in History*, 31.2 (June 2011), 141.
116 Biscotti, 176; John Hawkes, *The Meynellian Science; or, Fox Hunting upon System* (Brooklyn: Privately Printed for Ernest R. Gee, 1926), 23–24.
117 Anthony Trollope, "About Hunting," *Saint Paul's: A Monthly Magazine*, Volume 1 (November 1867), 208.
118 Raymond Carr, *English Fox Hunting* (London: Weidenfeld and Nicholson, 1976), 60.
119 Davidoff and Hall, 13.
120 Davidoff and Hall, xviii; Amanda Gilroy, "The Habit and the Horse, or, the Suburbanization of Female Equitation," in Amanda Gilroy (ed.), *Green and Pleasant Land: English Culture and the Romantic Countryside* (Leuven: Peeters, 2004), 46, 55.
121 Dipesh Chakrabarty, *Provincializing Europe: Postcolonial Thought and Historical Difference* (Princeton: Princeton University Press, 2008); Gayatri Chakravorty Spivak, "Can the Subaltern Speak?" in Cary Nelson and Lawrence Grossberg (eds.), *Marxism and the Interpretation of Culture* (Urbana: University of Illinois Press, 1988).

122 Catherine Hall and Sonya O. Rose, *At Home with the Empire: Metropolitan Culture and the Imperial World* (Cambridge: Cambridge University Press, 2006).
123 Sarah E. Stockwell, *The British Empire: Themes and Perspectives* (Oxford: Blackwell Publishing, 2008).
124 William Thackeray, *The Newcomes: Memoirs of a Most Respectable Family, Volume 1* (London: Bradbury and Evans, 1854), 52.
125 Ronald Hyam, *Empire and Sexuality: The British Experience* (Manchester: Manchester University Press, 1990), 141; see also Antoinette Burton, *Burdens of History: British Feminists, Indian Women, and Imperial Culture, 1865–1915* (Chapel Hill: University of North Carolina Press, 1994); Mrinalini Sinha, *Colonial Masculinity: The "Manly Englishman" and the "Effeminate Bengali" in the Late Nineteenth Century* (Manchester: Manchester University Press, 1995); Philippa Levine, ed., *Gender and Empire* (Oxford: Oxford University Press, 2004); Angela Woollacott, *Gender and Empire* (New York: Palgrave Macmillan, 2006).
126 Margaret Strobel, *European Women and the Second British Empire* (Bloomington: Indiana University Press, 1991); Margaret Strobel and Nupur Chaudhuri, *Western Women and Imperialism, Complicity and Resistance* (Bloomington, IL: University of Illinois Press, 1992).
127 Edward W. Said, *Orientalism* (New York: Vintage Books, 1979).
128 Anne McClintock, *Imperial Leather: Race, Gender and Sexuality in the Colonial Contest* (New York: Routledge, 1995), 6–7.
129 J.A. Mangan and Callum C. McKenzie, *Militarism, Hunting, Imperialism: "Blooding" the Martial Male* (Abingdon: Routledge, 2009). See also J.A. Mangan, *"Manufactured" Masculinity: Making Imperial Manliness, Morality and Militarism* (London: Routledge, 2012).
130 J.A. Mangan and Callum McKenzie, "'Pig Sticking is the Greatest Fun': Martial Conditioning on the Hunting Fields of Empire," in J.A. Mangan (ed.), *Militarism, Sport, and Europe: War without Weapons* (London: Frank Cass, 2003), 100.
131 Mary A. Procida, "Good Sports and Right Sorts: Guns, Gender, and Imperialism in British India," *The Journal of British Studies*, 40.4 (October 2001), 462; Mary A. Procida, *Married to the Empire: Gender, Politics, and Imperialism in India, 1883–1947* (Manchester: Manchester University Press, 2002).
132 Rahul Bedi, "'Tally Ho!' cries the huntsman… in India?," *BBC News*, July 20, 2004, http://news.bbc.co.uk/2/hi/south_asia/3907861.stm
133 John MacKenzie, *The Empire of Nature: Hunting, Conservatism, and British Imperialism* (Manchester: Manchester University Press, 1988).
134 Procida (2001), 474.
135 E.I. Steinhart, "Hunters, Poachers and Gamekeepers: Towards a Social History of Hunting in Colonial Kenya," *The Journal of African History*, 30.2 (1989), 247–264; William K. Storey, "Big Cats and Imperialism: Lion and Tiger Hunting in Kenya and Northern India, 1898–1930," *Journal of World History*, 2.2 (Fall 1991), 135–173; Joseph Sramek, "'Face Him like a Briton': Tiger Hunting, Imperialism, and British Masculinity in Colonial India, 1800-1875," *Victorian Studies*, 48.4 (Summer 2006), 659–680; Angela Thompsell, *Hunting Africa: British Sport, African Knowledge and the Nature of Empire* (New York: Palgrave Macmillan, 2015); Vijaya Ramadas Mandala, *Shooting a Tiger: Big-game Hunting and Conservation in Colonial India* (New Delhi: Oxford University Press, 2019).
136 Philippa Levine, ed., *Gender and Empire* (The Oxford History of the British Empire Companion Series) (Oxford: Oxford University Press, 2004); Andrew Thompson, ed., *Britain's Experience of Empire in the Twentieth Century* (The Oxford History of the British Empire Companion Series) (Oxford: Oxford University Press, 2012), 10–11.

137 Sir Humphrey F. De Trafford, Bart., *The Horses of the British Empire* (London: Walter Southwood and Co., Limited, 1907); Greg Bankoff and Sandra Swart, eds., *Breeds of Empire: The "Invention" of the Horse in Southeast Asia and Southern Africa, 1500–1950* (Copenhagen: NIAS, 2007); and James L.A. Webb, Jr., "The Horse and Slave Trade between the Western Sahara and Senegambia," *The Journal of African History*, 34.2 (1993), 221–246.

138 Horace A. Laffaye, *The Evolution of Polo* (Jefferson, NC: McFarland and Company, Inc., 2009), and *Polo in Britain: A History* (Jefferson, NC: McFarland and Company, Inc., 2012); Patrick McDevitt, "The King of Sports: Polo in late Victorian and Edwardian India," *International Journal of the History of Sport*, 20.1 (2003), 1–27; Eliza Riedi, "Brains or Polo? Equestrian Sport, Army Reform and the Gentlemanly Officer Tradition, 1900–1914," *Journal of the Society for Army Historical Research*, 84 (2006), 236–253; Luise Elsaesser, "'Dashing about with the greatest gallantry': polo in India and the British metropole, 1862–1914," *Sport in History*, 40.1 (2020), 1–27.

139 "Indian Paper-Chase," *The Illustrated Sporting and Dramatic News* (April 19, 1879), 101.

140 Laura Doan, "A Challenge to 'Change'? New Perspectives on Women and the Great War," *Women's History Review*, 15.2 (April 2006), 337–343.

141 For example, see Clare Midgley, *Women against Slavery: The British Campaigns, 1780–1870* (London: Routledge, 1992) and Seth Koven, *Slumming: Sexual and Social Politics in Victorian London* (Princeton: Princeton University Press, 2004).

142 Alison Light, *Forever England: Femininity, Literature, and Conservatism Between the Wars* (London: Routledge: 1991), 9.

143 Claire Langhamer, *Women's Leisure in England, 1920–60* (Manchester: Manchester University Press, 2000).

144 Ina Zweiniger-Bargielowska, "The Making of a Modern Female Body: Beauty, Health, and Fitness in Interwar Britain," *Women's History Review*, 20.2 (April 2011), 299–317; Ina Zweiniger-Bargielowska, *Managing the Body: Beauty, Health and Fitness in Britain, 1880–1939* (New York: Oxford University Press, 2011).

145 Adrian Bingham, "An Era of Domesticity? Histories of Women and Gender in Interwar Britain," *Cultural and Social History*, 1 (2004), 225–233.

146 Patricia M. Thane, "What Difference did the Vote Make? Women in Public and Private Life in Britain since 1918," *Historical Research*, 76.192 (May 2003), 268–285.

147 Julia Bush examines the anti-suffrage campaigns but does not examine sporting women. See Julia Bush, *Women Against the Vote: Female Anti-Suffragism in Britain* (Oxford: Oxford University Press, 2007).

148 Richard Holt, *Sport and the British: A Modern History* (Oxford: Clarendon Press, 1989); Tony Mason, ed., *Sport in Britain: A Social History* (Cambridge: Cambridge University Press, 1989); Dennis Brailsford, *Sport, Time, and Society: The British at Play* (New York: Routledge, 1991); Dennis Brailsford, *British Sport: A Social History* (Lanham, MD: Barnes and Noble Books, 1992); Dennis Birley, *Land of Sport and Glory: Sport and British Society, 1887–1910* (Manchester: Manchester University Press, 1995); Dennis Birley, *Playing the Game: Sport and British Society, 1910–1945* (Manchester: Manchester University Press, 1996).

149 Richard Holt, "Sport and History: The State of the Subject in Britain," *Twentieth Century British History*, 7.2 (1996), 231–252.

150 For example, see Richard Holt, *Sport and the Working Class in Modern Britain* (New York: Manchester University Press, 1990); John Lowerson, *Sport and the English Middle Classes, 1870–1914* (New York: Manchester University Press, 1993); J.A. Mangan, ed., *A Sport-loving Society: Victorian and Edwardian Middle-Class England at*

Play (London: Routledge, 2006); Mike Huggins, "Sport and the Upper Classes," *Sport in History*, 28.3 (2008), 351–363.
151 Holt (1988), 8.
152 J.A. Mangan, ed., *Making European Masculinities: Sport, Europe, Gender* (London: Frank Cass, 2000); Patrick F. McDevitt, *May the Best Man Win: Sport, Masculinity, and Nationalism in Great Britain and the Empire, 1880–1935* (Houndmills: Palgrave MacMillan, 2004).
153 J.A. Mangan, *Athleticism in the Victorian and Edwardian Public School: The Emergence and Consolidation of an Educational Ideology* (New York: Routledge, 2000).
154 Kathleen E. McCrone, "Play Up! Play Up! And Play the Game! Sport at the Late Victorian Girls' Public Schools," *The Journal of British Studies*, 23.2 (Spring 1984), 106–134.
155 Jean Williams, *A Contemporary History of Women's Sport, Part One: Sporting Women, 1850–1960* (London: Routledge, 2014), 13–17.
156 Kathleen E. McCrone, *Playing the Game: Sport and the Physical Emancipation of English Women, 1870–1914* (Lexington: University Press of Kentucky, 1988).
157 Jennifer Hargreaves, "'Playing Like Gentlemen while Behaving like Ladies': Contradictory Features of the Formative Years of Women's Sport," *The British Journal of Sports History*, 2.1 (1985), 40–52.
158 Parratt (1989), 140–157.
159 Carol A. Osborne and Fiona Skillen, "The State of Play: Women in British Sport History," *Sport in History*, 30.2 (June 2010), 189.
160 Sheila Fletcher, *Women First: The Female Tradition in English Physical Education 1880–1980* (London: Athlone Press, 1984); Hargreaves (1985); J.A. Mangan and Roberta Park, eds., *From "Fair Sex" to Feminism: Sport and the Socialization of Women in the Industrial and Post-Industrial Eras* (London: Frank Cass, 1987); McCrone (1988); Parratt (1989); Kathleen McCrone, "Class, Gender, and English Women's Sport, c. 1890–1914," *Journal of Sport History*, 18.1 (Spring 1991), 159–182; Jennifer Hargreaves, *Sporting Females: Critical Issues in the History and Sociology of Women's Sports* (London: Routledge, 1994).
161 Fiona Skillen, *Women, Sport and Modernity in Interwar Britain* (New York: Peter Lang, 2013); Williams (2014).
162 Jean Williams, *A Game for Rough Girls?: A History of Women's Football in Britain* (New York: Routledge, 2003); Rafaelle Nicholson, *Ladies and Lords: A History of Women's Cricket in Britain* (New York: Peter Lang, 2019).
163 McCrone (1988), 52.
164 This is not to denigrate what are wide-ranging and important macrohistories of the role of the horse in history: Charles Chenevix-Trench, *A History of Horsemanship* (New York: Doubleday and Company, 1970); Kellock (1974); Connor (2003); Susanna Forrest, *The Age of the Horse: An Equine Journey through Human History* (London: Atlantic Books, 2016); Ulrich Raulff, *Farewell to the Horse: The Final Century of Our Relationship*, Ruth Ahmedzai Kemp, trans. (London: Penguin Books, 2017).
165 Thomas (1983), 100–101.
166 Harriet Ritvo, "The Animal Turn in British Studies," *Anglistentag 2007 Münster, Proceedings 29*, Klaus Stiersdorfer, ed. (Trier: WVT, 2008), 13–23; Linda Kalof and Brigette Resl, *A Cultural History of Animals* (New York: Berg, 2007); Linda Kalof, *Looking at Animals in Human History* (London: Reaktion Books, 2007); Sandra Swart, "'But Where's the Bloody Horse?': Textuality and Corporeality in the 'Animal Turn'," *Journal of Literary Studies: Ecocriticism*, 23.3 (2007), 271–292.
167 Kristen Guest and Monica Mattfield, eds., *Equestrian Cultures: Horses, Human Society, and the Discourse of Modernity* (Chicago: The University of Chicago Press, 2019).

168 J.H. Plumb, *The Commercialisation of Leisure in Eighteenth-century England* (Reading: University of Reading, 1973), 16, footnote 58.
169 Roger Longrigg, *The History of Horse Racing* (New York: Stein and Day, 1972); Wray Vamplew, *The Turf: A Social and Economic History of Horse Racing* (London: Allen Lane, 1976); Roger Munting, *Hedges and Hurdles: A Social and Economic History of National Hunt Racing* (London: J.A. Allen, 1987).
170 Mike Huggins, *Flat Racing and British Society, 1790–1914: A Social and Economic History* (London: Frank Cass, 2000); Mike Huggins, *Horseracing and the British, 1919–39* (Manchester: Manchester University Press, 2003); Mike Huggins, *Horse Racing and British Society in the Long Eighteenth Century* (Woodbridge: The Boydell Press, 2018).
171 Rebecca Cassidy, *The Sport of Kings: Kinship, Class, and Thoroughbred Breeding in Newmarket* (Cambridge: Cambridge University Press, 2002); David Oldrey, Timothy Cox, and Richard Nash, *The Heath and the Horse: A History of Racing and Art on Newmarket Heath* (London: Philip Wilson Publishers, 2016). For gambling, see Mike Huggins and J.A. Mangan, eds., *Disreputable Pleasures: Less Virtuous Victorians at Play* (New York: Frank Cass, 2004) and Mike Huggins, *Vice and the Victorians* (New York: Bloomsbury Academic, 2016); Esther Harper, "Fast Horses: The Racehorse in Health, Disease and Afterlife, 1800–1920," Ph.D. Dissertation, King's College, London (2018).
172 David C. Itzkowitz, *Peculiar Privilege: A Social History of English Foxhunting, 1753–1885* (Hassocks, Sussex: The Harvester Press Limited, 1977); Raymond Carr, *English Fox Hunting* (London: Weidenfeld and Nicholson, 1976); Roger Longrigg, *The History of Foxhunting* (New York: Clarkson N. Potter Inc., 1975).
173 Jane Ridley, *Fox Hunting* (London: Collins, 1990); Michael Clayton, *Foxhunting in Paradise* (London: J. Murray, 1993).
174 Alison Plumb and David Marsh, "Beyond Party Discipline: UK Parliamentary Voting on Fox Hunting," *British Politics*, 8.3 (2013), 313–314.
175 Emma Griffin, *Blood Sport: Hunting in Britain since 1066* (New Haven: Yale University Press, 2007).
176 Jonathan Finch, "'Grass, Grass, Grass': Hunting and the Creation of the Modern Landscape," *Landscapes*, 5.2 (October 2004), 41–52; Jonathan Finch, "'What more were the pastures of Leicester to me?' Hunting, Landscape Character, and the Politics of Place," *International Journal of Cultural Property*, 14.3 (August 2007), 361–383; Mandy de Belin, *From the Deer to the Fox: The Hunting Transition and the Landscape, 1600–1850* (Hatfield: University of Hertfordshire Press, 2013).
177 Michael Tichelar, *The History of Opposition to Blood Sports in Twentieth Century England: Hunting at Bay* (New York: Routledge, 2017).
178 John Clark, *The Medieval Horse and its Equipment, c.1150–c.1450* (Woodbridge: The Boydell Press, 2004); Richard Almond (2009); John G. Cummins, *The Art of Medieval Hunting: The Hound and the Hawk* (Edison, NJ: Castle Books, 2003).
179 Peter Edwards, *Horse and Man in Early Modern England* (London: Continuum, 2007).
180 Karen Raber and Treva J. Tucker, eds., *The Culture of the Horse: Status, Discipline, and Identity in the Early Modern World* (New York: Palgrave Macmillan, 2005).
181 Donna Landry, *Noble Brutes: How Eastern Horses Transformed English Culture* (Baltimore: Johns Hopkins University Press, 2008); Donna Landry, "The Making of the English Hunting Seat" in Mary Garrett, Heidi Gottfried, and Sandra F. VanBurkleo (eds.), *Remapping the Humanities: Identity, Community, Memory, (Post)Modernity* (Detroit: Wayne State University Press, 2008).
182 Nicholas Russell, *Like Engend'ring Like: Heredity and Animal Breeding in Early Modern England* (Cambridge: Cambridge University Press, 1986); Margaret E. Derry, *Horses in Society: A Story of Animal Breeding and Marketing, 1800–1920* (Toronto: University of Toronto Press, 2006); Kristen Guest and Monica Mattfeld, eds., *Horse*

Breeds and Human Society: Purity, Identity and the Making of the Modern Horse (New York: Routledge, 2020).
183 Peter Edwards, Karl A.E. Enenkel, and Elspeth Graham, *The Horse as Cultural Icon: The Real and Symbolic Horse in the Early Modern World* (Leiden: Brill, 2012); Louise Hill Curth, *"A Plaine and Easie Waie to Remedie a Horse": Equine Medicine in Early Modern England* (Leiden: Brill, 2013); Kevin De Ornellas, *The Horse in Early Modern English Culture: Bridled, Curbed, and Tamed* (Madison, NJ: Fairleigh Dickinson University Press, 2013); Anastasija Ropa and Timothy Dawson, *The Horse in Premodern European Culture* (Kalamazoo: Medieval Institute Publications, 2019).
184 Pia Cuneo, "The Reformation of Riding: Protestant Identity and Horsemanship at North German Courts," *The Court Historian*, 24.3 (2019), 235–249; Pia Cuneo, "Equine Empathies: Giving Voice to Horses in Early Modern Germany," in Sarah D. P. Cockram and Andrew Wells (eds.), *Interspecies Interactions: Animals and Humans between the Middle Ages and Modernity* (New York: Routledge, 2018).
185 Treva Tucker, "From Destrier to Danseur: The Role of the Horse in Early Modern French Noble Identity," Ph.D. Dissertation, University of Southern California, 2007; Daniel Roche and Daniel Reytier, *À cheval!: écuyers, amazones & cavaliers du XIVe au XXIe siècle* (Paris: Association pour l'académie d'art équestre de Versailles, 2007); Daniel Roche, "Equestrian Culture in France from the Sixteenth to the Nineteenth Century," *Past and Present*, 199 (May 2008), 113–145.
186 Gaby Hermsdorf, *Frauen zu Pferde Geschichte und Geschichten der Reiterinnen* (Hamburg: Philippe-Verl., 1998); Catherine Tourre-Malen, *Femmes à cheval: la féminisation des sports et des loisirs équestres: une avancée?* (Paris: Belin, 2006); Rosine Lagier, *La femme et le cheval: des siècles d'histoire* (Janzé: C. Hérissey, 2009); Susanna Hedenborg and Gertrud Pfister, "Écuyères and 'Doing Gender,' Presenting Femininity in a Male Domain – Female Circus Riders 1800–1920," *Scandinavian Sport Studies Forum*, 3 (2012), 25–47; Hilda Nelson, *The Great Horsewomen of the 19th Century Circus* (Franktown, VA: Xenophon Press, 2015); Veauvy, de Savray, and d'Amécourt (2016).
187 Lida Fleitmann Bloodgood, *The Saddle of Queens: The Story of the Side-Saddle* (London: J.A. Allen and Co., 1959); Rosamund Owen, *The Art of Sidesaddle: History, Etiquette, Showing* (Saltash, Cornwall: Trematon Press, 1984).
188 Buxton (1987), and Caroline Ramsden, *Ladies in Racing: Sixteenth Century to the Present Day* (London: Stanley Paul, 1973).
189 Janet Arnold, "Dashing Amazons: The Development of Women's Riding Dress, c. 1500–1900," in Amy de la Haye and Elizabeth Wilson (eds.), *Defining Dress: Dress as Object, Meaning, and Identity* (Manchester: Manchester University Press, 1999); Cally Blackman, "Walking Amazons: The Development of the Riding Habit in England during the Eighteenth Century," *Costume: The Journal of the Costume Society*, 35 (2001), 47–58; Alison Matthews David, "Elegant Amazons: Victorian Riding Habits and the Fashionable Horsewoman," *Victorian Literature and Culture*, 30.1 (2002), 179–210.
190 Monica Mattfield, *Becoming Centaur: Eighteenth-century Masculinity and English Horsemanship* (University Park, PA: The Pennsylvania State University Press, 2017).
191 "Sport, n.1." *OED Online*, Oxford University Press, September 2020, www.oed.com/view/Entry/187476.
192 Williams (2014), 4.
193 Dennis Brailsford, *A Taste for Diversions: Sport in Georgian England* (Cambridge: The Lutterworth Press, 1999), 7.
194 Chris Chase, "Which Olympic Sport Is the Hardest? Fourth-Place Medal Ranks All 32," *Yahoo Sports*, July 11, 2012, https://ca.sports.yahoo.com/blogs/olympics-fourth-

place-medal/olympic-sport-hardest-fourth-place-medal-ranks-32-195706044--oly.html
195 Susanna Hedenborg and Manon Hedenborg White, "Changes and Variations in Patterns of Gender Relations in Equestrian Sports during the Second Half of the Twentieth Century," *Sport in Society*, 15.3 (2012), 302–319; Birgitta Plymoth, "Gender in Equestrian Sports: An Issue of Difference and Equality," *Sport in Society*, 15.3 (2012), 335–348; Katherine Dashper, "Together, Yet Still Not Equal? Sex Integration in Equestrian Sport," *Asia-Pacific Journal of Health, Sport and Physical Education*, 3.3 (2012), 213–225; Deborah Butler, "Not a Job for 'Girly-Girls': Horseracing, Gender and Work Identities," *Sport in Society*, 16.10 (2013), 1309–1325; Susanna Hedenborg, "Gender and Sports within the Equine Sector - A Comparative Perspective," *The International Journal of the History of Sport*, 32.4 (2015), 551–564.
196 John L. Firth, "Equestrian Injuries," in R.C. Schneider, J.C. Kennedy, and M.L. Plant (eds.), *Sports Injuries: Mechanisms, Prevention, and Treatment* (Baltimore: Williams & Wilkins, 1985), 431–449.
197 John Butler, *The Horse; and How to Ride Him: A Treatise on the Art of Riding and Leaping* (London: Baily Brothers, 1861), 5.
198 William H. Brooks and Doris M. Bixby-Hammett, "Prevention of Neurologic Injuries in Equestrian Sports," *The Physician and Sportsmedicine*, 16.11 (1988), 84–95; Firth, 431–449.
199 Malia Wollan, "How to Fall Off a Horse," *The New York Times*, April 25, 2018, https://www.nytimes.com/2018/04/25/magazine/how-to-fall-off-a-horse.html
200 Firth (1985); E.H. Carrillo, D. Varnagy, S.M. Bragg, J. Levy, and K. Riordan, "Traumatic Injuries Associated with Horseback Riding," *Scandinavian Journal of Surgery*, 96 (2007), 79–82.
201 William Shakespeare, *Henry IV, Part 1*, Act 4, Scene 1, Lines 109–100, in David Bevington (ed.), *The Complete Works of Shakespeare* (New York: Longman, 1997), 793.

Chapter 1

Ladies, Hunting, and the Sporting Revolution in Britain, 1772–1825

The late eighteenth century was an era of widespread and talented female horsemanship. Many women excelled at equestrian sports, especially fox hunting. Contemporary authors and commentators often wrote about and praised these huntresses. The foremost was Mary Amelia "Emily Mary" Cecil, the first Marchioness of Salisbury. She was considered "the epitome of Tory society," only comparable to her Whig rival, the Duchess of Devonshire.[1] The Marchioness was the first woman to appear in an illustration for *The Sporting Magazine,* and her skillful, if daring, equestrian feats graced its pages frequently. In January 1796, Lady Salisbury's Hertfordshire Hunt had a smashing run of over three and a half hours for two foxes over 40 miles of country. *The Sporting Magazine* recorded:

> Out of a field of fourscore [eighty riders], only *nine* were in at the earth, at the head of whom was Lady Salisbury. After giving honest Daniel, the old huntsman, the go by, she pressed Mr. Hale *neck* and *neck*; – soon blowed the Whipper-in, and contrived indeed, through the whole chace to be always nearest the *brush!*[2]

This hunt was actually of relatively brief duration, only about a third of the time of the usual all-day affair. Riders traveled over 11 miles per hour, the speed of a fast trot or slow canter. In April of the same year, "The Marchioness was foremost, as usual, in taking all the *dashing leaps* that came before her" in a field of an estimated 400 people.[3] Despite the limitations imposed by the two-pommeled sidesaddle when jumping over fences and galloping at speed, the Marchioness rode brilliantly, and she was joined by the best riders of the day, including Hugo Meynell, founder of the Quorn Hunt, and the Duke of Wellington.[4]

Well known for her superb horsemanship, the Marchioness was also the first female Master of Foxhounds (M.F.H.), having taken the office of Master from her husband in 1775 and holding it until 1819, when she was 70 years old.[5] She maintained her own pack of dwarf foxhounds, renowned for their sensible demeanors and delicate noses, as well as coursing greyhounds and a pack of harriers.[6] She regularly hosted fields of 40 to 80 riders, consisting of guests who lodged with her at Hatfield House, as well as many local farmers and horse dealers, who were welcome to ride along, thus showing the early localized and democratic nature of the sport.[7]

In 1802, *The Sporting Magazine* reported, "The Marchioness of Salisbury's dwarf foxhounds are in high reputation: they have had a succession of fine runs this season, in which her Ladyship, by dint of superior jockeyship, had generally contrived, with the Squires of the Chase – 'to leave them at a distance behind.'"[8] Her hunts were both successful and popular, not only due to her social reputation and personal charisma, but also for her experienced and no-nonsense hunting expertise. In 1807, it was declared, "her Ladyship is said to be the best *sportsman* in that sporting country!!!"[9] Rather than being perceived as less respectable as a woman for following the hounds, the Marchioness was considered much more, receiving the ultimate compliment of being so talented that she was actually better than her fellow athletes, the men.

Even as she grew older, the Marchioness continued her favorite pastimes of riding and hunting, although she was less aggressive in the saddle. As *The Sporting Magazine* concluded, "Lady S-----, one of the boldest female riders in the kingdom, relaxes a little with her own foxhounds; some few years ago since she almost invariably went *over the gate*; she now waits with more prudence and patience till the gate is opened."[10] The Marchioness continued hunting until 1830 when she was 80 years old and had to be literally tied to the saddle due to blindness, following a special groom who not only piloted her in the field, but led her horse on a leading rein. When they reached a jump in the field, the groom would reportedly shout, "Damn you, my lady, jump!" and together they would leap across the obstacles.[11]

What was the standard of eighteenth-century femininity? What role could – and did – women play in public? How did women push at the boundaries of the proper, and how were they limited by demands of the acceptable? By the mid-eighteenth century, women imitated men in several new and potentially radical ways – in theater, politics, and sports. Actresses on stage could imitate men with devastating and convincing effect, and sometimes even carry those roles into real life. In politics, women such as Georgianna, Duchess of Devonshire, involved themselves in electioneering, campaigning, and canvassing. As Elaine Chalus notes, "openly political involvement was accepted, not because they were viewed as honorary men, but out of respect for their political capabilities."[12] Women were thus respected for their own abilities; their power reflected their femininity, and vice versa. In fact, politics and female equestrianism often mixed, as hunts often followed campaigning.[13]

Participating in horse sports was one way women pushed at the boundaries of their sex and expanded their horizons. In *A Vindication of the Rights of Woman* from 1792, Mary Wollstonecraft encouraged women to "take sufficient exercise and not [be] confined in close rooms," and then concluded: "Let us then, by being allowed to take the same exercise as boys, not only during infancy, but youth, arrive at perfection of body, that we may know how far the natural superiority of man extends."[14] Occasionally women such as Lady Salisbury may have been viewed as an "honorary man" (in her case, "the best sports*man*") but women were more often respected for doing a man's work in their own quiet, capable, and unassuming feminine ways. Contemporaries often viewed women's roles and gender differences in far more intricate and malleable ways than a simple and definite separation between the sexes.[15]

All of these sporting and gendered changes in Britain must be placed in the context of the times. The emerging Industrial Revolution led to the development of new social classes and new ideals of domesticity, but foreign events also influenced such transformations. The eighteenth century was an era of British warfare. This martial focus affected many areas of society, including sports. From the Jacobite Rebellion to the Seven Years' War, from the American Revolution to the French Revolution, many British men fought in the wars. Defeats in India, America, and France led to a perceived decline in Britain's national character after mid-century, which was partly attributed to blurred distinctions between the proper roles and behaviors of both sexes.[16] Rather than intensifying ideals of masculinity, the defeats exacerbated the idea that British men had become effeminate and emasculated. In contrast, women had supposedly become fiercely masculine. These anxieties expressed the moral and social concern with clearly defined gender roles – or the lack thereof. Eighteenth century texts argued that the two sexes were naturally different, and that such differences should define their roles at home and in public.

By the 1790s, the French Revolution brought questions about proper female behavior to the forefront of public debate. These tensions only increased at the beginning of the nineteenth century when Britain became consumed in a struggle for existence during the Napoleonic Wars. Some explanations of the French Revolution viewed the overthrow of the patriarchal monarchy as the result of an inversion of gender roles and the weak effeminacy of the *ancien régime*. Not only were radical Frenchwomen suddenly in command – as in the March on Versailles – but the upper classes had lost all martial vigor and public respect by succumbing to the lure of luxury and idleness.[17] Frenchmen had been corrupted into effeminate softness. So, would British men follow suit, and where did British women fit in?

This chapter answers that question by examining women's place in equestrian sports from the late eighteenth to the early nineteenth centuries. It spans from the publication of Charles Hughes' *The Compleat Horseman* in 1772, the first riding manual to feature instructions for lady riders, to John Allen's *Principles of Modern Riding for Ladies* in 1825, when aspirational equestrianism and park riding had been well established. The shifting dynamics of politics, class, gender, fashion, and sport all contributed to public perceptions – both approval and disapproval – of female equestrianism. Advances in riding equipment and clothing enabled women to take a more active and efficient role on horseback. The publication of riding manuals for women and the opening of riding schools encouraged education and instruction on horseback. All of this led to the increase in women's participation in riding and hunting over the latter half of the eighteenth century.

Who were these riders? First were the aristocrats who were born to the saddle and could afford the cost of keeping horses for sport. The gentry and other rural residents followed in mounted country sports and accounted for an increasing number of female riders. Others included aspiring equestrians, including courtesans and other high-class emulators, whose passport to participation was their skill in the saddle. The Industrial Revolution also brought wealth to a new class who wished to emulate their social betters, and what better way to publicly do so than by riding and hunting? Yet just as women had made their mark and found their places in equestrian activities, sport and society changed. Hunting became faster, required the constant negotiation of fences, and became hyper-masculinized. These changes, influenced by the gendered nuances of the French Revolution and the beginning of the prescriptive ideology of separate spheres, now limited or barred female equestrian participation.

Ladies' Riding Equipment in the Eighteenth Century

Riding begins with the equipment needed to manage a horse, specifically the bridle and saddle. Sporting technology and equestrian equipage thus influenced and affected gender and social ideals. By the eighteenth century, changes in saddle design empowered women to ride more effectively. A new sidesaddle allowed them to take improved control of their mounts and engage in more collaborative horsemanship, whereby rider and horse worked more instinctively and harmoniously together. These changes resulted from practical innovations; riding equipment became less about lavish display and visual splendor and more about efficient equitation, or the art and practice of horsemanship. Advances in saddle construction changed for both men and women; such improvements illustrated how riding – and the specifically British saddles utilized – was used to promote a new and exceptional national identity in contrast to traditional European ideals.

First, saddles began to be made of leather rather than cloth. As riding in England shifted from a means of transport and royal ritual to being an urban pastime and countryside sport, more durable materials and construction were needed. Padded cloth saddles used for *haute école* in Continental riding schools could not hold up to either exposure in inclement weather or the rigorous use in hunting and racing. In the late 1600s, the only leather used for men's saddles was for coverings, stirrup leathers, and girths. By the early 1700s, however, full leather saddles had been adopted for daily riding; these saddles, made of finished and durable animal hides, could withstand the use and abuse of field sports. England therefore led the charge in saddle innovation, mainly because of the new emphasis on hunting which required a very different kind of saddle for a very different kind of riding.[18]

Riding equipment for women followed suit.[19] Full leather sidesaddles appeared by the 1780s, decades later than leather saddles for men. A few sidesaddles sported suede seats and pommels into the 1790s, but by the turn of the century, all ladies' saddles appeared to be smooth leather only, sometimes with a padded and occasionally embroidered knee grip on the flap toward the front of the saddle, similar to those on jumping saddles today.[20] Not surprisingly, this portion of the saddle was called the "safe." Besides being more durable, leather was also practical; it prevented the horse's sweat from seeping through the cloth saddle pads and spoiling ladies' expensive dresses.[21]

Second, bridles and other equipment evolved in more practical ways as well, usually by incorporating leather. Like men, women rode with a curb bit and two reins, or a double bridle. Soft leather reins were recommended because "silk, thread, or worsted reins soon twist, and are as disagreeable to the hand as a cord would be."[22] Advances did not come all at once: a 1775 painting by Sawrey Gilpin, entitled "A Bay Hunter tethered to a Tree," shows a fine horse standing to the near (left) side, wearing a two-pommeled sidesaddle lined with a light cloth or doeskin seat, and dressed with a long curb bridle with leather curb reins and light cloth snaffle reins with tassels.[23] So too does the 1780 painting of Josiah and Sarah Wedgwood at Etruria Hall by George Stubbs show Sarah with a white rein attached as the snaffle rein. But these examples seem to be outdated outliers.

Third and finally, a second pommel was added to sidesaddles, which was a major advantage (Figure 1.1). Before the eighteenth century, sidesaddles initially had a single horn near the center of the saddle; a woman hooked her left leg around this pommel for balance (Figure 0.3).[24] This invention of a second pommel, or crutch, was viewed as revolutionary at the time, as Charles Carter (writing as "Mr. Carter") indicated in his 1783 riding manual for women. As he explained:

> formerly saddles were made with pommels, two or at most three inches high, and set an inch and an half on the near [left] side, and the crutch straight, not turning up to the pommel; accidents were frequent; everything was calculated for the lady's being thrown off, instead of enabling her to keep on; every sudden motion of the horse was sure to throw the right knee over the pommel, by which means she fell, or on the pommel, when perhaps she escaped with only a severe bruise; the position in which she sat, the consequence of the bad make of the saddle, was most ungraceful; from the lowness of the pommel they were obliged to cling with the right knee, and for want of support from the crutch, and from the great sweep in the seat, they stooped and sunk in their right side at the hip, which gave rise to the invention of turn heads, to ride on either side of the horse, to prevent young ladies from growing deformed ...[25]

These changes in saddle construction not only enabled more effective equitation, but also fostered improvements in body posture and health. A woman no

Figure 1.1 James Ward, R. A., "A Lady's Hack" (1796): No image better illustrates a two-pommel sidesaddle than this painting by James Ward, circa 1796. The addition of a second pommel created a u-shaped "fork" at the front of the sidesaddle, through which a lady could wedge her right leg, while leaving her left to balance in a stirrup. Formerly women had sat perpendicular to the horse's head (90 degrees), but now they sat twisted to the front (the top half of their body facing forward, with the waist down turned 45 degrees to the side). The new pommel allowed forward-facing horsemanship, which enabled more effective equitation.

Credit: © Virginia Museum of Fine Arts, Richmond (Paul Mellon Collection), Photo: Travis Fullerton.

longer had to twist her leg around a single horn to maintain her position on horseback. The new pommel allowed a more secure and forward-facing horsemanship, which enabled women to ride more naturally and effectively, being more in sync with her mount.

While the double pommels were a significant advance, these saddles were not free from their own particular dangers. Tall, prong-like crutches could ensnare a lady and prevent her from falling free of her horse in case of an accident, while also dangerously bruising her internal organs and ribs if her horse stopped short and she was forcefully thrown against them. But smaller, shorter crutches were no more helpful, given that they were little more than molded leather bumps on the saddle. They offered her little security in keeping her seat, as any sharp movement could easily dislodge her right leg from its position, tip her off-balance, and cause a fall. That might result in being dragged if she could not free her foot from the stirrup first. As *The Sporting Magazine* noted, a woman's "balance is the only means she had of keeping her seat on horseback; which if she once loses, it is ten to one she comes to the ground."[26] As Richard Berenger, master of the horse for King George III, concluded in 1771, "and hard indeed is the *equestrian* situation of the sex! for if they are to be accused of indelicacy for riding after the *manner* of *men*, they certainly hazard their safety too much in riding after the *manner* of *women*."[27]

Though the two-pommel sidesaddle was an advance on riding pillion or sitting sideways on an oversized cushion, it still had many shortcomings (Figure 1.2). Women had little if any use of their legs, twisted to the side as they were, and though a stirrup was added for the left leg, the one not through the crutch, "the only use of it is to ease the leg a little, which, for want of practice might ache by dangling and suspension," as riding instructor John Allen noted.[28] Before the mid-eighteenth century, ladies' stirrups were attached by looping the leather around the pommel and crutch (Figure 0.5), rather than the more stable method of attaching it to the saddle tree via a stirrup bar under the leather flap as on a man's saddle. Supposedly, this practice prevented the leather from rubbing against a woman's shin bone, but these stirrups could easily become unhooked, leaving a woman without any balance for her left leg.[29]

Female riders typically used a slipper stirrup, which encased the front of the foot like a sleeve. Although this type of stirrup had the added benefit of "keeping the foot dry and warm in wet roads," this platform was less secure than a man's regular stirrup iron.[30] But some early examples show considerable ingenuity: Thomas Stringer's painting of a saddled bay hunter from 1772 depicts a modern-looking double-hooped safety stirrup, while John Nost Sartorius' painting of a ladies' hunter from 1788 shows a hinged stirrup iron that would have alleviated pressure on the foot to keep the heel down and leg in place.

The demand for these new sidesaddles and their prominent representation in images from the mid-eighteenth century confirms considerable female interest in horse sports. By the late 1700s, saddle manufacturers in Britain competed for business in making these new types of sidesaddles. In 1767, Whippy (Whippy Steggall & Co.) began selling its version, and in 1786, the firm Wilkinson and Kidd (later Champion and Wilton) added to the competition (the latter crafted a sidesaddle for Lady Salisbury in 1788).[31] Three girths were recommended to secure ladies' saddles, plus a surcingle (a girth that went over the saddle). Cruppers (which secured the saddle from the back around the tail) and breastplates or collars (which secured it around the front of the horse's chest) were used to keep everything right side up. A typical complaint was that grooms girthed ladies' horses too tightly, which caused sore backs, rubs, and even lameness, although there was no other way to keep the saddle on the horse's back without it slipping.

Riding instructor Charles Carter, in his 1783 manual for ladies' riding, noted that he had spent 14 years trying to improve sidesaddle construction. This either

Figure 1.2 Joseph Wright of Derby, "Mr. and Mrs. Thomas Coltman," about 1770–1772. Mounted on horseback, Mrs. Coltman looks down on her husband from a position of equestrian power. Her physical posture indicates the body positioning of a two-pommel sidesaddle; her right leg (left to the viewer) is wedged between the two high pommels, while her left rests loosely on an invisible stirrup beneath the folds of her skirt. Although the two-pommel sidesaddle was an advance on earlier platforms, this painting indicates why it was not a safe or secure conveyance for fast speeds or jumping.
Credit: © National Gallery, London/Art Resource, NY.

says much for the manifold problems of ladies' riding saddles, or little about his abilities to make progress.[32] But while the two-pommel sidesaddle was by no means perfect, it did enable women to sit facing forward and ride their mounts at more than an ambling pace. These advances enabled women to literally take the reins and control their own horses, and to dismiss the services of a groom to lead the horse. These developments, together with the new British riding style, provided a platform from which women could better pursue riding and other equestrian sports.

Riding Clothes for Women in the Late Eighteenth Century

Developments in riding clothing coincided with advances in saddlery and equipment. "Riding habits," or women's specific riding clothing, were established garments in many women's wardrobes. This kind of clothing was worn not only for riding, but also for traveling, walking, or as relaxed daywear. These versatile garments mimicked menswear, but included certain modifications such as a waist seam that allowed a comfortable fit over stays and the top of a wide skirt.[33] The jacket skirts were vented around the back to allow for "maximum moveability."[34] The most common garments for riding included a tailored jacket or redingote, a long skirt (still called a petticoat), waistcoat, and a ruffled necktie or cravat, together with special shoes, gloves, and headwear.

Fabric and color were important for these sporting garments. Worsted wool was the fabric of choice; it was warm and sturdy enough for the demands of riding and it allowed physical mobility. It also withstood the wear and tear of soiling and frequent washing. Jackets were often lined with linen or silk, faced with contrasting silk, and trimmed with satin or metal braid (gold lacing and braid were common). Red was the predominant color for ladies' habits throughout the late eighteenth century, followed by green, although both were displaced by blue at the turn of the century, which triumphed as the preferred color after 1801. Many riding habits were designed in the colors of a particular hunt: for example, Stubbs' paintings of the Countess of Conigsby (1759–1760) and of the Duchess of Richmond and her sister-in-law (1760) show the ladies all in the "Goodwood blue" of the Charlton Hunt.[35]

Military style influenced women's habits. Classic examples include Sir Joshua Reynolds' portraits of Lady Charles Spencer (1775) and Lady Worsley (1776). In her full-length portrait, Lady Worsley appears in a dashing red riding habit, specially adapted to match the uniform of the Hampshire Militia, her husband's regiment. A scarlet cutaway coat with black and white border is layered over a beige waistcoat and ruffled cravat, with a matching scarlet skirt. On her shoulders are silver epaulettes and tassels. This fashionable look was copied by many, including Mrs. John Musters, painted by George Stubbs in 1777; Mrs. John Montresor, painted by John Singleton Copley in 1778; and the now-lost portrait of Elizabeth, Duchess of Hamilton, also by Reynolds, in 1779.[36]

By the late 1770s, fears of a French invasion sparked the formation of voluntary militias led by aristocrats such as the Duke of Devonshire. One training camp was set up on Cox-Heath in Kent, and it was here that the Duke's wife, Georgianna, as well as other officers' wives, joined in the spectacle. Although women could not serve as officers or in the militia, Georgianna hit upon the idea of creating a female auxiliary corps.[37] The Duchess chose the look she wanted: a riding habit modified to emulate a regimental military uniform. "Her Grace the Duchess of Devonshire appears every day at the head of the beauteous Amazons on Coxheath, who are all dressed *en militaire*, in the regimentals that distinguish the several regiments in which their Lords, etc., serve, and charms every beholder with their beauty and affability."[38] She and other officers' wives demonstrated that women were also prepared to fight the French. In 1781, newspapers reported that Georgianna appeared both beautiful and admirable in "a smart cocked hat, scarlet riding habit and a man's domino [cloak]," adding that she looked "divinely."[39] Women, in such patriotic uniforms, displayed a fierce and strong female national character.

Such intentionally military styling of ladies' riding clothes masculinized women's wear, to the point of dressing ladies in "red coats and scarlet habits."[40] Lady Worsley herself dictated that her riding habit should copy her husband's military uniform, and when the pictures are compared side by side, the similarity is obvious. Grace Dalrymple Elliott, the Princes of Wales' mistress, procured her riding habits from Louis Bazalgette, her lover's tailor, as did Mrs. Fitzherbert and probably Lady Worsley.[41] These habits were made of dark colors (black, blue, and green), often with buff or black trim. This masculine and military clothing and portraits reveal a very public strength and confidence for women based on equestrian pursuits.

By the turn of the century, fashion trends in riding habits shifted again. The spencer jacket came into fashion; riding habits now consisted of a short, fitted jacket over a skirt and train. Fabrics also became lighter in weight: merino wool was popularly advertised. Military-style decoration, including frogging and braid, still remained fashionable. Footwear morphed from delicate slippers to kid boots that were not necessarily practical. A 1795 fashion plate advertised "purple Spanish leather spring heel slippers"; subsequent plates highlighted "purple Spanish leather shoes" (1797), "yellow elastic boots" (1799), and "demi-boots of purple kid, laced with jonquil cord" (1807). More fitting for riding were "half-boots of black Spanish or Morocco leather."[42] Gloves and hats of all sorts finished the look. These riding habits combined freedom of movement with fashion, but such outfits, while mixing both masculine and feminine dress, inverted gender stereotypes and often attracted scorn from more conservative commentators.

Equestrian Manuals and Riding Schools

The eighteenth century witnessed increased publication of sporting literature, especially material on the new sport of fox hunting. Volumes included Peter

Beckford's *Thoughts on Hunting* from 1781, followed by Hugo Meynell's *The Meynellian Science* in 1802, and Colonel John Cook's *Observations on Foxhunting* in 1826, though these works were devoted mainly to hound science.[43] But fox hunting was not the only equestrian pursuit to receive added attention. For example, Stubbs' painting "Two of Peter Beckford's Hunters" (1779) includes a horse with a two-pommel sidesaddle, likely for Beckford's wife, Louisa, who shared in the sport.[44] Advances in riding equipment and clothing showed a continuing yet newly enthusiastic engagement in – and demand for – female participation. A new kind of prescriptive literature, ladies' riding manuals, confirms this expanded interest. At least five such texts were published between 1772 and 1801. These guidebooks specifically advised women how to become proficient on horseback and served as pocket references in learning how to ride well.

The new manuals point to a new reading – and riding – audience. Ladies (and gentlemen) of the aristocracy were "born into the saddle"; they learned to ride as a natural matter of course, usually by family (or trusted servants') instruction. But by the late eighteenth century, following the first burst of the Industrial Revolution, an emerging group of the *nouveau riche* wished to emulate their social betters, especially in all things equestrian, which had long denoted a very public and visual social status. Equestrianism held a growing attraction for non-country people, as industrial cities sprung up across the country and those with money and leisure time looked for new ways to occupy themselves. This interest coincided with an increase of female literacy in Georgian England. Circulating libraries flourished after mid-century; by the 1790s there were more than one thousand.[45] This emphasis on reading, rather than experience, was a radical change from earlier methods of being taught by the family groom or coachman.

The need for equestrian instruction, then as now, was a very real requirement. No one could learn to ride by reading alone, but such instructions certainly helped. Riding horseback requires not only physical and mental strength, but also discipline, compassion, and an experienced understanding of how to manage and control a thousand-pound animal. It is never as simple as mounting and galloping off into the sunset, as generations of novices have learned. Such bravado often results in tears and upsets, to say nothing of real injuries and sometimes death. For women riding on two-pommel sidesaddles, this learning experience was even more fraught and full of jeopardy. As one instructor wrote in 1783, "Thus a lady, who at all other times was an object of admiration and praise, from attempting to ride on an unbroken horse, so badly accoutered, and without instructions, created the sensations of pity and fear, and too often of merriment and ridicule."[46] This appearance caused concern, both from the real issues of safety as well as the tangible repercussions of social embarrassment. Poor riding damaged female reputations and created a negative image of femininity as being outwitted and out of control. Such incidents confirmed public perceptions of women as weak and needing direct supervision.

The first riding manual with directions for female riders was published in 1772 by Charles Hughes. He explained that he published the book to help "unskilled" equestrians (of both sexes) ride safely and gracefully.[47] Hughes dedicated his book to King George III and Queen Charlotte, though it may have been directed more to the princesses, who rode regularly, especially Princess Amelia.[48] Though only three pages of his 61-page treatise focus on female equitation, he did set a precedent for other authors in encouraging women to ride, as well as shedding light on important issues such as proper dress (he urged shoes with a heel), how to hold the whip and reins (straight and gracefully), and how to mount (with assistance).[49]

Hughes included directions for women because he was teaching a new kind of British riding, in which they could take part. *Haute école* had devolved into circus spectacles in Britain and remained a military affair on the Continent, making the style unsuitable for respectable female participation. Hughes offered lessons and sold his book at his private riding school, near Blackfriars Bridge in London, which he tellingly named the British Riding Academy. Hughes considered female riders such an important contingent of both his sporting and reading audience that he was assisted in running his riding school by his wife and sister, both of whom likely taught female students. In fact, his wife, Mrs. Hughes (Miss Tomlinson), was featured in two of the nine woodcut engravings in the book, one on horseback beside him and one assisting her husband in teaching a student (Figure 1.3).[50]

Figure 1.3 Frontispiece from Charles Hughes' *The Compleat Horseman; or, The Art of Riding Made Easy ... with Directions to the Ladies to Sit Gracefully, and Ride with Safety* (London: F. Newbery, 1772): Hughes' volume was the first in Britain to include directions for ladies' riding. This first plate depicts Mr. and Mrs. Hughes as equally skilled equestrians; in another plate, Mrs. Hughes assists in teaching a student, thus demonstrating the popularity and prominence of female riders as accomplished equestrians and skilled instructors.

Credit: Image Courtesy of the National Sporting Library and Museum.

Hughes rejected the usefulness of *haute école* riding in his manual and focused on the British-centric activities of road riding and hunting, as befitting his British Riding Academy. As Hughes wrote, "Managed [manèged] horses that are taught their motions only for parade, are not fit for the road or hunting. And therefore this part of horsemanship is quite useless to the generality."[51] He encouraged instruction on "the *hunting* or *common saddle*," thus indicating his goal for novices under his tutelage was to become proficient horsemen (or women) in this style of riding.[52] He also expected a horse's head to be carried naturally, rather than collected artificially as in *haute école*.[53] He also instructed on body position for jumping, something that might be called for when hunting.[54] In fact, Hughes later staged a fox-hunting scene at the Covent Garden Theatre and supplied the horses, hounds, and requisite foxes.[55]

As early as 1772, therefore, the authors of riding manuals clearly understood and described a specific British style of riding in opposition to the Continental method. Hughes had begun his career as a featured equestrian performer with Philip Astley, the father of the modern circus, but they quickly separated and became rivals, especially when Hughes was the first to publish a riding manual.[56] The publication of Hughes' book, three years before Astley published his first volume in 1775, was probably to drum up business for his new teaching venture and cater to a new audience and generation of riders.

At the same time as riding manuals addressed female equestrianism, so too did a new kind of business – the riding school. In the few moments of peace between the Jacobite rebellions of the 1740s and before the French wars of the 1790s, former military officers and equestrian performers turned their talents to horseback instruction for a new audience: women. Twenty-six schools operated at various times between 1731 and 1835.[57] The number of riding schools increased every year until 1790, and a peak occurred between 1781 and 1795 when there were at least 11 houses operating simultaneously, many around the fashionable area of Hyde Park Corner.[58] By this time, *haute école* had been replaced by the new British hunting style of riding, leading to increased consumer demand and need for instruction.

Charles Carter opened his riding house in 1771, perhaps earlier than Hughes, but he did not publish an instruction book until 1783.[59] The resulting work of 31 pages, *Instructions for Ladies in Riding*, by "Mister Carter," was the first full-length treatment devoted exclusively to women's riding in Britain. He offered detailed directions for ladies about riding, including instructions for mounting, dismounting, body position, hand position, the seat at various gaits (including the trot), and information on horses, saddles, bridles, stirrups, and whips. Conspicuously, Carter did not offer advice on dress for riding, short of noting the necessity of appropriate footwear, as did Hughes. He did include specific directions for riding in a "modern" sidesaddle (one with two pommels) and opposed the use of "stuffed or quilted saddles," referring to earlier pad saddles.[60] Carter also gave directions to women who did not own their own horses, but hired them, thus hinting at the emergence of a new class of urban equestrians.[61]

Carter's riding school was located in the fashionable area near Chapel Street, Grosvenor Square.[62] His father, Captain Carter, had significant royal connections, having been "Equerry to his late Royal Highness, the Duke of Cumberland," as well as owning a separate riding house and stables. Upon his father's death, Carter junior returned from America, where he had been serving in the military. He then opened his own riding establishment in London, although there was already stiff competition from two established rivals in the area, Mr. Hall and Mr. Emmerson.[63] Emmerson had operated a school near Shepherd's Market, Mayfair, since at least 1769, while Hall and his son had an establishment near Hyde Park Corner.[64] Demand for instruction was high enough to sustain all three: Carter's school continued for 55 years, Halls' for 43 years, and Emmerson's for 26 years.[65]

Carter's father had sent him to Great Manège at Versailles for three years' training, but despite this *haute école* influence, he did not promote it. Instead, he touted his ability to train hunting horses for speed and jumping – and to instruct ladies.[66] The cost of ladies' lessons depended on purchasing them as part of a package deal. A single lesson was 5s, as was hiring a horse for park riding. But his fees for 12 lessons at one's own convenience were £2 2s, or 3.5s per lesson. A package of 16 regularly scheduled lessons in three weeks cost the same £2 2s, or only 2.6s apiece. However, these prices were at a time when average family income after mid-century was approximately £46 per year, rising to just under £100 per year in 1803.[67] By 1787, Mr. Carter claimed that "nine hundred ladies of the highest rank and fashion" had been taught to ride at his establishment alone.[68] The popularity of his lessons for ladies occasioned the caveat that "no gentlemen are admitted while the ladies are riding but their friends [while offering] a commodious room with a fire, to receive them."[69]

Riding lessons taken in private at a school might be segregated by sex, but the ultimate purpose was to graduate as a skilled equestrian who could ride in the sexually mixed areas of the road, park, or hunt field. In addition to teaching riding skills, Carter thus instructed women how to behave in the public spaces of a new and fashionable equestrian world. He offered specially trained horses for ladies (for purchase or hire) and appealed to image-conscious parents by advertising "proper horses for young ladies and gentlemen during their vacation from school."[70] Such activities appealed to the *beau monde* and aspiring classes, to whom riding was another public display of accomplishment and social status. Riding schools were not just about the "commercialization of equestrian recreation" but "shared much in common with other, more conventional venues of urban sociability, such as the Ranelagh Rotunda, the Pantheon and the Opera House."[71]

If it was not possible for a woman to take riding lessons, she could turn to additional manuals published from 1793 onward. Directions for female riders appeared in numerous equestrian guidebooks, such as *Lectures on Horsemanship*

Wherein Is Explained Every Necessary Instruction for Both Ladies and Gentlemen by "T.S.," who claimed to be a "professor of horsemanship," in 1793. The author asserted the mental and physical benefits of riding, including personal anecdotes of "young Ladies instead of growing crooked by learning to ride, have been greatly relieved from those complaints."[72] In 1799, John Adams also included a section on ladies' riding in his self-published three-volume set, *An Analysis of Horsemanship*.[73] As these volumes indicate, riding was promoted for health and well-being, as well as for providing immense social value.

In 1801, circus entrepreneur Philip Astley followed the example of his rival Charles Hughes by publishing an equestrian manual that included directions for ladies' riding. Further editions of *Astley's System of Equestrian Education* were printed in Dublin in 1802 and in London in 1802 and 1804; all included a significant section for female equestrians. His first book in 1775 had focused exclusively on equitation for male riders: *The Modern Riding-Master: or, A Key to the Knowledge of the Horse, and Horsemanship: with Several Necessary Rules for Young Horsemen*.[74] The changing times and demands encouraged Astley to shift the focus of his instruction to a new female audience. Yet his preference for *haute école* was clear: Astley complained that the practice was "so much neglected in this country."[75] Thus, his instructions, either written or in person, were more problematic and less applicable to women than those of other equestrian experts at the time. His circus spectacle made him a less than respectable public figure, and his books did not discuss one increasingly necessary skill: jumping.

Thus, female equestrians, albeit fairly well-to-do ones, were a target audience of equestrian products and services during this time, in both text and practice. While writers and instructors like Hughes and Carter had been trained in the *haute école* style, they did not teach it. They realized that advocating the new British style of riding was more popular and profitable. This increase in riding manuals and schools came at a time when fox hunting had begun its rise in popularity. Women also participated in this sport during the late eighteenth century, and the surge of guidebooks and lessons indicated a new demand for knowledge from a new audience of riders and readers. Manuals and mounted instruction were a way for women to educate and properly present themselves in public when mounted on horseback, thus demonstrating a skilled and popular sporting femininity.

Fox Hunting in the Eighteenth Century

After learning to ride, equestrians graduated from the private confines of the urban riding school to "riding out" in Hyde Park or on public roadways, and thence to the rural pursuit of fox hunting. Even before the French Revolutionary and Napoleonic Wars prohibited travel to the Continent, Britons turned inward to domestic travel, pastimes, and sports.[76] After mid-century, this new emphasis on fox hunting catalyzed changes in riding equipment, clothing, and instruction, and these changes enabled, supported, and confirmed further changes in the sport such as speed, duration, and strategy. Thanks to new saddles, specialized clothing, and informed instruction, women actively participated in mounted hunting during the late eighteenth century.

By this time, hunting had shifted from pursuing deer and hares to the faster and more wily fox. Stag hunting remained popular into the early 1800s, but it was for carted rather than wild deer. The deer population in Britain (and their forest homes) had been by then much reduced, requiring deer to be preserved, systematically released for a chase, and then safely recaptured at the end to be hunted another day.[77] The scarcity of deer meant that other game had to be found for mounted pursuit. Unlike many popular game animals, such as fowls, otters, and others, the fox was considered vermin and therefore was not restricted from being hunted under the Game Laws, which encouraged more people to join the hunt. Those beyond the aristocracy could now share in the sport.

Fox was ranked seventh for pursuit in *The Master of Game* in 1406, but by 1591, Thomas Cockayne, in *A Short Treatise on Hunting*, listed him first.[78] Initially fox hunting was considered poor sport since it culled common pests rather than procuring food or demonstrating martial prominence. As interest grew in hunting for sport rather than sustenance, the fox provided what other animals did not: speed. Hunting for deer in thick forests was a slow occupation, as was hunting hare, which ran in circles to evade pursuers. But the fox ran fast, straight, and long, providing an exciting chase. For all these reasons, many in England switched to hunting foxes, including the Prince of Wales (who stopped hunting stag and began chasing foxes instead by 1793).[79]

Not only did hunting before the late eighteenth century pursue different game, but it was also a different kind of sport. Hunting (for hare, fox, and other small animals) was a local, informal affair. Great houses and local gentry bred and formed their own packs of hounds for hunting, but they did not advertise their meets, and, as a result, only friends, neighbors, and personal guests attended. Packs were known at this point in time either by the owner's name or the area they hunted, for example, the Earl of Darlington's foxhounds, or the Hatfield harriers. Women could participate in hunting because it remained mostly a local and elite affair. Aristocratic women had joined hunts since medieval times, when they went hawking and coursing, so their presence in the field by the late 1700s was not unusual. More importantly, geographic proximity also enabled other local women to ride and hunt without discrimination against their class or sex.

In addition to being a homegrown occasion, it was also a leisurely one. As a nocturnal hunter, the fox only returned to his burrow, or "earths," at dawn. Therefore, meets began very early as hunters set their hounds after foxes that were returning from the night's feed with full bellies. When the foxes ran, they did so much more slowly than usual, which suited hunters since neither their heavyweight horses nor old Southern hounds could match even the speed of a slower fox. Hunts were therefore long, drawn-out "chases" that could last an entire day, as illustrated by the Duke of Richmond's record day in 1739 that covered 24 miles in ten hours (an average of 2.4 miles per hour). Some hunts did go faster: for example, the Grafton Hunt covered 60 miles in 12 hours in 1745 (an average of 5.0 miles per hour), but this is still slow when considering that a horse's walk averages 4 miles per hour (the Duke of Richmond was riding a horse appropriately named Slug).[80] In fact, hunts could literally walk a fox to death, which resulted in an unexciting though successful conclusion to the day's progression.[81]

Horses, hounds, and hunt strategy were not the only reason hunting was so much slower in the early eighteenth century. The landscape also prevented hunts from being the stereotypical fast dashes characteristic of the next century. Without proper drainage, ground remained wet and heavy, which made for slow and deep going, especially in the Midlands.[82] Although widespread drainage did create better conditions and revolutionized hunting, some areas remained problematic as late as 1870, when Augusta Fane recalled, "many of the pastures round Sixhills and Shoby Scolls were unrideable: horses sank up to their hocks in the boggy, deep clay-soil."[83] A gentle canter or workmanlike trot was the fastest speed possible in most places, and since most of the country was not yet enclosed, there were very few (if any) real fences to jump. Although gates, low hedges, and ditches may have been encountered, these were likely taken as standing rather than flying leaps, in which the horse took off from a standstill rather than a gallop (Figure 1.4). In fact, one sportsman recalled that there were no fences at all in the land between Nottingham Castle and Belvoir Castle, a distance of some twenty miles.[84] At this point, "second horses," or auxiliary mounts, were unheard of, and strenuous rattling gallops over such land would have exhausted both horse and rider almost immediately.

Although certainly not without its excitement, hunting of the early eighteenth century was a more leisurely recreation. The moderate pace and uncluttered landscape encouraged women's equal participation. The localized and informal nature of the hunt further enabled their acceptance in the field. Deep conditions, slower speeds, and fewer obstacles to jump allowed women to follow the hounds as easily as men. If women were limited by their two-pommeled sidesaddles, they were no more so than men with their long stirrups and high cantles, for it was not until the early 1700s that a reliable hunting saddle with a flat seat (with shorter stirrups for better balance) came into fashion.[85] If women could fall off, it was more likely that men could be castrated.

Female Huntresses

The women who participated in fox hunting before 1800 fell into three categories: aristocrats, country women, and courtesans. In the first category, a prime exemplar was the first Marchioness of Salisbury, but she was not exceptional in being the only renowned female rider of the time; she was simply deemed the best of a competitive group (Figure 1.5). Lady Jersey and Lady Conyngham also

Figure 1.4 "The Female Fox Hunter" (after John Collett), 1778: In this print, a fashionably dressed woman on horseback skillfully leaps a gate while raising a whip in her right hand (possibly to discipline horse or hound). In the background, two riders (man and woman) look pityingly on a man who has fallen off over a much smaller fence. Scholars have remarked on the world-turned-upside-down quality of Collet's prints as well as the erotic connotations of the chase, but these images also illustrate how women adopted and adapted male sports and clothing to advance their own comfort, pleasure, and freedoms. These prints show a public recognition of women's equestrian expertise (in fact, they rode better than men), and if not praise for, then at least complaisant acceptance of, female participation.

Credit: © The Trustees of the British Museum (2010, 7081.1044).

Figure 1.5 "Coursers, Taking the Field at Hatfield Park," by James Pollard, 1824. Two women lead the field away from Hatfield House in the background, one surveying the scene through an eyeglass mounted on the butt of her whip. Both wear the sky-blue livery of the Hatfield Hunt, and the lady in the foreground has a "seat-belt" strap across her lap to keep her skirt from blowing up indecently. By 1824, when Pollard completed the original oil painting, the first Marchioness of Salisbury was over 70 years old, so the female rider may be Frances, the first wife of the second Marquess of Salisbury.

Credit: © The Trustees of the British Museum (1939, 0714.17).

hunted with the Prince of Wales in the 1790s, and Lady Craven also hunted with the Craven hounds, maintained by her husband and the successive Earl of Craven, from 1739 to 1804.[86] On a run in November 1797, it was noted that hard riding "soon reduced the original sixty to *nine* or *ten*; in the midst of whom were Ladies, in such stile, of both courage and ability, as not to be exceeded by any Lady Salisbury of the past, present, or future century."[87] Lady Salisbury's name became synonymous with fine riding, and not a little pluck, and other female riders were compared to her. In 1796 *The Sporting Magazine* reported, "a young lady who rode the chace throughout, and displayed such a specimen of agility in following the hounds, through the enclosures, as would have surprised *Lady Salisbury* herself."[88] Aristocrats trained in horsemanship from youth and appeared in public from a position of equestrian power; equestrianism was therefore a performance and confirmation of the social hierarchy.

Other women who rode to hounds before 1800 included those who resided in the country and lived close to the hunts, regardless of their class status. Country sportswomen included representatives from the rural gentry like Juliana Ludford, of Ansley Hall in Warwickshire, who rode with Lord Donegall's, Mr. Kinnersley's, and Lord Belfast's nearby packs in the 1770s and 1780s.[89] Another equestrian was Phoebe Higgs, one of the mistresses of "Squire" George Forester, of Willey Hall in Shropshire. Together they hunted across the "clear field" of rolling lowlands near the Clee Hills to the flat plain of the River Severn.[90] Higgs was "renowned all round that countryside for her daring feats in the saddle" and for:

> taking the most daring leaps, beckoning [the Squire] to follow, till he vowed there was no woman in England to compare with her, and would offer to back her for 500 guineas to ride against any horsewoman in the world.[91]

Despite the limitations of the sidesaddle, Phoebe proved her worth on the hunting field not only against other horsewomen but also the finest male riders of the day, including the Squire's legendary whipper-in Tom Moody. Not only did she breakfast with the Squire at 4 a.m. on hunting days and stay out well past sunset, but she was also hailed locally for her charity, spending her free days tending to the poor.[92] Her unusual social status did not bar her from sporting participation, nor did her sex.[93]

Phoebe Higgs' sporting prowess was not thought incompatible with an admirable femininity both on and off the horse. During the eighteenth century, her public behavior as a hunting daredevil and the Squire's mistress did not strictly threaten her feminine reputation.[94] Many women hunted with their family's packs; for example, Miss Diana Draper hunted with – and even acted as whipper-in to – her father, Squire Draper, in Yorkshire. She was considered "invaluable" for her bold work in the field, and "escaping all perils of the hunting field she reached a good old age before death claimed her, and … 'she died with whole bones in her bed.'"[95] In 1798, a lady of Mr. Boldero's was "*well in* at the death" after a chase of 15 miles with a subscription pack of foxhounds,[96] while a note from 1803 pointed out that "There is a female Nimrod, of the name of Dussell, who constantly hunts with the King's staghounds; and being the best *flying leaper* of the field, is generally in at the head of the yeoman prickers when the stag is taken."[97] These country women were praised as enthusiastic and educated riders, and often described in proper, respectable, successful but masculine sporting terms. Gender construction in the late eighteenth century was therefore far more positive and malleable for sportswomen than it would become after the turn of the century.

Hunting and horsemanship were also avenues of enrichment and social improvement for aspiring women of the lower class or socially questionable status. The future king George IV switched from hunting deer to foxes in 1793, and he drew a considerable entourage in his wake. Henrietta Le Clerc was a noted equestrian who regularly rode with both the Duke of Richmond's foxhounds and the Goodwood hounds during the early 1800s.[98] Although she was the illegitimate daughter of Charles Lennox, the third Duke of Richmond, she was probably taught to ride by the Duke's sister, noted equestrian Lady Louisa Conolly.[99] She was "frequently in at the death, and never refused a leap. The gentlemen of the hunt had often a difficulty keeping pace with her; and her style of riding, so elegant and spirited, was the admiration of them all."[100] Despite her lowly birth, her fine horsemanship won her a successful marriage to Colonel John Dorrien of the Life Guards.[101] Equestrianism was therefore a valuable asset for upward social mobility.

This gendered flexibility of sporting participation is best seen in another famous equestrian of the time, Laetitia, Lady Lade, who was painted by George Stubbs, as commissioned by the Princes of Wales. Born of Gypsy background, Laetitia first worked as a cook before becoming the mistress of the notorious highwayman "Sixteen String Jack." Somewhere she learned to ride extremely well; Stubbs' portrait depicts a nonchalant horsewoman masterfully controlling a fractious, rearing horse. Her firm command of the reins of the double bridle, and her easy seat, demonstrates her competence on a troublesome mount.[102] Such composure and skill led to marriage to Sir John Lade, close confidante of the Prince of Wales. Like his wife, he was an accomplished equestrian, and perhaps the most talented of Regency whips, who even taught the future king to drive a carriage.[103]

Laetitia more than equaled her husband in horsemanship, and her expert equestrian skills were well known.[104] In June 1795, it was mentioned that she was "in the straw" (likely pregnant), but by November 1796, she was back in the saddle at the front of the pack.[105] *The Sporting Magazine* attested, "she is the first horsewoman in the kingdom, being constantly one of the only five or six that are invariably with the hounds," even on runs of 35 miles lasting over two hours (about 17 miles per hour, or a fast canter).[106] But this kind of riding was not without its dangers: in November 1797, Lady Lade suffered "a most sever[e] fall, which was reported to have fractured her arm, and dislocated her wrist."[107] Never down for long, by the next February, less than three months later, she was back in the field again.[108] The last reference to Lady Lade's riding appeared in the October 1799 edition of *The Sporting Magazine*, which mentioned a run of almost three hours for the royal deer. It was noted that "Lady Lade kept up the whole time – her fleet courser never fails."[109]

Lady Lade was often joined by her friend, Mrs. Hodges. In 1794, *The Times* remarked that the "two ornaments of Rotten Row" had ridden in "a severe stag hunt." On this occasion,

> Mrs. Hodges not only out leaped Lady Lade, but every gentleman in the field. Nothing stopped her. She flew over five barred gates with as much facility as she ever leapt into a lover's arms. It was remarked she had all the properties of a Diana – except her chastity.[110]

Riding well was a passport into high society. Like Grace Elliot, Anna Sophia Hodges was another mistress of the Prince of Wales (she first caught his eye when out hunting) and was a cousin to Mrs. Fitzherbert.[111]

The presence of these women in hunting fields in the late eighteenth century demonstrated not only the social permeability of hunts but also the social value of expert horsemanship. Though they did not inherit titles by birthright like Lady Salisbury, Henrietta Le Clerc and Lady Lade married into the most exclusive social set of the time, which included the Prince of Wales and the highest-ranking figures in England. The ticket to entry was their horsemanship which transcended their lowly upbringing. Though noble women had long participated in hunting as a traditional pastime befitting their social rank, hunting as a sport had evolved and so had the ability to participate. If the key to joining field sports had once been status, now it was skill and merit, a trend that would continue into the next century with a woman memorably named "Skittles."

A Sporting Revolution

Women were accepted in equestrian activities such as riding and hunting through the late 1700s, but changes in gender ideals, social values, and sporting strategy began to curtail their involvement after the early 1800s. One reason that fewer women hunted by this time was the changing nature of the hunt. The slower hunts of the eighteenth century had evolved by the early nineteenth century into faster chases with more and bigger obstacles to jump. Improvements in hound and horse breeding, as well as a revolution in landscape design following the enclosure movements, all created a different kind of sport that was more difficult for women to pursue, thus decreasing women's participation in hunting.

Hugo Meynell is widely credited with, although not solely responsible for, the veritable sporting revolution that transformed fox hunting after the mid-eighteenth century. Meynell, who took over as Master of the Quorn Hunt in 1753 and held it until 1800, focused primarily on breeding and developing a fast hound with a good nose for scent. Before the 1750s, hunters mainly pursued hare and, more rarely, stag. Hares rely on deception to evade their hunters. They double back and run in circles, which make horseback pursuit slow and uncertain. But the fox was another animal altogether, which used speed rather than trickery (despite Reynard's sly reputation) to escape. Harriers (hounds for hunting hares) had been bred to follow the hare's erratic path by smell, but not for speed.

In order to pursue this new quarry, hunters had to begin at dawn when the fox was returning to its burrows with a full belly, thus resulting in a slower run that regular hounds could still follow. This method of hunting created long, slow hunts that lasted from very early in the morning until very late in the evening, when the fox could finally escape his pursuers in the dark. Meynell, likely influenced by his neighbor Robert Bakewell's advances in selectively breeding farm animals, bred a new kind of hound for both speed and stamina to more effectively pursue foxes. Based on his successes, Meynell then initiated changes in hunt culture. Rather than gathering in the pre-dawn hours when full-bellied foxes crept home and the chase was slow, hunting shifted to mid-morning, after the fox had digested and could run more quickly.

This new style of hunting with faster dogs pursuing an even faster fox demanded a faster horse. By the mid-1700s, British horses (and hounds) had moved away from classification by types (based on purpose) to classification by breeds (based on scientific genealogy).[112] The assimilation of Eastern bloodstock with native horses led to the creation of the English Thoroughbred and hunter, but the emphasis on the faster type of sport horse was so great that it led to the disappearance of traditional heavier horses, such as the Leicestershire black horse, by the nineteenth century.[113] Whereas formerly crossbred horses (draft and Thoroughbred) sufficed for hunting, now nothing less than a full or 7/8 Thoroughbred would do. Such horses were both temperamental and expensive, requiring an experienced rider with a deep pocket.

Hunters were not bred to be as fast as racehorses, but bursts of action in the field required a horse that could gallop both fast and long. Whereas record chases in the early 1700s might cover 24 miles in ten hours (a walking speed of roughly 2.4 miles per hour), the pace now increased. The famous Billesdon-Coplow run in 1800, with Hugo Meynell as Master, covered 28 miles in two hours and fifteen minutes (over 12 miles per hour, or the speed of a canter).[114] This creation of horses and hounds bred specifically for hunting illustrates the importance placed on effective pursuit of the sport. Far from being the leisurely recreation of country gentleman or royalty, in which finding game was a haphazard affair and the horses used were multipurpose mounts, hunting was consciously developed into a science by a new social and sporting intelligentsia, to be pursued logically and efficiently over a changing landscape.

While the evolution of hunting and the breeding of faster horses and hounds revolutionized the sport, so too did the transformation of the English countryside by the enclosure movements of the late eighteenth century. Although the pace and acceptance of enclosure depended on local conditions and attitudes, the movement as a whole did create a new landscape of fenced or hedged pastures, in contrast to the medieval system of open fields and commons.[115]

Previously Leicestershire, the heart of hunt country, had been mainly composed of unfenced grassland, so runs were straight across country. If obstacles did appear, riders would either dismount or take them from a standstill. Sporting author Robert Smith Surtees himself wrote that no one "took pleasure in leaping."[116] By 1750, however, half of Leicestershire had been converted to fenced pastureland, and 50 years later, so was much of the rest.[117] This new arrangement encouraged faster riding because a fox's scent held better over grass than deep earth. By 1825, these new grassy enclosures were lush enough to support heavy grazers like cows instead of sheep, and by this time the cattle disease that had plagued the countryside had ended, making it possible and profitable to raise bovine stock.[118]

Unlike smaller animals, however, cows required stronger fences to keep them contained, leading to the construction of "double oxers" and "post and rail" fences – the former was a solid hedge with guardrails on either side, while the latter was a series of horizontal bars attached to vertical posts. These solid fences presented serious obstacles to horse and rider, causing the flurry of falls and injuries catalogued in hunting diaries of the time. New skills were needed to stay on the new sport horses: by 1783, Charles Carter, the riding instructor, touted his ability to train hunting horses for jumping (as well as the ability to show equestrians how to stay on).[119] Although young "swells" might appreciate the excitement of jumping all day, others did not: as "Wildrake" complained, "we do not think it is an erroneous calculation to suppose, that for every leap taken fifty years ago, ten leaps are taken now, and if things go on as they are now doing, we shall soon be 'flying,' or 'on and offing,' all day."[120] Hedges and obstacles became so prominent that any afflicted area was labeled "damned pewey-country" for its new similarity to box pews in a church: "Whole counties, that a hundred years ago possessed scarcely a fence from one end to the other, are now divided and sub-divided like pews in a church."[121]

Another aspect of the changing landscape was the careful creation of coverts – small patches of scrub and wooded cover – where foxes could live. One reason fox hunting was not more successful before the early 1800s was the lack of foxes available to hunt. Throughout the early to mid-1800s, *The Sporting Magazine* bemoaned the lack of foxes and harshly decried the practice of "bag foxes," whereby foxes were captured in one area and sold for hunting in another. Not only did this result in poor runs, as discombobulated foxes did not run well in unknown territory, but it caused the artificial extinction of fox populations in some areas and the overpopulation of others. Whereas hares flourished in open fields, foxes required adequate cover, and this forced many hunts to create new earthenworks planted with gorse and blackthorn to shelter them.[122] This new form of direct landscape management and animal conservation did result in more successful hunting: for example, the number of "blank days" without a chase for the Raby pack hunted by the Marquis of Cleveland between 1787 and 1832 fell from 5.8 days per season in the 1790s to 1.4 in the 1810s after such measures had taken effect.[123] As the number of blank days decreased for many packs, women who had formerly attended these off days with shorter, slower runs were now faced with hounds that could find a fast fox almost every time they went out.

Equestriennes Excluded?

After a half century of enthusiastic participation, women found themselves limited or barred from the hunting field by the turn of the nineteenth century. The new kind of hunting horse was not an ideal mount for women riding sidesaddle. As "Nimrod" (the sporting author Charles James Apperley) noted during his Yorkshire tour, "Lady Augusta Milbanke rode a thoroughbred horse, formerly in Mr. Maxse's stable, and one which but few women would have nerve for" – quite a compliment, given that Maxse was one of the hardest riders in Leicestershire.[124] Even if women could manage these fractious horses, the new requirement of galloping and jumping made participation extremely dangerous in a two-pommel sidesaddle. More than that, a new hyper-masculinity tinged the sport with a lack of respectability. Suddenly the hunting field was no longer a place for a woman.

Female equestrians may have been able to stay on faster horses and keep up with faster hounds despite the limitations of the two-pommeled sidesaddle, but their Waterloo was the increased size and number of obstacles they had to jump. In 1776, a French riding instructor "claimed that when he attempted to jump a fence in a woman's saddle he was obliged to stick his spur into the leather in order to retain his balance, and would have been unseated when the horse shied unexpectedly had he not immediately thrown his leg over the side."[125] The Sporting Magazine proudly proclaimed the equestrian feats of Lady Lade and the Marchioness of Salisbury, among others, but constant and substantial jumping was rare. Although some intrepid women attempted to solve the lack of security in leaping sidesaddle by grabbing the backs of their saddles for support as they went over the fences, most horsewomen would have to wait until the invention of the third pommel, or leaping head, to rejoin hunting fields after 1830.[126]

Changes in speed, strategy, and landscape limited women's ability to follow the hounds as they had done throughout the late 1700s, as illustrated by women such as the Marchioness of Salisbury, Lade Lade, Phoebe Higgs, and others. The sporting author "Nimrod" recorded that the celebrated horsewoman Mrs. Russell struggled to continue hunting with the East Sussex hounds by the 1830s:

> Mrs. R. used to be a bold rider I believe; but, like many of us, she is getting one of the "has beens," and she makes a poor fight of it without Mr. B. I saw her out with Col. Wyndham's hounds one day, attended by a Gentleman in *trowsers*, who was more timid a great deal than she was; instead of riding boldly at his fences, and making her follow, they kept looking at them together, he saying, "do you think we can manage this?"[127]

Even the Marchioness of Cleveland, who rode her renowned hunting horse Raby for seven years, could not keep up with the changes because, when faced with new obstacles, her "nerves are not so strong as they were."[128] Some women, like Mrs. Russell, persevered, and after a blazing run with Colonel Wyndham's hounds in July 1830, she was even presented with the brush, or the fox's tail.[129] But the pack hunted the rolling hills of the South Downs and estate parklands of Sussex, where little jumping was required.[130]

Though credited with initiating many of the changes that transformed hunting, Hugo Meynell was allegedly horrified by the results of his efforts.[131] People now did not so much ride to hunt, as hunt to ride. Hunting was no longer about the workings of the hounds but showing off one's equestrian skills before fashionable company. Although he had once been labeled the "worst sportsman and wildest huntsman" in his youth, Meynell was now appalled by the over-riding caused by foolhardy riders following fast hounds across a country.[132] He declared he "had not had a day's happiness" since the advent of what was alarmingly called "the splittercockation pace."[133] "Neck or nothing" became the motto of many of the "thrusters" who crushed anything – fence, hound, or horseman – in their quest to be up at the kill. The fox's brush, the ultimate reward in hunting, had initially been awarded to the rider first at the kill, but, given so much reckless and life-endangering competition for this prize, it now had to be awarded at the Master's discretion for the best ride, so as to discourage so much jostling and so many injuries.[134]

The increasingly rash riding, jumping, and general showing off resulted in the never-ending stream of broken bones, falls, and lamed horses recorded in hunting chronicles of the time. Captain John White, a famed Melton madcap, nearly drowned when "he jumped into a pond grown over with green weeds ... Mr. Warburton rode right on top of him, and both were submerged."[135] During Thomas Assheton Smith's last year following hounds in Leicestershire, he nearly ran over fellow rider, the same Captain White, who had become wedged in a fenced hedge that he wished to jump:

> they came to a fence so strong and high, that there was only one place where it appeared at all practicable, and this was in the line Mr. White was taking. The consequence was, Mr. Smith was obliged to turn to this place, expecting to find Mr. White well over; but instead of this, he found him what is called "well bull-finched," his horse and himself sticking fast in the hedge. "Get on," says Mr. Smith. "I cannot," said Mr. White, "I am fast." "Ram the spurs into him," exclaimed Mr. Smith, "and pray get out of the way." "Damn it," said Mr. White, "if you are in such a hurry, why don't you ride at me and charge me?" Mr. Smith did charge him, and sent him and his horse into the next field, when away they went again as if nothing had happened.[136]

Formerly a "science" that focused on the slow and careful working of hounds, the hunt became literally about *a* chase – and not necessarily *the* chase.

This is not to say that the new style found universal acceptance. In 1828 a letter published in *The Sporting Magazine* expressed doubts over this newfangled style:

> The more I hear of the present style of riding, the more I am confirmed in the argument I have so often held, that the school of old sportsmen was better than the modern school of wild, over-riding gentry. ... it is Bedlam let loose.[137]

This bedlam could explain why few women were present the field. In their unwieldy two-pommeled sidesaddles, they lacked the safety and security of seat needed for such wild dashes across the countryside, not to mention they could hardly be accepted into what was rapidly becoming a boys-only sporting club. As *The Ladies' Field* magazine pointed out, "hunting was the typical country gentleman's favourite amusement ... and, with a few exceptions, was a pastime 'for men only.'"[138]

Dianas Denounced

The 20 years between 1810 and 1830 have been described as a "golden age" for hunting in Leicestershire, but during this time the sport became less localized and more masculinized.[139] Previously, those who wished to hunt often lodged with their hosts, such as the Marchioness of Salisbury or Hugo Meynell, in their private homes. Here they were in a setting with more gender balance, pursuing sporting interests from a more domestic venue. Until the railways revolutionized travel, the primitive state of transportation to the country made short stays impractical. So, most, if not all, of the hunting field were known to each other personally. In this setting, women participated in riding, dining, and entertaining friends and neighbors. Domesticity, femininity, and sport were not – as yet – incompatible.

By the early nineteenth century hunting had expanded geographically. Expensive private packs had evolved into more cost-effective subscription packs, whose members (located anywhere) paid annually for the privilege to ride with a specific hunt, thus sharing the enormous cost of maintenance. Whereas Masters previously knew the majority (if not everyone) of those at the hunt, by the early 1800s, they might personally recognize few who turned up and paid to partake in the morning's sport. The later starting time allowed participants to journey from greater distances and still arrive before the action began. Such changes depersonalized hunting, as sportsmen did not need to stay with local friends or hosts in order to hunt, and often chose to reside in more convenient lodgings in a nearby town, which further decreased the opportunity for women to participate.

New hunting towns like Melton Mowbray were born to cater to sports*men*, typically young bachelors, and to all their lodging, dining, and entertaining needs.[140] Loughborough, just over ten miles above Leicester, had been the most centrally located town during the heyday of Meynell's Quorn Hunt, but most hunters stayed with him at Quorndon Hall because there were few residences or amenities available in town. But later, with these new hunts, Melton became the most central – it was within hacking distance of not one, but four of the best packs in Britain: the Quorn, the Belvoir, the Cottesmore, and the Pytchley. Hence, sportsmen could hunt six days a week from this location, and during hunting season, at least 300 hunters were stabled in the town.[141] Two hotels – the George and the Harboro – catered to these visitors, as did many "hunt clubs," where sportsmen took local lodgings to live communally.[142] As these circumstances suggest, there was no room for women. Hunting became the preeminent activity pursued by men only; there were no longer mixed social gatherings and activities because there were no days off from sport (except for Sunday).

These new towns and the behavior of their new sportsmen did not necessarily impress visitors. In 1812, Harriette Wilson went to Melton in pursuit of her latest lover, only to find what she termed "a very stupid life."[143] The men left early in the morning and returned only very late in the evening, when they proceeded to get drunk and then repeat the performance the next day. As Wilson noted, the only women in Melton were "a few wretched, squalid prostitutes" who the men slipped out to meet.[144] Given the new masculinized nature of hunting, the absence of respectable ladies was not unusual. Changes in hunting strategy and culture, as well as sporting equipment, catalyzed changes in gendered standards. As *The Ladies' Field* magazine pointed out retrospectively,

> In early days there were few ladies at Melton, and fewer still in the hunting field – the Duchess of Devonshire hunted with Mr. Meynell – nor would they have been welcome. It was not so much the want of will or power among women as for the manners and customs of the men in those days.[145]

Even outside of Melton, this male fraternity invaded hunting towns like Market Harborough and led to the development of private clubs, informal associations, and an exclusively male sociality where hunting was the first and often the only topic of discussion.

The doings of these bachelor societies made it obvious why few women were present. Drinking brandy and gin from glasses the size of stable buckets, men played juvenile pranks that defied belief. At one such celebration,

> the Bloody head of a Fox [was] immersed in a Bowl, or rather *Pond* of Punch, which was then stirred up with the Brush, the whole Party being next re-baptized with it dripping from the liquor, which was quaffed by all, with as real enthusiasm and *gout*, as could possibly be evinced by the Noble Duke, who devoured part of a Fox's head devilled![146]

On another famous occasion, the Marquis of Waterford and friends painted Melton Mowbray's nightwatchmen in red paint, nearly blinding them, before going on to cover many of the walls and doors of the town in the same color – hence the phrase "painting the town red."[147] Hunting madcap John Mytton's antics included sending a drunken man to bed with two bulldogs and a bear, and also riding the same bear to dinner in formal hunting attire.[148] According to

"Nimrod," "The animal carried him very quietly for a certain time; but on being pricked by the spur he bit his rider through the calf of his leg, inflicting a severe wound" (Figure 1.6).[149] On a bet, the Marquis of Waterford set up a four-foot field gate in the midst of his dining room and jumped his best hunter over it, though the unfortunate horse was led upstairs to the second level of the house later that night and had to be removed through the window and hoisted down days later.[150]

Throughout the early nineteenth century, this pervasive masculinity spread both geographically and socially: from the countryside to more urban environs, and from aristocrats to the aspiring classes. As late as the 1820s, the city of London was still intimately connected with the countryside, especially in sporting terms. Despite increasing urbanization, there were still green areas to pursue sport within a stone's throw of the City. Harrier packs hunted from Dulwich, Southgate, Finchley, Hounslow, and Sunbury.[151] Stag hunting with the Epping Hunt in the forest north of London was popular until the 1830s.[152]

Figure 1.6 "A New Hunter – Tally ho! Tally ho!" by Henry Alken, from *Memoirs of the Life of the Late John Mytton*, by "Nimrod" [Charles James Apperley], fifth plate in the 1835 first edition: According to "Nimrod," John Mytton kept a pet bear, and "he once rode this bear into his drawing room in full hunting costume. The animal carried him very quietly for a certain time; but, on being pricked by the spur, she bit her rider through the calf of his leg, inflicting a severe wound." Such private antics and public behaviors, as well as changing gender norms, limited the participation of women in fox hunting during the early nineteenth century.
Credit: Collection of the author.

An hour's hack brought riders to the country beyond Regent's Park, or toward the hounds that met from Streatham and Croydon.[153]

This easy proximity created a new type of participant: the "Cockney sportsman." Exemplified by Surtees' fictional character, John Jorrocks, he was a City man, often involved in trades or business, but with enough disposable income and leisure time to pursue activities like hunting. The Cockney sportsman knew little about the countryside, but he was determined to imitate and enjoy rural sport despite his lack of experience. Though much caricatured and often ridiculed for their unlearned behavior and inappropriate airs, such (fledgling) sportsmen were accepted (if not welcomed) into the field, based on their sex and ability to pay as hunt subscribers. The inclusion of these unschooled and much-lampooned sportsmen indicated that masculinity now trumped social standing and that sporting inclusion was based on the horizontal ties of sex and gender, not the vertical ties of class.

This transformation of hunting, horses, and landscape did not bode well for female participants, and the new exclusively masculine sociability sealed the deal. Public opinion turned against women riding and hunting by the early 1800s. By 1831, even the old standby, *The Sporting Magazine*, which had praised women's sporting activities from its inception in 1792, now reversed its position, stating "we profess that we are no approvers of FEMALE HUNTERS."[154] As the fourth most popular magazine in Britain by 1819, the opinions of its pages carried no small weight.[155] "I do not like to see women out with fox-hounds," Surtees wrote bluntly, "A man does not like riding before them, or leaving them in the lurch; and even if they do 'go along,' the whole field is kept in alarm lest an accident should happen."[156]

As the sport of hunting evolved, becoming ever more masculine in make-up, its practitioners condemned women who tried to join as unnatural and unsexed. By 1802, Lady Salisbury, who had formerly been so praised for her sporting prowess, was now depicted as a bedraggled demon in a print by John Collett (Figure 1.7). This caricature illustrated how participation in blood sports was now thought to irrevocably corrupt feminine virtues. As an author in *The Sporting Magazine* highlighted in 1830:

> I know of no Lady who feels a wish to follow hounds; while those who do, all I can say is, that it tells very much for their *temerity*, but very little indeed for their *taste*! and such I take it is the prevailing opinion – we regarding women who attempt to RIDE AFTER hounds much in the same light as they would us if engaged on a fine scenting morning sitting cross-legged at cross-stitch – saving that we should *pity* where they would *contemn*.[157]

It was no longer considered proper or womanly for female riders to go hunting. Ideals of respectable femininity had not changed, but the sport of hunting – and those participating – had. In fact, *The Sporting Magazine* concluded in 1830 that the only field sport a woman could participate in "without incurring the

Figure 1.7 "Diana Return'd from the Chace," print by James Gillray, 1802 (based on an amateur watercolor with the same title and caption): By the early nineteenth century, public opinion had turned against female equestrians. Even Lady Salisbury, so admired for her horsemanship, was not immune to criticism. Here she stands, victorious with the fox's brush, having beaten both hounds and horsemen to the kill, but resulting in a scandalous state of *dishabille* with tattered skirt, torn stockings, and bedraggled hair. The title of the print compares the Marchioness to Diana, goddess of the hunt, while the caption comes from the seventh book of Virgil's *Aeneid*, describing Camilla, the "Amazon" and "virgo bellatrix." The early 1800s witnessed changing gender ideals, but, even in satire, female equestrians never fully lost their power or prominence.
Credit: © The Trustees of the British Museum (1868, 0808.7001).

imputation of being thought masculine" was archery, and even that was hotly contested.[158] Equestrian events took women out of the home, now specified as a woman's proper place in the prescriptive ideology of separate spheres. As Surtees concluded, "A habit in the hunting-field was quite an unknown article in the [hunt] country, where nearly all the ladies had ample domestic duties to occupy them."[159] If the true measure of a woman and her worth were her cares and attention to the home, then women who abandoned the home for the field jeopardized not only their personal femininity, but also the family's well-being (and by extension, the nation's). As Surtees continued, he and "Mrs. Nim South" had followed the harriers when they were younger, but now such activities were not considered proper and when he went hunting, he confirmed that his wife "stays at home and mends my pens for me to write for the *Magazine*."[160]

Racing Rebels

Many British women also showed considerable interest in horse racing beyond being mere passive spectators, although more usually – as in the case of Queen Anne, who inaugurated the Ascot races – as trainers and owners, rather than riders.[161] As early as 1725, ladies were racing at places like Ripon in Yorkshire: a Ladies' Plate valued at £15 was offered, in which women paid one guinea to enter for three heats of twice around Ripon Common. According to the *Newcastle Courant*, "four damsels rode two-mile heats 'in jockey cappes, colored waistcoats, and with their shapes transparent.'"[162] But, by the early 1800s, equestrianism, sexuality, and femininity were not considered as compatible as they had been previously. Thus, by 1827, when "Nimrod" mentioned the Ripon Ladies' Plate, he did so to show its exceptional nature.[163]

By the early 1800s, the perceived incompatibility of respectable femininity with public horse sports like racing was illustrated by the exploits and public opinion of Alicia Thornton, the mistress and perhaps wife of Colonel Thomas Thornton. Thornton was a keen sportsman in the Prince of Wales' entourage and had even presented a gift of pistols to Napoleon Bonaparte.[164] Although she was also a famous huntress and bold driver, Mrs. Thornton's real fame grew from her horse racing. In 1804 and 1805, she rode in several high-profile match races, all while riding sidesaddle on her husband's Thoroughbred horses.[165] Based on these equestrian feats, she became a celebrity in the sporting world. Mrs. Thornton raced against Frank Buckle, the best jockey of the day, before audiences estimated between 30,000 and 100,000.[166] As *The Sporting Magazine* enthused,

> Mrs. Thornton took the lead, which she kept for some time; Mr. Buckle then put in trial his jockeyship, and passed the lady, which he kept for only a few lengths, when Mrs. Thornton, by the most excellent, we may say – horsemanship – pushed forwards, and came in in a stile far superior to any thing of the kind we ever witnessed, winning her race by half a neck. The manner of Mrs. Thornton's riding is certainly of the first description; indeed

her close seat and perfect management of her horse; her bold and steady jockeyship, amazed one of the most crowded courses we have for a long time witnessed; and on her winning, she was hailed with the most reiterated shouts of congratulation.[167]

To further celebrate her victory, *The Sporting Magazine* issued a rare portrait of Mrs. Thornton in January 1805. She was one of the very few female sportswomen whose portraits appeared in its pages. She even wrote a poem about her triumph which was published in the September 1805 issue.[168] Besides the popular press, Mrs. Thornton's feats appeared in Pierce Egan's *Book of Sports and Mirror of Life* and *Raciana*, as well as in Lord William Pitt Lennox's *Fifty Years' Biographical Reminisces*. Egan was unstinting in his praise for her exploits, calling her racing "a lasting monument of FEMALE INTREPIDITY."[169] According to the enthusiastic Egan, Mrs. Thornton's riding was superb, even better than Astley's, Nimrod's, and Chifney's – like the Marchioness of Salisbury, she was so expert that she could only be compared to – though she exceeded – men.[170] Her prowess became so well known that some races were conceded without ever being run, as in Mr. Bromford's forfeit at the York August meetings in 1805.[171]

Figure 1.8 Thomas Henry Nicholson, "A Ladies' Horse Race," 1839: Female equestrians raced competitively and publicly by the eighteenth century, but the most well-known female jockey was Alicia Thornton, whose racing in the early 1800s Piece Egan called "a lasting monument of FEMALE INTREPIDITY." But, by this time, respectable femininity was deemed incompatible with public horse sports like racing and riding for money.

Credit: © Virginia Museum of Fine Arts, Richmond (Paul Mellon Collection), Photo: Sydney Collins.

Nonetheless, public opinion soon turned against her. Racing in public for money was a publicity stunt; it was a spectacle as unrespectable as performing in a circus (Figure 1.8). In 1804, Mrs. Thornton had participated in a race against Mr. Flint, her brother-in-law, at the York August meeting, wagered for 500 guineas over a four-mile course. According to Egan, Mrs. Thornton's race originated out of a family argument, since the two wives, the Colonel's and Mr. Flint's, were sisters. In this case, she lost to Mr. Flint, but reportedly only because her girth loosened and her saddle slipped, forcing her to pull up during the last mile. She held the lead until this point, but this turn of events illustrates the unstable nature of the sidesaddle as well as Mrs. Thornton's adventurous and skilled horsemanship in pursuing such activities regardless. Mrs. Thornton immediately challenged Mr. Flint to another race, which he declined, though Egan stated that Flint, "a man of gallantry ... ought to have permitted his fair opponent to have won the race."[172] The only reason he did not, Egan intimated, was that he felt his masculinity would have been threatened if he lost to a woman.

This race, and Mrs. Thornton's example, marked a turning point in gender and sporting relations. In an "An Old Woman's Observation, on Reading the Account of Mrs. Thornton's recent Race at York," Olivia Oldstock declared that British grandmothers, who only ever rode pillion, were aghast at the disreputable behavior of women contriving "to vie with men in every manly grace." Far from riding soberly and gently, Olivia wondered, "What would [women of generations past] say, to see the modern maid, / Which jockey sleeves, and velvet cap array'd, / Dashing thro' thick and thin, to gain the post, / And swearing, when she finds her wishes cross'd!"[173] Even Egan admitted that though many ladies cheered on Mrs. Thornton as a member of their own sex, there were others – whom he labeled "a few old maids" and "rather squeamish" – who believed it was inappropriate for a female to race on a public track for a cash prize in front of an audience. Accordingly, these detractors believed Mr. Thornton should have stopped his wife from racing for propriety's sake.[174] Such public sporting displays, especially when gambled on, were not considered appropriate for ladies, with a husband's approval or not.

The gendered aspects of Mrs. Thornton's racing were brought even further into the public eye by her husband's sensational court case against Mr. Flint. The lawsuit originated when Colonel Thornton, due to the unfair circumstances, refused to pay a wager of £1000 for his wife's race against Mr. Flint. Mr. Flint, believing himself the victor, assaulted Colonel Thornton with a horsewhip at the York races over the non-payment. At the Court of King's Bench on February 3, 1806, Mr. Flint averred that, "The conduct of Col. Thornton, in suffering Mrs. Thornton to ride a match at the York Races, had been such, that the Court could not consider itself called upon to interpose its extraordinary powers, by granting a criminal investigation for an assault originating in such a subject."[175] It was so unthinkable that a man would support and encourage his wife to indulge in such spectacles that the court declined to intervene in the matter. However, public opinion had already decided the case. In March, Mr. Eskine, the lawyer for Mr. Flint, "took the occasion to deprecate the spectacle of a lady riding in a race."[176] The impropriety of a woman racing was at the heart of the controversy; the perceived unnaturalness of such performances prejudiced the public against all women's riding.

Public outcry and criticism of Mrs. Thornton's unfeminine behavior continued to grow. This criticism appeared to be vindicated with the asterisk included in an October 1807 article, which claimed in a footnote that the female jockey had run away with her groom to France: "The lady, who was always a devil of a sportswoman, had lately '*stole away*,' and given her *keeper* the slip. – Such dashers are generally of the Eel species; rather slippery: and when a woman once mounts a racer, she will inevitably be run away with."[177] Thus, female involvement in horse racing was now classified as deviant sexuality, rather than sporting prowess.

Separate Spheres?

Was the decrease of women's participation in equestrian sports by 1825 an illustration of – and caused by – the emergence of the separate spheres ideology? As shown by female involvement in riding and hunting through the late eighteenth century, women continued to participate in a wide variety of sports, activities, and social events. However, such participation diminished by the early 1800s. "The times are changed," the *Lady's Magazine* lamented in 1825, women:

> now seek only to exercise their virtues in domestic retirement. The wise (and those who are entitled to that appellation happily form the majority) perceiving the bad taste manifested in striving for mastery with man, are contented with truly feminine occupations...

The article lamented that "women have fallen from their high estate, and dwindled into comparative insignificance."[178] This damning verdict was an exaggeration, but gender ideals had changed by the early 1800s. Hannah Barker and Elaine Chalus have argued that the eighteenth century did not see the stereotypical development of separate spheres but rather more complex forms of gender construction whereby men and women were considered naturally different and those biological differences shaped the sexes' roles in society.[179] Yet, as Lawrence Klein has argued, "binary opposition does not adequately explain the complexities of discourse, let alone those of human experience in practice."[180] Although women were certainly influenced by social paradigms and prescriptive criteria, there was some flexibility in terms of equestrian participation, even if in a far more limited way than previously.

Participation in military or sporting activities traditionally demonstrated martial masculinity, a prowess in fighting, hunting, and triumphing in ancient survival skills. By the late eighteenth century, however, anxiety over military defeats and social disruptions caused gendered panic. For men, "foppery," connotating vanity and idleness, was seen as deviant masculinity, compensating for an "unimpressive physique" with fashionable and expensive clothing, accessorized by excessive hair and make-up. This lifestyle revolved around sedentary activities, such as patronizing coffee houses and theaters, activities which might have stimulated intellectual but not physical fitness. The rise of the "Cockney sportsman" was one attempt to lose this urban flab. While the sporting fraternity at Melton Mowbray exhibited very different qualities – muscular athleticism and excessively chauvinistic male sociality – it was evident that *female* physicality, prowess, and authority was now troubling to many.

These fears indicated the challenges of building a new urban culture against the fabric of traditional rural life. The separate spheres ideology sought to confine women into the safe and private space of the domestic home, although this demarcation was clearer in theory than practice. Polite society encouraged female activity, though preferred it be limited to the urban public spaces of parks, museums, shops, or some assembly rooms.[181] Riding in urban places like Hyde Park occurred in the mixed-gender public sphere of leisure, but even this activity was naturally circumscribed by the space. Women and horses were more easily constrained and controlled by definite barriers such as park railings or defined pathways. In contrast, hunting took place in the masculine sphere of sport, in an unlimited and untamed wild space rather than the civilized domestic home. Providing a female rider could negotiate gates, hedges, or other obstacles in the newly enclosed landscape, there was no limit to how far she could go on her own, without a chaperone. Here any boundaries could simply be galloped across or jumped over – but such unbridled enthusiasm could overturn the entire social order.

By the early 1800s, female sportswomen were caricatured for being over-enthusiastic. Riding has always been linked to sexual activity. Illustrations often depicted women as "wearing the breeches" or accused of "over-riding" with the predictable sexual connotations, as in the works of John Collett titled "A Soft Tumble after a Hard Ride" and "The Rising Woman and the Falling Man." Such inversions were meant to uphold gender roles through ridicule, and though such reversals were always temporary, they showed "in an extraordinarily positive fashion, the idea that gender identity is artificial and mutable."[182] Gender inversions for sporting women were more positive than for men, as women might be depicted as assertive, but thoroughly skilled, whereas men were often shown as foolish and drunken louts.

By the late eighteenth century, however, male patriarchy and dominance had prevailed, and female independence diminished, hence the decline in women's equestrian participation. As historian Donna Landry has argued, the idea of the British countryside was formed between the 1671 Game Laws and their subsequent repeal in 1831, but how should this new landscape be used for sport, and by whom?[183] More importantly, was it a proper place for women? The answer in the first third of the nineteenth century was no. But even if views about sport and gender hindered women from pursuing more demanding equestrian sports such as hunting and racing, female equestrians did not abandon riding altogether. Lady Lade lived until 1825 and the Marchioness of Salisbury until 1835, but their reputation lived much longer and inspired new generations of female riders.[184]

Down but Not Out

The evolution of British women's participation in equestrian sports between 1772 and 1825 is a story of inclusion to exclusion. Prior to 1800, women had freely and openly participated in riding and hunting. The development of the two-pommel sidesaddle had enabled women to pursue more demanding equestrian sports, while specialized clothing for riding and hunting enabled freer movement in the saddle. The corresponding production of riding manuals and the increase of riding schools illustrates how riding evolved from being a mere mode of transport to a new and defining activity of class and gender status.

Revolutionized by Hugo Meynell, fox hunting had become a fashionable pursuit that was more than rural pest control. During the late 1700s, the chase had been elevated from a country hobby to a desirable and popular sport. But, without improved roadways or train transportation, it remained a semi-private and localized activity. In this way, it was not limited by class, but rather by geography, and women were well able to ride with men. Female huntresses were not limited to aristocrats like the Marchioness of Salisbury, as other sporting females came from a variety of social backgrounds and also joined in the chase. Women such as Laetitia, Lady Lade, and Phoebe Higgs demonstrated that status was less important to joining such activities than skill and merit. Riding and hunting well was the ticket to inclusion in such sports, not class. Such widespread involvement of women also indicates that femininity was initially compatible with sporting participation, not jeopardized by it.

Up to the nineteenth century, the press coverage of women as riders was exceedingly positive. Most, if not all, mentions of their exploits come across in glowing, even ravishing, terms. In 1804, Mrs. Stoddard, who rode with the Prince's harriers near Brighton, was admiringly described as:

> one of the best female equestrians we ever saw; a descent at full speed from the highest hill alarms her not; graceful and easy in the saddle, she manages the reins with all possible agility, and seems to acquire additional fortitude when difficulties present themselves; difficulties which – as on Wednesday – unhorse the Cockney sportsman, but call her powers pleasingly into action, and give fresh cause for admiration and surprise.[185]

But by the 1810s, such mentions were the stuff of the past and coverage dwindled and diminished until the 1830s. A few appear in Nimrod's accounts of 1824 concerning the Marquis of Cleveland's daughters, but they had been specially raised by their father to ride and hunt in the rural countryside south of Durham.[186] This decrease was not popular among all sportsmen: a note from a male subscriber in *The Sporting Magazine* of November 1829 implored, "I do wish the ladies in our neighbourhood (for we have some excellent horse-women among us) would a little oftener favour us with their company."[187]

By the early nineteenth century, however, both sporting practices and gender ideals had changed. The strategy of sport had been modernized, horses and hounds became faster and more strategically bred, and landscape was modified through enclosure. All these changes merged to close the formerly open nature of the field and to limit women's participation, though of all factors, gender ideals mattered most. By the early 1800s, hunting had become formally masculinized in ritual and practice, and women's involvement was no longer proper or acceptable. Women might have found the courage and skill to negotiate fearsome fences in their sidesaddles, but few were willing to risk social ostracization or jeopardize their reputations.

Women's participation in hunting, long accepted as a traditional pastime for ladies, was increasingly condemned after the early 1800s. It was believed that hunting eroded natural feminine character through its exposure to rough violence, whether natural (killing the fox) or human (male manners). Its sordid associations and the base behaviors of a few (such as Alicia Thornton running off with her groom) gave rise to the negative stereotypes about female riders as a whole in the early 1800s, thus making it harder for ordinary women to participate. Sporting prowess was one thing, but social reputation and respectability were another. By the end of the eighteenth century, these two factors were no longer compatible as they had been previously, thus leading to a decline in female equestrianism. Men no longer wanted to see women in the field, putting them to shame in their pursuits. As *The Ladies' Field* magazine noted, "Had the first Lord Forester or Sir James Musgrave, members of the old club, found a copy of THE LADIES' FIELD on his table one fine morning, they would have thought the world was coming to an end." Adrian Harvey has argued that after Alicia Thornton, women had little impact on sport and that female participation ended with her, but that not the case.[188] Happily, the exclusion of women from the hunting field was never complete, and there were women – country-born and not – who continued to ride and follow the hounds through the first half of the nineteenth century – and the world did not end.

Notes

1 David Cecil, *The Cecils of Hatfield House* (London: Constable, 1973), 188–189.
2 *The Sporting Magazine*, Volume 7 (January 1796), 176.
3 *The Sporting Magazine*, Volume 8 (April 1796), 52.
4 *The Sporting Magazine*, Volume 53 (February 1819), 251.
5 Meriel Buxton, *Ladies of the Chase* (London: The Sportsman's Press, 1987), 38; Lida Fleitmann Bloodgood, *The Saddle of Queens: The Story of the Side-Saddle* (London: J.A. Allen and Co., 1959), 19. The sporting author and historian "Thormanby" states that the Marchioness resigned only in 1828, giving the hounds to the county and the mastership to Thomas Sebright. See "Thormanby" [Wilmott Willmott-Dixon], *Kings of the Hunting Field* (London: Hutchinson and Co., 1899), 257.
6 In October 1807, *The Sporting Magazine* proclaimed, "The Marchioness of – hunted on Thursday with *her* harriers …" (28) – italics in the original.
7 "Coursers Taking the Field at Hatfield Park, Hertfordshire, the Seat of the Marquess of Salisbury," Tate, https://www.tate.org.uk/art/artworks/pollard-coursers-taking-the-field-at-hatfield-park-hertfordshire-the-seat-of-the-marquess-t03434.

8 *The Sporting Magazine*, Volume 21 (December 1802), 164.
9 *The Sporting Magazine*, Volume 31 (October 1807), 28.
10 *The Sporting Magazine*, Volume 15 (December 1799), 150 (but incorrectly printed as page 15).
11 See Cecil, 192–193. Elaine Chalus, "Cecil [née Hill], Mary Amelia [Emily Mary], marchioness of Salisbury (1750–1835), political hostess and sportswoman," *Oxford Dictionary of National Biography*.
12 Elaine Chalus, "'That Epidemical Madness': Women and Electoral Politics in the Late Eighteenth Century", in Hannah Barker and Elaine Chalus (eds.), *Gender in Eighteenth-Century England: Roles, Representations and Responsibilities* (London: Longman, 1997), 155.
13 Chalus (1997), 157, Duchess of Devonshire to Lady Spencer, Chatsworth, October 21, 1783.
14 Mary Wollstonecraft, *A Vindication of the Rights of Woman* (Boston: Peter Edes, 1792), 152.
15 Hannah Barker and Elaine Chalus, eds., *Gender in Eighteenth-Century England: Roles, Representations and Responsibilities* (London: Longman, 1997), 2.
16 John Brown, *An Estimate of the Manners and Principles of the Times* (London: L. Davis, and C. Reymers, 1757).
17 Linda Colley, *Britons: Forging a Nation, 1707–1837* (New Haven: Yale University Press, 2005), 250–252.
18 E.M. Kellock, *The Story of Riding* (London: David and Charles, 1974), 58.
19 Lauren Gilmour, "Saddles of the Stuart Period," in Lauren Adams Gilmour (ed.), *In the Saddle: An Exploration of the Saddle through History* (London: Archetype, 2004), 81; John W. Waterer, *A Short History of Saddles in Europe* (Brighton: The Museum of Leathercraft, 1975).
20 Bloodgood, 28.
21 Mr. Carter [Charles Carter], *Instructions for Ladies in Riding, By Mister Carter* (London, 1783), 27–28.
22 Carter, 20.
23 "Gilpin, Sawrey, 1733–1807," Paul Mellon Centre for Studies in British Art Photographic Archive.
24 Anonymous, *The Young Lady's Equestrian Manual* (London: Whitehead and Company, 1838), 18–19. Robert Healy's sketch of Lady Louisa Conolly and Groom (1768, at Castletown House, Ireland) shows a leather saddle with one horn – the stirrup leather is looped over the horn rather than attached under the skirt, with crupper and overgirth (no balance strap).
25 Carter, 25–27.
26 *The Sporting Magazine*, Volume 21 (January 1803), "Observations on the Construction of Stables, Choice of a Lady's Pad, Breaking of Horses, &c. &c.: From T.H. Morland's *Treatise*, entitled, Every Man His Own Judge, &c.," 219.
27 Richard Berenger, *The History and Art of Horsemanship*, Volume 1 (London: T. Davies and T. Cadell, 1771), 106.
28 John Allen, *Principles of Modern Riding for Ladies; in Which All Improvements Are Applied to Practice on the Promenade and the Road* (London: Thomas Tegg, 1825), 40.
29 Carter, 29. See also "T.S.", *Lectures on Horsemanship Wherein Is Explained Every Necessary Instruction for Both Ladies and Gentlemen* (London: 1793), 30.
30 Carter, 29.
31 Lindsay Smith, "The History of Development of the Side-Saddle," in Lauren Adams Gilmour (ed.), *In the Saddle: An Exploration of the Saddle through History* (London: Archetype, 2004), 86; Rhonda C. Watts Hettinger, *The Illustrated Encyclopedia of the*

Sidesaddle (Wilton, NH: Sidesaddle Source, 2009), 25; Sally Mitchell and Nick Creaton, *A Brief History of the Side Saddle* (Palette Press, 2019), 114.
32 Carter, 25.
33 "Riding coat," *Victoria and Albert Museum Collections*, http://collections.vam.ac.uk/item/O84125/riding-coat-unknown/.
34 "Riding coat, ca. 1760," *The Met Collections*, https://www.metmuseum.org/art/collection/search/81754.
35 Judy Egerton, *George Stubbs, Painter: Catalogue Raisonné* (New Haven: Yale University Press, 2007), 16–17.
36 H. Wilberforce Bell, "The Vicissitudes of a Picture by George Stubbs," *Country Life*, September 26, 1936, lii–liv. The Reynolds painting was destroyed in a fire in 1988, but contemporary notes described Elizabeth wearing a red riding habit and a remaining black and white image shows the style to be similar in cut. David Mannings, *Sir Joshua Reynolds: A Complete Catalogue of His Paintings* (New Haven: Yale University Press, 2000), 235.
37 Amanda Foreman, *Georgiana, Duchess of Devonshire* (New York: Modern Library, 2001), 64.
38 *Morning Post*, July 18, 1788, cited in Foreman, 64.
39 *Morning Herald and Daily Advertiser*, June 11, 1781, cited in Foreman, 88.
40 *The Sporting Magazine*, Volume 71 (February 1828), 278.
41 Joanne Major and Sarah Murden, *An Infamous Mistress: The Life, Loves and Family of the Celebrated Grace Dalrymple Elliott* (Barnsley: Pen and Sword History, 2016), 124–125. See also Charles Bazalgette, *Prinny's Taylor: The Life and Times of Louis Balzalgette (1750–1830)* (Salmo: Canada: Tara Books, 2015), 45, 90, 102, 107.
42 "Fashionable Riding Habits for July 1799," plate III, *The Lady's Monthly Museum* (London: Vernor & Hood, 1798–1828), Volume 3 (July 1799), description on page 60.
43 M.L. Biscotti, *Six Centuries of Foxhunting: An Annotated Bibliography* (London: Rowman & Littlefield, 2017), xiv.
44 Egerton, 209.
45 Chris Evans, *Debating the Revolution: Britain in the 1790s* (London: I.B. Tauris, 2006), 31 and 34.
46 Carter, 26.
47 Charles Hughes, *The Compleat Horseman; or, the Art of Riding Made Easy; Illustrated by Rules Drawn from Nature, and Confirmed by Experience; with Directions for the Ladies to Sit Gracefully, and Ride with Safety* (London: F. Newbery, 1772), 8.
48 John Van der Kiste, *King George II and Queen Caroline* (Stroud: Sutton Publishing, 1997), 107. See also William Tyte, *Bath in the Eighteenth Century* (Bath: G. & F. Pickering, 1903), 24.
49 Hughes, 60–61.
50 John M. Turner, "Hughes, Charles (1746/7–1797), Equestrian and Circus Proprietor," *Oxford Dictionary of National Biography*.
51 Hughes, 7.
52 Hughes, 8.
53 Hughes, 11.
54 Hughes, 14.
55 Philip H. Highfill, Jr., Kalman A. Burnim, and Edward A. Langhans, *A Biographical Dictionary of Actors, Actresses, Musicians, Dancers, Managers and Other Stage Personnel in London, 1660–1800* (Carbondale: Southern Illinois University Press, 1982), 22.
56 Marius Kwint, "The Legitimization of the Circus in Late Georgian England," *Past and Present*, 174.1 (2002), 72–115. See also Highfill, 19.

57 Thomas Almeroth-Williams, "Horses & Livestock in Hanoverian London," PhD thesis, University of York (2013), 280–281.
58 Almeroth-Williams, 282–284.
59 Carter, iv.
60 Carter, 12 and 25.
61 Carter, 18–19.
62 Carter, title page.
63 Carter, iv.
64 Almeroth-Williams, 280–281.
65 Almeroth-Williams, 280–281.
66 Carter, vi–vii.
67 Mike Huggins, *Horse Racing and British Society in the Long Eighteenth Century* (Woodbridge: The Boydell Press, 2018), Further Matter (previous to page 1).
68 Almeroth-Williams, 291, from *World & Fashionable Advertiser*, October 9, 1787 and December 13, 1787.
69 Carter, viii.
70 Carter, viii.
71 Almeroth-Williams, 274 and 309.
72 "T.S.", 34.
73 John Adams, *An Analysis of Horsemanship* (London: M. Ritchie, 1799).
74 Philip Astley, *The Modern Riding-Master: or, a Key to the Knowledge of the Horse, and Horsemanship: with Several Necessary Rules for Young Horsemen* (London: 1775).
75 Philip Astley, *Astley's System of Equestrian Education* (Lambeth: C. Creed, 1801), 15.
76 Colley, 172.
77 Emma Griffin, *Blood Sport: Hunting in Britain Since 1066* (New Haven: Yale University Press, 2007), 105–107.
78 Raymond Carr, *English Fox Hunting* (London: Weidenfeld and Nicholson, 1986), 25–27.
79 Carr, 25.
80 Jane Ridley, *Fox Hunting* (London: Collins, 1990), 18. See also Buxton, 34.
81 William Scarth Dixon, *The Sport of Kings* (London: Grant Richards, 1900), 60.
82 Jonathan Finch, "'Grass, Grass, Grass': Hunting and the Creation of the Modern Landscape," *Landscapes*, 5.2 (2004), 45.
83 Augusta Fane, *Chit-chat* (London: Thornton, Butterworth, Limited, 1926), 122.
84 The recollection by Lord Wilton (Second Earl), in Fane, 121.
85 Carr, 30; Buxton, 34.
86 Buxton, 36.
87 "The Royal Chace," *The Sporting Magazine*, Volume 11 (November 1797), 56.
88 "Royal Chase," *The Sporting Magazine*, Volume 9 (October 1796), 7–8.
89 Buxton, 35–36.
90 Quote from John Randall, *Broseley and Its Surroundings* (Madeley, Salop: The Salopian and West Midland Journal Office, 1879), 267. See also "The Shropshire Landscape Typology," *Shropshire County Council* (September 2006), https://www.shropshire.gov.uk/media/1803/the-shropshire-landscape-typology.pdf.
91 "Thormanby," 31.
92 Buxton, 38.
93 "Thormanby," 31.
94 Buxton, 35–36.
95 "Thormanby," 5. The original notes are likely from "An Amateur Sportsman" [Pierce Egan], *Sporting Anecdotes: Original and Select* (London: J. Cundee, 1807), 449–451.
96 *The Sporting Magazine*, Volume 13 (November 1798), 65.

97 *The Sporting Magazine*, Volume 23 (December 1803), 159.
98 *The Sporting Magazine*, Volume 27 (January 1806), 209.
99 Rosemary Baird, *Goodwood: Art and Architecture, Sport and Family* (London: Frances Lincoln Limited, 2007), 114, 117–118.
100 "A Good Huntsman – Luke Freeman," *The Sporting Magazine*, Volume 5 (March 1822), 277. See also Baird, 143.
101 "A Good Huntsman – Luke Freeman," *The Sporting Magazine*, Volume 59 (March 1822), 277. See also Baird, 154–155.
102 George Stubbs, "Laetitia, Lady Lady" *The Royal Collection Trust (RCIN 400997)*, https://www.rct.uk/collection/400997/laetitia-lady-lade-d-1825.
103 Buxton, 36. She was an expert carriage driver (as her curricle matches attest). The final mention of Lady Lade in *The Sporting Magazine* occurs in July 1809, for a curricle accident, rather than her riding. See *The Sporting Magazine*, Volume 34 (July 1809), 260. It should be noted that she was not driving; her husband was.
104 This is not to say that she did not have her rough edges as well, as she was notorious for her foul language; to swear "like Letty Lade" meant to spout extensive profanity. See J.H. Plumb, *Men and Centuries* (Boston, Houghton Mifflin, 1963), 86.
105 *The Sporting Magazine*, Volume 6 (June 1795), 168.
106 "Account of the Royal Chace," *The Sporting Magazine*, Volume 9 (November 1796), 61.
107 "The Royal Chace," *The Sporting Magazine*, Volume 11 (November 1797), 57.
108 "Royal Chace," *The Sporting Magazine*, Volume 11 (February 1797), 239.
109 "Sporting Intelligence," *The Sporting Magazine*, Volume 15 (October 1799), 45.
110 Anonymous, *Fifty Years of London Society, 1870–1920* (London: Eveleigh Nash Co. 1920), 102.
111 Roger Powell, *Royal Sex: The Scandalous Love Lives of the British Royal Family* (Stroud, Gloucestershire: Amberley Publishing, 2013), 186–187.
112 Donna Landry, *Noble Brutes: How Eastern Horses Transformed English Culture* (Baltimore: Johns Hopkins University Press, 2009).
113 David C. Itzkowitz, *Peculiar Privilege: A Social History of English Foxhunting, 1753–1885* (Hassocks, Sussex: The Harvester Press Limited, 1977), 48. See also Nicholas Russell, *Like Engend'ring Like: Heredity and Animal Breeding in Early Modern England* (Cambridge: Cambridge University Press, 1986), 60–61, 111, 219.
114 Ridley, 18–19.
115 Finch (2004), 42.
116 John Patten, "Fox Coverts for the Squirearchy," *Country Life* (September 23, 1971), 738.
117 Colin B. Ellis, *Leicestershire and the Quorn Hunt* (Leicester: Edgar Backus, 1951), 60. See also Itzkowitz, 8.
118 H.G. Hunt, "The Chronology of Parliamentary Enclosure in Leicestershire," *The Economic History Review*, New Series, 10.2 (1957), 266.
119 Carter, vi.
120 "Full Cry," *The New Sporting Almanack*, "Wildrake" (ed.), (Rudolph Ackermann, 1843), 52.
121 Patten, 738. See "Full Cry," *The New Sporting Almanack*, 52.
122 Patten, 736–738.
123 Finch (2004), 48.
124 *The Sporting Magazine*, Volume 71 (February 1828), 278–279.
125 Bloodgood, 18–19.
126 Buxton 34 and 43.
127 *The Sporting Magazine*, Volume 76, First Series/Volume 1, Second Series (June 1830), 103–104.

128 *The Sporting Magazine*, Volume 71 (February 1828), 280. For praise of her early skills, see *The Sporting Magazine*, Volume 19 (April 1827), 391.
129 *The Sporting Magazine*, Volume 76, First Series/Volume 1, Second Series (July 1830), 234.
130 G.E. Mingay, *Parliamentary Enclosure in England: An Introduction to Its Causes, Incidence and Impact, 1750–1850* (London: Longman, 1997), 17.
131 Ridley, 18.
132 Colonel John Cook, *Observations on Fox-Hunting* (London: Edward Arnold and Co., 1922), 127.
133 "The Druid" [Henry Hall Dixon], *Scott and Sebright* (London: Frederick Warne and Co, 1862), 375. See also William C.A. Blew, *The History of the Quorn Hunt and Its Masters* (London: John C. Nimmo, 1899), 48.
134 Buxton, 45.
135 "Thormanby," 160.
136 "Thormanby," 60–161.
137 "A Letter from 'An Old 'Un' in Paris to 'A Young 'Un' in Leicestershire," *The Sporting Magazine*, Volume 71 (March 1828), 348.
138 "Manners and Customs: Hunting, etc.," *The Ladies' Field*, Volume 4 (February 4, 1899), 356.
139 Itzkowitz 42–45, Ridley, 21.
140 Ridley, 21.
141 Ridley, 21.
142 Blew, 11. See also Stephen Butt, *Melton Mowbray through Time* (Stroud, Gloucestershire: Amberley Publishing, 2012).
143 Buxton, 48.
144 Buxton, 48.
145 "Melton: The Story of its Rise, I," *The Ladies' Field* (November 10, 1900): Supplement: Sports and Pastimes, unpaginated.
146 William Henry Scott, *British Field Sports* (London: Sherwood, Neely, and Jones, 1818), 398.
147 Carr, 72.
148 "Nimrod" [Charles James Apperley], *Memoirs of the Life of the Late John Mytton, Esq.* (London: Rudolph Ackermann, 1837), 27.
149 "Nimrod," 27.
150 Buxton, 49.
151 Leonard Cooper, *R.S. Surtees* (London: Arthur Baker, Ltd., 1952), 31–32.
152 Frederick Watson, *Robert Smith Surtees: A Critical Survey* (Norwood, PA: Norwood Editions, 1978), 38–39. The Epping Hunt was finally disbanded in 1853.
153 Cooper, 31–32.
154 *The Sporting Magazine*, Volume 77, First Series/Volume 2, Second Series (January 1831), 192.
155 *The Sporting Magazine*, Volume 53 (February 1819), 251.
156 "Nim South's Southern Tour," *The Sporting Magazine*, Volume 77, First Series/Volume 2, Second Series (December 1830), 120.
157 "A Dorsetian Sketch, II, by A Native," *The Sporting Magazine*, Volume 77, First Series/Volume 2, Second Series (December 1830), 101.
158 "Origin, Progress, and Present State of Archery," *The Sporting Magazine*, Volume 77, First Series/Volume 2, Second Series (December 1830), 81.
159 Robert Smith Surtees, *Mr. Facey Romford's Hounds* (London: Bradbury and Evans, 1865), 66. See also Surtees, *Analysis of the Hunting Field* (London: Methuen and Co., 1904), 291.

160 "Nim South's Southern Tour," *The Sporting Magazine*, Volume 77, First Series/Volume 2, Second Series (December 1830), 120.
161 Rebecca Cassidy, *The Sport of Kings: Kinship, Class and Thoroughbred Breeding in Newmarket* (Cambridge: Cambridge University Press, 2002), 15. See also Caroline Ramsden, *Ladies in Racing: Sixteenth Century to the Present Day* (London: Stanley Paul, 1973), 15–20.
162 William Fawcett, *Riding and Horsemanship* (New York: Charles Scribner's Sons, 1935), 146. See Frederic Shoberl, *Horse-Racing: Its History and Early Records of the Principal and Other Race Meetings* (London: Saunders, Otley, and Co., 1863), 138–139.
163 See "Nimrod's Yorkshire Tour," *The Sporting Magazine*, Volume 20 (1827), 287.
164 Arthur G. Credland, "Colonel Thornton's Gift to Napoleon Bonaparte and Further Notes on his Career," *Arms & Armour*, 6.1 (2009), 62–78.
165 For stag-hunting, see *The Sporting Magazine*, Volume 25 (January 1805), 173. For driving, see *The Sporting Magazine*, Volume 26 (July 1805), 225.
166 Pierce Egan, *Book of Sports and Mirror of Life* (London: T.T. and J. Tegg, 1832), 130.
167 *The Sporting Magazine*, Volume 26 (August 1805), 234.
168 For the portrait, see *The Sporting Magazine*, Volume 25 (January 1805), 171. For the poem, entitled "The York Match – A New Jockey Song," see *The Sporting Magazine*, Volume 26 (September 1805), 319.
169 Egan, 129.
170 Egan, 130.
171 *The Sporting Magazine*, Volume 26 (August 1805), 234.
172 Egan, 131.
173 *The Sporting Magazine*, Volume 25 (December 1804), 168.
174 Egan, 131.
175 *The Sporting Magazine*, Volume 27 (February 1806), 224. See also *The Sporting Magazine*, Volume 26 (August 1805), 235.
176 *The Sporting Magazine*, Volume 27 (March 1806), 296.
177 *The Sporting Magazine*, Volume 31 (October 1807), 27; D. Brailsford, "Thornton [Meynell], Alicia (fl. 1804), horsewoman," *Oxford Dictionary of National Biography*.
178 "Woman," *The Lady's Magazine; or, Mirror of the Belles-Lettres, Fine Arts, Music, Drama, Fashions, &c.* (London: S. Robinson), February 28, 1825, 65.
179 Barker and Chalus, 1.
180 Lawrence E. Klein, "Gender and the Public/Private Distinction in the 18th Century," *Eighteenth Century Studies*, 29.1 (Fall 1995), 98.
181 Colley, 240–241.
182 Robert B. Shoemaker, *Gender in English Society, 1650–1850: The Emergence of Separate Spheres?* (London: Longman, 1998), 38.
183 Donna Landry, *The Invention of the Countryside: Hunting, Walking and Ecology in English Literature, 1671–1831* (New York: Palgrave, 2001).
184 Her exploits were the inspiration for the character of the "Amazon" in George W.M. Reynolds, *The Mysteries of the Courts of London* in 1849. According to Donna Landry, the character appears in Volume 1, page 56 and consistently throughout. See Landry (2001), 163.
185 *The Sporting Magazine*, Volume 25 (October 1804), 42.
186 *The Sporting Magazine*, Volume 63 (March 1824), "Sporting Intelligence," 347. See also Volume 67 (February 1826) for Nimrod's account of Lady Shakerley, 263; and Volume 99 (April 1827), on Mrs. Russell, 391.
187 *The Sporting Magazine*, Volume 75 (November 1829), 35.
188 Adrian Harvey, *The Beginnings of a Commercial Sporting Culture in Britain 1793–1850* (Burlington, VT: Ashgate, 2004), 198.

Chapter 2

Horseback Riding as Exercise and Female Accomplishment, 1805–1857

The author Sir Walter Scott illustrated the rising popularity of female equestrianism in his depiction of Diana Vernon in his popular book, *Rob Roy*, published in 1818. Narrated by Frank Osbaldistone in the 1760s, the story is set during the Jacobite Rebellion of 1715–1716.[1] Exiled from London to Osbaldistone Hall in Northumbria, Frank's first experience in his new home is to encounter a fox hunt in full cry. Here he sees for the first time the excellent horsewoman (and his future wife), Diana:

> It was a young lady, the loveliness of whose very striking features was enhanced by the animation of the chase and the glow of the exercise, mounted on a beautiful horse, jet black, unless where he was flecked by spots of the snow-white foam which embossed his bridle. She wore, what was then somewhat unusual, a coat, vest, and hat, resembling those of a man, which fashion has since called a riding-habit.[2]

Throughout Scott's novel, Diana pushes at the boundaries of respectable femininity through her horsemanship and hunting prowess. She appears in riding clothes designed on masculine lines and participates in what was considered – by 1818 – to be a masculine sport.[3] *She* even acts as pilot for *him*, leading him across an imposing jump. "There are hopes of you yet," she concludes, noting that her equestrian skill had far outshone his.[4]

Though the fictional Diana flaunted contemporary feminine conventions, scholar Ian Duncan shows that readers then – as well as successive generations – "adored" her, even though she was apparently everything that female prescriptive literature condemned.[5] The first edition of *Rob Roy* sold out its first print run of 10,000 copies in two weeks, and four more editions were printed in 1818 to meet demand.[6] A review of Scott's novel in *The Edinburgh Magazine* proclaimed it "altogether glorious and resplendent."[7] Harriet Martineau even praised the author: "he has advocated the rights of woman with a force all the greater for his being unaware of the import and tendency of what he was saying."[8]

Although Diana Vernon, her love of horsemanship, and her challenging of feminine norms scored points with a British audience, such behavior did not find favor in France. In Auguste-Jean-Baptiste Defauconpret's French translation, the all-important hunting scene is radically reinterpreted, and a more feminine Diana does not challenge Frank to horseback feats of jumping fences.[9] The different depictions of Diana Vernon for both British and French audiences not only pointed to the differing social, cultural, and gender norms in both countries, but also their sporting disparities. While the French concentrated on the military applications of *haute école*, in which women found few opportunities to involve themselves, British women, by contrast, participated widely in hunting and riding. In fact, the positive reception of Diana Vernon in 1818 pointed to the beginnings of a new British acceptance of women as riders and a new era of female horsemanship. The character was therefore caught in a moment of history, representing of an older way of life that was more supportive of women's sporting participation, while also serving as a role model for a new generation of hunting women yet to come.

Perhaps encouraged by Diana's example, British women's participation in urban riding increased during the early 1800s, even though the number of women hunting had decreased. Gone were the days of Phoebe Higgs and Lady Lade galloping across the countryside, and certainly no sane woman would attempt such feats in crowded city streets. As *The Young Lady's Equestrian Manual* stressed in 1838:

> No lady of taste ever gallops on the road. Into this pace the lady's horse is never urged, or permitted to break, except in the field; and not above one among a thousand of our fair readers, it may be surmised, is likely to be endowed with sufficient ambition and boldness, to attempt "the following of hounds."[10]

In previous times, riding on horseback had been mainly for travel or public display, while mounted sports like fox hunting had been limited to rural areas for utilitarian purposes. By the turn of the nineteenth century, however, new equestrian activities had spread widely into cities and to urban areas like Hyde Park's Rotten Row, where British riders were acclaimed as the best in the world (Figure 2.1).[11]

The rise of female riders instigated the transformation of riding clothes for women, which became safer and more practical. These clothes, called "riding habits," gave women greater liberty and agency on horseback, and these innovations were paralleled by the invention of the leaping head, a third pommel on sidesaddles. Together with changing social, gender, and sporting ideals, advances in women's riding clothes and saddles enabled them to pursue more demanding equestrian activities and rejoin fox hunting fields. Women made hunting their own again by reshaping not only the sport itself through their "civilizing influence" but also reshaping ideas about proper femininity and female behavior. In doing so, they augmented the development of hunting as a national sport and its contribution to a specifically British identity.

90 Exercise and Female Accomplishment

Figure 2.1 "Rotten-Row, Hyde-Park," *The Illustrated London News* (May 24, 1851), p. 462. In 1690, King William III established "Rotten Row" as a safe byway through Hyde Park, linking Kensington Palace and St. James' Palace. The name may have come from the French *"route du roi,"* meaning "king's road," or the English "rotten" as a soft or decayed surface (being unpaved). This wide dirt track through the most prominent park in London became *the* fashionable place to ride and be seen by the early nineteenth century. Ladies were especially encouraged to ride as a healthy exercise, and this illustration shows several female riders, controlling high-spirited horses amidst the crowding and confusion of urban park riding.
Credit: Collection of the author.

This chapter examines the upsurge in urban riding for women and how female equestrians made their triumphant return to fox hunting. It highlights the years between the publication of John Adams' *An Analysis of Horsemanship* in 1805, with a significant section on ladies' riding that encouraged jumping, to the appearance of Mrs. J. Stirling Clarke's *The Ladies' Equestrian Guide; or, The Habit and the Horse: A Treatise on Female Equitation* in 1857, the first equestrian manual for women written by a woman. Traditionally, the early Victorian era has been viewed by historians as a period when opportunities for women decreased and ideals of femininity were inextricably linked to the home and family, as illustrated by Sarah Stickney Ellis' works, including *Women of England* published in 1839. However, as argued by Linda Colley, Amanda Vickery and others, this ideology of separate spheres may have intensified *because* women's opportunities and activities outside the home were increasing so dramatically.[12] Even as some women may have retreated into separate, private, and domesticated spaces, others were also exploring new opportunities outside the home, including increased participation in equestrian activities.

Riding for Health

Though women's participation in fox hunting decreased by the early 1800s, that decline was compensated by a marked increase in ladies' park riding, or what Amanda Gilroy has called "aspirational recreational riding."[13] Riding on the road or in a park was called "hacking," for the use of an easy-going horse called a "hack."[14] This designation, in contrast to a carriage-horse or racehorse, became popular at the end of the eighteenth century, especially as leisurely "park riding" became more popular.[15] Riding became an attractive activity not only as opportunities for women to go hunting declined, but also for its own benefits.

Urban riding was lauded as a healthy exercise, as well as social accomplishment, for ladies. Its popularity was highlighted not only by the example of the newly crowned Queen Victoria but also by a flurry of riding manuals specifically for female readers and riders. After the turn of the nineteenth century, these manuals not only gave detailed directions on how to ride, but how to behave properly in the social settings of a new public equestrian sphere. Women did not stop riding simply because they were discouraged from fox hunting. In fact, by being excluded from hunting, they made urban riding a popular and socially attractive activity.

Outdoor and field sports had originally been urged as a beneficial recreation for both men and women, especially the former. It encouraged gentlemen to remain in the country to look after their affairs, and it brought together the wider social community, if not in equality, then at least in proximity. But as industry and pollution spread across Britain, more well-to-do families lived in urban or suburban areas where there was little space for outdoor refreshment, so other means had to be found to take the place of field sports. William Pitt the Elder had declared parks "the lungs of London," and the use of open space was encouraged for exercise.[16] The values of country life – which instilled courage, strength, and hardiness – against the city's corruption, vice, and effeminacy were considered especially important in the age of increased industrialization and urbanization.[17] Even as women were excluded from hunting, their participation in recreational riding brought the benefits of the country to the city.

British women were considered the frailer sex due to their allegedly delicate physiology. Early Victorian medical doctors believed that the female body was by nature both sick and weak. Women were seen as particularly vulnerable (and in need of supervision) due to their reproductive capacity.[18] Fears of over-exertion often led to over-coddling and enforced sheltering in place – especially for middle class women – in the domestic home. "We English matrons are a far more feeble race than our grandmothers, or even our mothers, were," the author of *The English Matron* lamented in 1846, "Witness our pallid faces … or witness our over-fed and over-expanded forms, enfeebled by indolence, and suffering the worst species of debility—the debility of *fat*."[19] Restrictive fashions, including corsets and "tight lacing," also caused problems.[20]

Beyond physical maladies, there were also concerns for female mental health, especially female hysteria or "madness." If women's bodies were frailer than men's, so too, it was assumed, were their brains, thus being more susceptible to breakdown. Women in the early nineteenth century purportedly suffered from "melancholy," "occasioned by a sedentary life and solitude," according to Lewis Mansey in *The Practical Physician* in 1800.[21] One of the causes of such nervous diseases was urban existence, with too much sociality and stress.[22] This idle indoor existence was worsened by darkened rooms, scant ventilation, and little exercise, leading to a myriad of eye, muscle, lung, and heart troubles for both growing girls and adult women.[23] Female illness and invalidism were common, for "God never intended us to be inactive."[24]

Riding was one way to address these problems. It improved mental well-being as well as physical health. According to a 1798 article entitled "Riding on Horseback Recommended":

> Riding is not only conducive to health and long life, but to study and speculation. It not only braces the nerves of the body, but enlivens the faculties of the soul, the one being actuated by the other, and their sensations so woven together and intermixed, that where the proper temperament of the body is not preserved, the faculties of the soul cannot exert themselves with vigour.[25]

Exercise from horseback riding, one of the few outdoor and energetic activities that respectable ladies could pursue, boosted a rider's composure, confidence, and self-control. As Queen Victoria claimed, riding was "good for the nerves."[26] As we know now, riding (and other physical exercise) mediates depression by releasing endorphins and other brain chemicals to regulate mood swings and increase feelings of well-being. As famed actress Fanny Kemble confirmed, riding was one of "my best remedies for the blue devils" of her depression and anxiety.[27]

After the turn of the nineteenth century, riding was encouraged as the ladies' exercise *par excellence* in comparison to other sports, games, or recreations. In 1805, riding master John Adams asserted, "the exercise of riding is more salutary to the constitution ... Hence, the chamber-horse, the swing, the skipping-rope, the dance, and numberless other exercises, calculated to promote circulation, are found inferior and very inadequate to riding."[28] Twenty years later, this belief was still going strong. In 1828, the sporting author "Nimrod" espoused the healthful benefits of riding for women: "The Ladies Augusta Milbanke and Arabella Vane are constant attendants on the Raby pack three times a fortnight, which is pretty good work for the softer sex; but there is nothing like horse exercise for the human economy. As old Juvenal says, it keeps the body sound and the understanding clear."[29] He praised the ladies' horsemanship and promoted riding for ladies, but he did not generally believe in female participation in hunting at this time.

In 1838 riding master George Reeves called horse exercise "that accomplishment which is calculated, above all others, either as a recreation or an exercise, to impart health and strength to the more delicate sex."[30] Riding developed core strength of the back, abdomen, and pelvic muscles, important for posture and reproduction. Sidesaddle riders were constantly reminded to sit squarely in their saddles. Writing from the perspective of the horse, Thomas Craige advised: "Do not sit on my back like a politician, all on one side."[31] In other words, female riders should balance evenly without relying on stirrups or reins, thus using core muscles to achieve control through coordination and stability.[32]

At the same time, wider acceptance of women's equestrianism was hindered by fears that riding only on one side of the horse would deform women's bodies. Riding put stress on all parts of the body, but most specifically on the spine and hips, which took the brunt of impact in the saddle.[33] The artificial position of riding sidesaddle put additional stress on bones and muscles, and, as a result, many novices became "saddle sore" after even mild exertion. Even Fanny Kemble, an avid equestrian, complained, "I have taken two riding lessons and like it much, though it makes my bones ache a little."[34] The resulting strain could have lasting consequences. "The most universal of these deformities," according to Donald Walker, author of several Victorian exercise guides, was "lateral curvature of the spinal column."[35] Walker's *Exercises for Ladies*, published in 1836, specifically targeted the activities deemed most harmful in causing this "one-sidedness": standing, sitting, writing, drawing, guitar and harp playing, riding, and sleeping – which begs the question, what female pursuit did *not* purportedly cause deformity?[36] Women were trapped: it was not proper for them to ride in anything but a sidesaddle (with their legs demurely closed), but riding sidesaddle was believed to deform their musculature.[37]

One solution was to take everything in moderation, including horseback riding. Any excess – whether in idle leisure or intense exercise – was deleterious, although early Victorians preferred that women err to the former rather than the latter. For example, in "Memoirs of a Celebrated Sporting Lady," published in 1803, Lady Dareall, a passionate huntress, was described as "sun-tanned and weathered" from exercise, despite being not quite forty, having "done everything to preserve her health, and destroy her beauty." Though she was "still a fine woman," it seems that part of her attraction had been irrevocably damaged through continued exposure to the elements.[38] When "Nimrod" met the celebrated horsewomen Mrs. Russell in 1830, he wrote in a slightly disapproving tone that, "from the state of her hair and glow of her complexion, [she] had evidently been going 'the pace that kills.'"[39] Hunting, masculinized as it had become by the early nineteenth century, damaged not only a woman's physical appearance through weather and over-exertion, but also her inner qualities. It eroded her beauty and health from the outside in, and her femininity from the inside out.

One common sense solution was for women to purchase and use a sidesaddle that could be adjusted to ride on either side of the horse. Charles Hughes had encouraged this practice in 1772, and John Lawrence encouraged it again in 1829.[40] Such saddles prevented women from always having to ride in one position, thus developing a balanced musculature. Directions such as Lawrence's also demonstrated that ideas about proper health, exercise, and gender ideals were changing; ladies were being encouraged to demonstrate respectable femininity through approved recreations like horseback riding. Backward ideas à la Walker were not popular in this atmosphere of increased female participation in horse sports, as illustrated by the beautiful and healthy young Queen, who publicly partook of horse exercise. By 1842, horse sports were "never so much practiced as at present."[41]

Negative medical opinions on ladies' riding were publicly challenged by *The Sporting Magazine* in 1842, five years after the young Queen had come to the throne:

> Addison declaring, in his admirable *Spectator*, that fox hunting is a remedy for every evil under the sun, even for *love*; observing, "There is no kind of exercise which I would so soon recommend to my readers *of both sexes* as riding, as there is none which so much conduces to health, and is every way accommodated to the body…"[42]

There was considerable push-back against spurious declarations that horse exercise was not beneficial physically and mentally. Walker's *Exercises for Ladies* was evidently not nearly as popular as its companion piece for men, *British Manly Exercises* published first in 1834. Unlike the latter, which went through ten revised editions to 1860, *Exercises for Ladies* was only printed twice, in 1836 and 1837, signaling a lack of interest and demand.[43] Riding manuals that encouraged fresh-air physical activity for women found favor during this time, but backward-looking texts that deprecated nearly all exercises for ladies did not find a ready audience.

Riding as Accomplishment

The second reason for riding's increased popularity among women in the first decades of the nineteenth century was the view that it was a valuable feminine "accomplishment."[44] Despite swapping the country for the city, the horse still remained "a highly effective promoter of sociability."[45] As author Edward Stanley asserted in 1827, "A knowledge of the Art of Horsemanship [is] essential in a Lady's education."[46] He added that, "Riding, as an accomplishment, is indisputably one of the most elegant a Lady or Gentleman can possess."[47] Even as women were discouraged from hunting on horseback, they were urged to pursue gentle equestrianism like park riding. Unlike other parks in London that were limited to private use, Hyde Park had been opened to the public since the reign of James I. Thus, open places such as Hyde Park – green, urban, and polite – replaced wild, rural spaces like the fox hunting fields of the countryside.[48]

In an age of public social display, women could not appear at greater advantage than when on horseback. Such dignity and elegance excited "universal admiration."[49] Thus, female equestrians flocked to the park on their steeds during the social Season from April to August. Riding was a highly public and visual form of social deportment; riding in urban spaces became what hunting had been previously: a way of emulating high society and a meaningful key to social advancement. Riding was a public performance, and one's deportment on horseback was judged as critically as that in "commercial venues such as assembly rooms, pleasure gardens, and even art exhibitions."[50] Yet unlike these places, where social mixing or mingling resulted in exclusivity, horseback riding was a greater equalizer of classes and sexes.

However, equestrianism was a double-edged sword: performed well, it was a ticket to widespread appeal and notice, but performed poorly, it led to social embarrassment and shame, if not actual injury. "Nothing can be more detrimental to the grace of a lady's appearance on horseback than a bad position," a conduct book concluded, adding that, "it is a sight that would spoil the finest landscape in the world."[51] J. Rimmel Dunbar, in his 1859 volume on park riding, favored equestrianism because "a lesson in riding is a lesson in deportment."[52] Horseback activity trained female riders how to behave gracefully and properly. Therefore, the emphasis on women's equestrianism increased during the early nineteenth century not only due to its health benefits, but also its social perks.

For women of the upper and aspiring middle classes, public acclaim and social eminence was a coveted goal, and riding was a means to attain it. Horseback riding was a transferable activity – it could be relocated from the private confines of the riding school to the public spaces of city parks and suburban roads. Though park riding was largely an urban phenomenon, given the close proximity of riding schools for lessons and well-maintained spaces like Hyde Park, equestrianism, for leisure rather than transport, increased in suburban and rural areas as well. In this way, female equestrians re-populated the same countryside where they had been discouraged from hunting. These skills and knowledge of the landscape would serve them well in increasing their horsemanship and justifying their inclusion in field sports once more.

Horse sports were well-regarded because they required both time and money to pursue, and they attracted traditionally upstanding participants. These activities necessitated a significant investment, not only for the horse and proper training, but also for dress, accoutrements, and saddle. An 1821 estimate placed the price of a lady's horse around 25–50 guineas, compared with the price of middling hunters at 80–100 guineas and middling racers at 250 guineas or more, but ladies' horses (especially good ones) were still not cheap.[53] In this way, riding in the early nineteenth century was still largely limited to the upper and aspiring middle classes who could afford not only the costs of such activities but also had the leisure time to pursue them. Equestrianism was not something that could be picked up like a tennis racquet or croquet mallet; it required a real investment of time, effort, and energy.

Riding for ladies was considered so necessary to female education in the early Victorian era that it was featured in conduct guides like *The Young Lady's Book* (1829). This tome, weighing in at over 500 pages, included other proper pursuits such as horticulture, mineralogy, conchology, entomology, aviary matters, the toilet, embroidery, painting, music, dancing, archery, and correspondence. But among all the subjects, equestrianism held a place of prominence: riding was an art in "the first class of exercises."[54] It taught the right behaviors and feminine qualities – patience, kindness, and sympathy. But the book chided amateurs, noting that equestrianism was an accomplishment that required time and effort to learn well or a lady would appear embarrassingly ignorant.[55] A minute of carelessness might lead to a lifetime of regret and reputational loss.

The value of riding as a social accomplishment was also enhanced by Queen Victoria's public example. When she was a child, Victoria adored horses, but her mother, the Duchess of Kent, prohibited her from riding because she feared for her daughter's safety. It was not until 1831 that a teenage Victoria took up riding, including lessons from the famous instructor Mr. Fozard.[56] On August 18, 1838, Victoria recorded in her journal, "I rode 'Uxbridge,'" who went delightfully, and "I had a new & comfortable saddle, which made the whole difference."[57] With her self-appointed guardians, Lord Melbourne and the Duke of Wellington, as well as her husband Albert in later years, Victoria pursued equestrian excursions around Windsor and in London, despite increased traffic and congestion.[58] She enjoyed riding, and did so frequently, as indicated by the wear visible on her sidesaddles today.[59]

Victoria's equestrian pursuits also aided the revision of gender ideals after 1837, although her influence was in many ways short-lived, as she stopped riding regularly in 1840 after she became pregnant with her first child. But under

Victoria, femininity was once again viewed as compatible with horse exercise, and the monarch's equestrian excursions catalyzed a new audience of interested riders – women from the aspiring and well-to-do middle classes.[60] As Mrs. J. Stirling Clarke acknowledged in 1857:

> Some years ago, riding was by no means general amongst the fair sex; then ladies on horseback were the exception and not, as now, the rule, but "*grace à notre charmante Reine*," [thanks to our lovely Queen]/Whose high seal for healthy duties/Set on horseback half our beauties/there is now scarcely a young lady of rank, fashion, or respectability, but includes riding in the list of her accomplishments; and who … is not ambitious of being considered by her friends and relatives, "a splendid horsewoman."[61]

In 1859, *The What-Not, or Ladies' Handy-Book* listed riding as the "No. 1" female accomplishment.[62] Riding *was* an accomplishment; indeed, one that took as much (or more) effort and time to learn as playing the piano or creating intricate needlework. Anyone could mount a horse, but few did so *well*.

Not only did ignorance and incompetence reflect badly on female riders themselves – for inept riders looked foolish – but it was also dangerous. As London and other urbans spaces became more congested, riding became more difficult and precarious. Victoria recorded in 1838 on an outing with Mr. Fozard and others: "I rode my dear favourite Tartar who went perfectly and *most delightfully*, never shying, never starting through all the very noisy streets, rattling omnibuses – carts – carriages, &c., &c."[63] Just 12 years later, the dangers of urban riding hit home when Sir Robert Peel, the former Prime Minister, was thrown from his horse while riding on Constitution Hill in Green Park, dying just days later.[64]

Victoria was lucky; not all women could possess such perfect and unflappable mounts. So many horses, carriages, and pedestrians crammed together in such confined spaces, combined with so many inexperienced riders, could only lead to disaster – and often did. Horses bolted or shied, ladies (and gentlemen) were run away with or fell off, and pedestrians were often threatened by misbehaving equines, which sometimes tried to jump out over Hyde Park's iron railings. The experience of dealing with such challenges – and becoming proficient horsewomen – was not something women could learn in the private confines of the riding school. It was one thing to ride in the safe and quiet space of a school, but quite another to ride in crowded public streets and parks. Thus, new riding manuals included "rules for the road," regarding safe and appropriate conduct when riding in public.[65] There was a whole realm waiting to be explored, and what was needed – and duly provided – were riding manuals to show women how to ride safely and correctly in this brave, new equestrian world.

Riding Manuals for Ladies, 1805–1857

Given these circumstances, it is not surprising that a flurry of riding manuals for women appeared throughout the first decades of the nineteenth century. The purpose of these manuals was to show women how to ride safely and proficiently, for public display and their own well-being. In the 52 years between 1805 and 1857, at least 15 riding manuals were either published specifically for women or contained separate chapters for female equestrians. Of these, seven appeared in multiple reprints during this time, bringing the total available volumes to 22, or about one every other year.

In 1805, John Adams included a significant section on ladies' riding in his three-volume set, *An Analysis of Horsemanship*. Adams began his career in the Light Dragoons, served as adjutant for the Mid-Lothian Cavalry in Edinburgh, and became Master of the Royal Riding School before his premature death in 1804.[66] He first self-published his book in 1799 ("for the author"), but it became well-known only in 1805 when it was re-published by James Cundee in Paternoster Row, the heart of London's thriving book trade.[67] Adams criticized early riding masters for teaching only *haute école*, when it was clear that the demand was for "jockey riding."[68] "The *manège* is not the style of riding for travelling, hunting or racing," Adams concluded, nor was it suitable for female equestrians.[69] Adams' inclusion of ladies' riding as a legitimate topic spoke to increased demand: "The custom for ladies to ride becomes daily more and more prevalent."[70] He explained why riding was so fashionable at the turn of the nineteenth century:

> All whose condition in life, afford them the means, are no longer restrained by the former prejudices of "bold, masculine, and indelicate for ladies to ride"; but may enjoy a recreation which exhilarates the spirits, invigorates the body, amuses the mind, gratifies the eye, and contributes so much to the felicity of the gentlemen who are honoured with the care and attendance of our fair countrywomen in these salutary exercises.[71]

Riding was popular because it was so invigorating; and it was respectable, having shed its late eighteenth-century association of being "bold" or "masculine." Even before the leaping head appeared, John Adams encouraged women to learn to jump: "In leaping the bar, the hand and body act in like manner as the gentleman's; a firm grip with the right knee must be observed, but no stress to be put in the stirrup."[72] Such instructions indicated an exciting new direction in female equitation, and one which subsequent authors would endorse and encourage.

After an interval of 20 years – the time during which women's riding was normalized as a respectable activity – the next riding manual for ladies appeared in 1825. John Allen's *Principles of Modern Riding for Ladies* was published in London, Glasgow, and Dublin. Allen was a riding master at Seymour Place in

Bryanstone Square, just north of Hyde Park. He opened the business in 1819, and after his death, his son eventually sold the school to Mr. Haines who operated it into the twentieth century.[73] Allen was "at the head of his profession in London, his manège was attended by all the best people, and he made, by his great ability as a teacher, an ample fortune."[74] Allen's book promised riding tips for "the promenade and the road," and he focused on fashionable park riding and the social visibility of equestrian sports. Allen sought to educate women in "simple and intelligible language" with lavish illustration (23 plates), although much of his text was lifted from John Adams' earlier work.[75] Three of the images depicted different methods of leaping for ladies, implying that jumping had only increased in popularity since the early 1800s.

Two years later, in 1827, Edward Stanley, "late of the Royal Artillery," published *The Young Horsewoman's Compendium of the Modern Art of Riding*, "comprising a progressive course of lessons."[76] Stanley was also the proprietor of a riding school at the "Horse Bazaar" on King Street, in Portman Square, which he operated from 1830 until 1834.[77] Again, the object of his publication was to give female equestrians a way to learn to ride if they could not take lessons at a riding school.[78] He included a chapter on leaping, with instructions for the "flying leap," given that so many ladies "[felt] disposed to practice it out of doors" – or, to go hunting where jumping was required.[79]

By the 1820s, riding was so fashionable that directions even appeared in conduct books for young ladies. An important chapter appeared in *The Young Lady's Book* from 1829, and this information was revised and expanded into a new book as *The Young Lady's Equestrian Manual* in 1838.[80] Author J.G. Peters tried to include two chapters on female equestrianism in *A Treatise on the Art of Horsemanship* in 1835, but his publisher baulked, claiming that he had already submitted too much material.[81] The purpose of conduct books was to illustrate proper, respectable, and admirable behaviors; the inclusion of riding in these largely domestic books shows how valuable the activity was in fashioning the ideal woman. As these texts show, riding was no longer limited to the sporting community, but was considered a valuable recreation and accomplishment that merited careful attention and practice by Victorian girls and women.

In 1838, George Reeves published *The Lady's Practical Guide to the Science of Horsemanship*, which achieved a third edition by 1847. Reeves listed himself as a "riding master" of the Montpellier Riding School in Cheltenham, the fashionable spa town, which he operated until at least 1860.[82] His first edition was published one year after Victoria's accession: the dedication praised her riding in hope that others would educate themselves to follow in her example. Reeves later noted that he had "been careful not to get up a large book," as his goal was "to simplify the art to his pupils."[83] The 1847 edition was published in his hometown, where he was teaching pupils. Those who visited Cheltenham could gently partake in its mineral waters and also pursue more active recreations like riding to improve their health.[84] Both visits to the baths and outdoor activities like riding brought together elite society, and the spa location demonstrated the geographical spread of fashionable equestrianism outward from London.

A year later in 1839, Colonel George Greenwood, an officer in the Life Guards of the Household Cavalry, published *Hints on Horsemanship, to a Nephew and Niece*. He encouraged riding for both sexes not only for health, but to promote a national method and brand of equestrianism. King William IV even sent him horses to train and declared him "the most accomplished rider in the British army."[85] Greenwood wrote, "The English hunting seat ... is the best adapted to common riding. It unites, in a greater degree than any other, utility, power, and grace."[86] This helpful and instructive book proved exceedingly popular with readers: a second edition appeared in 1844, a new edition in 1861, and a final edition in 1871.[87]

By the 1840s, at least two other manuals had appeared on the market. In 1842, Captain M*****, whose identity remains unknown, issued *The Handbook of Horsemanship*, a reprinted edition of his previous book, *The Equestrian*, from 1840.[88] Demand was clearly high for additional equestrian texts, and was, as yet, unsatiated. As the author stated,

> The equestrian education of ladies is too frequently incomplete, either from its being entrusted, in the country, to the care of some confidential domestic in the park or paddock, or to a few scanty lessons in a riding-school, and the riding-master's "matter-of-course" compliments on their equestrian abilities.[89]

The captain implied that "masters" flattered pupils with exaggerated compliments when they should have been correcting and properly instructing them. Also, in 1847, Professor [Paul Henry] Furbor issued *The Lady's Equestrian Companion; or, The Golden Key to Equitation*.[90] Furbor, formerly of the 11th Hussars, was a military man and riding master located in Brighton, another spa town with a history of healthy recreation. Furbor asserted that the "off-crutch" was "obsolete," thus affirming the general use of sidesaddles with leaping heads by that time. Accordingly he instructed that ladies should learn how to gallop and leap.[91] Furbor's book was published by subscription, and subscribers included Prince Albert (the only man listed) and 46 female parties.[92]

Several additional volumes on women's riding appeared around mid-century. Samuel C. Wayte's *The Equestrian's Manual* (1850), Nicholas Wiseman's *Horse Training Upon New Principles* (1852), and Captain Mervyn Richardson's *Horsemanship; Or, The Art of Riding and Managing a Horse* (1853) all included sections on ladies' riding.[93] But the real bestseller was Mrs. J. Stirling Clarke's *The Ladies' Equestrian Guide; or, The Habit and the Horse* first printed in 1857. It not only received subsequent English printings but was also translated into German and French.[94] In fact, information on ladies' riding expanded well beyond its epicenter in Britain. Another manual – T.A. Jenkins' *The Lady and her Horse* – was printed in Madras, aimed at British women in the Empire as well as to those at home.[95] Several ladies' riding manuals that were originally published in Britain were also subsequently published in America. For example, Willis P. Hazard's *The Lady's Equestrian Manual*, published in Philadelphia in 1854, had first appeared in London in 1838, under the title, *The Young Lady's Equestrian Manual*, which had been published in Philadelphia and New Orleans in 1839.[96] Thus, the British style of riding for ladies spread across the world.

Riding Lessons for Ladies

One impetus to the publication of so many riding manuals during this time was that riding schools had fallen from favor and popularity in Britain during the French Revolutionary and Napoleonic Wars. Instructors with military backgrounds had been called away for service, and many never returned or went back into business. Of the eleven riding schools operating in London between 1772 and 1801, all but four had closed by 1798.[97] Only after the British victory at Waterloo did out-of-work cavalrymen need to take up new employment. It was only in 1817 that new riding schools began operating again, peaking at 12 schools by 1830, when hunting and the English style of riding were practiced by both men and women.[98]

Many women patronized urban riding schools during the 1820s and after. In the 1830s, actress Fanny Kemble rode at Captain Fozard's school near Grosvenor Gate on Park Lane, adjacent to Hyde Park. Kemble recorded the proprietor's intense training techniques:

> Fozard's method was so good that all the best lady riders in London were his pupils, and one could tell one of them at a glance, by the perfect squareness of the shoulders to the horse's head, which was one invariable result of his teaching. His training was eminently calculated to produce that result, and to make us all but immovable in our saddles. Without stirrup, without holding the reins, with our arms behind us, and as often as not sitting left-sided on the saddle, to go through violent plunging, rearing, and kicking lessons, and taking our horses over the bar, was a considerable test of a firm seat ....

The lessons were popular – the school's multiple instructors gave some 20 private lessons a day for a duration of 1–2 hours each.[99] Three lessons (of 2 hours each) cost 8 shillings a piece, and attracted a significant, if well-to-do, audience.[100] On December 19, 1831, Kemble recorded: "Went to Fozard's, and had a pleasant, gossiping ride with Lady Grey and Miss Cavendish. While I was still riding, the Duchess of Kent and our little queen that is to be came down into the school" – thus, the budding actress met the future Queen, who also took her early riding lessons at Fozard's establishment.[101]

Even though equestrianism was an eminently popular recreation, ladies still faced challenges in learning how to ride. Not all instructors were like Fozard, with a smart reputation and prestigious clients, and not every novice rider could afford the luxury of his teaching. Many would-be equestrians were plagued by the "generally troublesome lessons of riding-masters."[102] "Generally troublesome" was an understatement, for it seemed many "riding masters" were hardly masters of anything at all. As Samuel Wayte argued in 1850, most were

> *generally retired* stable keepers and grooms, who, having saved a little money, immediately become metamorphosed into "riding masters," without the anatomical and scientific knowledge of the nature, temperament and characteristics of the horse, and *whose former position in life has precluded* (generally speaking) *education*, except of the *most meagre* description.[103]

Having shifted from one line of equestrian business to another, few were qualified with more than practical experience to teach students, little of which was applicable to women riding sidesaddle. Not only did such "masters" lack the ability to teach, but more importantly they lacked the reputation and respectability required for ladies to patronize their establishments. One way for an instructor to distinguish himself was to publish equestrian guidebooks, thus demonstrating the depth of his knowledge and indicating his status as a literate professional.

Even after mid-century, Clarke, the author of *The Ladies' Equestrian Guide*, argued that riding as a study would be more encouraged if riding masters and schools were more respectable.[104] Riding manuals for women filled a gap in ladies' educations. Daughters of the aristocracy might learn from family members, but this new surge in female riders did not come from the upper classes, or those with traditional equestrian backgrounds. Because they were unable to patronize riding schools – for lack of respectability or geographic distance – or were unable to gain a thorough education from the few proper ones, women could supplement their knowledge through these riding guidebooks. These sources, therefore, transcended prescriptive literature and provided necessary, and likely even lifesaving, information to the great number of women who followed their monarch's example on horseback.

The most obvious reason why many riding masters were ill-equipped to teach female pupils was that very few men actually rode sidesaddle or understood the style well enough to teach it. Some men did attempt to ride sidesaddle, out of curiosity or for a lark, but such shenanigans did not qualify them as experts (Figure 2.2). For example, in 1838, Queen Victoria recorded that two of her male courtiers demonstrated leaping in a sidesaddle "uncommonly well," but neither would have had the expertise to teach others how to do so.[105] Men also had no proper understanding of women's clothing, and therefore were at a loss to instruct on it or properly discuss it in female company. In fact, before 1857, every riding manual on women's equestrianism was written by a man. Of the several volumes published anonymously, nothing points to their authorship by a woman, though the possibility is tantalizing. Who had the motivation and knowledge necessary to write an equestrian guidebook for women? And why

Figure 2.2 Sir Francis Grant, P.R.A. (1803–1878), "Gentleman Riding Sidesaddle," pen sketch (undated): Although it was unusual for men to ride sidesaddle, it was not unheard of. In 1838, Queen Victoria recorded that two of her male courtiers rode and jumped sidesaddle as a lark ("uncommonly well"), and some male riding instructors likely attempted the style for pedagogical purposes. But the sidesaddle was also a saving grace for men who had been injured or had wounds that prevented them from riding astride in an age before modern medicine and advanced prosthetics. As equestrian author Robert Henderson recorded, "As regards a man riding in a sidesaddle, I may say that some years ago a young friend of mine, now deceased – than whom there was never a better man to hounds – hunted in a sidesaddle for three or four seasons before his death. He had injured his right foot so badly in a fall as to necessitate amputation at the instep, and he preferred the sidesaddle seat to the awkward and disagreeable feeling occasioned by trusting to a cork foot in the off-side stirrup."
Credit: © Sally Mitchell/Museum of the Horse (Tuxford).

write under a pseudonym when the point of publishing a manual was usually to profit by gaining clientele? Only in 1857, when Mrs. J. Stirling Clarke published *The Ladies' Equestrian Guide*, did women begin writing for women under their own names.

Although Clarke was not initially identified as the author, the work appeared "Under Royal Patronage" in England.[106] Clarke herself was aware of her volume's importance, writing that "It is constantly remarked that, although many books have been published which successfully impart a knowledge of riding to gentlemen, not one has appeared that can be regarded as a sufficiently comprehensive treatise for ladies."[107] Clarke would have known about the plethora of earlier manuals on ladies' riding, so either this comment was a marketing ploy or she genuinely disagreed with the quality of instruction offered in these texts. As she pointed out, women required specific information on riding that men could not provide, and she likely felt that no male author had provided adequate written instructions to date. "As a woman, I write exclusively for the guidance of my own sex," she explained, mainly because women sorely needed it. Changes in social and gender norms may have propelled an increase in female equestrianism, but few likely realized how much practice was required to put in a good appearance, or the specialist skills that could only be gained through experience.

Leaping Ladies

Most of the guides published until the 1850s focused on riding, not hunting. Directions usually included the basic methods of equitation at the walk, trot, and canter, as well as instructions on clothing, equipment, and behaviors. Riding manuals were useful, but they could never replace expertise gained through practice and experience in the saddle. Handling the reins alone – the principal method of control over a horse – was complicated. Women rode with a double bridle, which had two bits and therefore four reins, and they were expected to hold all four reins in one hand, with each finger controlling one rein.[108] This was but one small part of learning to command and control a horse, to say nothing of doing so well.

One major difference between earlier riding manuals for ladies and those published after 1805 was the inclusion of directions for jumping.[109] The practice became standardized after the turn of the century because, after Adams' volume, every subsequent riding manual encouraged it. *The Young Lady's Equestrian Manual* from 1838 noted that women tended to learn jumping as a matter of course in riding schools: "The practice is certainly beneficial; as it tends to confirm the seat, and enables the rider more effectually to preserve her balance."[110] In 1838, Reeves also included a chapter on leaping and encouraged ladies to learn the art.[111] "As the lady increases in confidence and address, so may the frequency and size of the leap be also increased," concluded Mervyn Richardson, author and instructor, in 1853.[112] Despite the disadvantages of the sidesaddle, Richardson's directions for jumping were the same as for men. This new emphasis for women indicated a change in riding methods: it encouraged a strength and determination previously unknown. For example, women were directed to persevere when a horse refused a fence and to use strength and willpower (and possibly even her whip) to make him jump: "she must remain firm and kind, and compel him to clear it."[113]

In 1853, Richardson wrote that if women could handle themselves well in schools or controlled circumstances, then they were "well fitted" for hunting.[114] In leaping and hunting, Richardson advised women to shorten stirrup-leathers one hole, and he elaborated on how to find the perfect length for hunting. Only the correct length of stirrup – and hence, leg position – would result in a balanced seat on horseback for such strenuous jumping: a long stirrup would result in a loose, swinging leg with little grip, while too short a stirrup would cramp the leg, result in sores, and cause skeletal and muscular pain. Richardson's hunting advice was explicit– "always ride clear of the crowd, and select your own line of country."[115] Richardson encouraged an independent rider: "ride in opposition to no one, and seldom follow the judgment of another in preference to your own."[116] The goal of any woman was clear: "if both horse and rider acquit themselves satisfactorily over a small leap in cool blood, they are well fitted for larger performances when under the excitement of company or the chase."[117] Jumping therefore gave women a new autonomy and very real independence on horseback.

Habiliments for Horsewomen

Like riding equipment, riding clothing for women saw manifold advances during the early 1800s. By the late 1700s, fashion plates of riding clothes were appearing in the most popular magazines alongside other female apparel. These images, often in expensive color, illustrated the popularity of park riding undertaken in fashionable locations with sometimes impractical clothing. As riding became popular as a social accomplishment and a healthful exercise for women, there was a corresponding transformation of female riding clothes. During the early 1800s, the purpose of such clothes was not to allow women to participate in rough sport but to express a proper and pleasant – yet still powerful – femininity.

Throughout the first half of the nineteenth century, women's riding dress consisted of long, flowing skirts that looked beautiful in pictures, but were not practical on horseback. Skirts were made of four yards of cloth, but this excessive length was dangerous.[118] Not only could the horse step on the garment, but the lightweight fabric could also flap against his sides and scare him, resulting in accident and injury. As Stanley advocated in 1827, "The Skirt to the Riding Habit should not be too long, as there is a possibility of its getting between the Horse's fore-legs, or being blown across them, so as to check his action, and throw him down."[119] At the very least, such clothing quickly became very dirty, thus presenting a less than appealing appearance. A woman's position on horseback would always be dangerous and insecure if she was perpetually entwined by – paradoxically – both restrictive and billowing clothing.

The point of riding clothing for women – especially during the Napoleonic Wars – was to illustrate a strong but respectable femininity. British women should be strong, healthy, progressive, and patriotic, but – above all – not revolutionary or radical like Frenchwomen. *Ackermann's Repository*, the venerable magazine published by Rudolph Ackermann, included three fashion plates of riding habits between 1809 and 1829. The first riding dress appeared in December 1811, accessorized with military-style frogging and a beehive hat with curtain veil. The dress was further accessorized with kid half-boots (to match the "pale lead or olive" color of the habit), brown gloves, and a fur pelerine for colder weather.[120] The second plate, entitled "The Glengary Habit," appeared in September 1817, and featured even more military styling, with "richly ornamented" frogging on the sleeves and neck, epaulettes, and a braided jacket.[121] The last habit appeared only a year later in July 1818, and also featured rich soldierly braiding and details.[122] Military detail remained popular – especially after the British victory at Waterloo – but the garments themselves became ever more unsuitable for physical activity. These habits were the only specialized sporting clothing illustrated in *Ackermann's* pages, but they were designed to showcase unmistakably female bodies.

The excessive ornamentation and length of such garments meant that women were more restricted and endangered by their clothing on horseback than they had ever been. The predicament of dressing for fashion rather than sport resulted in some novel ideas. One (truly terrible) idea was that that long skirts be pinned up for riding, to prevent the fabric from getting in the way. John Adams (foolishly) recommended fastening the skirt under the rider's foot, with pins "long enough to pass several times through the garment."[123] Even these "habit brooches," however, were not a safe solution to the problem, as pinning the skirt trapped a woman in her saddle, literally "pinning" her into place. If a woman fell or the pin came undone, she was likely to be stabbed by a massive needle. Another (terrible) idea was to use lead shot to weigh down a skirt. As Adams wrote in 1805, "pouches in the skirts of the habit, with leads in them, are very convenient; the habit then flows more gracefully than when pinned; and the [petticoats] may be pinned under the skirt, if the lady prefer it."[124] Twenty years later, riding instructor John Allen encouraged the same thing, copying his text directly from Adams.[125] Other authors followed suit: "You can sew small quantities of shot in small pieces of muslin, and tack them around the inside of the skirt at equal distances on the front breadth."[126] This might prevent indecent exposure but it also unbalanced a woman by pulling her all to one side.

Not everyone agreed with this approach, however, and two years later, in 1827, Stanley encouraged women to have their skirts tucked under their feet in the stirrup, rather than using pins to fasten it, or lead to weigh it down.[127] Although the skirt would release from this informal position if a woman fell, it was still dangerous in practice because it was only held in place by the pressure of a woman's foot in the stirrup, which resulted in her losing traction on the stirrup bar.[128] Given these restrictions, it is not surprising that *The Young Lady's Book* in 1829 described the process of dismounting from a horse as "the perfect disentanglement of the clothes from the saddle."[129] Later, authors like Samuel Wayte strenuously railed against pinning skirts as antithetical to the necessary liberty required by a woman on horseback.[130] The dangers of this trend had been so criticized, that while the 1829 edition of *The Young Lady's Book* featured instructions to pin the skirt, these directions were removed in the subsequent

1838 edition.[131] Although riding clothing was often at the front line of sartorial innovation, not all inventions were safe or successful.

The development of more specialized sporting clothing for women complemented equestrianism's growing status as a sport rather than a hobby or leisure activity. A woman could not wear the same clothes for riding as she did for indoor activities like sewing or painting, nor could she use garments meant for outdoor amusements such as croquet or archery. One of the first real advances was to focus on women's comfort and safety on horseback, rather than only her appearance. In 1827, Edward Stanley wrote, "Great care must be observed, that the Habit and undergarments are particularly full and easy, in order that the Lady may be at perfect liberty, and not, in the most trifling degree, confined by them."[132] Equestrian author Thomas Craige went even further and advised: "Your riding dress should be made of something that will not change its color if it should happen to get a sprinkle of rain. ... If your dress be too tight, you cannot ride with comfort and it injures your health."[133]

Thus, riding habits were designed more with function – rather than fashion – in mind. T.A. Jenkins opined that "A *lady's riding dress*, should be neat, and compact, and at the same time she should carefully avoid the slightest approach to a *mannish* appearance."[134] Clothes for riding needed to withstand multiple demands, from pressures of the saddle to environmental challenges like dirt, water, and prickly greenery. Male sporting garments were already crafted to these specifications: the trick was to take the cut, fabric, and designs of riding clothes for men and make them feminine. Riding was one outdoor activity where all feminine embellishment was eschewed. "All that is gaudy, needless, or even elaborate, is vulgar," instructed *The Young Lady's Equestrian Manual*, "Perfect simplicity, indeed, as regards, not only her own costume, but 'the trappings of her palfrey,' is expected, at the present day, on the part of every well-bred female equestrian."[135] Neither end of the sartorial spectrum – masculine utilitarianism nor feminine ornamentation – would do; what female riders (and clothing designers) had to do was chart a middle road of simplicity, practicality, and functionality. They had to look like ladies while dressing like men.

What Clarke recommended was a male tailor, familiar with sporting garments, rather than the traditional female dressmaker.[136] The demand for sporting clothing had created specialized makers and suppliers; male tailors had thus long crafted male riding clothes and were familiar with sartorial requirements for sporting demands. They knew how to cut and design garments to provide the necessary ease and comfort for riding well. For propriety, female attendants were employed at many firms to assist and take measurements, and often a model horse, complete with saddle, was available to test the fit of a habit.[137] Ladies' riding clothes were thus aesthetically similar to men's, often being crafted of the same fabrics and colors. This meant that riding habits were completely distinctive and distinguishable from a woman's other clothes. These new habits were no longer made of lightweight feminine fabrics decorated with

Figure 2.3 "Fashions for London and Paris, May 1857," Fashion plate from *The London and Paris Ladies' Magazine of Fashion*: This fashion plate features female dresses, including a riding habit. The latter stands out starkly in contrast to the elaborate ruffles, lace, and decoration of ordinary daywear for women. Dark colors, sturdy fabrics, and innovative designs contributed to the construction of a practical uniform for female riders. Undergarments were especially important when riding: "white frillies" are just visible underneath the hem of this riding habit. But petticoats caused significant problems and discomfort when riding. The eventual rejection of petticoats was the first move to adopting riding trousers and eventually enabling women to "wear the breeches."
Credit: © Victoria and Albert Museum, London.

masculine ornamentation like epaulettes and frogging, as in *Ackermann's*, but were constructed of – and cut on the same lines as – men's. Ladies' riding clothes imitated menswear, but in a different and respectable way.

A series of advances in riding habit design before mid-century increased physical mobility and personal safety for women. The first advance was to shorten the length of skirt, as advocated by both Samuel Wayte and Mrs. J. Stirling Clarke in their riding manuals from 1850 and 1857 respectively. Wayte argued that a lady's riding skirt should be "full" but "neither should the Habit be so long as it is frequently worn (nearly touching the ground), because it prevents *that liberty so indispensable to security* in the sudden plunging of the horse."[138] Once skirt length decreased, there was no further need for skirts to be dangerously pinned, tied, or weighted with lead.[139] Clarke agreed, noting while "ample folds" might be aesthetically attractive, they were not practical for sport. In 1859, *The What-Not, or Ladies' Handy-Book* also urged shorter skirts for both hygiene and safety.[140]

Second, undergarments were equally important (if not more so) in riding, as both Wayte and Clarke pointed out. Petticoats were the earliest underclothes for riding (Figure 2.3), but pantaloons had been adopted by many as the undergarment of choice by the 1820s, and riding trousers (the precursors of modern breeches) a decade later.[141] Wayte recommended comfortable undergarments, "on which *depend* so much the requisite ease and graceful appearance."[142] Although Clarke was also adamant that a "superfluity of underclothing" should be avoided, she also wrote that it was just as bad to avoid all under-clothing, and to appear as "one of the beauties of the reign of George the Second, when we are informed it was "*la mode*" for ladies to vie with each other in the scantiness of their nether garments."[143] The eventual rejection of petticoats was the first move to adopting riding trousers and eventually enabling women to "wear the breeches."

Third, special corsets were designed for riding. During the early Victorian era, many men wore corsets for back support when riding or hunting, although for women, they were a daily sartorial necessity.[144] By the 1830s, "stays" were made with steel rather than whalebone, although this could be problematic in damp areas. In 1835, Emily Eden, writing from India, requested "a silver busk, because all steel busks become rusty and spoil the stays," due to the humidity and weather.[145] For women, corsets ensured a smaller waist and smoother silhouette, but achieving a proper hourglass form might require dangerously tight lacing, which was to be eschewed at all costs when riding. Nicholas Wiseman specifically warned against the dangers of the practice, writing,

> The shape of a woman is no where so defined and exalted as when dressed in a close fitting riding habit, and mounted on horseback; and we hope our fair readers will pardon the presumption of giving an opinion on their angelic shapes, which is perhaps the opinion of most men. We do not like to see a woman with a waist like a wasp, or a toy with a small stalk connecting two large ends, called a Devil, played with a cord and two sticks. I should not like such a woman as the mother of my children.[146]

Women's riding corsets were thus cut high over the hips to allow movement in the sidesaddle. They were also crafted with elastic gores for extra flexibility.[147] Clarke further advised that the habit-jacket should fit a woman's bust comfortably in order to give the necessary room for the chest to expand.[148] While Donald Walker had argued 20 years earlier that riding was unhealthy for women, Clarke sallied back that it was not the sport but the constrictive clothing that was so destructive.[149]

Headgear also evolved for female riders, although it was still a century away from the hard hats and safety helmets of the twentieth century. By the early 1800s, ladies' hats had grown increasingly large, varied – and problematic. As *The Young Lady's Equestrian Manual* stated,

> To ride in a bonnet is far from judicious. A hat, or neat undress military cap, is indispensable to the female equestrian. It should be secured most carefully to the head: For, the loss of it would not merely be inconvenient, but, perhaps, dangerous, from the startling effect which its fall might produce on the sensitive temperament of the horse.[150]

Nearly all authors urged female riders to "secure the hat," so it did not blow off and frighten the horse, possibly resulting in a fall.[151]

Another concern was the use of long veils, which, like long skirts, could upset the horse and cause alarming accidents. As Stanley wrote in 1827, "Long veils are also dangerous on Horseback, as they get entangled with the reins, confuse the Rider, and cause her to lose command of her Horse."[152] Only short or moderate veils should be used when riding, safely attached and without ornament.[153] In the same vein, women were urged to carefully dress their hair closely to the head, so it too did not fall down and distract the rider. Female equestrians were strictly instructed to take care with their toilet: "The hair should be plaited; or, if otherwise dressed, so arranged and secured, that it may not be blown into the rider's eyes; nor, from exercise, or the effect of humid weather, be liable to be so discomposed, as to become embarrassing."[154] Astley had encouraged this as early as 1801, but subsequent manuals repeated these important directions.[155]

Clothing for female riders thus became standardized by mid-century. All items that interfered with physical mobility and active riding were eschewed. Dark colors, sturdy fabrics, and innovative designs contributed to the construction of a practical uniform for female riders. Proper and specialized sporting clothing allowed greater liberty of physical movement and increased safety, enabling female equestrians to move beyond park riding to pursue more demanding equestrian activities.

The Leaping Head

The rise in ladies' equestrianism over the first half of the nineteenth century was also aided by a revolutionary advance in sidesaddle construction: the introduction of the "leaping head," or a third pommel to the near (left) side and below the central crutch (see Figure 3.2). As described by one contemporary:

> The third or hunting pommel is screwed into the tree of the saddle a little below the near pommel, and is intended to lie across or span the left leg just above the knee, to prevent the rider from being thrown forward, or on the

neck of the horse.[156]

Whereas the older two-pommel sidesaddle forced a woman to place her right leg between two curving forks at the center of the saddle, the leaping head enabled a new position. In these sidesaddles, the right leg curled around the upper pommel on the center of the saddle, pushing the right thigh around the crutch, while the left leg was tucked up underneath the leaping head. The resulting grip attained through muscle leverage, called "the purchase," kept a woman securely in the saddle. An even stronger "emergency grip" was obtained by pressing the right calf against the pommel and bringing the left leg up under the leaping head; the right heel was shoved back toward the left leg, and the right shoulder shifted backward. This pretzeled position effectually locked a woman into place; she could not fall off or be thrown from her mount. These improved sidesaddles enabled a new kind of riding at speed and over fences, which in turn aided the development of a reconceptualized sporting femininity. From this revolutionary improvement in sporting equipment came additional health, safety, sociability, and sporting engagement.

The true origins of the leaping head are unclear. There is much contemporary support in Britain for the claims of Thomas Fitzhardinge Oldaker, huntsman to the Earl of Berkeley (1788–1820). Oldaker (sometimes spelled Oldacre) was knowledgeable about saddlery, a trade he passed down to his son. As *Baily's Magazine* noted, "he had the rare advantage of experience to teach him what was easiest for a horse to carry, and for many years not a M.F.H. [Master of Foxhounds], or indeed any man who had once tried them, used any saddles but Fitz Oldaker's."[157] His motivation for inventing the leaping head is murky: either he broke his leg and needed the grip of the new pommel to stay on over fences in his job as huntsman, or he did it on a bet.[158] As *Baily's Magazine* recorded, the leaping head may have been developed by:

> the outcome of a wager between Mr. Oldaker, a very practical saddler, and some person whose name is now forgotten. The conditions of the bet were that they were to ride a steeplechase, "catch weights," on ladies' saddles. Mr. Oldaker, uncertain of his ability to keep his seat, conceived the idea of the leaping head; he negotiated the course, without his leg once slipping, and was first past the post. The leaping-head, or third pommel, or crutch, being found so advantageous, was generally adopted for cross-country riding; two heads being found sufficient, the off-head was gradually discarded.[159]

Regardless of the cause of its development, the intention was to allow women to gain additional security while going over fences, especially in hunt country.[160]

Two Frenchmen, riding masters Jules-Charles Pellier and François Baucher, also claimed credit for the innovation.[161] Pellier declared that he invented the leaping head – in French, called a "third fork" – in the early 1830s and to have exhibited a three-pommel version almost 30 years later at the Paris Exhibition in 1855. Léon Gatayes, writing in *Le Siècle*, claimed that this saddle was:

> *Inventee en 1828 un habile écuyer (l'éminent professeur qui dirige et a donné son nom au magnifique et célèbre manége Pellier), la selle à trois fourches est devenue d'un usage général, non-seulement en France, en Angleterre, mais dans le monde entier* [Invented in 1828 by a skillful rider (the eminent professor who directs and gave his name to the magnificent and famous manége Pellier), the three-forked saddle became of general use, not only in France, and in England, but in the whole world].[162]

Yet his colleague François Baucher contested this claim in the second edition of his book, *Dictionnaire raisonné d'équitation*, in 1851: "*FOURCHE (la troisième), appliquée aux selles de femmes est encore de mon invention*" [FORK (the third), as applied to women's saddles, is again my invention].[163] He did not claim credit in the first edition published in 1833, and Pellier said, in his own book, *La selle et le costume de l'amazone* (1897), that the leaping head was a collaboration between Baucher, Pellier *père*, and Pellier *fils*:

> *Sans vouloir renouveler une discussion qui date de loin, et dont les deux antagonistesne sont plus de ce monde, disons que certainement nous devons la découverte de la troisième fourche à l'heureuse collaboration de mon père, un écuyer artiste de premier ordre, et de M. Baucher, un écuyer savant qui a fait époque.* [Without wishing to renew a discussion which dates from a long time ago, and in which the two antagonists are no longer of this world, let us say that we certainly owe the discovery of the third fork to the happy collaboration of my father, a first-rate artist rider, and of M. Baucher, a learned rider who made an era].[164]

It is not clear why French instructors would have felt the need to invent a third pommel, when French two-pommel sidesaddles were perfectly adequate for the kind of riding pursued in France, and, in fact, were used throughout the nineteenth century. It makes more sense that such an innovation would occur in Britain, where the galloping and jumping required in the hunt field mandated a better and more secure saddle. In 1852, Alfred Roger had credited the two-pommel sidesaddle as an English invention ("*la selle anglaise avec ses deux fourches*" [the English saddle with its two forks]), so why not the third pommel as well?[165] As Pellier himself noted, "*Avec la troisième fourche, les dames ne sont plus obligées de rester aux petites allures. Elles peuvent toutes trotter à l'anglaise, galoper dans tous les sens, supporter les changements de pied et sauter des obstacles*" [With the third fork, the ladies no longer have to stay at low speeds. They can all trot in the English style, gallop in all directions, withstand changes of foot and jump over obstacles].[166] But French instructors deprecated the "English style" of riding, deriding English huntresses as unsexed "steeplechase jackeys."[167]

Even if the "leaping head" pommel was invented in France, it does not appear to have caught on there for female equestrians,[168] and it was not listed as standard equipment in riding manuals that appeared from the 1830s to 1850s.[169] In 1842, Comte Savary de Lancosme-Brèves did mention a "third fork" in *De l'équitation et des haras*, but he discouraged its use. He deprecated the use of the saddle for jumping and decried the danger of women's skirts catching on the extra pommel and causing injury or death.[170] Also in 1842, P.A. Aubert's *Équitation des dames* referenced only the two-pommel saddle and illustrated it in plate 13: "*Cheval De Femme, Régulièrement Équipé*," as standard equipment.[171] Ten years later, in 1852, only the two-pommel saddle was mentioned by Alfred Roger,[172] and in the third edition of A.D. Vergnaud's *Nouveau manuel complet d'équitation à l'usage des deux sexes*, published in 1860, all instructions and images still describe a two-pommeled sidesaddle; there is no mention of a third pommel or leaping head.[173] Further, Vergnaud urged French ladies to use English saddles when learning to ride: "*Dans toutes les leçons du manège pour les dames, le cheval sera en bride et en selle anglaise à fourches*" [In all the lessons of the manège for the ladies, the horse will be in bridle and in an English saddle with forks], or a two-pommel sidesaddle.[174]

One reason that the leaping head may not have been popularly adopted in France is its connection with the circus. In *La selle et le costume de l'amazone*, Pellier mentioned that his student, *la première écuyère de haute école* Caroline Loyo, was using a three-pommel platform to perform at the Cirque Olympique in 1833.[175] Loyo received instruction from both Pellier and Baucher, and her performances became the rage in Paris.[176] Loyo's use of such a saddle may have discouraged respectable women from adopting riding equipment that was utilized by a circus celebrity. Loyo may have had the need for a more secure saddle to perform her trick riding and jumping, but reputable Frenchwomen would not have required such security for their ordinary equestrian activities. Loyo later performed in London, and only returned to France in 1846 – by which time the leaping head sidesaddle was well-established in England – so it is possible that saddlery advances were shared between French and English equestrians.[177] Englishman James Greaves patented his version of a "leaping horn" sidesaddle in 1856. Perhaps the fairest assessment is from scholar Lindsay Smith, who concludes, "It is possible that they arrived at the same result at the same time to correct or lessen a serious difficulty."[178]

The more important question is when the new invention became standardized and popularized in Britain. If the new saddle was not popularly adopted in France, it was embraced and endorsed in Britain from the 1830s onward.[179] In 1839, Colonel Greenwood in his *Hints on Horsemanship, to a Nephew and Niece* praised the utility of the leaping head: "A side-saddle should have no right-hand pommel. It is useless to the seat, and impedes the working of the right hand. The appearance when mounted is infinitely improved by the absence of it. It should have what is called a third pummel, or leaping horn."[180] The leverage of the new leaping head created a safer and more secure seat for women: "A wonderfully strong grasp is obtained, much stronger than the grasp obtained by the

114 Exercise and Female Accomplishment

Figure 2.4 John Frederick Herring, Senior, "Hunting Scenes: A Hunting Morn, ca. 1840": This painting, completed before mid-century, is the earliest known depiction of the leaping head in British sporting art on the horse in the center. This third pommel gave women unprecedent security on horseback and enabled them to pursue more challenging activities. This revolutionary advance amounted to what Lida Fleitmann Bloodgood has called "the horsewoman's Magna Carta or Declaration of Independence."
Credit: © Virginia Museum of Fine Arts, Richmond (Paul Mellon Collection), Photo: Travis Fullerton.

mode in which men ride."[181] As Greenwood pointed out, the leaping head was actually a boon for women riders – not only did it give them more stability in the seat than the two-pommel saddle, but it actually gave them an arguably firmer position than men. Greenwood wrote, "I find I am much stronger in a side-saddle than in my own."[182]

The new saddle also began to appear in British sporting artwork. A third pommel was depicted in John Frederick Herring's painting, "Hunting Scenes: A Hunting Morn," circa 1840 (Figure 2.4).[183] Print and visual sources show that this new style was prominent – if not already in general use – well before the mid-nineteenth century when Pellier claimed to have exhibited his version in Paris.[184] The new saddle was popular for giving women more control over their mounts, being less likely to give internal injuries in case of accident, and for allowing a straighter, more balanced, and more correct equitation in the saddle. The new posture enabled women to sit more naturally, which benefitted not only the rider but the horse as well, because it allowed them to work more in tandem and less disconnected or out of sync.

The leaping head offered several tangible advantages. One was that it was less likely to cause grave internal injury in case of accident. A real danger of the two-pommel saddle was that women could be thrown onto the two forks if the horse stopped suddenly or bucked, thus causing serious injury to a women's abdominal area and internal organs.[185] The leaping head also enabled straighter posture in the saddle, a hallmark of fine equitation.[186] This was important because it countered medical opinions that riding caused spinal curvature. Sidesaddles could also be modified by adding the leaping head to the side of the saddle, thus enabling a woman to ride either to the left or right, avoiding the muscular strain of always riding on one side. Many authors encouraged women to ride on both sides, near and off, by having a saddle with moveable crutches and a leather saddle skirt on each side.[187] Such practice "[improved] the pliancy of the body,"[188] and, by the 1830s, such saddles were widely available from saddlers.[189]

With an additional pommel, sidesaddles were becoming rather cluttered conveyances. The second, or off-side, crutch was not abandoned immediately, and some transitional saddles had three pommels – the fork of the two upright ones, and the leaping head below. As Richardson directed:

> The lady's saddle ought to have three crutches or pommels. The third or hunting pommel is screwed into the tree of the saddle a little below the near pommel, and is intended to lie across or span the left leg just above the knee, to prevent the rider from being thrown forward, or on the neck of the horse.[190]

These saddles illustrated the new professional nature of female riders. "Three pommels," said a male rider about a hunting lady, "then she must be a goer."[191] After mid-century, a "goer," or serious rider, was indicated by the lack of the off-side crutch, which was called a "useless eyesore."[192] Samuel Wayte was in favor of this change, writing that ladies' saddles should have only two pommels and no "off head" or left crutch.[193]

While some argued that taking away this left crutch deprived a woman of a point to steady herself on, Wayte replied that a nervous or novice rider had "no business" using her hand to hold onto this protuberance.[194] This method of artificially balancing by the off pommel was not only dangerous but also ill-advised for lady riders. As Wayte argued:

> when holding on by the head [the left crutch], she loses the use of one hand, and her horse goes into the ditch, or any other place he may choose; secondly, she can never get her hands down to get a fair pull at the horse's mouth; thirdly, look at the fair rider's poor wrists, which in hunting are everlastingly being bruised by it (the head), to say nothing of the chance of breaking them.[195]

By mid-century Wayte laid out clearly what Greenwood and earlier authors had only hinted at: this new saddle gave women the security to gallop and jump – in short, to hunt.

After the turn of the nineteenth century, sidesaddles also featured another new element, the balance strap. This was a leather strap that connected the hind part of the saddle on the off/right side to the girth (visible in Figure 2.6). This made the saddle more secure on the horse's back and less likely to flip up or slip sideways at the slightest shift of the rider's weight. In 1805, Adams wrote:

> Ladies' saddles, when properly fitted, will not require cruppers more than gentlemen's, but the girths crossed from the hind part of the saddle to the front, will keep them more steady; or a strap from the hind part of the saddle to the fore girth on the off side, may prevent the saddle twisting to the near side, as it usually does.[196]

In 1824, George Wycherley patented a y-shaped balance strap that ran from the off-side of the saddle to the stirrup leather on the near side; when a lady mounted, the pressure in the stirrup (which would normally pull the saddle to one side) was balanced by the strap exerting pressure to the opposite side of the saddle.[197] Allen promoted a single-strap balance girth in 1825, which had become standard by that time.[198] Combined with the leaping head, the balance strap added greater safety and balance while mounted, which was an advantage for female riders who wished to pursue more demanding equestrian activities.

How much of an advantage was the leaping head? As Samuel Wayte asserted, "no one who has ridden with the leaping head will ever be without one."[199] When the acclaimed horsewoman, Victoria, Countess of Yarborough, began hunting with the Brocklesby pack in 1859, she initially used a two-pommel sidesaddle: when jumping all manner of fences, "she held on with her left hand to the saddle behind," using only her right hand to hold the reins and guide her horse.[200] Mary Richardson (the sister of the Countess' second husband) had no difficulty jumping fences because she owned "a saddle which possessed one of the first three crutches, or leaping heads."[201] As Mary Richardson recorded,

> How well I remember that day out hunting..., when [the Countess] came up to me and said, "How do you manage to sit your pony over fences without holding on to the back of your saddle? I cannot." Then I remember it suddenly dawned upon me that it might possibly be the new saddle my grandmother had given me, with its delightful and safety three-crutch leaping head, which gave me this most unfair advantage. .... Then I remember how astonished we both were when, jumping down from my pony when the hounds checked, she discovered that wonderful new third crutch, and I that her saddle did not possess one. How well I remember, too, with what pride I lent her my saddle, and how she loved her day's hunting upon it; how a saddle with the leaping head was obtained for her as soon as it were possible ....[202]

As Richardson confirmed, "Oh, the joy of security in jumping which that third crutch gave."[203]

Although brave sportswomen had hunted and jumped in two-pommel sidesaddles, such activities were perilous at best and lethal at worst. A French riding master found his position in the two-pommel sidesaddle so precarious when jumping that he resorted to stabbing his spur into the saddle leather in order to stay on, and when his horse spooked, he threw his leg over in order not to fall off.[204] By 1857, Mrs. J. Stirling Clarke confirmed that the leaping head was "now so generally adopted" that few rode without it.[205] As she advocated, it "certainly possesses great advantages; for, if properly used, it gives immense security to the seat in all critical situations."[206]

Clarke pointed out that these advances had certain downfalls as well: "Its chief disadvantage lies in the uninitiated rider's depending entirely upon it for security, instead of on her own skill in the management of herself, and horse."[207] Therefore Clarke advised ladies desirous of learning how to ride to begin on a saddle *without* a leaping head so they could attain balance, hand position, and seat without "this artificial aid."[208] The leaping head did give female riders unprecedented security, and with it, an immense confidence, but the audacity it encouraged could have serious consequences. The security of the new saddle was not a substitute for real horsemanship and equestrian education, though it was certainly a welcome complement to it.

Female Fox Hunters

The leaping head was more popular with women who hunted (and therefore needed it) than with ordinary park riders, who could easily manage slower and more controlled paces with the older crutch saddle. J. Rimmel Dunbar's 1859 book *Park Riding* confirms this, as the author does not refer to the leaping head, mentioning only the traditional "crutch." According to him, women were already familiar with their positions in the saddle and did not need any new instruction: "The position of the right leg being governed by the crutch, which is a lady's chief dependence, requires no direction."[209]

As equestrian and author Alice Hayes confirmed, looking back from the turn of the twentieth century, "The leaping head, third crutch, or third pommel, as it was first called in England, came into use in this country in the forties, and with its aid ladies felt themselves endowed with sufficient ambition and boldness to follow hounds."[210] Mervyn Richardson confirmed this in his 1853 manual, in which he (likely the first to do so) specifically called the leaping head a "hunting pommel,"[211] as did T.A. Jenkins in his riding manual for ladies in 1857.[212] While the benefits of riding in terms of health and social advancement had been confirmed by mid-century, it was the leaping head that aided the return of women to the hunting field. "When a lady is seated in the saddle [with a leaping head]," one author wrote, "she is about as safe as a gentleman, and it is just as difficult to get her out of the saddle as it would be to displace a gentleman."[213] Now women were able to escape the constraints of gentle urban riding to the more demanding galloping and jumping of the countryside.

Women had not stopped participating in field sports during the first 50 years of the century, though their numbers had declined since the late 1700s (Figure 2.5). In the first quarter of the nineteenth century, Augusta Fane recorded sparse female attendance: only "a few married ladies who lived in the country seem to have come out with their husbands."[214] But participation soon increased. In 1829, author John Lawrence confirmed, "Lady Craven, upon Pastime, never shrunk from either fence or timber, reasonably passable; and Lady Hester Stanhope may be now hunting upon her Arab, in those howling wildernesses."[215] According to John Elliott in *Fifty Years of Fox-Hunting*, Mrs. Loraine Smith, her two daughters, and a Miss Stone were among the women out in 1838, and a painting of "The Loraine Smith Family" by John Ferneley, Jr., shows three women with the hounds behind them.[216] By 1841, Nelly Holmes, later Lady Rivers, was often out hunting, "topping the fences like a bird to the admiration of all; and when we came to the brook, over she went"[217]; she "had just begun to show them what a habit could do in the hunting field."[218] Although there may have been fewer ladies out in the early 1800s, others soon followed: "There is one certainty about ladies, what one does another will do, if it be worth the doing. Very soon others were at the game, and many have played it well since."[219] By 1844 *The Sporting Magazine* listed the "Countess of Wilton, Mrs. Colonel Wyndham, and other Ladies" as gracing the chase.[220]

Not everyone approved of the increased female presence. In 1829, Lawrence admitted, "Assuredly, the male seat on horseback is the most secure ...; although our huntresses ... have always retained their proper seat; ... All that I have to say further on this point is, I have never been an advocate for women riding to hounds."[221] Sporting author Robert Smith Surtees was particularly against women in the hunting field. He firmly supported female riding, and he encouraged

Exercise and Female Accomplishment 119

Figure 2.5 Charles Loraine Smith, "The Rendezvous of the Quor'n Hounds at Grooby Pool," 1826. A chimney-sweep – like the one depicted here on the far right – rode with the Grafton Hunt for many years. Despite his workaday profession, Adam Sherwood was a "great authority" on fox hunting – even the Duke of Grafton asked for his advice in the field. Although "his steed was not exactly thoroughbred" and his hunting costume was a much-crushed "chimney-pot hat" with "green smock-frock," the sweep was a welcomed member of the chase. Fox hunting was, in the eighteenth century, a socially inclusive – if not fully democratic – activity. As John Hawkes asserted in 1802, fox hunting "links all classes together, from the Peer to the Peasant. It is the English man's peculiar privilege." As the ladies in this image show, it was an *Englishwoman's* privilege as well.
Credit: © Virginia Museum of Fine Arts, Richmond (Paul Mellon Collection), Photo: Troy Wilkinson.

women to come to the meet (before the hounds moved off). Such riding was a good way to get exercise and a fine way to meet prospective husbands, while also being an excellent excuse for some (less adventurous) men to leave before the hunt began.[222] Surtees' pretense for prohibiting female riders from hunting was that their presence in the field would exhaust all topics of conversation during the day, leaving nothing to talk about over dinner at night.[223]

But Surtees also discouraged women from hunting because their skilled performances might make the male riders look bad. Surtees divided female huntresses into two groups: those that "go" (experienced huntresses that could gallop and jump), and those that did not. Those who "went" put men to shame: "Pretty dears who would scream at the sight of a frog or mouse, will face a bullfinch from which many men would turn away."[224] Because it was a point of honor that men must go over what women did, Surtees' objections suggest that men did not have the nerves or skills to negotiate such obstacles successfully.[225] Surtees flagged these "palpable inconveniences" in his sporting novels: when Lucy Glitters hunted, men were obliged to follow her example: "Whatever Lucy took, the young [men] felt constrained to take, for the honour and credit of the hunt. So there was more dashing riding and heavy fencing on this occasion than usual."[226] More explicitly, Surtees asserted, "But for the inconvenience of being beaten by a lady, very few of them would have risked a ducking [in the brook]."[227]

Surtees also resented the fact that women might pip men to the finish and to the ultimate "prize" in fox hunting: receiving the brush. According to practice, if the fox was killed, the huntsman would intervene and remove the mask (head), pads (feet), and brush (tail) of the fox, as the inedible parts, before throwing the body (meat) to the hounds. The master would then decide who among those at the finish were most worthy of receiving these "prizes."[228] If *any* lady was present at the kill, the only polite thing to do was present the "trophy" to her, whether she deserved it or not.[229] A gentleman (and a Master had to be one) could do nothing else, although only the *first* person to arrive at the kill deserved that honor. As more women were often present at the kill than men, women were more likely to receive the prize, which upset the male sportsmen. As Surtees concluded rather callously:

> Some men ... would rather have a wife staying at home looking after the house than tearing about the country after the hounds. Besides, it is possible you might beat him, and *men don't like being beat by their wives in the field, any more than wives like being beat by their husbands in the house*.[230]

This criticism points to a major flaw in male equitation: men simply could not equal women as riders. To prevent their own embarrassment and salve their fragile egos, they attempted to keep female equestrians from joining them in the hunting field. "Separate sexual spheres were being increasingly prescribed in theory, yet increasingly broken in practice," concluded historian Linda Colley, "the boundaries supposedly separating men and women were, in fact, unstable and *becoming more so*."[231] Riding and hunting brought men and women into ever closer contact, showing both the progress and friction resulting from these opportunities.

Civilizing Influences

Some contemporaries attributed the increase in female equestrian participation to Queen Victoria's example, as she came to the throne in 1837 and lent her influence to equestrian sports.[232] Certainly the Queen's example was important, but she hunted only rarely, whereas other women were making a much more significant impact. Victoria's sidesaddles were of the two-pommel variety; there is no evidence that she ever rode in a saddle with a leaping head. Thus, it was left to other British women to catalyze and then normalize advances in equestrianism.

For the hunting world, the 1830s began a period of transformation as revolutionary as that of Hugo Meynell in the eighteenth century. Moving on from the "golden days" of the boys' club "painting the town red" at Melton Mowbray, women's appearance in these centers improved and refined them. As *The Ladies' Field* noted,

> As soon, however, as wives and daughters of Meltonians began to winter there, and later to go hunting, a great change came over the place for the better, and its growth in fashion was so rapid that not only were the houses in and about the town, such as Craven Lodge, Melton Lodge, Staveley Lodge, and the Old Club, all rapidly taken up, but the neighbouring villages of Darby, Ashfordby, and Somerby were occupied by visitors, who formed and still form a great part of Melton society.[233]

If men had created Melton as a hunting town, it was women who made it a respectable and flourishing social and sporting scene.[234] They did this by rejoining hunts and making the sport respectable, certainly no small task given its rakish reputation and masculine character. As novelist Anthony Trollope argued, "The oftener that women are to be seen 'out,' the more will such improved feelings prevail as to hunting, and the pleasanter will be the field to men who are not horsey, but who may nevertheless be good horsemen."[235] This shift occurred during the first third of the nineteenth century; therefore, as depicted in sporting art (à la Herring) and described in manuals (à la Greenwood), it would seem likely that the leaping head was already in popular usage by the 1830s to enable such an increase of female participation (Figures 2.6 and 2.7).

By the 1830s, women had begun residing at Melton with their husbands and riding with hunts. In 1829, John Lawrence recounted that "Miss Catharine Arden, I am informed, is regular at the Melton hunt; and Miss. H. of Staffordshire, not only hunts, but sees the end of it, as often as the most crack male rider in the field"[236] Alice Hayes also dated the reemergence of women hunters in Britain to this time,[237] and *The Ladies' Field* magazine recalled:

> It was about 1831 that ladies began to winter at Melton. Among the first were Lady Sarah Ingestre, Lady Edward Thynne, Lord Stormont, and Mrs. Floyd. There were, however, some local ladies of position hunting, for "Nimrod" relates a certain Miss Manners declined to go home before the end of a run on the ground that "Papa would be very angry with me if I did so."[238]

Women joined their husbands and family members in hunting centers, even if they did not ride, and this female company gave such areas a respectability and

Figure 2.6 Francis Calcraft Turner (c. 1782–1846), "Gone Away," from the series "Hark Forward, Away!" (undated, nineteenth century): F.C. Turner died in 1846, so this series must have been completed before mid-century. Both prints highlight a female rider in a sidesaddle, possibly a three-pommel saddle still with an off-side crutch, and indicate an increased female presence in contemporary sport and sporting art.
Credit: © Virginia Museum of Fine Arts, Richmond (Paul Mellon Collection), Photo: Troy Wilkinson.

prominence they had previously lacked. In this way, the civilizing influence of women became important to hunting culture even off the horse.[239] As one author proudly bragged:

> I have only to evidence Melton's proudest boast – the Ladies – who are delighted to accompany their husbands, and remain during the winter perfectly happy and content. Were fox-hunters such as some would fain represent them would husbands take their wives, the mothers of their children, to breathe the same atmosphere with beings so depraved?[240]

By at least mid-century, then, if not much earlier, the worst excesses of the sport had been consciously reformed – and by those who had been previously

Figure 2.7 Francis Calcraft Turner (c. 1782–1846), "Tally-Ho!" from the series "Hark Forward, Away!" (undated, nineteenth century): This third plate in the series shows the female rider skillfully negotiating a fence on her way to follow the hounds, while a gentleman to her right has already fallen off. The fourth and final print in the series shows the lady receiving the brush at the kill to the admiration of her fellow sportsmen.
Credit: © Virginia Museum of Fine Arts, Richmond (Paul Mellon Collection), Photo: Troy Wilkinson.

excluded, women. This was a deliberate and conscious refashioning of sport by women to include women.[241] This "taming" of hunting (on the human side, at least) occurred much earlier than the comparable taming of the political sphere in the late nineteenth and early twentieth century.[242]

Not only was the atmosphere in hunting centers becoming far more respectable, but so too were the types of women present there. Far from the few prostitutes that had hung around the dark corners of Melton during the 1820s, by 1834 it was asserted that, "there are Ladies at this moment at Melton of such unsullied purity of character that not even Malignity has ever dared asperse with its pestiferous and blighting breath, or Envy dreamed of tarnishing, is a fact beyond dispute."[243] As Trollope confirmed, the presence of ladies in the field made the sport more respectable for all participants: "Their presence tends to take off from hunting that character of horseyness – of both fast horseyness and slow horseyness – which had become, not unnaturally, attached to it, and to bring it within the category of gentle sports."[244] The more respectable the sport became, the more women could participate in it without fear of losing their reputations.

These changes helped demolish the previously masculine dominance of fox hunting. Sportsmen were no longer able to join or find acceptance on the basis of gender alone. Hunting was no longer a solely male sport, and merit and skill became more important than sex. While innovations such as the leaping head and advances in riding clothing were vital in enabling women to hunt, another important factor that increased their involvement was the public acceptance of women into the field. The confluence of riding manuals and women's participation in riding, for health or social reasons, increased the number of skilled horsewomen who were interested in hunting. General interest in hunting surged from the 1830s onward and sometimes resulted in fields of over 500.[245] New saddles and specialized riding clothes aided women in this endeavor, as did the shifting gender ideals in which hunting was no longer incompatible with respectable femininity.

Hunting as the National Sport

In rejoining hunting fields, women transformed the sport both in manners and in thought. Hunting had become extremely popular and fashionable in the early 1800s, but it was not until after the 1830s, when women began staying in hunting centers and rejoining the fields, that it truly became known as Britain's athletic activity of choice. Historian David Itzkowitz argues that "between 1800 and 1830, hunting began to emerge as a great national sport."[246]

Certainly the impact of the Napoleonic Wars and the subsequent anti-French feeling went far in focusing British entertainment on domestic pursuits and field sports through the mid-nineteenth century. But, even before the Napoleonic Wars, British equestrians consciously defined themselves against French practicioners of *haute école*. After 1815, however, these distinctions became more important, as did the role women played in sustaining them. As scholar Adrian Harvey has argued, between 1793 and 1850 a unique sporting culture developed and expanded in Britain. The Napoleonic Wars limited foreign contacts and created the conditions necessary for a specialized domestic leisure culture in the countryside.[247] This further catalyzed the turn away from Continental riding styles and the development of a distinctive British equestrianism. In fact, it was this British style of riding that was credited with defeating Napoleon's Cuirassiers at Waterloo.[248] Whereas the French rode with long stirrups, toes down, and relaxed legs – "like a sugar tongs astride upon a poker" – the British rode with shortened stirrups, stronger seats, and better balance.[249] These techniques made them more effective riders when galloping after fox and hounds as well as for military charges and repelling counter-attacks.

Britain's shift away from the military style of *haute école* in favor of a freer and faster style of hunting enabled women to ride and hunt because such equestrian activities were separated from their exclusively military (and therefore masculine) associations. Following the end of the Napoleonic conflict, *haute école* was labeled French and therefore to be avoided at all costs: "it looks very well at Astley's [circus], but on the road it is altogether unseemly."[250] Riding manuals published throughout the first half of the nineteenth century illustrate this divide, as instructions focus not on the elevated collection and fancy movements of *haute école* but the more practical "hunt-seat" style based on the free motion of the horse. In his 1839 manual, Greenwood even refused to use French terminology to describe riding maneuvers.[251] By the 1830s, circuses in Britain, which were based on Continental *haute école* practices, had also declined in popularity.

At the same time, and in contrast with sporting developments in Britain, Napoleon's rule in France had led to a revival of older traditions of classical equitation, and with them, an absolute rejection of the new English ideas about free and forward riding from hunting and racing. When author Nicholas Wiseman visited a French riding school around mid-century, "The riding master, finding I was no spooney, took much pains to persuade me that the English knew nothing of horsemanship. He began capricoling upon a horse, which he held by reins, attached to a very severe bit, and by way of horsemanship making summersaults like the clown at Astley's."[252] Wiseman was not impressed by such trick riding. Even after Napoleon's defeat, French riding remained firmly focused on such practices, further restricting French women from pursuing equestrian sports with the same ease and flair as their British sisters.[253]

This British style of riding allowed female equestrians to canter on Rotten Row as well as join their male sporting companions in the hunt field. Publicly displaying their horsemanship, women were an important part of a specific and fiercely proud national identity. Whereas formerly women had been discouraged from hunting and urged to avoid the public gaze, now they were encouraged to fly the flag for British superiority. As Clarke concluded, "every noble stranger, who, charmed with a '*coup d'oeil*' such as no other country can boast, will doubtless on returning to his native land, descant on horsemanship, or excellence in riding, as not the least amongst the many valued attributes of Albion's daughters."[254]

In contrast to the supposed idleness of French women, British women were encouraged to ride and hunt as they had done previously in the 1700s. As "Nimrod" wrote in 1828,

> The condition of women is one of the most remarkable in the manners of all nations, and a decisive criterion of the stage of society at which they have actually arrived. Cleopatra hunted with Antony, and drank with him afterwards – quite in character with that dissolute age; but, in more modern times, such is the refinement of manners and language, the exercise of riding, and riding after hounds, have not been considered incompatible with the highest pitch of female delicacy.[255]

Female riders in Britain could prove their respectability and contribute to the nation by being skilled horsewomen. Their sporting prowess could make both them and Britain stronger. By the mid-nineteenth century, hunting grew in importance not only in numbers, but in the strength of feeling it attracted, among both hunters and non-hunters alike. Both men and women therefore came together to promote hunting as Britain's national sport. Captain M****** opened his chapter on ladies' riding in 1842 by noting that the sidesaddle is "the graceful and admirable fashion of English ladies," thus pointing to a particular nationality of which women were an intrinsic part. It confirmed gendered ideals that included riding as a necessary accomplishment.[256] Horses had long been a part of this special British sporting identity; in 1800, a French author had noted that "The English in general have a degree of friendship and affection for horses, which few men shew even to their own species."[257] Contemporaries believed that women with their fine delicacy in handling horses, drawn from their innate feminine qualities, were an important part of this national construction.

Hunting was a part of a national identity based on horse sports in even more concrete ways. Whereas the first editions of Donald Walker's *British Manly Sports* had not included hunting or rural sports, the 1840 edition was specifically revised to include them. In 1846, Surtees paraphrased Peter Beckford, the renowned author of *Thoughts on Hunting*, writing "Hunting is quite the peculiar taste of Britons, and let people say what they will, it must exercise a most beneficial influence on the national character."[258] These beliefs pointed to the masculine attributes of the sport, but if hunting influenced a larger national character, then women were also part of it. In this way, despite his personal lack of enthusiasm for women hunting, Surtees and others like him helped open the door for women as riders to become part of something bigger than themselves through equestrian sport. Riding had increased the popularity of horse exercise for women, both for new social classes and in new locations. The way was thus paved for a truly national sport, of both sexes, across Britain.

"The Horsewoman's Magna Carta"

Then as now, riding instilled a sense of power and authority. The last thing a woman on horseback should present was "an air of timid *gaucherie*."[259] A successful female rider could not be a wallflower or shrinking violet; after all, "an unsteady hand is sure to produce an unsteady Horse."[260] Rather, a female rider had to take command not only of herself but also her mount, for her own safety and that of others: "the rider must, in all her wishes, be obeyed."[261] Yet such obedience came not from brute strength or masculine assertion, but from quiet and steady firmness: "a lady cannot rival him [a horse] in physical strength, but she may conquer him by mere ingenuity, or subdue him by a calm, determined assumption of superior power."[262] The ultimate goal in riding was that the mistress became the master.

Through horseback riding, women gained a new sense of self-possession. As military leaders had demonstrated for centuries, the horse was a conduit to power.

Not only did the horse give additional height and stature, but the command of a powerful animal visibly demonstrated one's authority and leadership. It was not enough to passively sit and stay on a horse's back; an equestrian's power resulted from becoming one with the horse and not separating from him even in challenging conditions. As riding master John Allen agreed, "to have a good seat on horseback, she must be in unity with her horse, and as firm and easy as though they were one body."[263] This centaur-like attitude aided the development of women's physical, mental, and personal strengths: "as she begins to collect and unite her horse, so she collects and unites herself."[264] The key to success in horseback riding was to develop one's own personal assets (mental, moral, and physical) in preparation for managing others – whether animals or humans. These qualities – and the "assumption of superior power" – endured well after a rider had dismounted and influenced other areas of her life.

The transformation of riding clothes and the addition of the leaping head to sidesaddles enabled women to pursue more demanding horseback activities, such as galloping and jumping, thus leading them back to fox hunting. These changes amounted to what writer and rider Lida Fleitmann Bloodgood has called "the horsewoman's Magna Carta or Declaration of Independence."[265] As equestrian author Robert Henderson wrote retrospectively in 1874, "Looking back at those days, the only wonder to me is, how ladies managed to ride at all. That they did is proof (if any were wanting) of their courage and perseverance under difficulties."[266] By exercising what Victorians regarded as their natural female qualities and "civilizing influence," women transformed hunting as a sport. In this way, women contributed to the making of fox hunting as the national sport of Britain, leading to their equal participation and involvement in the chase. But they still had far to go, and after mid-century, they continued advancing the large-scale sporting revolution they had begun.

Notes

1 Ian Duncan, "Introduction," Sir Walter Scott, *Rob Roy* (Oxford: Oxford University Press, 2008), xxix.
2 Sir Walter Scott, *Rob Roy* (Oxford: Oxford University Press, 2008), 101–102.
3 Scott, 385.
4 Scott, 104.
5 Duncan, xiv.
6 Duncan, xii.
7 Review of *Rob Roy*, *The Edinburgh Magazine* (January 1818), 45.
8 Harriet Martineau, "Scott as Moral Hero," *Tait's Edinburgh Magazine* (1833), in John O. Hayden, *Walter Scott: The Critical Heritage* (London: Routledge, 1996), 340.
9 Scott, 21.
10 *The Young Lady's Equestrian Manual* (London: Whitehead and Company, 1838), 84.
11 Joyce Bellamy, *Hyde Park for Horsemanship* (London: J.A. Allen, 1975), 11.
12 Amanda Vickery, "Golden Age to Separate Spheres? A Review of the Categories and Chronology of English Women's History," *The Historical Journal* 36.2 (June

1993), 383–414; Linda Colley, *Britons: Forging the Nation 1707–1837* (New Haven: Yale University Press, 1992), 262–263.
13 Amanda Gilroy, "The Habit and the Horse, or, the Suburbanization of Female Equitation," in Amanda Gilroy (ed.), *Green and Pleasant Land: English Culture and the Romantic Countryside* (Leuven: Peeters, 2004), 46.
14 "Hack, *v*.3" and "Hack, *n*.3 (and *adj*.)," OED Online. Oxford University Press, March 2020.
15 Jean Froissard and Lily Powell Froissard (eds.), *The Horseman's International Book of Reference* (London: Stanley Paul, 1980), 415.
16 Michael Symes, "William Pitt the Elder: The Gran Mago of Landscape Gardening," *Garden History* 24.1 (Summer 1996), 128. See also Sitting of 30 June 1808, https://api.parliament.uk/historic-hansard/commons/1808/jun/30/hyde-park.
17 Donna Landry, *The Invention of the Countryside: Hunting, Walking and Ecology in English Literature, 1671–1831* (New York: Palgrave, 2001).
18 Patricia A. Vertinsky, *The Eternally Wounded Woman: Women, Doctors, and Exercise in the Late Nineteenth Century* (Urbana: University of Illinois Press, 1994).
19 *The English Matron*, by the author of "The English Gentlewoman" (London: H. Colburn, 1846), 133–134.
20 Patricia Branca, *Silent Sisterhood: Middle Class Women in the Victorian Home* (New York: Routledge, 1975), 66.
21 Lewis Mansey, M.D., *The Practical Physician; Or, Medical Instructor* (London: J. Stratford, 1800), 349 and 351.
22 Andrew Scull, *Hysteria: The Biography* (Oxford: Oxford University Press, 2009), 49–50.
23 Hilary Marland, *Health and Girlhood in Britain, 1874–1920* (London: Palgrave Macmillan, 2013).
24 Barbara Harrison, "Women and Health," in June Purvis (ed.), *Women's History: Britain, 1850–1945: An Introduction* (New York: Routledge, 1995), 124. Quote from *The English Matron*, 142.
25 *The Sporting Magazine*, Volume 12 (September 1798), 302.
26 Bellamy, 44.
27 Frances Ann Kemble, *Records of a Girlhood* (New York: Henry Holt and Company, 1879), 291.
28 John Adams, *An Analysis of Horsemanship* (London: James Cundee, 1805), Volume 2, 85.
29 *The Sporting Magazine*, Volume 71 (February 1828), 280–281.
30 George Reeves, *The Lady's Practical Guide to the Science of Horsemanship* (Bath: Myler and Son, 1838), iv.
31 Thomas Craige, *A Conversation Between a Woman and Her Horse* (Philadelphia: Thomas Craige, 1851), 35.
32 *The Sporting Magazine*, Volume 71 (February 1828), 280–281.
33 Jolene Zaia, "Saddle Sore: Skeletal Occupational Markers of Habitual Horseback Riding," *Senior Honors Thesis* 269 (2019), https://digitalcommons.brockport.edu/honors/269.
34 Kemble, 248.
35 Donald Walker, *Exercises for Ladies Calculated to Preserve and Improve Beauty* (London: T. Hurst, 1836), ix and 26.
36 Walker, xiv.
37 Mathias Roth, M.D., *The Prevention of Spinal Deformities, Especially Lateral Curvatures* (London: Groombridge and Sons, 1861), 71.
38 *The Sporting Magazine*, Volume 22 (June 1803), 137.

39 *The Sporting Magazine*, Volume 76, First Series/Volume 1, Second Series (June 1830), 103.
40 Charles Hughes, *The Compleat Horseman* (London: F. Newbery, 1772), 61. See also John Lawrence, *The Horse in All his Varieties and Uses* (London: M. Arnold, 1829), 184–185.
41 Captain M*****, *The Handbook of Horsemanship: Containing Plain Practical Rules for Riding, Driving, and the Management of Horses* (London: Thomas Tegg, 1842), 1.
42 "The Quorn Hounds, by Clio," *The Sporting Magazine*, Volume 100, First Series/Volume 25, Second Series (December 1842), 586–589. Underlined italics mine.
43 A separate addendum volume entitled *Games and Sports; Being an Appendix to Manly Exercises, and Exercises for Ladies* was published in London in 1837 by T. Hurst and in 1840 by J. Thomas.
44 Mrs. J. Stirling Clarke, *The Ladies' Equestrian Guide; or, The Habit and the Horse: A Treatise on Female Equitation* (London: Day and Son, 1857), 4.
45 Thomas Almeroth-Williams, "Horses & Livestock in Hanoverian London" (PhD thesis, University of York, 2013), 320.
46 Edward Stanley, *The Young Horsewoman's Compendium of the Modern Art of Riding* (London: James Ridgway, 1827), iii.
47 Stanley, vi.
48 Bellamy, 18.
49 "Observations on the Construction of Stables, Choice of a Lady's Pad, Breaking of Horses, &c.," *The Sporting Magazine*, Volume 21 (January 1803), 219. For London's social Season, see Leonore Davidoff, *The Best Circles: Women and Society in Victorian England* (Totowa, NJ: Rowman and Littlefield, 1973).
50 Hannah Greig, "'All Together and All Distinct': Public Sociability and Social Exclusivity in London's Pleasure Gardens, ca. 1740–1800," *Journal of British Studies*, 51.1 (January 2012), 51.
51 *The Young Lady's Book: A Manual of Elegant Recreations, Exercises, and Pursuits* (London: Vizetelly, Branston, and Co., 1829), 434.
52 J. Rimmel Dunbar, *Park Riding, with Some Remarks on the Art of Horsemanship* (London: Saunders, Otley, and Co., 1859), 11.
53 "State of the Horse Market," *The Sporting Magazine*, Volume 59 (December 1821), 138.
54 *The Young Lady's Book* (1829), 427.
55 *The Young Lady's Book* (1829), 427.
56 *The Morning Post* (London) reported that Victoria's first riding lesson at Fozard's occurred on Wednesday, December 21, 1831. See *The Morning Post* (London), Thursday, December 22, 1831, page 3, accessed via Newspapers.com. See also "A Lady," *Anecdotes, Personal Traits, and Characteristic Sketches of Victoria the First* (London: William Bennett, 1840), 182. See Viscount Esher, ed., *Girlhood of Queen Victoria* (London: John Murray, 1912), 219–220.
57 Journal Entry for Saturday 18th August 1838 (Buckingham Palace), from Princess Beatrice's copies, Volume 4 (1st June 1838–1st October 1838), 218. Accessed via *Queen Victoria's Journals* database, October 15, 2013.
58 "Queen Victoria as a Horsewoman," *The Ladies' Field*, Volume 12 (February 2, 1901), Supplement, 2.
59 Victoria Green, "Queen Victoria's Sidesaddle," https://nationalleathercollection.org/spotlight-on-queen-victorias-saddle.
60 *The English Gentlewoman: A Practical Manual for Young Ladies on their Entrance into Society* (London: James Hogg and Sons, 1861), 166.
61 Clarke, 2.
62 *The What-Not, or, Ladies' Handy-Book* (London: Piper, Stephenson, and Spencer, 1859), 38–39.

63 Esher, 292.
64 Norman Gash, *Sir Robert Peel: The Life of Sir Robert Peel after 1830* (Totowa, NJ: Rowman and Littlefield, 1972), 697–698.
65 John Allen, *Principles of Modern Riding for Ladies; In Which All Late Improvements Are Applied to Practice on the Promenade and the Road* (London: Thomas Tegg, 1825).
66 John Kay, *A Series of Original Portraits and Caricature Etchings, Volume 1, Part 2* (Edinburgh: Hugh Paton, 1838), 410.
67 John Adams, *An Analysis of Horsemanship* (London: M. Ritchie, 1799).
68 Adams, Volume I (1805), xvii.
69 Adams, Volume I (1805), xxi.
70 Adams, Volume II (1805), 85.
71 Adams, Volume II (1805), 85–86.
72 Adams, Volume II (1805), 107.
73 Bellamy, 55.
74 M. Horace Hayes, *Among Men and Horses* (London: T. Fisher Unwin, 1894), 325.
75 Allen, vi.
76 Stanley, title page.
77 *The Portfolio; or, a Collection of State Papers*, Volume 1 (London: James Ridgway and Sons, 1836), see advertisement at the end of the book on page 9. See also Almeroth-Williams, 281.
78 Stanley, vii.
79 Stanley, 93.
80 *The Young Lady's Equestrian Manual* (Philadelphia: Haswell, Barrington, and Haswell, 1839) and (New Orleans: Alexander Towar, 1839).
81 J.G. Peters, *A Treatise on the Art of Horsemanship, Simplified Progressively for Amateurs* (London: Whittaker and Co., 1835), xlvii.
82 *The Cheltenham Annuaire for 1860* (Cheltenham: Henry Davies, Montpellier Library, 1860), 213, 237.
83 Reeves, 57.
84 See Thomas Rowlandson, "Comforts of Bath, Plate 5" (January 6, 1798), in the collections of the Metropolitan Museum of Art, https://www.metmuseum.org/art/collection/search/739142.
85 Richard J. Chorley, Antony J. Dunn, Robert P. Beckinsale, *The History of the Study of Landforms: Volume 1; Geomorphology Before Davis* (Abingdon, Oxfordshire: Routledge, 2009), 364.
86 Colonel George Greenwood, *Hints on Horsemanship, to a Nephew and Niece; or, Common Sense and Common Errors in Common Riding* (London: Edward Moxon and Co., 1839), 69.
87 Colonel George Greenwood, *Hints on Horsemanship, to a Nephew and Niece; or, Common Sense and Common Errors in Common Riding* (London: Edward Moxon, 1861, 1871).
88 Captain M*****, *The Equestrian: A Handbook of Horsemanship* (London: Darton and Clark, 1840).
89 Captain M***** (1842), 55–56.
90 Professor Furbor, *The Lady's Equestrian Companion; or, The Golden Key to Equitation* (London: Saunders and Otley, 1847).
91 Furbor, 18, 60–63, 72–79.
92 Furbor, 133–136.
93 Samuel C. Wayte, *The Equestrian's Manual; or, The Science of Equitation* (London: W. Shoberl, 1850); Nicholas Wiseman [pseudonym], *Horse Training upon New Principles, Ladies' Horsemanship, and Tight Lacing* (London: W. Clowes and Sons,

1852); Captain (Mervyn) Richardson, *Horsemanship; or, The Art of Riding and Managing a Horse* (London: Longman, Brown, Green, and Longmans, 1853).
94 Based on Clarke's English edition, *Das Pferd und die Amazone* appeared in 1860, 1862 and 1865, based on an earlier French edition, while *Le cheval et l'amazone* was published in 1861 and 1894.
95 T.A. Jenkins, *The Lady and Her Horse* (Madras: Pharoah and Co., 1857).
96 Willis P. Hazard, *The Lady's Equestrian Manual* (Philadelphia: Willis P. Hazard, 1854); *The Young Lady's Equestrian Manual* (Philadelphia: Haswell, Barrington, and Haswell, 1839) and (New Orleans: Alexander Towar, 1839).
97 Almeroth-Williams, 280–281.
98 Almeroth-Williams, 283.
99 Bellamy, 42.
100 Bellamy, 38.
101 Kemble, 474–475.
102 Captain M*****, 2.
103 Wayte (1850), 3.
104 Clarke, 4–5.
105 Journal Entry for Saturday 29th December 1838 (Brighton, Royal Pavilion) from Lord Esher's typescripts, Volume: 9 (3rd December 1838-4th April 1839), 129; Accessed via *Queen Victoria's Journals*, database October 15, 2013.
106 Clarke, title page.
107 Clarke, iv.
108 Stanley, 15; Allen, 67.
109 Adams, Volume II (1805), 107.
110 *The Young Lady's Equestrian Manual* (1838), 87.
111 Reeves, 38.
112 Richardson (1853), 95.
113 Richardson (1853), 94.
114 Richardson (1853), 95.
115 Richardson (1853), 47, 53, 58.
116 Richardson (1853), 65.
117 Richardson (1853), 95.
118 "The Evolution of the Riding Habit," *The Ladies' Field*, Volume 44 (January 2, 1909), 216.
119 Stanley, 111–112.
120 "Ladies' Riding Habit," *The Repository of Arts, Literature, Commerce, Manufactures, Fashions and Politics, by Rudolph Ackermann*, Volume 1 (December 1811), 358.
121 "The Glengary Habit," *The Repository of Arts, Literature, Commerce, Manufactures, Fashions and Politics, by Rudolph Ackermann*, Volume 2 (September 1817), 178.
122 "Ladies Riding Dress," *The Repository of Arts, Literature, Commerce, Manufactures, Fashions and Politics, by Rudolph Ackermann*, Volume 2 (July 1818), 53.
123 Adams, Volume II (1805), 94–95.
124 Adams, Volume II (1805), 96.
125 Allen, 31.
126 Craige, 47.
127 Stanley, 111.
128 *The Young Lady's Book* (1829), 456.
129 *The Young Lady's Book* (1829), 456.
130 Wayte (1850), 111.
131 *The Young Lady's Book* (1829), 430; *The Young Lady's Equestrian Manual*, 40.
132 Stanley, 8.
133 Craige, 46–47.

134 Jenkins, 2.
135 *The Young Lady's Equestrian Manual*, 31.
136 Clarke, 21.
137 H.J. and D. Nicholl, *A Lady's Horse: With a Few Words on the Proper Costume for Riding, Walking, Dining* (London: J. Tallis, 1859), 16, 40.
138 Wayte (1850), 80.
139 Captain M*****, 59.
140 *The What-Not, or Ladies' Handy-Book*, 38.
141 Rhonda C. Watts Hettinger, *The Illustrated Encyclopedia of the Sidesaddle* (Wilton, NH: Sidesaddle Source, 2009), 196.
142 Wayte (1850), 79–80.
143 Clarke, 23.
144 "A Lady" [Sarah Josepha Buell Hale], *The Workwoman's Guide* (London: Simpkin, Marshall and Co., 183), 83. See also Valerie Steele, *The Corset: A Cultural History* (New Haven: Yale University Press, 2001), 38.
145 Violet Dickinson, ed., *Miss Eden's Letters* (London: Macmillan and Co., Ltd., 1919), "Miss Eden to Lady Campbell" (August 1835), 253.
146 Wiseman, 32.
147 Steele, 56; Clarke, 22.
148 Clarke, 18.
149 Clarke, 34.
150 *The Young Lady's Equestrian Manual*, 31.
151 Reeves, 6.
152 Stanley, 112.
153 *The Young Lady's Equestrian Manual*, 32.
154 *The Young Lady's Equestrian Manual*, 31; Craige, 46–47.
155 Philip Astley, *Astley's System of Equestrian Education* (Lambeth: C. Creed, 1801), 88.
156 Richardson (1853), 84–85.
157 "Our Van," *Baily's Magazine of Sports and Pastimes*, Volume 43 (October 1884), 121–122.
158 "The Modern Side Saddle," *Saddlery and Harness, A Monthly Trade Journal*, Volume 1 (June 1892), 190.
159 "Saddles," *Baily's Magazine of Sports and Pastimes*, Volume 70 (November 1898), 346. Historians Shedden and Apsley also credited Oldaker: see Lady Diana Shedden and Lady Viola Apsley, *"To whom the goddess ...": Hunting and Riding for Women* (London: Hutchinson and Co., 1932), 102. So does Charles Chenevix Trench, *A History of Horsemanship* (New York: Doubleday and Company, 1970), 277. See also "Riding for Women: The Cross and the Side Saddle (From a Correspondent)," *The Times* (London) Friday, July 4, 1913 (Issue 40255), page 11, which unequivocally admitted "what a debt of gratitude all hunting women owe to Mr. Oldaker."
160 German literature appears to support Oldaker as well: Daniela Kabele, "Relationship Between Woman-Horse from the Antique till Now," presentation at the International Congress of the World Association for the History of Veterinary Medicine (September 10–13, 2008), www.damensattel.cc/Damensattel/Documents/Poster_4.pdf.
161 Alice M. Hayes, *The Horsewoman: A Practical Guide to Side-Saddle Riding* (London: Hurst and Blackett, Limited, 1903), 33. Historian Lida Fleitmann Bloodgood also credited Pellier: Lida Fleitmann Bloodgood, *The Saddle of Queens: The Story of the Side-Saddle* (London: J.A. Allen and Co., 1959), 9 and 42–43.
162 Léon Gatayes, "Exposition universelle: harnachment des chevaux dans l'Antiquité," *Le Siècle: journal politique, littéraire et d'économie sociale* (November 10, 1855). Pellier

cites Gatayes in his own book, J. Pellier fils, *L'équitation pratique* (Paris: L. Hachette et Cie, 1861), 128–129.
163 François Baucher, *Dictionnaire raisonné d'équitation* (Paris: Chez L'Auteur, 1851), 157.
164 François Baucher, *Dictionnaire raisonné d'équitation* (Rouen: D. Brière, 1833); Jules Pellier, *La Selle et le Costume de l'Amazone: Étude Historique et Pratique de l'Équitation des Dames* (Paris: J. Rothschild, 1897), 112–114.
165 Alfred Roger, *Livre de l'équitation des dames et de la gymnastique* (Paris: Ch. Ploche, 1852), 7.
166 Jules Pellier, *La Selle et le Costume de l'Amazone: Étude Historique et Pratique de l'Équitation des Dames* (Paris: J. Rothschild, 1897), 114.
167 Pellier (1861), 127-128.
168 Isabelle Veauvy, Adélaïde de Savray, and Isabelle de Ponton d'Amécourt, *Cavalières Amazones: Une Histoire Singulière* (Paris: Swan, 2016), 134.
169 It does not appear in M. Lebrun, *Manuel complet du bourrelier et du sellier* (Paris: L. Laget, 1833), though two-pommel saddles are discussed (pages 150–153) and illustrated (plates 2–3).
170 Le Comte Savary de Lancosme-Brèves, *De l'équitation et des haras* (Paris: Chez Rigo frères, 1842), 388, 400.
171 P.A. Aubert, *Équitation des dames* (Paris: Chez l'auteur, 1842), 93.
172 Roger, 7.
173 A.D. Vergnaud, *Nouveau manuel complet d'équitation à l'usage des deux sexes* (Paris: De Roret, 1860), 188, 189, 192 and Figures 19–24. Previous editions were published in 1834 and 1842.
174 Vergnaud, 184.
175 Pellier (1897), 114.
176 De Vaux, 107–108.
177 De Vaux, 110–111.
178 Lindsay Smith, "The History and Development of the Side-saddle," in Lauren Gilmour (ed.), *In the Saddle: An Exploration of the Saddle Through History* (London: Archetype, 2004), 87.
179 John Malsbury Kirby Elliott, *Fifty Years' Fox-hunting with the Grafton and Other Packs of Hounds* (London: H. Cox, 1900), 7. Alice Hayes cites Elliott in her agreement with the date; Hayes (1903), 305 and 430.
180 Greenwood (1839), 86 and (1861), 60.
181 Greenwood (1839), 86 and (1861), 60.
182 Greenwood (1839), 61 and (1861), 87.
183 See John Frederick Herring (British, 1795–1865), "Hunting Scenes: A Hunting Morn, ca. 1840," now at the Virginia Museum of Fine Arts, Richmond, Paul Mellon Collection, https://www.vmfa.museum/piction/6027262-8150151/.
184 "Ladies Side Saddles – No. 2698," *English Patents of Inventions, Specifications: 1856* (London: H.M. Stationery Office, 1856), 1–2.
185 Greenwood (1839), 61 and (1861), 87. Minor grammatical differences in 1861 text, but meaning identical to 1839.
186 Greenwood (1861), 88–89.
187 Greenwood (1861), 88–89; Stanley, 101.
188 Stanley, 101.
189 *The Young Lady's Equestrian Manual*, 18.
190 Richardson (1853), 84–85.
191 "A Man from the Next Country," *Baily's Magazine of Sports and Pastimes*, Volume 23 (April 1873), 209.
192 Mrs. Harry Allbutt [Annie Blood-Smyth], *Hints to Horsewomen* (London: Horace Cox, 1893), 30.

193 Wayte (1850), 166–167.
194 Wayte (1850), 166.
195 Wayte (1850), 167.
196 Adams, Volume II (1805), 150. A crupper is a strap that goes under the horse's tail and attaches to the back of the saddle, to keep it from slipping forward.
197 W. Newton, *The London Journal of Arts and Sciences: Containing Reports of All New Patents*, Vol. XI, No. LXIX (London: Sherwood, Jones, and Co., 1826), 352–353. Wycherley's patent is No. 5049, dated December 4, 1824. A later version of this kind of balance strap is seen in Thomas Woodward's "August Röting with 'Barb'," one of the horses Queen Victoria rode in the early 1840s, now in The Royal Collection Trust, https://www.rct.uk/collection/407266/august-roting-with-barb.
198 Allen, 11.
199 Wayte (1850), 166–167.
200 Mary E. Richardson, *The Life of a Great Sportsman (John Maunsell Richardson)* (London: Vinton and Company, Ltd., 1919), 47.
201 Richardson (1919), 47.
202 Richardson (1919), 48.
203 Richardson (1919), 49.
204 Bloodgood, 18–19.
205 Clarke, 62.
206 Clarke, 62.
207 Clarke, 62.
208 Clarke, 62.
209 Dunbar, 19.
210 Hayes (1903), 305. Hayes continued, "it was not until the introduction in 1830 of the leaping head that women were able to ride over fences" (430).
211 Richardson (1853), 84.
212 Jenkins, 47.
213 Craige, 66.
214 Augusta Fane, *Chit-chat* (London: Thornton, Butterworth, Limited, 1926), 106. She mentions Mrs. Turner Farley as one of them (107).
215 Lawrence, 182.
216 Guy Paget, *The Melton Mowbray of John Ferneley* (Leicester: Edgar Backus, 1931), photo of painting after page 10.
217 George F. Underhill, *A Century of English Fox-Hunting* (London: R.A. Everett and Co., 1900), 142. See Elliott, 7 and 14 (quote).
218 J. Nevill Fitt, *Covert-side Sketches; or, Thoughts on Hunting Suggested by Many Days in Many Countries with Fox, Deer, and Hare* (London: Sampson Low, Marston, Searle, and Rivington, 1879), 132.
219 Elliott, 14.
220 Colin B. Ellis, *Leicestershire and the Quorn Hunt* (Leicester: Edgar Backus, 1951), 109.
221 Lawrence, 181–182.
222 Robert Smith Surtees, *The Analysis of the Hunting Field* (London: Methuen and Co., 1904), 291.
223 Surtees (1904), 291.
224 Surtees (1904), 292.
225 Surtees (1904), 293.
226 Robert Smith Surtees, *Mr. Facey Romford's Hounds* (London: Bradbury and Evans, 1865), 70.
227 Surtees (1865), 74.
228 "Sketch of a Fox-Hunt," *The Edinburgh Literary Journal*, 64 (January 30, 1830), 69.

229 Surtees (1904), 35.
230 Surtees (1904), 295. Italics mine.
231 Colley, 250.
232 Dunbar, 1.
233 See "Melton: The Story of its Rise, I," *The Ladies' Field* (November 10, 1900): Supplement: Sports and Pastimes, unpaginated.
234 "The Influence of Women in Hunting Countries I," *The Ladies' Field* Volume 32 (January 20, 1906), 283–284. See also "Melton," *The Ladies' Field* Volume 16 (January 11, 1902), 199–200.
235 Anthony Trollope, *Hunting Sketches* (London: Chapman and Hall, 1865), 32.
236 Lawrence, 186–187.
237 Hayes dates women hunting in Britain to 1830 "it is only within about the last seventy years that ladies have ridden across country" (quote 304, see also 305, 430). Hayes' first edition was published in 1893; hence, she dates women hunting to around 1823.
238 "Melton: The Story of its Rise, I."
239 *The Sporting Magazine*, Volume 71 (February 1828), 280
240 "Present Race of Fox-hunting Gentlemen," *The Sporting Magazine*, Volume 83, First Series/Volume 8, Second Series (January 1834), 236.
241 *The Sporting Magazine*, Volume 67 (February 1826), 277.
242 James Vernon, *Politics and the People: A Study in English Political Culture, c. 1815–1867* (Cambridge: Cambridge University Press, 1993).
243 "Present Race of Fox-hunting Gentlemen," *The Sporting Magazine*, Volume 83, First Series/Volume 8, Second Series (January 1834), 236.
244 Trollope, 31.
245 "The Quorn Hounds, by Clio," *The Sporting Magazine*, Volume 100, First Series/Volume 25, Second Series (May 1842), 17.
246 David C. Itzkowitz, *Peculiar Privilege: A Social History of Foxhunting, 1753–1885* (Hassocks, Sussex: The Harvester Press, 1977), 15–16.
247 Adrian Harvey, *The Beginnings of a Commercial Sporting Culture in Britain 1793–1850* (Burlington, VT: Ashgate, 2004).
248 Wiseman, 25.
249 Wiseman, 31.
250 *The Sporting Magazine*, Volume 59 (February 1822), 215.
251 Greenwood (1839), 13.
252 Wiseman, 25.
253 W. Sidney Felton, *Masters of Equitation* (London: J.A. Allen and Co., 1962), 34.
254 Clarke, 15–16.
255 *The Sporting Magazine*, Volume 71 (February 1828), 281.
256 Captain M***** (1842), 55.
257 "English Horse Races and Other Sports, Described by a French Author," *The Sporting Magazine*, Volume 16 (June 1800), 123.
258 Frederick Watson, *Robert Smith Surtees: A Critical Survey* (Norwood, PA: Norwood Editions, 1978), 51 and 155.
259 *The Young Lady's Equestrian Manual*, 45.
260 Stanley, 50.
261 Reeves, 42.
262 *The Young Lady's Equestrian Manual*, 59.
263 Allen, 40.
264 Allen, 46.
265 Bloodgood, 42.
266 "Vieille Moustache" [Robert Henderson], *The Barb and the Bridle* (London: The "Queen" Office, 1874), 49.

Chapter 3
Fox Hunting and Sporting Emancipation for Women, 1857–1913

In 1859, a stunning horsewoman appeared in Hyde Park. Her skillful equitation, combined with her perfect appearance, immediately set her apart from other riders. Her riding was so incredible that curious spectators flocked to see her and vast traffic jams were created just to catch a glimpse of her (Figure 3.1).[1] She literally brought London to a standstill.[2] "With slackened rein swift Skittles rules the Row," wrote Alfred Austin in *The Season: A Satire*.[3]

But everything was not as it seemed. "Skittles," or Catherine Walters, belonged to the *demi-monde*, or those beautiful but less-than respectable women kept by elite men for entertainment. Socialite Augusta Fane called them "ladies of the 'half-world,'" though they inhabited the same world as everyone else and with more notoriety than most.[4] Walters' fame culminated in being crowned "Anonyma" in print, for though ironically she may have been anonymous by birth, she was made famous by riding. Despite her reputation – or perhaps because of it – she personified the transition from ladies' riding in urban parks to female participation in the hunt field.

Walters not only became one of the famed "pretty horsebreakers," but the best of them. These were professional courtesans who exhibited themselves through their expert horsemanship.[5] In 1861, a dramatic sketch entitled "The Pretty Horsebreaker" defined its popularized subject as "a horsebreaker – a heartbreaker – a general smasher up of me and all belonging to me – in that pork-pie hat and blue riding habit."[6] Wearing ravishing riding clothes ("Skittles" started a fashion craze for pork-pie hats) and easily managing the most unmanageable steeds, these women, though low by birth and profession, mingled (and often married) into the highest of London society thanks to their expert equestrianism. In fact, Rotten Row became known as the human equivalent of Tattersalls, the auctioneers of fine equine bloodstock.

Men were besotted by the beauty and skill of these equestrians, but London's Society women were less enthusiastic. "Pretty horsebreakers, forsooth! Pretty hearth and hope breakers!"[7] criticized some. But, as another pointed out, "How many ladies have we known, who have won their husbands by a graceful seat, and a good hand upon a well-united horse – elegant horsemanship in the Park has subdued as many hearts as graceful acting upon the stage."[8] In 1861, Walters

Figure 3.1 Photograph of Catherine Walters, known as "Skittles." Walters was a famed equestrian and courtesan during the mid-nineteenth century. Though lowly by birth, "Skittles'" passport into high society was her skill in the saddle. From park riding to fox hunting, Walters gained social acceptance via sport that she could not obtain through other means. She also helped establish a public precedent of acceptance and admiration for female riders that would see such participation increase after mid-century.
Credit: © The Fitzwilliam Museum, Cambridge.

accomplished another great coup when she (or her image) "breached the forbidding walls of Burlington House" when Sir Edwin Landseer's painting "The Shrew Tamed" became the Royal Academy's "picture of the year." The subject was said to be Miss Gilbert, a respectable horsewoman, but she looked nothing like the figure in the painting, which everyone knew was really "Skittles." "For the Painter-Laureate of the Victorian middle class to exhibit a picture of a well-known whore was an astonishingly bold gesture," but the *Annual Register* claimed that the painting was one of the two most popular of the year.[9] While the gesture may not have been appreciated by some, few did not admire the horsemanship of the woman portrayed.[10]

It was through equestrianism, then, that Walters rode to the top of London society. She intuitively understood that riding well was the best way to display her wares, which, as a courtesan, was herself. She was following the tradition of many women before her such as Lady Lade and Miss Le Clerc, who had also used their skills in the saddle to achieve social recognition and success. As biographer Henry Blyth pointed out, "A prostitute on a horse was somehow different; and all the more different because she was able to look like a lady in the saddle. ... Her passport was her poise in the saddle."[11] Through her horsemanship, Walters gained social acceptance via sport that she could not obtain through other means.

To display her equestrian skills to their best advantage, Walters chose to hunt. In 1863, she headed to the "Shires" to hunt with the Quorn, then the best hunt in England. Along for the ride was her chosen pilot, James "Jem" Mason, the winner of the first Grand National Steeplechase in 1839.[12] Now in his forties, Mason was still considered one of the best riders of his day. As a pilot, Mason's duty was to provide a lead for the woman who followed him by choosing the best places to jump fences and avoid trouble spots. Mason did not hold back in the field, and, to Walters' credit, she kept up, though at the end of one day, she is said to have remarked about her sore posterior, "Jem, if you go on like this, my — will be as red as a beef-steak."[13]

Her presence upset no one more than the wife of the Master of the Quorn, Lady Stamford. Whether it was due to jealousy over Walters' prowess in the field or the fact that "Skittles" attempted to greet her as an equal, Lady Stamford demanded that her rival be removed from the field. This was largely a case of the pot calling the kettle black, as Lady Stamford had also been a courtesan before her marriage, and a circus rider to boot.[14] Sensitive to her new social status and keen to downplay her Cremorne Gardens ties (the London pleasure gardens where prostitutes gathered and she had performed as a trick rider), Lady Stamford demanded that her husband, as the Hunt's Master, "dispatch that improper woman home." Walters reputedly shot back: "I don't know why she should give herself such airs, she's not even head of our profession; Lady Cardigan is."[15]

Walters did leave the meet as requested, but as chance would have it, the hounds ran across her path on the way home and the temptation to follow them was irresistible. Her excellent riding during the run won the day. Lord Stamford praised her horsemanship and invited her to continue hunting with the Quorn, despite his wife's disapproval.[16] Though she had by then separated from her lover, Spencer Compton Cavendish, Lord Hartington, he stood up for

"Skittles'" right to join sport and society. Hartington, who became the eighth Duke of Devonshire, condemned "the stupid people in Leicestershire" for their rude treatment of Walters, labeling them "snobs."[17] Thus, Lady Stamford bore the brunt of popular derision for both her hypocrisy in trying to escape her own background and also breaching the unwritten rule of a democratic hunting field, which had been to include and welcome all whose abilities enabled them to participate.

Having scored a victory with the Quorn, Walters soon moved south to what eventually became the Fernie hunt under the Mastership of W.W. Tailby, who had taken the hounds in 1856. What occurred was *déjà vu*. According to Tailby's personal hunting diary, "a certain nobleman" objected to Walters' presence out hunting, and directed Tailby to see that hounds were taken home should she appear. As Master, it was Tailby's job to see that the hounds were hunted to the best of his abilities in providing both community service by killing foxes and also good sport for those following the hunt; thus, this demand challenged Tailby's authority and competence to rule the field and decide who contributed (and who did not) to the execution of those duties. As Tailby recorded in his private hunting diary,

> I took my stand on the broad principles that "the hunting field is open to all the world," that "I am not the censor of morality of the hunting field," that I have "no right to disappoint others to gratify the prejudices of an individual," – and that, in short, nothing should induce me to take the hounds home merely because "Skittles" is out. I am encouraged to this the more that I never hear any complaints of her conduct in the hunting field, or that she is in any way objectionable to the ladies who come out.[18]

Tailby recorded nothing further in his journals, and it appears that "Skittles" kept hunting without further ado.

Walters' appearances with these prestigious Hunts – and the increased involvement of women in general – forced a decision about hunting as a pursuit, and about who could (or should) legitimately join in the sport. If Masters could exclude women, would a similar axe fall on the lower classes of male fox hunters as well? Tailby was widely known as having "gained the support of all classes," and the fear of ruining what many believed was a "democratic" sport appeared very real.[19] As Tailby recorded, "Skittles" horsemanship and etiquette in the field were irreproachable, and he refused to send anyone home who behaved well while hunting, no matter how they behaved elsewhere. Women went to the theater and paid to see such women perform on stage, he noted, so they could see them on the hunt field – for free – and without complaining.[20] Hunting might well be based on "sufferance" rather than absolute "right" but if a woman "suffered," who was not to say a man would as well? Therefore, as *Baily's Magazine* concluded in 1861, "fox hunters cannot be accused of being exclusionists," for to exclude one was to open up a slippery slope of excluding all and thereby destroying the sport.[21] Thus, this chapter examines women's involvement in fox hunting from 1857 to 1913, or from the publication of Mrs. J. Stirling Clarke's *The Ladies' Equestrian Guide* in 1857, that encouraged women to hunt (sidesaddle), to the release of Mrs. Stuart Menzies' *Women in the Hunting Field* in 1913, that urged women to hunt and ride astride – like men.

Horsewomen and Hunting

"Skittles" helped establish a precedent of acceptance for female equestrians that would see their presence increase after mid-century. Though British women had made great progress in advancing their participation in equestrian activities throughout the first half of the nineteenth century, such pursuits had been limited to quiet hacking, or sedately riding in urban parks or on roads. Local female involvement in fox hunting, especially in the Midland Shires and around Melton Mowbray, had increased since 1830, but the real explosion in female interest and participation in equestrianism came after mid-century, when railroads opened the country to outside participation. This involvement led to a reevaluation and revision of the passive and domestic ideal for Victorian women. Before the rise of lawn games in the 1870s or bicycling in the 1890s, British horsewomen had been quietly and effectively transforming social, cultural, and gender ideals through equestrian sports. As twentieth-century observer and Leicestershire native Colin Ellis argued, female riders "probably did quite as much as the pioneers of Newnham and Girton to convince men that women could compete with them on equal terms."[22]

How much did female participation in horse sports increase during the mid-nineteenth century? Although there are no exact figures, there was an increase in horse ownership in general. In 1861, Henry Mayhew, in his survey of *London Labour and London Poor*, concluded that "two persons in every seven of those who are of independent means keep a riding or carriage-horse," and he believed that the increase in horses over the last decade was "a remarkable sign of the times."[23] Based on F.M.L. Thompson's calculations, non-agricultural horses (including riding and hunting horses) increased from one third of the total in 1811 to more than half in 1902.[24] The British horse population as a whole more than doubled from 1.3 million (1811) to 3.3 million less than a century later (1901).[25] In the seven decades from the 1830s to the 1900s, the horse/town-dweller ratio increased from 1:30 to 1:20, while the horse/country-dweller ratio increased from 1:15 to 1:6.[26] By the 1870s, there were so many horses in London alone that domestic hay specialists could only meet a third of the demand for roughage.[27] In this situation, even if people did not personally own horses themselves, they were in constant contact with people who did ride and with equine representations in press and print.

By 1865, the novelist and hunting enthusiast Anthony Trollope noted, "the number of such ladies is very much on the increase" in the hunting field.[28] At the moment when more women became more interested in fox hunting, the sport again became more fraught with difficulties. Though railways opened the country to non-locals, landscape changes resulted in larger fences and greater speeds for the chase, requiring more knowledgeable and skilled equitation, especially for women riding sidesaddle. Because of these challenges, ladies' riding manuals that focused on hunting were increasingly published after 1850. Over 20 books, many of which ran into several editions, were published for female riders during this time, and authors Nannie Power O'Donoghue, Alice Hayes, and Eva Christy led the charge in advocating, advancing, and educating women about hunting, with O'Donoghue stating that the goal of every rider was to hunt.[29]

Two factors led to increased female participation in horse sports after mid-century. As discussed in the previous chapter, these were cultural and technological changes: the wider acceptance of women into the hunting field and the invention (and utilization) of the third pommel on sidesaddles (Figure 3.2). The leaping head was critical to this process, and it was no coincidence that well into the 1890s it was also called the "hunting crutch."[30] This invention opened a new world of sporting opportunities for women.[31] Alice Hayes credited the invention of the leaping head for making hunting for women possible again, thus contributing to a decline of park riding as women pursued more adventurous activities.[32] In tandem with the leaping head, other advances such as the balance strap – which kept the saddle on straight – and any number of "safety" stirrups, leathers, and bars (by which the stirrup was attached to the saddle) were also introduced as demand increased. *Baily's Magazine* estimated that safety stirrups, which would (theoretically) free a woman's foot in case of a fall, thus preventing her from being dragged by the horse, typically appeared at a rate of about one per month.[33] Many contemporary sporting authors credited these innovations with enabling women to hunt more safely and successfully, while at the same time, decreasing the popularity of regular riding, or hacking, for ladies.[34]

Further, Faster, and Higher

As women became more interested in hunting after 1850, the sport became more fraught with difficulties. By mid-century, the number of people coming to hunt (called the size of the field) had increased exponentially due to the expansion of the railroads. By the 1870s, the equestrian author "Cecil" confirmed that "the journey from London only cost a few sovereigns which had rendered the society at Melton much less exclusive and aristocratic."[35] These new connections brought more people out into the country to hunt, thus making crowding and the need to ride well in order to avoid injury and/or embarrassment more of an issue. At the same time, landscape changes transformed hunting country, and fences grew bigger and more demanding, with wire fencing becoming a dangerous problem. Lastly, horses and hounds were being

Figure 3.2 Sidesaddle with leaping head pommel, plate XXII (following page 32) from Col. J.E. Hance, *School for Horse and Rider* (London: Country Life, Ltd., 1932): The utilization of the third pommel ("leaping head") on sidesaddles gave women a much stronger position on horseback. By pushing her left knee and thigh up into the leaping head, and pressing the right leg and thigh down onto the upper pommel, and then pulling that leg backward on the saddle flap, a woman "locked" herself into position on horseback. In this position, it was virtually impossible to become unseated. Such innovations opened a new world of sporting opportunities for women by enabling them to gallop, jump, and hunt on horseback.
Credit: Collection of the author.

continually better bred, so sport became faster, and holding one's own demanded skill and experience in staying on the former and staying with the latter.

If there was a "golden age" of hunting, it was arguably linked with the "railway age." Railways made it possible for people to travel and hunt across England no matter where they lived. As Anthony Trollope confirmed, this new transportation had "done so much for hunting that [it] may almost be said to have created the sport anew on a wider and much more thoroughly organized footing than it ever held before."[36] Railways catered to a new traveler – the fox hunter – by offering quick, easy, and affordable transport for man and horse across the country. Previously hunting had been limited to those who were local, or those who could afford rent and stabling to live in the area during the season. By the 1870s, if not well before, ladies were taking special advantage of this new transportation, according to equestrian author and former cavalry officer, Robert Henderson, writing under the pseudonym "Vieille Moustache,":

> They left St. Pancras at eight o'clock in the morning, in a saloon carriage, arrived at Melton at half-past ten, and were at the meet at eleven, with military punctuality. They enjoyed a capital day with the Quorn hounds, left Melton at half-past six, after riding a considerable distance back, and arrived in town at nine o'clock.[37]

As Surtees' Jorrocks had observed, "the iron horse is the best kiver 'ack [covert hack] in the world."[38] A "covert hack" was a horse ridden from home to "covert" where he would then be exchanged for a hunter to follow the hounds.

This new mode of transportation opened up the sporting world for female riders and enabled them not only to hunt but to leave the more sheltered and private home for a public world. But this is not to say that newcomers were automatically accepted into what had been a largely limited and rural sporting association. The easy accessibility provided by railways to hunt caused class contact and social friction, especially in the popular Shires which felt the brunt of the conflict. According to the hunting commentator "Scrutator" (or Knightly William Horlock), the problem with railways was that they brought "to every meet a host of evil-doers from manufacturing towns, garrisons, and fashionable watering-places, to override and perhaps maim the hounds, ruin the sport, and try the patience of the most even-tempered Masters."[39] Many of the newcomers were ignorant of the unwritten codes of sporting conduct, which increased agitation over – and sometimes protest against – these novices. The local and rural microcosm of hunting had been punctured by metal and wheels, and there were both benefits of, and problems with, this new association. While railroads did encourage class and community mixing and opened up new sporting possibilities for women, they also contributed to class and community conflict regarding the future of fox hunting and who should be allowed to participate.

These social issues were dwarfed – literally – by landscape changes and the increasing size of obstacles found in the hunting field as well as the new dangers of negotiating them. As Nannie O'Donoghue recalled by 1881,

> fences, if not stronger, are far more numerous than they were, and if some of the land rides lighter from being drained, there is more plough to contend with, as well as increased crowds, crushing and jostling for the practicable places; so that, taking things all round, it is more difficult to ride well now than formerly ...[40]

After the enclosure movements of the late eighteenth century, further agricultural improvements took the form of adequate drainage. As historian Jonathan Finch notes, the soil around Melton Mowbray, the premier hunting center in the Midlands, was a heavy, waterlogged clay which was prohibitive to galloping for horses and holding scent for the hounds. Surface drainage systems created in the nineteenth century resulted in large drains, or yawning muddy ditches, that had to be jumped.[41]

As drainage increased the quality of grassland, farmers began to keep more profitable cattle rather than sheep, but this type of larger livestock naturally required thicker, bigger fences around pastureland. Original enclosure fences had been built of timber rails protecting small hedges. These fences became known as "oxers," with the rail in front of the hedge to prevent stock from devouring the shrubs, or "double oxers," if there was a rail on either side. From small beginnings, these hedges often grew into impregnable "bullock fences" – or "bullfinches" – which had to be jumped *through* rather than *over*.[42] As they grew, these permanent hedgerows were then trimmed into massive cut-and-laid obstacles, by which the four-foot scrub was braided through itself.[43] Fences grew so large that Augusta Fane recorded hunters sending out their grooms the night before to saw into the rails so they would break if (inevitably) hit.[44] At morning meets before the hunt, alcoholic stimulants, commonly called "jumping powder," fortified the nerves – this could be ale, sherry, cherry brandy, or similar alcoholic tonics.[45] These fences in the hunting field were so massive that female riders were directed to learn leaping "until you can sit with ease over a jump of five feet," which was certainly no small feat when riding sidesaddle (Figure 3.3).[46] In comparison, the *maximum* fence height for show jumping at the Olympic Games today is 1.65 meters, or just over five feet high.[47] Thus, Victorian women riding sidesaddle were regularly jumping fences as large – or larger – than today's Olympic competitors.

Added to these fearsome obstacles was the real concern of the age: wire. Hunters deemed it "our phantom, too often our embodied, enemy."[48] *Country Life* magazine lamented, "the modern devotees of Diana have a grinning skeleton present at their sport."[49] Barbed-wire fencing had been introduced around 1850, but became a genuine nuisance a decade later when farmers switched to using it as a cheaper alternative to pasture fencing: it cost only about 1/10th of a wooden fence. It was estimated that wire costing £14 could replace wood fencing valued at £100.[50] The increased use of wire highlighted growing tensions between those who farmed the land and the ballooning numbers of those who rode over it. Wire was nearly invisible unless well-flagged and marked by the farmers who used it, and as a result, it caused many falls, injuries, and even deaths.[51] Because horses could not see it, they had to be trained to jump higher and wider to avoid being tangled in it. Injuries from wire – for horse and rider – were often fatal due to infection of the wound and blood poisoning.[52]

While fences were growing bigger and railways were transporting more people to hunt, the sport was getting faster because horses and hounds were being better

Figure 3.3 "Over the Five Bars," by J. Sturgess, *The Illustrated Sporting and Dramatic News* (March 24, 1877), page 20: This image shows a self-possessed horsewoman easily managing a tricky obstacle, a five-barred gate. Female equestrians, riding sidesaddle, were directed to learn leaping "until you can sit with ease over a jump of five feet" before they attempted fox hunting. In comparison, the maximum fence height for show jumping at the Olympic Games today is 1.65 meters, just over five feet high. Thus, Victorian women riding sidesaddle were regularly jumping fences as large – or larger – than today's Olympic competitors of either sex who ride astride.
Credit: Collection of the author.

bred. Following the advances of Hugo Meynell in the late eighteenth century, a second wave of breeding improvements occurred during the nineteenth century. "Railways, telegraphs, and steamboats have taught us to do everything at speed. Both hounds and horses have had to conform to the times," Mrs. Kennard, a sporting author, noted.[53] In 1886, the Hunter Improvement Society was formed to promote the better breeding of hunter horses, as were other similar breed-type societies.[54] Hunting horses were transformed from steady weight-carriers needed to power through heavy soils to clever, agile, and high-strung Thoroughbreds bred to run and jump at speed. These temperamental animals required an experienced rider to guide them through a more challenging countryside.

As more people hunted, the demand for good hunting horses increased and so too did their price. Even with an unlimited budget, however, "horses with perfect mouths and manners are, like angels' visits, few and far between."[55] Because of this, many less wealthy women who wanted to hunt were forced to ride other types of cheaper horses. These women (and men) often turned to renting horses, called "hirelings," to save on expenses, though these horses necessarily required more riding skills because they were so poor in quality.[56] As hunting enthusiast George Underhill recalled, "The habit of mounting ladies on thoroughbreds, which have been weeded out of racing stables, is dangerous to a degree bordering on crime. Yet, even now it is no uncommon thing to see a young girl riding a broken-down polo pony."[57] Discarded racehorses and decrepit polo ponies were hardly safe conveyances, especially for novice riders. The possession of an expensive ladies' hunter demonstrated class status in a sporting world where social indicators like fashionable clothing had disappeared. The skillful handling of inferior horses was yet another opportunity to prove one's merit and stand out in the field.

Although hunting enabled class mingling, it did not necessarily encourage class mixing. Often the worst critics and judges of female hunting participants were not men, but rather other women. As Alice Hayes commented, "I have heard female voices audibly 'picking holes' in a lady's mount, which is very unkind; for their poorer sister was doubtless riding the best horse she could get, and the hearing of such rude remarks may entirely spoil her day's pleasure."[58] When she was mounted on a cart horse, Mrs. Philip Martineau recalled being made fun of by the well-mounted lady riders – "I tried to persuade myself I didn't mind, but I did."[59] Thus, push-back for some female riders came not from their male colleagues, but from upper-class women discriminating against their lower-class sisters. Although the new spaces of sport and the hunting field had been opened for them, many women needed further instruction to take advantage of these opportunities.

Hunting Handbooks

To this end, a new kind of book was published after mid-century in vastly increased numbers. This was the ladies' riding manual, which sought to educate women not just on riding, but on hunting, horsemanship, and stable management – topics which had previously been considered unfeminine. Much of this impetus reflected the fact that despite so many women wanting to hunt, most ventured out knowing very little about riding, to say nothing about hunting, jumping, and basic horse care. As Mrs. Philip Martineau related, when she began hunting in the 1880s, "So little did I know about it that I didn't even put my left knee under the crutch, but over it. And to this day I don't know how I stuck on."[60]

While such enthusiasm was surely commendable, lack of knowledge and experience often caused dangerous problems in the field and could create negative feelings about women's participation. For example, one woman appeared in the field and committed the unforgiveable sin of overriding the hounds – getting in front of the pack ruined the scent of the fox and might terminate the day's sport altogether if the hounds were unable to pick up the trail again. The uneducated rider sent her horse galloping at a fence where a hound was slowly tracking the scent. The frustrated Master yelled, "Can't anyone stop that damned bitch?" Then, more quietly, he added, "I am afraid she's getting in the way of the lady jumping that fence."[61]

To counter such ignorance, the best of these manuals were written by experienced horsewomen, who imparted their own knowledge and experiences to educate other women and create a better and more positive atmosphere. In 1857, Mrs. J. Stirling Clarke's work catalyzed the beginning of a much larger trend of educating women riders, one which other female authors were not slow to follow. Clarke "indulged much" in hunting; she was "enthusiastically fond" of it, and she encouraged other proficient women to do the same, though she cautioned novices.[62] Between 1857 and 1899, ten entirely new titles appeared on women's riding, with another ten that contained chapters or significant sections on ladies' equitation. Several titles were reprinted in multiple editions, bringing the total of available books to 32 titles in 42 years.

The 1870s witnessed a flurry of books for female equestrians. Several books were published from collections of articles on ladies' riding that had appeared in popular periodicals such as *The Field* and *The Queen*, including the works of "Impecuniosus" (1872) and "Vieille Moustache" (1874).[63] Both encouraged women's hunting, as did Samuel Sidney in *The Book of the Horse*. Sidney's text first appeared in monthly parts, contributing to its vast length of over 600 pages when collated and published in 1875. It was so popular that it appeared in four more editions through 1893, reaching a final length of 680 pages. Sidney was the hunting correspondent for the *Illustrated London News* from 1847 to 1857 (as well as a commissioner for the Great Exhibition), and he was an enthusiastic proponent of ladies' hunting.[64] As Sidney wrote,

> A lady who can gallop without losing her breath or her nerve, who can sit her horse in comfort over average leaps, will, even in a flying country, with the assistance of the numerous hand-gates that are put up in all the

fashionable counties, and the many gaps that are established by the advanced guard of men, can see a great deal of sport, and have quite as much riding as is good for most women, without doing anything to be talked about.[65]

Sidney saw nothing improper or unfeminine in women riding to hounds. He considered hunting important socially: "which in its way is quite as important for success in society as the etiquette of the drawing and dining room."[66] It was a healthy activity and accomplishment that displayed admirable female qualities.

By the 1880s, even more manuals appeared for a female audience interested in hunting. Nannie Power O'Donoghue was one of the foremost horsewomen of her time, and she penned a series of articles concerning "ladies on horseback." Published by *The Illustrated Sporting and Dramatic News*, the series first appeared on October 2, 1880, with the articles later compiled into the celebrated book, *Ladies on Horseback*, which was published in 1881 and ran into five editions by 1896.[67] The information was so popular that a single book could not satiate demand for it, so O'Donoghue was commissioned by the *Lady's Pictorial* magazine to write another series of articles on ladies' equestrianism and horse management. This second series ran weekly under the heading "The Common Sense of Riding," with the first article appearing on May 21, 1884. After meeting with "generous favor," a number of publishers asked for the copyright to publish the articles as a book, and O'Donoghue accepted an offer from W. Thacker and Co. This series, with revisions, appeared in book form as *Riding for Ladies, with Hints on the Stable* in 1887.[68] The focus of these books was on O'Donoghue's great passion, hunting, and her goal was to educate other women riders to enjoy the sport as much as she did, which could only be accomplished by learning how to ride well.

By the 1890s, several other equestrian manuals with a hunting focus had appeared for ladies. These included W.A. Kerr's *Riding for Ladies* in 1891, Mrs. Harry Allbutt's *Hints to Horsewomen* in 1893, and Alice Hayes' *The Horsewoman: A Practical Guide to Side-Saddle Riding* also in 1893.[69] The latter was exceedingly popular and went into several subsequent editions.[70] A chapter on "Ladies' Riding" had appeared in Hayes' husband's edition of *Riding: On the Flat and Across Country* in 1881, but a separate book allowed further expansion on important topics.[71] In a nod toward the prevailing interest of the time, "and Hunting" was later added to the subtitle. Hayes' book was based specifically on her seven years' experience as the "rough-rider" at her husband's horse-breaking demonstrations throughout "India, Ceylon, Egypt, China, and South Africa" as well as her hunting experiences throughout Leicestershire and Cheshire.[72] Given her unique background, there was no question that Hayes knew her subject well: her book weighed in at nearly 500 pages in length and covered nearly every equestrian topic imaginable. Like O'Donoghue's works, Hayes' volume was very well received; in the Preface to the third edition, Hayes acknowledged the "hearty reception" from "horsewomen in all parts of the world."[73]

In 1899, Eva (E.V.A.) Christy published *Side-Saddle Riding: A Practical Handbook for Horsewomen*, which was soon followed by several more editions.[74] When she wrote almost two decades earlier, O'Donoghue claimed – perhaps for marketing purposes – that her books were the only ones on the subject of ladies' riding. This was not true, but by the turn of the century, O'Donoghue may have realized that new information was needed.[75] Thus, she did endorse Eva Christy's *Sidesaddle Riding* as a "very useful and sensible little manual. Admirably illustrated ... and giving good advice. Miss Christy writes very nicely on some delicate but essential subjects."[76] O'Donoghue was 56 years old by this time, and had not ridden for the last 20 years due to injury. As women's participation in horse sports progressed – and progressed very rapidly indeed – much of O'Donoghue's advice was old-fashioned at best, or obsolete at worst. Though Christy's advice mirrored what other female authors had written about riding and hunting sidesaddle, her books reflected a modern outlook on women's riding and hunting and about the sporting equality attained via these pursuits.

All these manuals had one thing in common: they pointed out that there was no substitute for experience if hunting was a woman's goal. But these printed texts were viable complements for women to teach themselves about riding and hunting. As H.G. English wrote in *The Art of Riding*, "The most valuable and effective lessons, however, are those obtained in the hunting field, when riding hard to hounds."[77] Catherine Walters and other female riders had raised the bar in terms of horsemanship, for both men and women, but the process of learning to ride well was not an easy or quick one. As author and rider Mrs. Stuart Menzies recalled,

> People are prone to underestimate the talents of the "Skittles" of every generation. They say, "Oh, that sort of success is easy enough for a pretty woman by those methods!" But is it? I think not. That is a great mistake ... I maintain there must have been real talent in "Skittles" besides good looks and easy ways.[78]

Walters' prowess demonstrated very clearly what Samuel Sidney had bluntly pointed out in 1875: the best horsewomen in Britain were the "professional amazones" because they spent the time and effort to learn to ride and hunt well, often by taking lessons from an instructor.[79] Ladies of the upper classes could not expect to compare favorably with the "pretty horsebreakers" on Rotten Row or in hunting fields if they too had not invested similar energy into perfecting their own horsemanship. Complain as they might – and did – the fact remained that "the virtuous daughters of Belgravia stood neglected in the background, practically wiped out of the picture by the popularity of the London lassie."[80] Hunting put this fact into even clearer relief: whereas a lady might flaunt her social status in a ballroom, it was hard to garner any man's attention or admiration when a rider like "Skittles" soared away from the rest of the field while they had ignominiously fallen off at the first fence.

Thus, these manuals were not just prescriptive literature but valuable tools for women in expanding their sporting knowledge and spatial horizons. There were not always local riding-schools outside London or major cities where ladies could practice jumping. It was also questionable whether riding in a school could provide adequate experience for hunting anyway. Hunting was a sport with unwritten rules of behavior; these guidebooks provided women with the insider knowledge needed to participate properly. Therefore, these manuals and the education they imparted enabled women to participate in a new public sphere. Here, they reinvented the traditional feminine ideal in a new space.

Self-Possession

The new space of the hunting field enabled women to develop personal autonomy as well as the masculine qualities of assertion and authority. Riding and hunting promoted personal (if not class) emancipation well before other sports or political progress. "Hunting," Lady Greville concluded "... is the best way of learning to be independent."[81] Rather than the cosseted Victorian hot-house flower or "angel of the house," female equestrians were role models for healthy, physical exercise as well as free thought. No one could navigate the challenges of the hunt field without a mind of her own. The Victorian ideal of passive domestic femininity was increasingly questioned: Nannie O'Donoghue argued, "I do not believe that anybody really admires a stuffed doll on horseback."[82] Hunting not only demanded that women ride well, but it also required that a woman was "capable of looking after herself," which was a complete reversal from being protected by socially mandated chaperones.[83] "I as matron was my own care-taker," recorded O'Donoghue, and her words reflect the change from being looked after by others to looking after oneself that riding and hunting necessitated of women.[84]

The emancipation of women via horse sports galloped forward after the mid-nineteenth century. Prescriptive literature advised women to cultivate and rely on their own strengths, rather than rely on the assistance of grooms, servants, and other male riders. This included being able to mount a horse themselves, rather than being boosted into the saddle by a male assistant, as had traditionally been advised in earlier manuals.[85] A woman should also be able to settle and arrange her own skirts, adjust her stirrups, and tighten her horse's girth.[86] As one sportswoman agreed later, "One of the most useful things for a woman to learn, is to be able to get on her horse off the ground by herself. If you cannot do this, you are so utterly dependent on the kindness of the long-suffering man."[87] Even the father of the Victorian conduct book, Samuel Beeton, concluded that every female rider should know the parts of her horse's equipment and how to bridle and saddle her own mount. "The dependence upon men for every service of this kind is ridiculous," he wrote in 1876, "When they are at hand make them useful, but be able to do without them when needful."[88]

These initial steps, seen throughout equestrian books and manuals in the 1870s, were important in not only giving women more control over themselves and their activities, but also in changing gender norms, which made it acceptable for a woman to assume and exercise command based on her own authority. As Sidney wrote in 1875, "A girl who is afraid of the common objects of the farm and the field, who screams on the slightest possible excuse, who flies from a peaceful milch cow, and trembles at a mouse, is not fit to mount a horse."[89] His statement showed the development of a new ideal of Victorian femininity, from the formerly over-closeted and cosseted female to a more robust and strong example, physically and mentally. Nannie O'Donoghue wrote that of all feminine qualities, courage was the one required most for riding. She stated unequivocally, "Courage is indispensable, and must be there from the outset. All other difficulties may be got over, but a natural timidity is an insurmountable obstacle,"[90] for "a timid horsewoman will never be a successful one."[91] O'Donoghue even went so far as to write that a true horsewoman was "not afraid of tumbling off, and so she does not look as though she were so."[92] A woman should face all physical, mental, and sporting problems on her own.

By the 1870s, further instructions appeared to show women how to embody independence and authority. On horseback, the mistress had to be the master. In 1876, Samuel Beeton wrote that a woman's relationship to her horse must be to "make him suit your own purposes."[93] As Samuel Sidney indicated,

> The lady who has mastered the first lessons in the equestrian art ... is then in a position to decide whether she will learn to rule her horse, or whether she is content to pass through life dependent for her comfort on the temper of her steed or the close, nurse-like attention of some groom or gentleman.[94]

His statement points to the value of personal equanimity for women that was not only supported but also encouraged by later authors like O'Donoghue. In her opinion, if a horse refused to jump a fence, a woman had to take steps to make him follow her will. This included whipping, the ultimate bugbear of "unsexed" women, as illustrated in Mary Elizabeth Braddon's novel, *Aurora Floyd*.[95] After all, yielding and using an object of punishment was a man's perogative; Sherlock Holmes used a hunting crop to bring criminals into line.[96] Yet a woman had to retain control and mastership of her mount, and this included usurping patriarchal power and the right to discipline and punish. As O'Donoghue instructed, "provoked though you may be, do not allow yourself to be vanquished. If you do not now gain the victory your horse will always be your conqueror."[97] In her opinion – which was certainly an opinion that carried weight, given the many editions of her works – women should never be "overpowered" by an animal "conqueror" because, as she directed, "allow them to vanquish you once, and they will pursue their advantage to their lives' end."[98] This experience gained via interactions with horses thus transferred to everyday interactions with people.

For women, hunting helped foster what many authors described as "self-possession."[99] This was, at its most basic, a personal autonomy, ability, and confidence to control one's destiny. By the 1890s, Eva Christy's advice for women hunting built on decades of similar work. Her directions spoke to a capable, independent woman, who could manage a variety of challenging situations whether on or off her horse. In her books, female riders were directed that a horse should "not get out of hand and master her."[100] Christy advised: "never hesitate at a jump,"[101] "don't lose presence of mind,"[102] and "never lose temper with a horse; for many a good animal turns stubborn and will not obey if the rider loses self-control."[103] "Use your own judgment," these commentators all summed up.[104] Trust, confidence, authority, self-possession – these were all masculine qualities that women came to embody through riding, and through them, emancipated themselves via horse sport.

Lead or Follow?

But how did women become "self-possessed" and create new identities for themselves? How did this transformation work in practice as opposed to prescription? One way women did this was to eschew the use of pilots in the hunt field and ride their own line, sometimes called "cutting out the work." In layman's terms, this meant riding for one's self, choosing where to ride, what to jump, and how to follow the hounds during a run, though it is far more complicated than this description makes it sound. It required a thorough knowledge of the landscape and countryside, of one's horse and his capabilities, of hunting as a sport and hound work, and last (but by no means least) an honest evaluation of one's own skills and judgment, the physical and mental qualities which made a sportswoman and rider. Given the increased challenges of bigger fences, more wire, faster horses, and more crowded fields all jostling for the best positions in chasing a fox, cutting out the work and finding one's own way was no small feat.

Many authors during this era urged women to select an experienced pilot before attempting to hunt, and previously even the best riders in England, such as Catherine Walters, had pilots to lead them on and show them where to go. A pilot was a "man whose duty or pleasure it was to choose a line for her, to pick places in the fences, to prevent her from riding over impractical parts of the country, and generally to enable his charge to see as much of the fun with as little risk as possible."[105] Though some local women did hunt on their own (though not necessarily by themselves, as a male chaperone or family member would usually accompany them), the majority of female riders were traditionally "expected to *follow*, not to *lead*" in the hunting field before mid-century.[106] Initially, this was thought to be a great boon for women, as the pilot was charged with all the difficult work and the lovely lady was only along for the ride. Even George Whyte-Melville and Samuel Sidney, great supporters of women riding and hunting, advised women to follow a pilot for safety's sake in the 1860s and 1870s.[107]

This advice was likely due to the increased size of the fields, the rougher going across country, the larger fences, and a lack of personal knowledge about the landscape the women were riding over. When hunting had been restricted only to the local community, those female riders who joined the hunt possessed as much knowledge of the country they were hunting as did the men. They knew where to cross streams or negotiate fences, where the going was bad or where the footing was better. In the early 1870s, Mrs. Jacobs, riding with the Cheltenham Staghounds, was regarded as "perfectly independent, can choose her own line, and never requires the assistance of anybody,"[108] while Mrs. Pole, in the Vale of the White Horse, "could take her part over a country without a pilot or gate-opener."[109]

However, when railroads opened the country up to hunting, the people who came to hunt (both men and women) had little experience with the local landscape and did not know or understand its dangers. "It is usual to say that women cannot take their own line over a country," one sporting author pointed out, "Of the majority this is doubtless true, but, so far as I can see, it is equally true of the majority of men."[110] This lack of knowledge was of less concern to men, who could blunder and fall off without being seriously hurt (most of the time), but it was a more serious issue for women riding sidesaddle, who were more likely to be injured in a fall. As Whyte-Melville put it, "It is at least twenty to one in our favour every time we fall, whereas with her the odds are all the other way, and it is almost twenty to one she must be hurt."[111]

For all these reasons, many equestrian authors urged ladies who wanted to hunt to follow a pilot in the field. The assumption behind all these instructions was that readers/riders were novices who required such services – at least, until they became experienced, both on horseback and with a particular landscape. As O'Donoghue noted, she had done without a pilot many times, but added, "then I am not a beginner, and I am surmising that *you* are."[112] And yet, if left alone when hunting, O'Donoghue did not advise following the field but rather riding for oneself: "Cut out a line for yourself, and follow the pack."[113] Pilots could easily get lost in the fray, or fall off themselves, so authors instructed women how to make do in such situations.[114] O'Donoghue reiterated this advice in her second book in 1887, writing that if a woman hunting had not secured a "trustworthy leader," it was better to "dispense altogether with the services of one, and cut out a line for yourself."[115]

Others, such as Alice Hayes, did not believe that women needed pilots at all. As she wrote:

> I have not enlarged on the subject of hunting pilotage, because, truth to tell, I have never indulged in the luxury of a pilot, as I have preferred to

know the capabilities of my mount and to see and act for myself. I believe that any woman who can ride and manage her horse with intelligent forethought, has no more need of a paid pilot than has the small boy who takes his chance on his pony.[116]

By the late 1800s, women were hunting on their own and doing it very well. If new to a country, it was prudent to follow a pilot until better acquainted with the landscape,[117] but overall women were expected to – and did – largely take care of themselves. Dispensing with the need to pay a pilot also opened hunting to less wealthy women who could rely on their own skills, not their purses. No woman could claim to be a first-rate horsewoman without being able to ride on her own and handle herself with confidence in the field.[118] In fact, the trend of cultivating women's independence and authority through sport reached its zenith in the hunting field. Lady Greville concluded that women did not need men at all. "It is, I suppose," she wrote, "a want of independence in the feminine character that makes most women follow some particular man."[119] Female riders took this advice to heart, for by the end of the century, it was widely noted that female riders "were making their way over the country quite as ably and readily as the men."[120] As T.F. Dale pointed out, "One of the most notable features of hunting in grass countries is the number of women in the field. Nor is the way in which they cross the country less remarkable. Of women who hunt a larger proportion ride at the top of the hunt than of men."[121]

The transition from following a pilot to riding for one's self exemplified the new equality women gained through riding and hunting. To be truly equal was to completely disregard any privileges of sex, which were the hallmark of the Victorian age and separate spheres ideology, and the basis for the patriarchal social order. Riding and hunting abolished the differences of sex in favor of merit and expertise. Riding without pilots was one way female riders aided this transformation, for as Alice Hayes pointed out, "It would be absurd for her to expect casual aid at every turn, in a large field composed chiefly of strangers, especially when its giver would be deprived of his place in a run."[122] Yet initially this had been the expectation, which caused no small amount of sporting grief. As one novel expressed, "Plucky young ladies, with no fear and no skill, are the curse of the hunting-field, if they only knew it. They are always in the way or else coming to grief, and then we men are expected to pick them up and set them straight. It ain't fair on a fellow, it really ain't."[123] For women to ride equally and on their own was the reverse of Victorian etiquette of the day, when gentlemen or chaperones scrupulously looked after women in their care. It was also contrary to advice given about urban riding, where women had once only been able to ride when escorted by "the care of a father, brother, or some near relative" and where gentlemen were instructed to pay all tolls and hold all gates when riding with a lady.[124]

To avoid such complaints in the field, women were encouraged – and encouraged others – to ride better and develop self-reliance when hunting. Such negative feelings could only destroy the delicate acceptance women had worked so hard to achieve, and also destroy the sport and the successful practice of it. As Captain Edward Pennell Elmhirst, soldier and Master of Hounds, wrote of hunting in 1877–1878,

> when ladies cast in their lot with the rougher sex, lay themselves out to share in all the dangers and discomforts incidental to the chase, and even compete for honours in the school of foxhunting – they should in common fairness be prepared to accept their position *on even terms*, nor neglect to render in some degree mutual the assistance so freely at their command, and that men in a Leicestershire field so punctiliously afford to each other.[125]

If anything untoward happened – losing a hat or a stirrup, or taking a tumble – women were expected to look after themselves. Women should not demand precedence at the start of a run, neither were they to be given the right of way at fences, gaps, or gates merely because of their sex.[126] "The accepted creed amongst the masculine members [was] that women who hunted ought to count as 'good fellows,' and be able to shift for themselves," wrote sporting author Mrs. Kennard in 1883.[127] Demanding the courtesies and politeness due to them in other social situations caused friction in the hunting field, where everyone on horseback was – to a great extent, despite class or gender – equal. Mrs. R.M. Burn, daughter of Colonel John Anstruther-Thomson, one of the century's great Master of Hounds, wrote, "Women out hunting should take their chance with the rest, and never trade on the chivalry of the opposite sex, for this is what makes them unpopular in the hunting field."[128] Women needed to actively contribute to the sport, not merely passively participate. Riding well and being unobtrusive or not interfering was not enough; women were called on to deliberately assist in the practice of sport. One way in which they did so was by assisting with the hunt in practical matters, by catching loose horses, helping those in need, or tending to the injured.[129]

In addition, women were expected to be financially equal, by paying the same hunt subscriptions as men, or paying to become an annual Member of a Hunt, and therefore being entitled to appear at its fixtures and meets. The rising prices of keeping hounds resulted in the formation of subscription packs in the nineteenth century. It also resulted in the professionalization of hunting, whereby the hunt, its hounds, and its staff were maintained by the money of its paying members. The packs of many country families and smaller farmers had provided popular amusements in rural areas where there were not many other attractions. These packs formed the basis of community identity and sociality, so that participation was not limited by class but rather by geography and residence. But as the great expense of keeping packs proved prohibitive to both great and small, the number of such private packs decreased over the early 1800s.

The decline of family-based packs such as the Raby hunt or personally owned hounds such as the Hatfield hounds removed the opportunity for women to ride as members of the family associated with them. But subscription packs were open to those who could afford to join them, and thus enabled women from families who subscribed to participate. In this way, they enabled class mixing – within limit. In *Records of the Chase*, "Cecil" shows an increase in subscription packs from about 25 in 1800 to at least 100 by 1854, when his book was published.[130] This massive increase of subscription packs by mid-century removed the requirement of residence to participate, though it instilled a new bar of wealth to join. It also opened such sports to a new audience – socially broader and more geographically widespread – that included women. For a few pounds sterling, women could subscribe and ride with the hunt for the whole season, or they could pay as they went for even less.[131] These measures did open hunting to a much broader social group of participants.

Initially women were exempted from paying such fees, but as they became more equal in other ways, so too did they financially. As *The Ladies' Field* explained,

> For a long time women were the guests of the hunt, we gave way to them at gates or gaps, and never thought of asking them for a subscription. The hunt was honoured by their presence, but occasionally embarrassed by the honour. *The first step was for women who hunted to place themselves by their own act on an equal footing with men*; and when they beat us over a country they themselves felt that they must take their turn at gaps, catch the gates – which most of them do very deftly – and in all respects conform to the etiquette of the hunting-field. The request for subscriptions soon followed, and now in many hunts it is demanded from them as a matter of course.[132]

By the beginning of the twentieth century, this practice had become standardized, with women subscribing equally with men, though hunting women had always been ahead of their time, as in earlier days "a majority of those ladies who hunted regularly did subscribe."[133]

"Capping," or the payment by non-members to join a hunt per day, was instituted first in the Midland Shires, but it was a controversial technique as it could lead to disenfranchising less well-off locals like farmers, over whose very land the hunt rode and with whom the hunt needed to maintain good working relations.[134] The increased size of the fields was to blame, due to the new social cachet of the sport, and capping did help thin out the numbers and make hunting less of a mad rush and bedlam. Capping led to further sporting equality for women, for as huntsman George Underhill noted, "in these days of feminine independence," ladies were often out by themselves and could pay for their own participation.[135] It also enabled a woman who could not afford a full year's subscription to come out as often as she could afford by paying per day. In fact, if a woman wanted to hunt and had "no menkind to arrange such business for her," she should pay her own subscription or capping fee by writing to the hunt secretary for information and using *Baily's* (the hunting reference book) as a guide.[136]

If men had initially objected to women's presence in the hunting field, they certainly had less ground to complain by the late 1800s, given that female riders were paying their own way, riding better, and contributing to the sport. As Alice Hayes pointed out,

> it seems rather superfluous for men to assure [women] that they do not object to their presence in the hunting field, an announcement which appears in print so often that it sounds like protesting too much. We never hear of hunting women recording the fact that they do not object to the presence of men ...[137]

Women had therefore proven their skills and were accepted as sporting colleagues in equestrian activities long before other sports were similarly transformed. The self-possession they gained through riding and hunting naturally transformed other areas of their lives and furthered the expansion of personal liberty, freedom, and fulfillment.

The Spectacle of "Sisi"

Just as British horsewomen had achieved an egalitarian footing in hunting fields, their advances were obscured by the arrival of a foreign celebrity. Elizabeth, the Empress of Austria, arrived in Britain in 1876 to hunt in the British fashion. "Sisi," as she was known, had learned to ride in royal *haute école* fashion in Bavaria, where her father, Duke Max, reportedly told her, "if we had not been born princes, we would have been circus-riders."[138] After her marriage to Emperor Franz Joseph in 1854, she indulged in hunting around the Hungarian countryside near Gödöllő, the royal summer residence. But this was not hunting in the British style: as one rider noted, "It is a delicious ground to ride over, all sandy fields, except when you come near a bog ... there is practically no jumping, a few little ditches now and then."[139] Thick woodland prevented fast runs, foxes often went to ground, the season was short (about two months from September to November), and there was almost no jumping.[140]

Many commentators, both then and now, have claimed that Elizabeth's participation in hunting was what ultimately made the sport popular for women in the last quarter of the nineteenth century.[141] But the Empress, in fact, made far less impact on equestrian sports for women than had Catherine Walters; in truth, she only built on the successes of women in Britain well before her time. As Underhill pointed out, "the ladies who loved sport had ridden to hounds for many years before the Empress visited England, and were thoroughly familiar with the orthodoxy of the hunting field."[142] Although the Empress was often touted as a good rider, she was not a fine horsewoman. She cared little for the horses she rode; to her, they were disposable goods to serve her pleasure. She often rode them to a lathered standstill and later commented that many had died by her hard riding.[143] Nor did she ride at the same caliber as British equestrians, having only to stay topside on the most experienced and expensive ladies' hunters of her day. Thus, her arrival in English and Irish hunting fields in the 1870s was not the boon to women's participation in the sport that has traditionally been argued.[144]

"Sisi" did garner vast media attention, but she was not admired for her eccentricities. She had been taught in the Continental *haute école* style and formed extremely close (scandalously so) relationships with European *écuyères* Elisa Renz and Emilie Loisset.[145] She even earned the disreputable sobriquet "the circus rider" in Viennese society circles.[146] In Britain, she was satirized in sporting fiction by Mrs. Edward Kennard in *The Catch of the County*. In this sporting novel, "Princess Vera Bogosloffsky" initially achieved acclaim in the hunting field, but was later revealed and reviled as a nothing more than a Parisian circus performer.[147] Trick riding and *haute école* were still deemed disreputable in Britain, a sentiment that would not change until the late twentieth century.

In preparation for hunting in England, the Empress ordered that large fences – the size of those in British hunting fields – be constructed on the public racecourse in Vienna. Here she practiced jumping without any chaperone except her English groom, Allen, which caused an uproar among Austrian society.[148] Her behavior was often thoughtlessly rude and uncommonly reckless; she was saved only by her title, her husband's money, and sheer luck. When she demanded a similar course of fences be constructed when she was visiting in France, she suffered a bone-jarring fall on hard ground, miraculously resulting in only a concussion.[149] More eccentric were her fitness and beauty regimes, including rigorous gymnastic exercises. "Body conscious" was an understatement when it came to the Empress, and, by today's standards, she would probably be considered anorexic, going through periods of starvation and liquid diets to maintain her 20-inch waist.[150]

Her arrival in England did not create the positive atmosphere she might have wished. In 1876, Queen Victoria wrote with disapproval in her journals that "The Empress has been in England a week & has taken a place in Northamptonshire, merely for hunting! She spoke with delight of having hunted each day since she arrived (!!)." The Empress detested stuffy English customs and left the royal meeting immediately upon seeing the Queen, rather than visiting in the usual diplomatic custom.[151] After hunting from Easton Neston in Northamptonshire in 1876, the Empress returned in 1878 to hunt further north with the Pytchley from Cottesbrooke.[152] By this time, she had achieved celebrity status, and crowds and photographers vied to see her. Her appearance caused a sensation, though she used a fan to shield her face from curious onlookers.[153]

At a time when British horsewomen had achieved independence by eschewing pilots, the Austrian Empress required this assistance. Captain "Bay"

Middleton, military officer and amateur jockey, was selected as her pilot. He had won the Irish Grand Military Gold Cup at Punchestown, Ireland, in 1873 and 1874, and was considered "the best rider to hounds since James [Jem] Mason," who had piloted Catherine Walters.[154] Initially, Middleton refused to pilot the Austrian ingenue: "What is an Empress to me?" he queried, "She'll only hold me back."[155] Yet, he was eventually persuaded into his duties. In her first hunt with Middleton as pilot, the Empress fell so hard with her horse into a muddy ditch that she broke the pommel on her saddle (although, luckily, nothing else).[156] The Empress could be a bold but not always brave rider: "Remember, I do not mind the falls," she told him, "but I will not scratch my face."[157] Middleton thus had to jump off and break holes through thick bullfinches and challenging fences for her to jump.[158]

"Sisi" was better prepared to be a success in the hunting field than anyone else. She purchased only "the best and safest hunters that money could buy," paying up to £500 per horse, and keeping a stable of 12 or more.[159] She even took lessons with Fred Allen, son of John Allen, at the famous Seymour Place school in London.[160] Society papers lavished praise on her riding, but fellow horsemen and women were not as thrilled. One huntsman recalled that she could not control her mount, writing that once she:

> was on a hot-headed one that wanted to be in front, and I was on one of the same sort, so as the hounds were running like blazes down-hill, I let him out to ease my arms. "Oh," said the Empress, "do let me be in front, for I cannot hold my horse!" so I had to pull in a bit.[161]

Even Middleton was frustrated with her inability to ride well, and specifically her failure to make her horses gallop (thus making both of them miss the hunt). He reportedly shouted at her, "Oh, come along, Madame, do come along!"[162] In times of trouble, she always needed instruction and assistance.[163]

Unlike British women who understood that their sex granted them no special privileges in the hunting field, the Empress always expected – and received – special, preferential treatment above and beyond anyone else, man or woman. She ignored the unwritten rules of the sport and participated as and when it suited her. As Underhill recalled, "it was also considered a breach of etiquette for anybody to ride in front of her, either at her fences or on the flat."[164] She was sewn into her undergarments and habit before every appearance, a process that could take up to three hours, and she kept the hunt waiting until she was satisfied with her appearance.[165] She was even guilty of the ultimate sin of overriding the Master and jumping on hounds: "You arrived an hour late and you've ridden over my hounds all day," Lord Willoughby de Broke complained to Middleton about the Empress' rude behavior – behavior which would not have been tolerated by anyone else.[166] "Sisi" found no greater favor among the ladies, who universally looked down on the Empress' riding skills. "How absurd to cry her up as a rider," one said, "Why, she cannot go without a pilot *and I can.*"[167] Thus, the Austrian Empress was not the positive role model to female equestrians that Catherine Walters had been, despite their vast social differences. But whereas "Sisi" may have failed in advancing equestrian sport for women, her British sisters did not.

Hazards for Horsewomen

One hundred years after the Marchioness of Salisbury's fine example, women's positions in British hunting fields had been firmly established. Yet, for all the ground they had gained and all the ways in which they had advanced, women who rode and hunted were still at a serious disadvantage compared to their male counterparts in one fundamental way – they rode aside rather than astride. As many noted, "There is, however, some room for improvement in saddles. There is no doubt that the present sidesaddles – great advances as they are on those of our mothers and grandmothers – are still not wholly satisfactory."[168]

Sidesaddles *had* advanced, especially with the addition of the leaping head, but the fact remained that women were still positioned sideways on a horse in dangerously restrictive clothing. Many late Victorian doctors, following earlier examples like Donald Walker, believed that sidesaddles caused a "crooked" spine in growing children and uneven muscle development in women, due to the unnatural position on horseback. Such posture supposedly caused "a great disfigurement, [and is] not unfrequently a cause of serious accident, for if your horse suddenly throws up his head, he hits you upon the nose, and deprives you of more blood than you may be able to replace in a good while."[169] Though such deformity was popularly denied, women were often encouraged to switch sides (from near to off) in riding, if they could afford a second saddle or a more expensive one with movable pommels. They were also urged to take up gymnastic stretching and flexibility exercises to counteract any of these possible dangers.[170] In fact, by the late 1800s, mechanical horse-exercise machines (fitted with real sidesaddles) provided in-house work-outs; these machines were even installed on transatlantic ocean liners such as the RMS *Franconia* and the ill-fated RMS *Titanic*.[171]

The problem with the sidesaddle was not necessarily the position on horseback, but what might become of a rider should she lose balance and topple sideways. The leaping head had made the seat more secure, but it was so secure that a woman could hardly fall off at all. This security was a great tool for instilling confidence in novice riders, but it was a dangerous liability as well. A woman was virtually trapped in the saddle if her horse came down over a fence or into a stream. Even if they avoided major injury, riders did not escape unscathed. As Nannie O'Donoghue recalled, when she followed her pilot too closely, her horse fell into a stream: "The fall involved the loss of the run, the loss of a habit, the loss of many odd shillings to wreckers, the loss of my temper, a wound from the boat-hook, and a heavy cold, the result of immersion on a perishing winter day."[172] She was not the only woman to suffer in the field: Mrs.

Edward Kennard displayed a broken stirrup leather in her home, as a reminder of an accident which caused her to be "dragged at a gallop over a ridge-and-furrow field, breaking her arm in two places." Kennard was later crushed beneath her horse in a ditch, and her husband recounted that these were "the two worst accidents he ever witnessed in the hunting field."[173]

There were many serious or fatal injuries that a woman might suffer from hunting sidesaddle. Mrs. Philip Martineau witnessed "a young woman out hunting ... killed by her horse rearing and falling back on her in a road, driving the pommel of the saddle through her."[174] Such gory deaths were not uncommon: the famous French écuyère, Emilie Loisset, was "impaled" on the pommel of her saddle when her horse fell over backward on top of her.[175] Fellow écuyère Fanny Ghyga fell and was dragged when her foot caught in the stirrup; gangrene set into her injured leg and she died at the age of 24 years.[176] Concussive injuries or head trauma were also common in an age before safety helmets. Lady Harrington, who rode with the Quorn, took such a bad fall on her head that she lost sight in one of her eyes.[177] According to hunting historian Guy Paget, she kept, "all over the country a-riding in these ladies' point-to-points" and took another fall, which miraculously returned her vision.[178]

Worst of all were spinal injuries. Many ladies broke their backs due to falls received in the hunting field. The sad numbers of these women included the popular Lady Apsley who rode with the Fernie,[179] as well as Miss Astor and Lady Willoughby de Eresby who rode with the Pytchley.[180] Mrs. John Bunbury, with the Island and Carlow in Ireland, had an "accident that deprived [her] of her hunting," describing in veiled terms the same paralyzing fate.[181] Such falls disabled, but did not kill these sportswomen, but many others did not survive. Female fatalities in the field included Mrs. Mason who hunted well until she broke her neck.[182] Sporting magazines grimly but truthfully recorded such distressing injuries in ever-increasing numbers as the nineteenth century wore on.

Nannie O'Donoghue, the foremost equestrian author of the mid-Victorian period, was not immune from serious injury. In her riding manuals and other texts, she wrote about many falls she had experienced when out hunting.[183] But little is known about the accident that caused her to give up riding and hunting altogether. According to biographer Olga Lockley, in December 1880, having sold her favorite hunting horse, Pleader, O'Donoghue was left only with two young mounts. In taking one out, she was bucked so hard against the pommels that she fainted and was thrown against a tree. Left unconscious, she was later rescued by a search party. On January 1, 1881, the editor of *The Sporting and Dramatic News* quoted her as saying, "I cannot move without awful pain but, thank Heaven, my head and hands are free." Just a week later, by January 8, 1881, she dismally concluded, "I know not when I shall ride again."[184] The extent of her injuries was not known but her spine was probably damaged. Her doctor likely recommended an end to all riding (which she did). O'Donoghue referred to it as "the accident which has disabled me"[185] and "the accident that deprived me of the power of ever riding [horses] again."[186] Nothing short of a life-threatening injury could have made such a splendid horsewoman give up what she so loved, but knowing that a second fall could have crippled or killed her, she did just that.[187] She was only 37 years old.[188]

Safety Skirts or "Death Traps?"

O'Donoghue's case raised important questions about ladies' riding and hunting clothes and how to make them less hazardous. Although there had been significant advances, riding habits were still "real murderous things …, long and heavy."[189] Riding clothes were a good place to start now that sidesaddles had also advanced with the addition of the leaping head:

> Safety habits and safety stirrups have reduced accidents to a minimum. To save the life of a lady dragged head downwards through a turnip field is an opportunity which comes but rarely now. Some years ago a lady relative of mine, on finding herself in this predicament, tried to free herself from her flowing habit and imposing pommel by clutching at the turnips as she passed. At last one especially staunch swede achieved the object desired.[190]

But it was no joke that women were still being injured, maimed, and killed pursuing equestrian sports, largely because they rode sidesaddle.

The stimulus began with redesigning safer riding clothes for female equestrians. As *Baily's Magazine* pointed out in 1884, "So many sad accidents have happened to ladies in the hunting field this season, that it is time someone who has studied how best to obviate them should take up a pen and try to give experience to those interested."[191] The most common hunting injury for a lady was being dragged by the horse when her skirt caught on the protruding pommels. Mrs. Kennard, no stranger to the hunting field, expressed the situation best in one of her novels, whereby her character Dulcie hung "over the off-side of the saddle. Her habit was apparently tightly held by the third crutch, and detained her firmly in that perilous position."[192] As *Baily's Magazine* reported, such injuries were distressingly of "constant recurrence."[193] Being strung upside down with no way to right oneself, the injury a galloping horse could do by metal horseshoe or other concussive impact was immense.

Thus, riding habits began to change as more women began to hunt and to demand better garments. As Samuel Sidney remarked, "When a young lady undertakes to ride in earnest, she must discard every article of her previous attire, except her stockings, and re-clothe herself from head to foot."[194] To ride well and hunt (which required strenuous galloping and jumping), women needed new flexibility and comfort on horseback. "If she cannot lace her own boots and put up her back hair," Sidney directed, "she may give up the idea of becoming a horsewoman, or anything better than a stuffed doll on horseback. A woman who means to ride well can neither afford to cramp her muscles nor to impede the circulation of her blood."[195] Every item of a woman's riding outfit was to be made with functionality and comfort in mind. Not only would such clothes enable a woman to perform better, but it made her a healthier woman overall and increased her enjoyment of activities that contributed to her feminine appeal and character. As Sidney summed up, "the *amazone* cannot be elegant if she 'suffers.'"[196] A woman could not display her full range of sporting skills without being first released from the cage of fashion.

First, the long, trailing skirt had to go. Full skirts often caught on the saddle's pommels during a fall, resulting in many women being dragged by their horses when they could not free themselves. Whereas riding skirts had previously been made by banding together up to 4 yards of cloth so that it would drape in folds over the crooked knee,[197] by the early 1870s such garments were shortened to just long enough to cover the left foot when mounted.[198] This was done:

> By making a seam from the waist to the knee and taking V's out of the cloth at the point where the knee was bent, as well as by large cuts and considerable shaping underneath, the skirt fitted close over the pommels, and both the shape of the knee and thigh were now clearly defined, the skirt hanging straight down without any superfluous material.[199]

These new skirts were called "hunting skirts," much the same way the leaping head was called the "hunting crutch."[200]

Another challenge was the material itself. The fabric needed to withstand the English landscape and climate. It had to be tough enough to survive mud and briars, while also being waterproof and warm to protect against cold and rain because hunting took place between November and April. Women's hunting habits were made of black Melton wool cloth, although navy was sometimes acceptable, or very rarely a dark green.[201] Any other color or ornamentation was firmly discouraged.[202] Though every once in a while a trend started for women to wear scarlet, the traditional "pink" worn by male riders, these were only passing fads and quickly discouraged as too circus-like to be appropriate.[203] The color red was "too bright for general costume," being considered an "ostentatious" shade.[204]

To complement and contribute to such functionality, riding habits were meant to be severely plain, with no embellishment whatsoever. In contrast to the vibrant color and adornment of Victorian women's wear, female riding dress was simplified to the point of austerity: no ribbons, flowers, or fancy whip handles.[205] Whereas in other public settings decoration might signify status and social class, in the hunting field "a gaudy 'get up' (to make use of an expressive common-place) is highly to be condemned, and at once stamps the wearer as a person of inferior taste."[206] Only those who did not know better – or who did, and purposefully ignored sartorial strictures – dressed lavishly. "Bear in mind that the more plainly you are dressed, the quieter your appearance, and the less obtrusive your style, the more ladylike you will appear," advised Nannie O'Donoghue, "and consequently the more to be commended and admired. It is only horsebreakers and women of inferior social standing who seek to attract attention by conspicuous action and costume."[207] Some might complain that all hunting women dressed alike, but in looking alike, those who stood out the most were the ones who rode best, regardless of class, as Catherine Walters had shown. As Mrs. Harry Allbutt (Annie Blood-Smyth, writing under a pseudonym) concluded, "Indeed, it is generally easy anywhere to pick out a woman who means 'going' by the simplicity and plainness of all her appointments."[208] The anonymity provided through similar riding clothes meant that riders were judged more on merit than on fashion.

Equestrian accessories were also improved. Functional gloves and stout boots (rather than delicate slippers) were required after mid-century. A proper riding outfit also included an elastic corset, to give support without overly compressing the lungs and vital organs. To expect a riding habit to fit over a regular corset was "as great a piece of injustice as to expect an artist to paint a picture with broken brushes, or a cook to furnish a banquet without the proper materials."[209] H.D. Nicholl and Co., habit-makers to the Royal Family, even added "elastic and concealed bands" into the bodice of the habit, to allow greater flexibility and "to permit expansion at the chest, even to the extent of several inches."[210] On no account were tight lacing or the use of "riding belts" encouraged.[211] In 1861, John Butler warned of the consequences of such practices: "The first symptom of tight lacing, with strong exercise, is pain in the right side: the second redness at the tip of the nose: the third, debility and loss of flesh; which ultimately ends with rapid consumption."[212] In contrast to regular daywear which required tight and elaborate corsetry, loose lacing was encouraged for breathability and arm movement when riding.[213] Riding corsets were thus made short all around, but especially at the front, or a rider would not be able to put her knee over the pommel without considerable abdominal discomfort.[214]

In addition, petticoats and "white frillies" were strictly discouraged in favor of female breeches or riding trousers to be worn underneath the skirt.[215] A few progressive women had adopted such clothes as early as 1829, but they came into widespread usage around mid-century.[216] Clarke had recommended trousers (cut to the ankle and worn with short boots) in 1857, and by 1868, "riding trousers are now invariably worn," reported a tailoring guide.[217] Trousers were made of the same dark fabric as the habit or of thin, soft Chamois leather. By the 1870s, trousers had been abandoned for masculine breeches (fitted to the knee and worn with top or tall boots).[218] As Captain Pennell Elmhirst wrote, the time to be shocked about ladies' underclothing had passed:

> the feminine breeches-and-boots of Anno Domini 1884 are as little likely to shock the eye of the chance observer, as the mention of them is to bring a blush to the face of the fair wearer herself when ordering them. They are known to exist, in all propriety as in all necessity – and, as far as the requirements of delicacy and possibly even of elegance are concerned,

might well dispense with their dangerous coverings, the cause of these accidents.[219]

Having served throughout the British Empire, where etiquette was less important than safety, Pennell Elmhirst radically suggested that hunting women simply do away with the "dangerous coverings" that entrapped them and move to wearing boots and breeches as men did. Yet few were willing to listen to such clarion calls of common sense.

More needed to be done than just shortening the length and bulk of hunting skirts and improving accessories. Thus, by the 1870s, riding habits evolved with the invention of "safety skirts."[220] The term encompassed numerous variations, almost always patented by individual designers, but it was at its most basic a skirt with an open seam down the back which was supposed to release and free the wearer in case of accident. As *The Ladies' Field* explained,

> the portion [of the skirt] which fitted over the pommels was boldly cut away and the cloth slit down to the bottom of the skirt, the two parts being held together with thin elastic braces. At the knee the skirt was attached by a short gaiter partly over the thigh, the idea being that, should a lady be thrown, there would be nothing to catch and the elastic lacing would break away, freeing the wearer as she fell from the pommels of the saddle.[221]

The Ladies' Field credited this invention to a sporting tailor, Mr. Höhne, in 1884, although Augusta Fane credited Mrs. Arthur of Market Harborough for riding with a safety skirt nearly a decade earlier in 1875.[222] Almost immediately countless other variations were available from sartorial rivals.[223]

Such advances meant that riding skirts no longer were weighted with lead in the hem (to keep them from flapping in the breeze). Nor was it advisable to have them lined with leather (which would not tear in case of a fall). Instead skirts now had elastic or rubber loops sewn into the hem which were slipped over the feet to keep the skirt in place.[224] Though necessary to keep one's skirt from blowing up inopportunely, the loops were troublesome for female riders. Elastics were supposed to break in case of a fall, but they often broke during hard riding when no fall had occurred. "One of the elastic straps in my skirt gave way," wrote Mrs. Edward Kennard, "It caused me infinite trouble; for, do what I could, the skirt no longer kept in its place."[225] However, these elastic loops also made it difficult to dismount (and remount) in the field, and a hasty dismount might cause the elastics to snap.[226] As one sporting novelist recorded, as in real life, when a woman got caught in a bullfinch, she had to climb out, "freeing her feet from the straps of her habit" before she could get back on. "How tiresome those straps are," Nellie, the character, complained.[227]

Worse than troublesome or tiresome, these inventions could be more dangerous than helpful. Elastic loops could be just as unsafe as bulky skirts if they did not break away in case of a fall. After his wife had a serious accident caused by her elastics,

Fig. 53.—Off side of The Hayes' Safety Skirt.

Fig. 55.—Apron skirt open for mounting.

Figure 3.4 "Off side of The Hayes' Safety Skirt" (Fig. 53) and "Apron Skirt open for mounting" (Fig. 55), from Alice Hayes' *The Horsewoman*, pages 93 and 97: Early riding habits were called "real murderous things," but were new designs any better? Rider and author Alice Hayes condemned some late nineteenth-century innovations as "death-traps." By the 1870s, the first "safety skirts" had appeared, basically a skirt with an open seam down the back which was supposed to release and free the wearer in case of accident, and, by the 1890s, an "apron" skirt was also popular with sidesaddle riders. Hayes created (and patented) her own version of a safety skirt. Her two main objectives were "absolute safety" and "decent covering" so that it could be worn appropriately whether on or off the horse.
Credit: Collection of the author.

one Master of Foxhounds found that he could put the entire weight of his 14 stone (nearly 200 pounds) on the loops "for some time" before they broke.[228] Even so-called "safety skirts" were no help; one maker patented a skirt with "glove-like fingers, which were made to fit over the upper crutch and the leaping head!" This hideous garment was rightly called a "death-trap."[229] Such inventions harkened back to the days of sidesaddles that included a leather "seat-belt" to tie women onto the saddle (see Figure 1.5); now, a woman might be tied to the saddle by her skirt at a time when the whole point of sidesaddle riding was to allow a woman to free herself in case of a fall. Thus, women could be injured by the very inventions that were supposed to protect them and save their lives.

By the 1890s, there were three main kinds of safety skirts: the skirt with patent fasteners, the half-apron skirt, and the apron skirt (Figure 3.4).[230] At least a decade previously, all lacings and fastenings had been done away with, so that the skirt had become an "apron," which fastened around the waist and provided a fig-leaf covering over breeches and top boots. This was deemed "the greatest of all changes … and, indeed, ceased to be a skirt at all."[231] The "apron skirt" came onto the market in the mid-1890s and was popular among hunting women before the turn of the century, as characters in sporting novels frequently wore them.[232] They were literally an "apron" covering that appeared like a skirt when mounted, but which could easily come away (and leave a woman in her acceptable dark breeches) in case of a fall. The garment was created by doing away with all the lacings, fastenings, and fabric of a regular safety skirt, thus cutting out the entire bottom or underside of the skirt, and using a single gaiter or elastic loop around the thigh to keep it in place.[233]

This was not to say that the apron skirt was immediately accepted. Some objected to its scantiness, and there were the obvious issues of its appearance when not on horseback.[234] "My habit is not a habit," a character in a sporting novel confessed, "it is a mere apology."[235] But the garment was admittedly popular, as one rider noted, having tried multiple safety habits and experiencing being "hung up both on the near and the off side," she wrote, "but since I took to the apron I have had no more danglings."[236] This sartorial immodesty (in the eyes of some) was well worth such safety. As many pointed out, "better a live lady in breeches than a dead one in a habit."[237] It might be embarrassing to stand in a field and watch one's horse fly away with a skirt clinging to the pommels, but it was undoubtedly worse to be dragged, injured, or killed.

These changes in riding habits had been heartily endorsed and adopted by female riders earlier than the 1880s. As *Baily's Magazine* recorded in 1878,

> Ladies who hunt have *emancipated themselves* by abandoning the dangerous long habit, which caused many accidents, and have adopted shorter skirts and Napoleon boots, have thrown away their chignons and head incumbrances, and develop the natural beauty of the head, and wear a little round pot-hat.[238]

Such garments fostered a new appreciation for merit in sport. Without expensive garments to distinguish them, women riders had to be judged on the basis of their skills rather than their wealth or appearance. Yet, at home in Britain, women wearing breeches – and only breeches – was still considered unacceptable. This was an interesting paradox, because if a safety skirt came away in a fall, a woman was left stranded in nothing but her breeches.[239] This happened frequently (luckily) and was depicted often, but, for women, wearing *only* breeches was still not considered respectable, as portrayed by sporting author and illustrator Georgina Bowers (Figure 3.5). The change that would make such clothing acceptable would have to come from elsewhere, and it did.

The demand for better and safer riding clothes increased as more women took up equestrian activities, and the sport broadened as a whole. The upside of such demand for new riding clothes was that it created competition for the best and

Figure 3.5 "Give Me My Skirt," from G. Bowers, *Mr. Crop's Harriers* (London: Day and Son, 1891), 25: Sartorial immodesty (in the eyes of some) was well worth such safety. "Better a live lady in breeches than a dead one in a habit," or as Nannie O'Donoghue advised, "Better be a live dog than a dead lion." It might be embarrassing to stand in a field and watch one's horse fly away with a skirt clinging to the pommels, but it was undoubtedly worse to be dragged, injured, or killed.
Credit: Collection of the author.

safest product – hence the numerous varieties of safety skirts. It also created a market for second-hand clothing, so that lesser well-off women could peruse sporting magazines for lightly used habits which allowed less wealthy women from lower classes to ride and hunt. As Nannie O'Donoghue directed,

> Look carefully over the columns of the various leading journals which contain an "exchange and mart," and you will be almost certain to see some advertisements of riding habits made by high-class makers and only worn a few times – occasionally never worn at all ... I have known one or two ladies with very moderate dress allowances who secured really excellent riding habits in this way.[240]

A few alterations would thus secure a much cheaper yet near-custom riding habit for a woman of lesser means. Alternately, O'Donoghue also advised women that they might borrow a habit from a friend and copy the pattern themselves.[241] These thrifty suggestions enabled women without deep pockets to participate in horse sports.

Women popularized equestrianism through their participation, gained increased independence and authority for themselves by doing so, and, as a result, forced the evolution not only of sporting clothing but of social values as well. As *The Ladies' Field* noted,

> Doubtless the cause of this evolution in the riding-skirt, dating from the eighties, was due to the fact that the fascinations of sport were being more generally appreciated by the fair equestriennes, who, not content with the monotony of the Row, were ambitious of extending their practice in horsemanship from the Park to the hunting-field. The reduction in railway rates for boxing and the facilities for travelling to hunting centres hitherto almost out of reach (such as Exmoor) gave great encouragement to the sport, of which ladies were not slow in availing themselves, and they settled down to hunting regularly in a business-like spirit and made their arrangements accordingly.[242]

This "business-like spirit" spoke to the strong, independent, and respectable femininity cultivated by these women, forcing positive revisions and new constructions of gender ideals during the late Victorian era. By the late nineteenth century, female riders were literally "wearing the breeches" (albeit beneath a skirt), and they had made their garments and conduct both acceptable and respectable.

A Woman's Province

Female equestrians made great strides in the hunting field after the mid-nineteenth century. "She has invaded the realms of sport," concluded *Baily's Magazine* in 1881, "and if she has not absolutely annexed them, she has made some brilliant conquests in this special domain of the greater man."[243] British women were riding in ever increasing numbers: by 1895, American visitor Caspar Whitney estimated that they were a major component of the nearly 50,000 people riding to hounds in England every week.[244] This estimate did not include those following harrier packs, so the figure was likely much higher.

This participation did not jeopardize a woman's femininity, but rather added to it by encouraging and developing the qualities of sympathy, confidence, and self-possession through riding. Nor was a female rider "unsexed" by sport or moving through these formerly masculine spaces. "The hunting-field is now almost as much a woman's province as the ball room or a box at Her Majesty's Theatre …" it was noted.[245] Sport was not feminized, but femininity could be achieved and demonstrated through sport. By their serious commitment and the advancing of their own skills, British women not only established new positions

Figure 3.6 "England," fox hunting postcard, early twentieth century: A hunting woman leads her fellow sportsmen over a fence as they follow the hounds on this undated but patriotic postcard. Victorian women had made riding and hunting their own, and in doing so, they had not only transformed gender ideals, but also inspired new conceptions of a national identity based on horse sports. As early as 1867, a commentator in *Baily's Magazine* wrote, "we frankly and freely acknowledge, that but for their sanction and support, fox hunting would not now be what it is – the sport of the nation."
Credit: Collection of the author.

and freedoms, but also furthered hunting as a sport by "civilizing" and modernizing its practice. "I believe that the more ladies who hunt the better it is for the sport ...," wrote Underhill,[246] while others noted how well women were going: "forward among them all, depending upon none of them, but riding each her own line easily, quietly, and successfully."[247]

Women had made riding and hunting their own, and in doing so, they had not only transformed traditional gender ideals, but also inspired new ideas about a modern national identity based on horse sports (Figure 3.6). As early as 1867, a commentator in *Baily's Magazine* wrote, "we frankly and freely acknowledge, that but for their sanction and support, fox-hunting would not now be what it is – the sport of the nation."[248] By mid-century, few riding manuals (for either sex) encouraged the Continental style of *haute école*, whereas fox hunting in the British style was socially and culturally necessary for women in contributing to the larger national character of sporting strength and respectable vigor. As Henderson noted,

It [equestrianism] is the one accomplishment in which they [British women] as far surpass the women of all other countries in the world as they outvie them in personal beauty. A German or French woman possibly may hold her own with an Englishwoman in a ball room or a box at the opera; but put her on horseback, and take her to the covert side, she is "not in it" with her English rivals.[249]

The idea of Britain as an "imagined community" of sportsmen and women was both pervasive and compelling. Britain's "ladies on horseback" were not a scandalous disgrace to their country, but rather a national bulwark against Continental effeminacy and weakness. The British cavalry and forward riding style might have defeated Napoleon, but, by the end of the century, it was British horsewomen who – as exemplars and mothers of the next generation – would triumph over a new empire.

Despite all they had gained, could women riders truly be independent in the hunting field if they continued to ride sidesaddle? Were they actually equal in the name of sport, being aside rather than astride? Despite the innovations in the sidesaddle and the general emancipation it gave women for hunting, it did not allow women to be truly equal in the field. As Whyte-Melville observed in 1875, "No man, till he has tried the experiment, can conceive how awkward and powerless one feels in a lady's seat."[250] Hampered by both saddle and skirt, women simply could not be as efficient as men.[251] As Alice Hayes wrote,

> An experienced hunting woman tells me that women should be as useful in the field as men; but I fear that is impossible, for we cannot get on and off our horses as easily as men, to render prompt help in cases of emergency; hold open a gate on a windy day, or perform the numerous kindly acts which fall to the lot of the mere male. Besides, however active and well-intentioned we may be, we are hampered by our dress, and still more so by the want of it, in the case of an apron skirt.[252]

While *Baily's Magazine* might conclude in 1881 that, "It is in the hunting field, however, that emancipated woman has perhaps achieved her most solid and enduring victories," female equestrians still had much further to go.[253] Hunting women might argue that they were "not made of sugar, to melt at the first drop of rain,"[254] but it was also true that many "ladies are no real good at galloping a horse. They never can send them along like a man, with a leg on either side", as Bay Middleton had complained.[255] Captain Pennell Elmhirst had decried the sidesaddle as early as 1884, bewailing "the cramped and unnatural position invented in deference to the overwrought sensitiveness of [our] grandmothers or grandfathers,"[256] but there was simply no other alternative for women that was socially accepted in Britain at this time.

Despite the innovations and advances women made for themselves through hunting, riding sidesaddle still remained dangerous, and injuries and accidents accumulated as the century wore on. Though women had gained a measure of egality through riding and furthered a certain emancipation for themselves through sport, true equality was elusive. As Lady Mabel Howard admitted, by the turn of the twentieth century, women had advanced through many sports and games, "but in hunting alone are they really successful, and can equal, and even on occasions surpass, men, in spite of the impediments of habits, pommels, and a one-sided balance."[257] Real equality could only come when women rode astride. British women had gone as far as they could go riding sidesaddle, which was very far indeed. To succeed further, they would need to contemplate the unthinkable – riding astride like a man.

Notes

1. The furor over "Anonyma," as she was called, appeared in James Matthew Higgins, *The Times* (London), Thursday, July 3, 1862, 12.
2. "A Woman of No Importance" [Amy Charlotte Berwicke Menzies], *Further Indiscretions* (New York: E.P. Dutton and Company, 1918), 306–307.
3. Alfred Austin, *The Season: A Satire* (London: George Manwaring, 1861), 28.
4. Augusta Fane, *Chit-chat* (London: Thornton, Butterworth, Limited, 1926), 76; Henry Blyth, *Skittles, The Last Victorian Courtesan: The Life and Times of Catherine Walters* (London: Rupert Hart-Davis, 1970), 17.
5. Trevor Fisher, *Prostitution and the Victorians* (New York: St. Martin's Press, 1997). For the more modern fictional take, see Barbara Cartland, *The Pretty Horse Breakers* (London: Hutchinson, 1971).
6. William Brough and Andrew Halliday, "*The Pretty Horsebreaker: An Apropos Sketch, in One Act*" (London: Thomas Hailes Lacy, 1861). According to printed notes, the sketch was first performed at the Adelphi Theatre, London.
7. "Charlie Thornhill; or, The Dunce of the Family," *Baily's Magazine of Sports and Pastimes*, Volume 5 (August 1862), 69.
8. Nicholas Wiseman, *Horse Training upon New Principles, Ladies' Horsemanship, and Tight Lacing* (London: W. Clowes and Sons, 1852), 30.
9. Cyril Pearl, *The Girl with the Swansdown Seat* (Indianapolis: The Bobbs-Merrill Company, Inc., 1955), 129.
10. "The Royal Academy and Water-color Societies," *Blackwood's Edinburgh Magazine*, Volume 90 (August 1861), 211.
11. Blyth, 57.
12. Guy Paget, *Rum'uns to Follow: Memories of Seventy Years in the Shires, by a Melton Roughrider* (London: Country Life, Ltd., 1934), 70.
13. Paget (1934), 72. See also F. Palliser De Costobadie, *Annals of the Billesdon Hunt (Mr. Fernie's), 1856-1913* (London: Chapman and Hall, Limited, 1914), 123. In this latter account, she is said to have remarked that "a certain portion of her anatomy would probably be of much the same hue as the [cherry ribbon] she wore round her neck."
14. Guy Paget, *Bad'Uns To Beat* (London: Collins, 1936), 125–126.
15. Her exact words were not recorded, but the meaning and intent were undoubtedly clear, and many similar variations of her reply exist. The fullest account is in "A Woman of No Importance" (1918), 304–307.

16 Augusta Fane fully recounts this episode in *Chit-chat*, 74–75.
17 Patrick Jackson, "'Skittles' and the Marquis: A Victorian Love Affair," *History Today*, 45.12 (December 1995), 49. See also Katie Hickman, *Courtesans: Money, Sex, and Fame in the Nineteenth Century* (New York: Perennial, 2004), 282.
18 Costobadie, 23–24. Costobadie had exclusive access to Tailby's private hunting diaries, in which he detailed records of each day's hunting over his 22 years as Master (1856–1878). See also Colin B. Ellis, *Leicestershire and the Quorn Hunt* (Leicester: Edgar Backus, 1951), 110.
19 Costobadie, 12.
20 Paget (1934), 70–71.
21 "Masters of Foxhounds," *Baily's Magazine of Sports and Pastimes*, Volume 2 (January 1861), 177.
22 Ellis, 153.
23 Henry Mayhew, *London Labour and London Poor*, Volume III (London: Griffin, Bohn, and Company, 1861), 360.
24 T.C. Barker, "The Delayed Decline of the Horse in the 20th Century," in F.M.L. Thompson (ed.), *Horses in European Economic History: A Preliminary Canter* (Reading: The British Agricultural History Society, 1983), 102. See F.M.L. Thompson, "Nineteenth-Century Horse Sense," *The Economic History Review*, 29.1 (February 1976), 60–81.
25 Barker, 102.
26 Keith Chivers, "The Supply of Horses in Great Britain in the Nineteenth Century," in F.M.L. Thompson (ed.), *Horses in European Economic History: A Preliminary Canter* (Reading: The British Agricultural History Society, 1983), 59.
27 Chivers, 66.
28 Anthony Trollope, *Hunting Sketches* (London: Chapman and Hall, 1865), 30.
29 Mrs. Power O'Donoghue, *(The Common Sense of Riding) Riding for Ladies, with Hints on the Stable* (London: W. Thacker and Co., 1887), 146, 167.
30 H.G. [Henry George] English, *The Art of Riding* (London: Simpkin, Marshall, Hamilton, Kent & Co., Limited, 1891), 128.
31 "Impecuniosus," *Unasked Advice: A Series of Articles on Horses and Hunting, Reprinted from "The Field"* (London: Horace Cox, 1872), 16.
32 Alice M. Hayes, *The Horsewoman: A Practical Guide to Side-Saddle Riding* (London: Hurst and Blackett, Limited, 1903), 16.
33 "Saddle Bars and Stirrups: Safety and Otherwise," *Baily's Magazine of Sports and Pastimes*, Volume 71 (March 1899), 186–189. Between May and June 1883, eight new patents for saddle bars alone had been granted.
34 Hayes (1903), 16–17, 30–31.
35 Fane, 126.
36 Frederick Smeeton Williams, *Our Iron Roads: Their History, Construction and Administration* (London: Bemrose & Sons, 1883), 393.
37 "Vieille Moustache" [Robert Henderson], *The Barb and the Bridle* (London: The "Queen" Office, 1874), 134. See also Fox Russell, *Cross Country Reminiscences* (London: Remington and Co. Publishers, 1887), 24–25. For Henderson's identity, see Alison Matthews David, "Elegant Amazons: Victorian Riding Habits and the Fashionable Horsewoman," *Victorian Literature and Culture*, 30.1 (2002), 184.
38 Russell, 24.
39 "The Science of Fox-hunting," *Baily's Magazine of Sports and Pastimes*, Volume 14 (February 1868), 229.
40 Mrs. [Nannie Lambert] Power O'Donoghue, *Ladies on Horseback* (London: W. H. Allen, 1881), 6.

41 Jonathan Finch, "'Grass, Grass, Grass': Hunting and the Creation of the Modern Landscape," *Landscapes*, 5.2 (2004), 45.
42 John Butler, *The Horse; and How to Ride Him: A Treatise on the Art of Riding and Leaping* (London: Baily Brothers, 1861), 34.
43 Finch, 46.
44 Fane, 122.
45 "Borderer," "Jumping Powder," *Baily's Magazine of Sports and Pastimes*, Volume 43 (December 1884), 204–211.
46 O'Donoghue (1881), 37.
47 See the guidelines for the Tokyo 2020 Equestrian Events: https://tokyo2020.org/en/sports/equestrian/.
48 Captain Pennell Elmhirst, *The Best Season on Record* (London: G. Routledge & Sons, 1893), 23.
49 "Wire in the Hunting Field," *Country Life Magazine* (September 18, 1897), 286.
50 Ellis, 102. See also Finch, 49; and De Costobadie, 112–113.
51 "A Man from the Next Country," *Baily's Magazine of Sports and Pastimes*, Volume 23 (April 1873), 215.
52 "Wire in the Hunting Field," *Country Life Magazine* (September 18, 1897), 286.
53 Mrs. Edward Kennard, *A Real Good Thing* (London: F.V. White, 1888), 81.
54 Sir Humphrey F. De Trafford, Bart., *The Horses of the British Empire* (London: Walter Southwood and Co., Limited, 1907), 204.
55 W.A. [William Alexander] Kerr, *Riding for Ladies* (London: George Bell and Sons, 1891), 44. See also O'Donoghue (1881), 148.
56 Russell, 6–7.
57 George F. Underhill, *A Century of English Fox-Hunting* (London: R.A. Everett and Co., 1900), 293.
58 Hayes (1903), 352.
59 Mrs. Philip Martineau, *Reminisces of Horses and Hunting, by A Fox-Hunting Woman* (London: Ernest Benn Limited, 1930), 34.
60 Martineau, 8–9.
61 Paget (1934), 13.
62 Mrs. J. Stirling Clarke, *The Ladies' Equestrian Guide; or, The Habit and the Horse: A Treatise on Female Equitation* (London: Day and Son, 1857), 211, 212.
63 "Impecuniosus," *Unasked Advice* (London: Horace Cox, 1872); and "Vieille Moustache," *The Barb and the Bridle* (London: The "Queen" Newspaper Office, 1874).
64 Samuel Sidney, *The Book of the Horse* (London: Cassell and Company, Limited, 1893), 5. See also Ernest Clarke, revised by Julian Lock, "Sidney [formerly Solomon], Samuel (1813–1883), writer on agriculture," *Oxford Dictionary of National Biography*, from https://www-oxforddnb-com.proxyau.wrlc.org/view/10.1093/ref:odnb/9780198614128.001.0001/odnb-9780198614128-e-25526.
65 Sidney, 456.
66 Sidney, 402.
67 The first edition of *Ladies on Horseback* appeared in 1881 (London: W.H. Allen & Co.); a third edition in 1889 (London: W.H. Allen & Co.); a new and revised edition in 1891 (London: W.H. Allen & Co.); and a fifth and revised edition in 1896 (London: J. Shiells & Co.).
68 Olga E. Lockley, *Nannie Lambert Power O'Donoghue, A Biography* (Preston: The Bee Press, 2001), 50–52. The first edition of *Riding for Ladies* appeared in 1887 (London: W. Thacker & Co.), with a second edition printed in 1905 (London: W. Thacker & Co.).

69 W.A. Kerr, *Riding for Ladies* (London: George Bell and Sons, 1891); Mrs. Harry Allbutt [Annie Blood-Smyth], *Hints to Horsewomen* (London: Horace Cox, 1893); Alice Hayes, *The Horsewoman: A Practical Guide to Sidesaddle Riding* (London: W. Thacker & Co., 1893).
70 A second revised and enlarged edition was published in 1903 (London: Hurst and Blackett), and a third revised and enlarged edition in 1910 (London: Hurst and Blackett).
71 M. Horace Hayes, *Riding: On the Flat and Across Country* (London: W. Thacker and Co., 1881), Chapter VI, 147–183.
72 Hayes (1893), 189–264. See also Hayes (1903), vii, 166, 458–9.
73 Hayes (1903), vii.
74 Eva Christy, *Side-Saddle Riding: A Practical Handbook for Horsewomen* (London: Vinton and Co., 1899; London: Vinton & Co., 1901); *Modern Side-Saddle Riding: A Practical Handbook for Horsewomen* (London: Vinton and Co., 1907).
75 O'Donoghue (1881), 13.
76 Lockley, 111.
77 English, 42.
78 "A Woman of No Importance" (1918), 302.
79 Samuel Sidney, *The Book of the Horse* (London: Cassell, Petter & Galpin, Limited, 1875), 316.
80 "A Woman of No Importance" (1918), 307.
81 Lady Violet Greville, *Ladies in the Field: Sketches of Sport* (New York: D. Appleton and Company, 1894), 40. This was published in London the same year by Ward & Downey.
82 O'Donoghue (1887), 182–183.
83 Greville, 13.
84 O'Donoghue (1881), 65; Sidney (1875), 351.
85 "Impecuniosus," 24.
86 "Vieille Moustache," 28.
87 Mrs. [R.M.] Burn, "Fox-hunting," *The Sportswoman's Library*, Volume I, Frances E. Slaughter (ed.), (Westminster: Archibald Constable and Co., 1898), 41.
88 Samuel Beeton, *Family Etiquette* (London: Ward, Lock, and Tyler, 1876), 71.
89 Sidney (1875), 343.
90 O'Donoghue (1881), 8.
91 O'Donoghue (1887), 30.
92 O'Donoghue (1881), 25.
93 Beeton, 72.
94 Sidney (1875), 361.
95 Mary Elizabeth Braddon, *Aurora Floyd* (Oxford: Oxford University Press, 2009), 138. The novel was first published in 1863.
96 Emelyne Godfrey, *Femininity, Crime and Self-Defense in Victorian Literature and Society* (New York: Palgrave Macmillan, 2012), 84.
97 O'Donoghue (1881), 122.
98 O'Donoghue (1887), 6–7.
99 Christy (1899), 10.
100 Christy (1899), 73. See page 75 in 1907 edition.
101 Christy (1899), 81.
102 Christy (1899), 81. See page 84 in 1907 edition.
103 Christy (1899), 72.
104 Burn, 22.
105 "Hunting in the Shires," *The Ladies' Field*, Volume 7 (December 30, 1899), 101.

106 "Ladies in the Hunting Field," *Baily's Magazine of Sports and Pastimes*, Volume 43 (March 1885), 397.
107 G. J. Whyte-Melville, *Riding Recollections* (London: Chapman and Hall, 1878), 117–118. See also Sidney (1875), 436.
108 "Country Quarters, The Cheltenham Staghounds," *Baily's Magazine of Sports and Pastimes*, Volume 23 (January 1873), 22.
109 "Country Quarters, The Vale of the White Horse," *Baily's Magazine of Sports and Pastimes*, Volume 23 (February 1873), 72.
110 T.F. Dale, *Fox-Hunting in the Shires* (London: Grant Richards, 1903), 277.
111 Whyte-Melville (1878), 118.
112 O'Donoghue (1881), 80, 101.
113 O'Donoghue (1881), 101.
114 O'Donoghue (1887), 187.
115 O'Donoghue (1887), 226–227.
116 Hayes (1903), 373–374.
117 Burn, 47. See also Hayes, (1903), 378; and "Hunting in the Shires," *The Ladies' Field*, Volume 8 (January 20, 1900), 237.
118 Greville, 47.
119 Greville, 50.
120 Captain Pennell Elmhirst, *The Best of the Fun, 1891-1897* (London: Chatto and Windus, 1903), 109.
121 Dale, 274.
122 Hayes (1903), 374.
123 Mrs. Edward Kennard, *The Hunting Girl* (F.V. White and Co., 1893), 164–165.
124 "Au Fait," *Social Observances: A Series of Essays on Practical Etiquette* (London: Frederick Warne and Co., 1896), 172; *Routledge's Manual of Etiquette* (London: George Routledge and Sons, 1860), 50.
125 Captain Pennell Elmhirst, *The Cream of Leicestershire* (London: George Routledge and Sons, 1883), 234. Italics mine. Belle Beach added: "When a woman hunts she enters a masculine field of sport, and in the hunting-field she is meeting men on their own ground and on even terms. In the hunting-field, therefore, a woman must expect to take her chances with the men, and she is not entitled to that courtesy and deference which she may expect on other occasions." See Belle Beach, *Riding and Driving for Women* (New York: Charles Scribner's Sons, 1912), 58.
126 Pennell Elmhirst (1883), 58–59.
127 Mrs. Edward Kennard, *The Right Sort, A Romance of the Shires* (London: Ward, Lock, and Co., 1886), 318.
128 Burn, 30.
129 Burn, 30.
130 Leonard Cooper, *R.S. Surtees* (London: Arthur Blake, Ltd., 1952), 34–35.
131 For an example of hunting costs for a later period, see "The Cost of Hunting," *The Ladies' Field*, The Ladies' Field Hunting Supplement, Volume 63 (October 4, 1913), 2.
132 *The Ladies' Field*, Volume 32 (January 20, 1905), 284. Italics mine.
133 Charles Richardson, *The Complete Foxhunter* (London: Methuen and Co., 1908), 101.
134 G.F. Underhill, *The Master of Hounds* (London: Grant Richards, 1903), 134.
135 Underhill (1903), 136.
136 Hayes (1903), 306–307.
137 Hayes (1903), 314.
138 John Welcome, *The Sporting Empress: The Story of Elizabeth of Austria and Bay Middleton* (London: Michael Joseph, 1975), 13.

139 Welcome, 73–74.
140 Welcome, 45.
141 Nannie O'Donoghue espoused such a view in *Ladies on Horseback* (1881). John Welcome argued this more recently in his 1975 biography, *The Sporting Empress,* as does Andrew Sinclair in *Death by Fame: Life of Elizabeth, Empress of Austria* (New York: St. Martin's 1999). See also Brigitte Hamann's *The Reluctant Empress* (New York: Knopf, 1986), translated from the German by Ruth Hein, and Katerina von Burg, *Elisabeth of Austria: A Life Misunderstood* (Windsor: Windsor Publishing, 1995).
142 Underhill (1900), 291–292.
143 Sinclair, 21 and 108.
144 Raymond Carr, *English Fox Hunting* (London: Weidenfeld and Nicholson, 1986) 174; David C. Itzkowitz, *Peculiar Privilege: A Social History of English Foxhunting, 1753-1885* (Hassocks, Sussex: The Harvester Press Limited, 1977), 56.
145 Sinclair, 72; Clara Tschudi, *Elizabeth, Empress of Austria and Queen of Hungary,* trans. E.M. Cope (London: Swan Sonnenschein and Co., 1901), 215.
146 Welcome, 13; Sinclair, 21.
147 Mrs. Edward Kennard, *The Catch of the County* (London: F.V. White, 1895).
148 Welcome, 49.
149 Welcome, 50.
150 Sinclair, 86; Jane Ridley, *Fox Hunting* (London: Collins, 1990), 88.
151 See entry for Sunday, March 12, 1876, accessed via *Queen Victoria's Journals* database. See also entries for Tuesday, March 9, 1880 and Monday, March 6, 1882.
152 Martin Haller, *Sisi: Die Kaiserin im Sattel* (Vienna: Morawa Lesezirkel, 2018), 79; H.O. Nethercote, *The Pytchley Hunt: Past and Present* (London: S. Low, Marston, Searle, & Rivington, 1888), 202.
153 Nethercote, 202.
154 Frederic Boase, *Modern English Biography*, Volume II (Truro: Netherton and Worth, 1897), 868.
155 Sinclair, 84.
156 Welcome, 60.
157 Paget (1934), 75.
158 Welcome, 96.
159 Lady Apsley, *Bridleways Through History* (London: Hutchinson and Co., 1948), 354; Welcome, 62 and 88.
160 M. Horace Hayes, *Among Men and Horses* (London: T. Fisher Unwin, 1894), 326.
161 "The Biography of a Huntsman," *Baily's Magazine of Sports and Pastimes,* Volume 30 (June 1877), 266.
162 "A Woman of No Importance" [Amy Charlotte Berwicke Menzies], *Memories Discreet and Indiscreet* (London: Herbert Jenkins Limited, 1917), 129.
163 Welcome, 92.
164 Underhill (1900), 290.
165 Welcome, 93–94.
166 Welcome, 95.
167 Welcome, 182–183.
168 "Women in the Hunting Field, 1907-8," *The Ladies' Field,* Volume 41 (May 2, 1908), 334.
169 O'Donoghue (1881), 28; O'Donoghue, (1887), 7.
170 Sidney (1893), 319–320.
171 Advert for Vigor & Co's Hercules Horse-Action Saddle (London: Dalziel & Co, 1894): http://www.bl.uk/onlinegallery/onlineex/evancoll/a/014eva000000000u07556000.html. For *Titanic* references, see Lawrence Beesley, *The Loss of the SS. Titanic* (Boston:

Houghton Mifflin, 1912), 12–13. See Getty Images, "Gymnasium, Titanic," for the sidesaddle machine (pommel visible behind pillar): https://www.gettyimages.com/detail/news-photo/photograph-of-the-gymnasium-on-the-titanic-passengers-could-news-photo/105870786.
172 O'Donoghue (1881), 102.
173 Helen C. Black, *Notable Women Authors of the Day* (London: Maclaren and Company, 1906), 180.
174 Martineau, 45.
175 Hilda Nelson, *The Great Horsewomen of the 19th Century Circus* (Franktown, VA: Xenophon Press, 2015), 98–99.
176 Nelson, 106.
177 Paget (1934), 7.
178 Paget (1934), 7.
179 Paget (1934), 57.
180 Paget (1934), 109.
181 Pennell Elmhirst (1903), 18.
182 Paget (1934), 57.
183 O'Donoghue (1881), 108, 113, 114.
184 O'Donoghue (1881), see the Correspondence section, 282.
185 O'Donoghue (1881), 75.
186 O'Donoghue (1887), 22.
187 Lockley, 85.
188 Lockley, 88.
189 Paget (1934), 72.
190 Underhill (1903), 233.
191 "Our Van," *Baily's Magazine of Sports and Pastimes*, Volume 42 (February 1884), 59.
192 Mrs. Edward Kennard, *Straight as a Die* (London: F.V. White, 1887), 56–57. This was first published in 1885.
193 "Our Van," *Baily's Magazine of Sports and Pastimes*, Volume 42 (February 1884), 59.
194 Sidney (1875), 345.
195 Sidney (1875), 346. O'Donoghue seconded Sidney's opinion, writing that "a lady dressed for riding ought to be able *when* dressed to take down or put up her hair, draw off her boots and put them on again, and walk a mile or two *with* them on, if required, without feeling any desire whatever to remove them after the exercise." See O'Donoghue, (1887), 183–184.
196 Sidney (1875), 318, 346.
197 "The Evolution of the Riding Habit," *The Ladies' Field*, Volume 44 (January 2, 1909), 216.
198 "Impecuniosus," 20.
199 "The Evolution of the Riding Habit," *The Ladies' Field*, Volume 44 (January 2, 1909), 216.
200 "Vieille Moustache," 124.
201 "Hunting Dress, Ancient and Modern," *Baily's Magazine of Sports and Pastimes*, Volume 73 (January 1900), 20.
202 "Hunting Dress, Ancient and Modern," *Baily's Magazine of Sports and Pastimes*, Volume 73 (January 1900), 20.
203 "Vieille Moustache," 95.
204 W. and G. Audsley, *Taste versus Fashionable Colours: A Manual for Ladies, on Colour in Dress* (London: Longman, Green, Longman, Roberts, & Green, 1863), 33 and 47.
205 Alison L. Goodrum, "A Severity of Plainness: The Culture of Female Riding Dress in America during the 1920s and 1930s," *Annals of Leisure Research*, 15.1 (2012), 87–105.

206 O'Donoghue (1881), 15; O'Donoghue (1887), 62.
207 O'Donoghue (1887), 62.
208 Allbutt, 30. For the pseudonym, see James A. Garland, *The Private Stable* (Boston: Little, Brown, and Company, 1903), 233.
209 O'Donoghue (1887), 51.
210 H.J. and D. Nicholl, *A Lady's Horse: With a Few Words on the Proper Costume for Riding, Walking, Dining* (London: J. Tallis, 1859), 16.
211 O'Donoghue (1887), 52, 57; also Sidney (1875), 321; Hayes (1881), 178.
212 Butler, 55.
213 Mandy Barrington, *Stays and Corsets: Historical Patterns Translated for the Modern Body* (New York: Focal Press, 2016), 220–222.
214 Mrs. Elizabeth Karr, *The American Horsewoman* (Boston: Houghton Mifflin and Company, 1884), 60–61.
215 Paget (1934), 72.
216 "Riding Habits, Past and Present," *The Ladies' Field*, Volume 51 (October 8, 1910), 197.
217 Clarke, 22; Edward Minister and Son, *The Gazette of Fashion and Cutting-Room Companion* (London: Simpkin, Marshall, and Co.), Volume XXII (April 1, 1868), quote on 96, 88.
218 T.H. Holding, *Ladies' Cutting Made Easy* (London: T.H. Holding, 1885), 38.
219 Pennell Elmhirst (1884), 193.
220 "Impecuniosus," 20. See also Alexander Mackay-Smith, et al., *Man and the Horse: An Illustrated History of Equestrian Apparel* (New York: Simon and Schuster, 1984), 67.
221 "The Evolution of the Riding Habit," *The Ladies' Field*, Volume 44 (January 2, 1909), 216.
222 Fane, 136.
223 "Saunters through the Shops, At Skinner's," *The Ladies' Field*, Volume 39 (October 5, 1907), unpaginated.
224 O'Donoghue (1887), 34–35; Sidney (1875), 323.
225 Mrs. Edward Kennard, *Sporting Tales* (London: F.V. White, 1896), 53.
226 Mrs. Edward Kennard, *The Right Sort: A Romance of the Shires* (London: Ward, Lock, and Co., 1886), 321.
227 Mrs. Robert Jocelyn, *The Criton Hunt Mystery* (London: Hurst and Blackett, Limited, 1890), 97–98.
228 "Our Van," *Baily's Magazine of Sports and Pastimes*, Volume 42 (February 1884), 59.
229 "Our Van," *Baily's Magazine of Sports and Pastimes*, Volume 42 (February 1884), 59.
230 Belle Beach, *Riding and Driving for Women* (New York: Charles Scribner's Sons, 1912), 108. See also "Riding Habits, Past and Present," *The Ladies' Field*, Volume 51 (October 8, 1910), 197.
231 "Duke of Beaufort's Hounds," *The Ladies' Field*, Volume 31 (November 11, 1905), 374.
232 Mrs. Edward Kennard, *At the Tail of the Hounds* (London: F.V. White and Co., 1897), 52.
233 "The Evolution of the Riding Habit," *The Ladies' Field*, Volume 44 (January 2, 1909), 216.
234 Underhill (1900), 299–300.
235 Mrs. Robert Jocelyn, *A Dangerous Brute* (London: Hutchinson and Co., 1895), 88.
236 Burn, 39.
237 Ellis, 113.
238 "The Female Slave," *Baily's Magazine of Sports and Pastimes*, Volume 32 (July 1878), 200. Italics mine.

239 *The Ladies' Field*, "Swears and Wells, Ltd., Safety Riding Skirt," Volume 25 (March 19, 1904), advertisement. See also, "Manias Safety Habits for Hunting, Park Riding," Volume 25 (March 19, 1904), xxxv.
240 O'Donoghue (1887), 194 195.
241 O'Donoghue (1887), 195–196.
242 "The Evolution of the Riding Habit," *The Ladies' Field*, Volume 44 (January 2, 1909), 216.
243 "Habited Habitués of Irish Hunting Grounds," *Baily's Magazine of Sports and Pastimes*, Volume 37 (May 1881), 131–132.
244 Caspar A. Whitney, *A Sporting Pilgrimage* (New York: Harper and Brothers, 1895), 26.
245 "Habited Habitués of Irish Hunting Grounds," *Baily's Magazine of Sports and Pastimes*, Volume 37 (May 1881), 131–132.
246 Underhill (1903), 18.
247 Pennell Elmhirst (1903), 33.
248 "The First of November," *Baily's Magazine of Sports and Pastimes*, Volume 14 (November 1867), 83.
249 "Vieille Moustache," 2.
250 Whyte-Melville (1878), 116. The first edition was published in 1875.
251 Hayes (1903), 176.
252 Hayes (1903), 176.
253 "Habited Habitués of Irish Hunting Grounds," *Baily's Magazine of Sports and Pastimes*, Volume 37 (May 1881), 132.
254 Mrs. Edward Kennard, *The Girl in the Brown Habit* (F.V. White and Co., 1887), 267.
255 Mrs. Edward Kennard, *A Professional Rider* (London: Anthony Treherne and Co., Ltd., 1903), 53.
256 Pennell Elmhirst (1893), 191.
257 Lady Mabel Howard, "Ladies in the Hunting Field," *Badminton Magazine of Sports and Pastimes*, Volume 4 (January 1897), 119.

Chapter 4

Horse Sports, Imperial Ideology, and Gender Construction in British India, 1850–1913

As historian John MacKenzie has argued, "sport was an obsession in British India."[1] More so than even in Britain, horse sports achieved the preeminent role as the social activity *par excellence*. Equestrianism was important in Britain, but options for women's participation were limited to ordinary riding or fox hunting. In India, British women rode and pursued equestrian sports like polo and competed in horseback games called gymkhanas. They also hunted from horseback for jackals, as the Indian subcontinent lacked the traditional British fox.[2] They even participated in that most dangerous mounted sport, pig sticking – or spearing a wild boar during a mounted chase.

Women embraced these new equestrian opportunities, which were, as MacKenzie concluded, "a powerful expression of female emancipation of sorts."[3] In doing so, these women publicly and intentionally created new, strong, and independent feminine identities – more strong and independent than they could form at home in Britain. More importantly, female engagement did not end there, as women brought the skills, authority, and independence gained through imperial experience back to Britain and transformed the British social, cultural, and sporting landscape.

Historians and scholars have traditionally regarded the British Empire as both male-dominated and critical to the formation of masculinity, with women either absent from, or irrelevant to, politics, military, and public life. As Ronald Hyam famously quipped, the empire was not acquired "in a fit of absence of mind, as much as in a fit of absence of wives."[4] But women were essential to the creation of empire, and to understanding how imperial gender identities were made. "The empire may have been masculine, but it certainly was not exclusively male," scholar Mary Procida argued.[5] Women's engagement with imperialism involved far more than their physical presence; it was active not passive. Women played significant roles in the Raj, as teachers, nurses, philanthropists, and wives.[6]

Female equestrians were among the most influential of women in the British Empire. Horsemanship was a necessary requirement, and female equestrianism transformed traditional gender, social, and sporting ideals. The impetus for riding astride for ladies had a long history in British India, going all the way back to William Hickey's recollections of a "Mrs. Bristow" in the 1780s. "Uncommonly elegant" and "highly accomplished," Mrs. Bristow was riding astride in Calcutta 100 years before the practice gained general popularity there. As Hickey recalled,

> instead of seating herself like other women on horseback, she rode like a man astride, would leap over any hedge or ditch that even the most zealous sportsmen were dubious of attempting. She rode several matches and succeeded against the best and most experienced jockeys.[7]

The freedom gained by this riding style was irresistible given the rough conditions in India. Although such "eccentric" practices might not have won universal approval, Mrs. Bristow was not condemned: rather, she was thought well-accomplished, including as a mother. She did not want to leave Bengal and wished to live there more than anywhere else – a sentiment that showed the attractions of the space and place to women beyond the pale of contemporary British femininity.

Horse sports have received insufficient attention in studies of empire or imperial sports, while games such as cricket have received much more examination. Many studies of imperial sport do not even mention equestrianism.[8] But horse sports were an essential and vital part of imperial life. For example, in the 1830s, Colonel Nesbitt raced to a ship that had just arrived in Calcutta from England and asked for the latest news. He was informed that new government Ministers had been selected; he immediately exclaimed, "Hang the Ministry! Is Nimrod's Yorkshire Tour arrived?"[9] referring to an eighteenth-century hunting serial that had achieved the same popularity as Conan Doyle's Sherlock Holmes a century later.

Horses were an important part of imperial life, not only for their practical value as transportation, but also for their role in fostering and securing a specific imperial identity. Horses were a part of home, of Britain, where sports such as riding, racing, and hunting were well-established facets of life. When Britons went abroad, they brought these interests with them to places like British India. They also imported their ideas about class; activities like riding and hunting publicly displayed one's place in society. In fact, horses (and the part of British life and identity they represented) became even more important away from home. Equestrian sports were a public and visual display of Britishness; they fostered a collective identity – an "imagined community" – among Britons far from British shores. Horse sport, and a mounted identity, were the preserve of a single white, ruling class, both male and female. In India, British men and women sought to form a united imperial front to demonstrate their power and authority over the native population.

Many scholars have argued that hunting emphasized a masculine physical culture, and in many ways that is true. Most guidebooks on big game hunting were aimed at a predominantly male audience. However, the transformation of British fox-hunting manuals in the nineteenth century shows that the target readers were often female. As ladies increased in numbers in British hunting fields, so did hunting literature written and directed to them. They likely also shared general texts because much sporting instruction and knowledge was equally applicable to both sexes. What is unique about imperial guidebooks is that British women were always implicitly equated with white male hunters. As social scientist M.S.S. Pandian points out, there was an unwritten but well-understood hierarchy for imperial hunters. The term and designation of "hunter" was the most prestigious, followed by the lesser "shooters" or, worse, "poachers."[10] In this way, women who hunted around the Empire, whether after jackal or tiger, with horse or with rifle, were called hunters, and they were verbally equated with British men at the highest level.

One of the most popular imperial sports, big game hunting, was limited in numbers, due to cost and therefore by class. This kind of hunting never truly lost its masculine associations.[11] Tiger hunting in particular was closely linked to native royal rulers, which many Britons sought to emulate, either consciously or unconsciously.[12] In this way, it was used to create and sustain a muscular imperial masculinity thought vital to powerful leadership. It was also traditionally done on elephants and remained ceremonial in many aspects, often drawing large groups of native spectators. In 1894, Kate Martelli, author of "Tigers I Have Shot," opened her essay with: "My personal experiences of tiger-shooting in India have been neither on a large scale nor of a very heroic and exciting nature."[13] Few women participated in these activities and those who did were largely exceptional in a way that female equestrians were not.[14] Female game hunters were also limited by physical strength in gun handling – guns could weigh over 12 pounds and have a powerful recoil – whereas the lack of brute strength in female riders enabled the development of more sympathetic modes of communication with, and control over, their mounts.[15]

Besides big game hunting, other sports were also important to the development of an imperial ideology. Cricket, the "imperial game," was foremost among these.[16] Imported from Britain, the sport was adopted by native Indians. Whereas sports like polo brought British and native players closer together, with the sporting illustrator "Snaffles" (Charles Payne) calling it "the game of Sahibs and Rajahs,"[17] a racial divide was far sharper and more evident in cricket. In fact, polo and cricket were often at odds with each other over playing spaces. As Ramachandra Guha argues, the "communalism" of competitive cricket actually "violated the idea of a shared citizenship" among Indians, "with teams composed on the basis of caste, ethnic group, race or religion" and thereby sowed the seeds of conflict between Britons and Indians.[18] For women, cricket did not provide the opportunities found in other sports, as it was only introduced for female play in 1913 in Britain and did not gain popularity until after the Second World War.[19]

Thus, horse sports shine greater light on many of the political, social, and gendered aspects of British India in the late nineteenth and early twentieth centuries. The British method of hunting on horseback for small, swift game did not become truly popular until after 1857. After the Indian Rebellion, social and political imperatives made it necessary to develop a separate British (or Anglo-Indian) identity rather than amalgamate with a native Indian one. The British began by purposely distancing themselves from the populated plains. The climate of India in British conclaves like the high-altitude hill stations was similar to that of home, thus providing a more healthful environment than the hot and arid plains, and also places better for the pursuit of British sports like hunting.[20]

In the seventeenth century, the British East India Company had encouraged cohabitation and intermarriage between military men and professionals with native women. This pragmatic strategy resulted in economic dominion, if not political. By the 1830s, evangelical fervor hardened against this racial mixing, and, by 1857, Britain took over the governance of India, requiring new constructions of gender, class, and empire.[21] Separate, superior, and different were the keywords of the day, and equestrian sports provided a means to publicly demonstrate these qualities. In the 1840s, Walter Campbell briefly mentioned hunting jackals in his chapter on the Ooty Hunt in *The Old Forest Ranger*, but additional information was sparse until mid-century.[22] "The Old Shikarri," G.A.R. Dawson, complained that many early sources did not mention jackal hunting but, after mid-century, new publications appeared rapidly. Captain Pennell Elmhirst, Master and Huntsman of the Neilgherry Hounds from 1875 to 1877, wrote that hunting was important because it enabled Britons:

> to forget they are in India. Even many of the time-honoured idiosyncrasies of Indian Society are left behind, and men _and women_ become more English-like and less colonial. The quaint and fantastic exactions of the world "à l'Indienne" being more or less laid aside, we are able to move and live more as we were wont in Lesser Britain …[23]

As Pennell Elmhirst stated, women were important to this collective construction of imperial white identity and the reinforcing of a superior imperial ideology. By riding well and joining hunts, they placed themselves in a gender-neutral community of British interests, as part of a seamless ruling class.

Hunting was intricately tied to the imperial project, in that hunters constructed a super-masculine "self" diametrically opposed to an effeminate, native "other."[24] Horse sports highlighted the differences between imperial rulers (male or female, white, and mounted), with the native ruled (colored and unmounted). Sex did not matter in this imperial classification. Many have defined this divide as one between masculine/feminine and colonizer/colonized categories; but British women blurred these distinctions by being both colonizer and female.[25] British women intentionally embraced the imperial ideology by riding, hunting, and then abandoning the traditional sidesaddle to ride like men. In doing so, they equated themselves with British male colonizers and leaders, as opposed to the native colonized. In this way, British women's participation in equestrian sports in India not only contributed to, but was crucial for, the reformation of gender, social, and sporting ideals before the First World War.

This chapter explores the influence of the British Empire in transforming horse sports for women between 1850 and 1913. It spans from the publication of

Augustus Frederick Oakes' *The Young Lady's Equestrian Assistant*, in Madras in 1850, the first riding manual published on ladies' riding in India, to Mrs. Stuart Menzies' *Women in the Hunting Field* in 1913, which highlighted that her own imperial experience was the reason for her abandonment of the sidesaddle for the cross-saddle. Although horses and equestrianism were integrated into colonial spaces such as Australia and Canada, no location illustrates how equestrianism transformed gender, social, and sporting ideals better than British India. In India, horse sports like polo and pig sticking became deeply entrenched in popular culture, and other mounted activities like hunting were specially adapted to the new location. Female equestrians were therefore essential for the preservation and future of British culture, values, and heritage.

Horses and Horse Ownership in India

One reason horse sports in India became so prevalent was because it was easier to own a horse there than in Britain. Horses were cheaper and more plentiful on the subcontinent. Beyond native breeds, many other mounts were shipped to India from Australia, especially New South Wales (these were called "Walers").[26] Stabling and grooms were also more affordable, despite the unwritten requirement that each individual horse needed its own personal groom (or "syce"), for care, and grass-cutter, for providing forage.[27] These factors led many such as Captain Younghusband to observe, "In England, only a man of fair means keeps a horse; in India, the least affluent officer keeps a pony as a natural part of his outfit."[28] He concluded that, in India, "sporting privilege ... is common to all, rich and poor alike."[29]

India was one of the few places in the British Empire that provided hospitable environs for horses, in contrast to the many locations around the British Empire that emphatically did not. As historian Sandra Swart has shown, diseases such as African Horse Sickness and trypanosomiasis prevented the development of widespread horse culture in Africa before the twentieth century.[30] John Singleton has demonstrated that in 1916 alone, animal mortality in East Africa was 290% of existing stock, with an average loss of 120%.[31]

Although horse ownership was virtually mandatory for military officers, if not as part of service then for sport and play, opportunities were available for women, as either wives of military men or civilians. As Lady Greville commented: "Everyone rides in India, for in many places it is the only means of transit."[32] Transportation, then, was a major reason for keeping horses, but no less important was the ability to get out of the home and participate in a healthy and social public activity – and one that visually demonstrated the power of the white ruling class.

A lady's horse, bearing a sidesaddle, required extensive training. A fractious or unbroken horse was not deemed a safe mount for a woman due to her delicate position on a sidesaddle. In Britain, ladies were continually advised only to ride perfectly-trained mounts for their own safety. In India, perfect mounts for ladies were few and far between, if they existed at all. Arabians, Walers, and country-bred horses were much smaller (usually pony height), thinner, and almost always more agile and high-strung than the well-trained park hacks and hunters of England. On these smaller horses (or even ponies), a normal sidesaddle was prone to slip and had to be readjusted lest it slide completely around the horse's belly, throwing the rider dangerously underneath her mount's hooves.[33] Unlike the broad-backed hunters of Britain, these horses had not been trained to carry a lady sidesaddle, and some horses would never take to this style.

Equines (and equestrians) in India also had to be prepared to face numerous surprises when out riding: "to canter over no particular road, and to go round elephants, and under camels, and over palanquins, and through a regiment."[34] Female riders had to adjust their riding skills to what was available – and make what was available do their bidding. As Samuel Sidney noted, "in India and the Colonies no precaution should be neglected for making the most of rough horses which [women] are frequently compelled to ride."[35] Former cavalry officer Robert Henderson seconded this: "a lady (especially in the colonies) may someday find herself on a bad-mannered animal that will 'set to' with her."[36] This was certainly the case more often than not, as Leonora Starr noted when she acquired "an ugly, bad-tempered, but extremely clever and comfortable little mare called Sharaz."[37]

Many women reveled in these new possibilities, and some were even surprised by them. Charlotte Canning, wife of the first Viceroy of India, wrote in shock that she suddenly possessed a stable of horses for her own use: "Another Arab horse has been bought for me, … only imagine me the possessor of three horses!"[38] Other women were more enthusiastic about sport and hunting, gladly joining their husbands to pursue opportunities less readily available to them in Britain. Whereas some British ladies only travelled to India with family, bound by familial responsibilities and duties, others willingly came for the adventure, the open space, and the sporting prospects. As Anna Chitty remarked on her journey to India, "Best of all I could begin riding, which I had yearned to do for many a long year."[39]

"Every Lady Rides in India"

In Britain, riding was an attractive social accomplishment and healthful exercise for ladies, but in the Empire, and especially in India, it was an absolute necessity. Many long journeys were completed or supplemented by horseback travel. Therefore, women were advised to take lessons before arriving in order to be prepared for their new lives. As Robert Henderson pointed out, "In the upper middle classes nothing is more probable than the marriage of one of the daughters of the house with a man whose future lot may be cast in the colonies, where if a woman cannot ride she will be sorely at a loss."[40] Despite climate and weather conditions (including scorching heat and drenching rains), the rough terrain, and difficulties of procuring well-trained horses, riding became the predominant social and sporting activity for women in the Raj. For those who had already enjoyed riding and hunting in Britain (and even for those who had not), the sport was a tonic for the strange conditions of India, a way to make the unfamiliar familiar.[41]

Riding was even taken up by Emily Eden, whose great-great-grandnephew was Prime Minister Anthony Eden. After the death of her parents, she and her sister Fanny went with their brother George, Lord Auckland, to India when he was appointed as Governor-General in 1835. Despite being depressed about leaving all she knew, fearing the five months' journey at sea, and anxious about the life that awaited her, she found India exciting and, in riding, a release from all her stresses.[42] From Simla, she wrote with excitement: "And then I have a new horse, ... which has turned out a treasure, and is such a beauty, a grey Arab. He is as quiet as a lamb, and as far as I can see, perfect."[43] Riding in India was different than in Britain, but Eden found comfort and normalcy in these British activities amid her new surroundings.[44]

Riding in India and at hill stations like Simla, as Emily Eden pointed out, was necessary for social purposes as well as transport. According to C.J. French in 1838, who served in Lord Auckland's encampment, riding on "the Mall" was "the pivot around which the Simla community revolved," for the Mall was the "nucleus" of the community, a place where this British interest brought cohesion to a group of expats.[45] Simla had a special place for equestrian display: "The Rotten Row of Simla is called the Mall, whereon fair equestrians sweep round the sharp curves at full gallop knowing well that there is no Hyde Park peeler at hand to prosecute them for riding furiously."[46] Calcutta also had a "Rotten Row" after its namesake in Hyde Park, while the promenade of Ootacamund (known as "Ooty") was called "the 'Rotten-row', where in the afternoon may be seen several hundred Anglo-Indians either on horseback or in vehicles of every description."[47] Britishness was imported to unfamiliar places by using familiar names, and, when possible, familiar places like racecourses that were not in use.[48]

While riding for the British in India was a social sport for public display and healthful exercise, it was also a visual gesture of British identity as necessary and appealing as it was comforting. This equestrian display was noted by Dr. Hoffmeister, the travelling physician who accompanied Prince Waldemar of Prussia on his travels in the East during the 1840s.[49] Though not British, he recognized the "Britishness" of horse sports, writing in 1848, "Every creature is on horseback; even the fair sex dash along on fine, spirited, Arab coursers; and many an English lady may be seen galloping down the street, followed by a train of three or four elegantly equipped officers."[50] By mid-century, therefore, Simla and other places were well populated by British women who took part in equestrian activities, and had "by no means a lack of young ladies."[51]

By mid-century, riding was so important that female riders were depicted in George Atkinson's popular work, *Curry and Rice* (On Forty Plates); Or, The Ingredients of Social Life at "Our" Station in India.[52] Three plates show ladies riding sidesaddle, and the title page depicts a woman in a long, trailing habit ready to set out for a ride (Figure 4.1). A female rider is part of the image of "Our Mall" – she is said to be "Mrs. Byle, wife of that artillery officer who is riding

Figure 4.1 Title page from "*Curry and Rice*" *(On Forty Plates); Or, The Ingredients of Social Life at "Our" Station in India*, by Captain George Francklin Atkinson, first published in London by Day & Son in 1859: George Atkinson served as Captain of the Bengal Engineers between 1841 and 1859, and his time in the Bengal Presidency influenced this very successful book published in the year of his death. British views of India changed after the Indian Rebellion of 1857. Britons now worked to consciously distance and differentiate themselves from their imperial subjects; one way in which both British men and women did so was through horse sports and by achieving a prominence and public power by being mounted on horseback.
Credit: Collection of the author.

with her." She wears a "white habit" (not necessarily the best color choice to keep clean, although certainly cooler than black fabric), and is said to be "a capital rider."[53] A woman is also seen galloping, accompanied by two young men. Although no description accompanied the illustration, the figure is likely Bella Clove, who was described as one of "our Spins," or, quite literally, fast women. According to Atkinson, she "rattles all about the cantonment on that little Arab of hers; scampers round the racecourse in the morning with the young ensigns; gallops at full speed down the Mall with a similar escort."[54] Clove upset the serenity of the carriage-driving ladies, the elderly females who preferred to take the air in a more sedate and less physically demanding fashion. Her athletic antics were not frowned upon as they would have been in Britain. Her frisky and frolicsome capers were more endearing than scandalous, and no one doubted her riding skills which enabled her boisterous behavior. India was a place where women could indulge in horseback activities more vigorously than in Britain, and this appealed to many female riders. Not only were these activities about personal and public admiration; they were a key public relations strategy for imperial rulers.

"Every lady rides in India," recorded Robert Henderson in 1874, "but a rattling gallop at gun fire, in the morning, over the racecourse at Ghindee or Bangalore, is quite a different matter to a gallop with the Pytchley hounds."[55] As he noted, riding had to be undertaken in new and different ways to suit the conditions, especially the heat. In India, women rode very early in the morning or very late in the evening, when the weather was cool(er), rather than partaking in traditional afternoon rides as in London. In India, ladies were advised to start before "gun fire," or the moment of sunrise, and ride for two to three hours' for the benefit of their health.[56] Even at these early hours, the heat was often still oppressive. In 1856, Charlotte Canning wrote: "This morning I had an experimental ride to try a little Arab [Charles] bought out of Lord Dalhousie's stable. Starting at a quarter to six, I had to be on at half-past, and oh, how hot I was! It took me an hour to cool."[57] After sunset, the heat was often just as bad. As Canning continued, "we ride at sunset, and always come home long after dark … it is terribly hot till the sun is quite low."[58]

These challenges did not lessen popularity of the sport. Women juggled other tasks and duties to ride out, sometimes even prioritizing equestrian activities over domestic ones. "You have no notion how difficult it is to squeeze time … out of the day's work," Canning wrote, "until the sun drops, and the hacks are at the door, and every moment of light (in these short twilights) becomes precious for one's ride."[59] Even though she admitted only a lukewarm enthusiasm for equestrianism, it became an established part of her daily repertoire, as it did for many other British women in India. In Calcutta, Canning complained constantly about the heat and dust, "except where the road is watered round a space like the ring in Hyde Park, where the whole English population rushes out for a half-an-hour at sunset."[60] Yet riding became her *modus operandi*. As she admitted, "These rides do me all the good in the world, and riding is the really pleasant thing to do here."[61]

Canning's accounts speak to how important equestrianism was, even to someone who was not previously an enthusiastic equestrian. She equated riding in India with precious and unencumbered freedom. Using a carriage required too many extra people and bothersome attendants – it was "wearisome" in a way that riding was not. She also stressed how respectable a social activity equestrianism was. "It is quite a mistake to suppose that society here is *bad*," she wrote from Calcutta in 1856, "I really believe hardly any woman but *me* goes out riding without her husband. It is really a very proper place."[62] She thought that India provided an open space for women to pursue such activities, even if some women took to riding with more dash and panache than usual. "Lady C. is become a perfect Amazon, considers it slow and dowagery to go for a drive, and when she gets on her horse generally starts off at a hand-gallop until she is too hot to bear it," Canning, ever prim and proper, wrote in admiration rather than censure.[63] Although such behavior would not have been tolerated on Rotten Row in London, where constables would have stopped such speedy riding, this kind of equestrian display was accepted and even provided a sort of release – a welcome amusement and excitement – from the ordinary run of Anglo-Indian life (Figure 4.2).

As the example of "Lady C." shows, by the 1860s women were certainly riding more adventurously in India than was possible at home in Britain. The letters of Sir Alfred Comyn Lyall, one of the most distinguished British civil servants in India, reveal the excellent horsemanship of his wife, Cora, and his pride in her abilities. Both husband and wife had experienced the Indian Rebellion first-hand, and after a period of rest in England, returned to India in 1863 when Lyall was posted to Agra as the Assistant Magistrate. Lyall noted with pride that his wife "acquired a certain social distinction" though her skill in riding.[64] After a sudden move to Hoshungabad, Lyall wrote that his wife was "encroaching daily on my stable," but "such qualities are very valuable."[65] Despite the duties of managing the house and raising their child, Lyall indicated that his wife was "riding again and getting into order my fidgety Arab mare."[66]

Horse-breaking and training was a time-consuming and complex process. Practically speaking, men did not have the time or experience to a train a horse for sidesaddle riding. Often, their wives had both. The challenges, as well as the rewards, of making a finished and finely-trained mount appealed to many, including women such as Cora Lyall, who were put to the task either by necessity or individual interest. It was almost unthinkable that a woman in Britain would possess the skill, time, or inclination to train horses. Those women who did so publicly were labeled "pretty horse-breakers" like "Skittles"; they were courtesans selling horses – and other pleasures – along Rotten Row. This reputation continued for any woman who took to riding imperfect mounts.

Cora Lyall's interest in horsemanship might have damned her to be considered "horsey" at best, or scandalous at worst, in Britain, but in India it made her an exceptional imperial wife. She carefully provided the time and effort in training horses that her husband did not have, and she was publicly admired for it. Lyall thought that his wife was the better rider of the two, and even said that

Figure 4.2 "Anglo-Indian Life: The Morning Ride," by R. Caton Woodville, from *The Illustrated London News* (September 26, 1891), page 412: This image shows a mother and daughter on a morning ride in India. Due to the heat, British women were advised to ride before "gun fire," or the moment of sunrise, and ride for two to three hours for their health. Many riding manuals advised on imperial riding for women, including Augustus Oakes in *The Young Lady's Equestrian Assistant* published in Madras in 1850, and T.A. Jenkins in *The Lady and her Horse* also published in Madras in 1857.
Credit: Collection of the author.

she would have made a fine man, yet he did not view her as any less feminine because of her sporting qualities.[67] In an 1867 letter of advice to his sister on sending her son to India, Lyall wrote, "Really it is as useful in life to be able to ride as to know most sciences, while a general knowledge of games brings a youth to the front wonderfully in society, but *riding* is of immense value."[68]

As Cora Lyall's example demonstrates, British women who traveled to India with their husbands had to possess a great deal of "self-possession." When mounted, women gained equal stature with their male counterparts, and their equestrian experience was a valuable asset both to their individual reputations and to the public image of the British ruling class in India.

Equestrian Manuals and Learning to Ride in India

Riding manuals published in Britain from the mid-nineteenth century onwards stressed how necessary it was for women to know how to ride before arriving at a far-flung point of the British Empire without the requisite skills for physical and social survival, and their own happiness. Robert Henderson could not have expressed the opinion more strongly, writing in 1874:

> I would respectfully impress upon every lady who is likely to go to India ... that they should avail themselves of every opportunity in this country of becoming efficient horsewomen. To be able to ride well is very desirable for a lady who is to pass her life in Europe, in India it is absolutely indispensable; and if the lady's equitation is neglected in the early days at home, she will find herself sadly at a loss when she arrives in India ...[69]

Henderson and other authors emphasized how important riding was to a woman's wellbeing, in terms of transportation, physical health, social acclimatization, and overall happiness – making many of the same points as equestrian authors did in Britain in the 1830s to encourage park riding for women.[70]

Should a woman arrive in India without knowing how to ride, her options could be limited. There were no enclosed riding schools in India, according to Augustus Oakes in 1850, so the best a woman could hope for was an open "circus," or schooling ring, in which to learn on her own or with some limited assistance.[71] She might enlist the aid of her male family to teach her, or she might beg instruction from British military officers. Despite the accepted idea that the best horsewomen learned to ride as children (and hence the impetus for teaching so many young British girls), Samuel Sidney wrote that he personally knew many fine female riders who learned to ride as adults: "our Indian Empire affords many examples of strong and graceful horsewomen whose first lessons were taken at the cavalry stations of the Indian army after marriage."[72] But many others cautioned against relying on the availability of such instruction. Henderson, for example, wrote that: "although there are plenty of thoroughly competent men there who could instruct her, their time is taken up with teaching recruits at the early time of the day at which a lady could avail herself of their services."[73]

Alternately, a woman might turn to textual resources such as riding manuals to learn how to ride. But few titles for ladies' riding were published for a British reading market in India. Augustus Frederick Oakes published *The Young Lady's Equestrian Assistant* in Madras in 1850, and T.A. Jenkins compiled *The Lady and her Horse* in Madras in 1857. As early as 1847, Professor Furbor, in Brighton, directed his manual to ladies in Britain, Ireland, "and its Colonies," and cited his equestrian experience in India.[74] Such titles for women were rare, despite the demand for information. In fact, Jenkins' work was largely a copy of *The Young Lady's Equestrian Manual*, published in Britain in 1838.[75] Importantly, both Oakes and Jenkins instructed women on leaping. In 1850, Oakes confirmed the importance of jumping, self-possession, and a sidesaddle with a leaping head: "Never put a horse at a jump, unless you have made up your mind that he shall go over it, and never jump your horse without a third crutch."[76]

After 1857, only two books for female equestrians appear to have been printed in the Raj, both published by the famous firm, Thacker, Spink and Co.[77] In 1887, Nannie O'Donoghue's *Riding for Ladies* was published in Calcutta and Bombay, and a second edition of the title was published in 1905 in Calcutta and Simla – eighteen years after it had first appeared in Britain.[78] Alice Hayes' *The Horsewoman* was also published in Calcutta and Bombay in 1893.[79] The main problem with these manuals was that they were specifically targeted to a British audience and focused almost exclusively on park riding and hunting. The appeal, and usefulness, of these guidebooks to imperial readers was limited, as details on wool habits and park riding procedure were not the best directions in imperial places. So few ladies' guidebooks were printed in comparison to the numerous books on horse management, training, and sports for a male audience in India, that many women likely turned to these texts for the information they could not get elsewhere.[80] In doing so, they were further encouraged to ride astride.

Despite these challenges, women adapted because riding was such a popular sporting and social activity for the British in India. "We have a nice long ride every afternoon," Lady Dufferin, renowned diplomatic wife of the eighth viceroy of India, remarked in 1887. She constantly noted daily equestrian activities in her memoirs.[81] "I felt that the happiness of my life here depended upon my having some thoroughly steady, safe, and yet fast means of locomotion," she wrote from Simla in 1885, and in due course she found a suitable mount.[82] She did not select an elegant Arabian but rather a "sensible and useful" mule. Begum, as she was named, was a "treasure" to Lady Dufferin because she could walk easily at a horse's pace and canter gently, even if she was, as her owner feared, "not Viceregal-looking."[83] But what Begum lacked in beauty, she made up for in temperament and sure-footedness on the rough pathways that included going "up and down staircases, and along the dry rough beds of rivers, and through streams and up narrow mountain paths."[84] Although Lady Dufferin would eventually switch to riding polo ponies, a more agile type of horse better ridden astride, the mule Begum provided a platform for learning to ride in India, and the Vicerene continued to remark that she found riding "delightful."[85]

In 1904, almost 20 years later, Lady Greville's book, *Ladies in the Field*, showed that little had changed. Her advice for lady riders was much the same as in the late 1800s, and Greville encouraged riding as a healthful activity.[86] Morning rides were still preferred: afterwards women were free to rest until 4 or 5 o'clock when the social rounds of tea, clubs, and calling began.[87] She appreciated the "space and liberty" this kind of equestrian lifestyle offered – because women independently looked after themselves and chose their own destinies. "There is a peculiar charm in Indian riding," she wrote:

> It is indulged in in the early morning, when the body is rested, the nerves strong, and the air brisk and fresh; or at eventide, when the heat of the day is over, and a canter in the cool breeze seems peculiarly acceptable. How delightful are those early morning rides, when, after partaking of the refreshing cup of tea or coffee, your "syce" or groom brings the pawing steed to your door, and once in the saddle, you wander for miles, with nothing to impede your progress but an occasional low mud wall, or bank and ditch, which your horse takes in his stride, or a thorny "nullah," up and down whose steep sides you scramble. There is something fascinating in the sense of space and liberty, the feeling that you can gallop at your own sweet will across a wide plain, pulled up by no fear of trespassing, no gates nor fences nor unclosed pastures with carefully guarded sheep and cattle, no flowery cottage gardens; the wide expanse of cloudless sky above you, the golden plain with its sandy monotony stretched out in front, broken only by occasional clumps of mango trees, or tilled spaces, where the crops grow, intersected by small ditches, cut for the purposes of irrigation – free as a bird, you lay the reins on your horse's neck, and go till he or you are tired.[88]

Greville argued that women could take part in these activities without becoming "unfeminine" and that they became better for it.[89] Women's riding had become far more than a social activity to alleviate boredom or a sport to promote physical wellness. It was singled out as a means to achieve independence and authority. Women's involvement in hunting only increased these opportunities.

Hunting in British India

The British took hunting on horseback with them everywhere they went, whether vicariously by reading Nimrod's latest installment, or by modifying the chase to pursue in new locations like India. Hunting was an established and important part of station life in India, so firmly entrenched in the British psyche and identity that it was adapted throughout the Raj to local circumstances. Without foxes, the quarry changed and Britons turned to chasing jackals. It was considered "a great attraction" and thrived throughout India, from Gulmurg, the capital of Kashmir in the north, to hill stations like Ootacamund in the south, and even on the hot plains of Bombay in the west and Calcutta to the east.[90]

According to G.A.R. Dawson, the "Old Shikarri" and author of *Nilgiri Sporting Reminiscences*, no surviving records reveal when foxhounds were first brought to India.[91] Scholar, soldier, and member of the Indian Civil Service J.K. Stanford argued that packs of hounds existed at Madras and Calcutta as early as 1738, and even dated a pack near Bombay to a century earlier.[92] Dawson estimated that the Madras Hunt had been around since 1800,[93] and, by 1829, foxhounds were recorded at Ootacamund, the summer capital for the Government of Madras.[94] In 1833, *The Sporting Magazine* stated that "bobbery packs" existed at all large military stations, as well as three regular packs of hounds at Bareilly, Tirhoot, and Calcutta.[95] The magazine noted large fields of participants, as many as 60 wearing hunting pink, and some 25 more in hunt colors.[96] Such numbers rivalled or surpassed all but the meets of the largest packs in the Shires.

In Britain, hunting packs were comprised of 30–50 couples (60–100) of purebred English foxhounds, but hunting in India was typically done with a "bobbery pack."[97] Hound mortality was considerable, due to climate and disease, and it was too expensive – over £1,000 – to annually import foxhounds from England to form a full pack.[98] Thus, dogs of any kind were needed as replacements. The term "bobbery" likely came from the Hindi "*bap ré!*" which means "look, father!" – "an expression denoting astonishment at anything unusual and extraordinary, and specially adaptable to the first appearance of a bobbery pack in a locality!"[99] Packs were often formed of any and all available dogs and could include everything from dachshunds to bull terriers to foxhounds. Walter Campbell mentioned hunting with a bobbery pack in the 1840s,[100] and so did George Atkinson in the 1860s in "*Curry and Rice*."[101] Bobbery packs remained an important part of hunting in India well into the early twentieth century.[102]

Hunting was especially popular in hill districts like Ootacamund. Ooty, as it was widely known, was famous for its European climate and served as a place of escape during the hot weather months.[103] "Hunting is pre-eminently the most popular form of sport of Ootacamund," proclaimed the *Call of the Nilgiris* in 1911.[104] The sport had become an established tradition in Ooty over a century earlier, drawing people from far and wide to join in. By 1835, the pack hunted sambur (Indian elk) and "jungle sheep" (muntjacs, also known as "barking deer"), and in 1845 the first Master of Foxhounds (M.F.H.) was appointed. Four years after the Indian Rebellion, in 1861, *Baily's Magazine* reported "in Ooty there is a well-established subscription pack of hounds for hunting the fox and jackal, besides several private ones of beagles, spaniels, and cockers for driving the covers."[105] Two years later, the 60th Rifles at Wellington maintained a bobbery pack that came to Ooty.[106] By 1864–1865, the Madras Hounds were brought up to Ooty, and finally by 1867, another subscription pack was formed, composed of hounds from Madras and Bangalore. By 1871 Ooty had a "bobbery pack" and regular hound breeding (rather than importing) began in

196 Horse Sports and Imperial Ideology

Figure 4.3 "Ooty Hunt Meet," plate 24 (following page 150) from "Old Shikarri" [G.A.R. Dawson], *Nilgiri Sporting Reminiscences* (Madras: Higginbotham and Co., 1880): Hunting was especially popular in hill districts like Ootacamund in British India. Ooty, as it was known, was famous for its European climate in the Nilgiri or Blue Hills and served as the summer capital for the Government of Madras. Foxhounds arrived in Ooty as early as 1829, and, by 1874, the hunt was well-established (the Maharajah of Mysore was a supporter), with a quarter of the field comprised of ladies. Here, three British women are shown after a challenging run where the jackal "went to earth" and escaped his pursuers.

earnest. By 1874, the hunt was well-established (the Maharajah of Mysore was a supporter), with a quarter of the field comprised of ladies.[107]

Dawson clearly and enthusiastically supported women hunting in India and hoped to see more (Figure 4.3). "Be a man fond of hunting as can be," he wrote in 1880, "his heart gladdens to see the ladies. God bless'em, taking their share of the run."[108] He lamented when women were not present at the meets, writing "it's pleasant to see the back of a good habit sailing along."[109] Although female equestrians had joined hunt fields in Britain in ever-increasing numbers by that time, support for them in India was much more passionate. Women were star participants in the sport. In the Peshawur Vale Hunt, women were avid members, including author Isabel Savory and many other women, as well as "the well-known Lady Harvey, [who] looks upon Peshawur as an Indian *Melton*, and brings her stud there regularly every season."[110] In many ways, hunting was more socially and culturally acceptable for women in the Empire because, in India, the sport contributed to a special imperial identity and buttressed the ruling ideology.

Hunting in India was popular for many reasons. Meets were held several times a week, and "jacks" (jackals) were plentiful, ensuring exciting draws and chases (Figure 4.4). Subscription fees to the hunt were "not excessive," and riders typically owned their own horses, due to their affordability. In some places, such as around Ooty, the landscape was mainly comprised of the Downs, extensive grass lands which formed "a field for sport that has no rival in any part of India or, indeed, throughout the Far East."[111] This landscape made the area an ideal hunting center, with lands that enabled much galloping, but required little jumping.[112] This was welcome for women riding sidesaddle, as well as for novice riders, who could gain experience and improve their horsemanship without the dangers of such formidable fences as in Britain.

In other places, however, the landscape required expert horsemanship and not a little nerve. According to Isabel Savory, the landscape of the Peshawur Vale varied greatly, from marshy areas (*jheel*) and paddy fields to "fresh meadows" and peach orchards.[113] There was a good deal of scrambling, tricky fences, and numerous, troublesome water crossings such as canals where many just swam their horses across. Paddy crossings were particularly dangerous: "one unfortunate lady whose pony 'forgot to jump' one of these grips [banks] was properly baptized from head to toe in mud and water."[114] Falling off was common, but most riders scrambled right back on.[115]

Savory highlighted one instance of hunting in India. When the rest of the field headed towards a bridge, a female rider guided her mare over seven big parallel dykes called the "Seven Sisters." This obstacle was a notorious "gridiron," or a series of artificial drainage ditches in parallel with a matching set of banks, described as "quite impassable for a horse" by the former Master of the Hunt.[116] "All glory to the lady and her good mare," Savory recounted, "for by some extraordinary skill they picked their way over each 'grave,' and landing on the little sound bit of turf between, neatly slipped over the next, jumping

198   Horse Sports and Imperial Ideology

Figure 4.4 "Jackal Hunting in India," from *The Illustrated Sporting and Dramatic News* (January 5, 1878), page 381: Oscar Wilde declared that fox hunting in Britain was the "the unspeakable in pursuit of the uneatable," but, "in India it is more a case of the unconventional in full pursuit of the unavailable." Here Britons hunted from horseback for jackals, as the Indian subcontinent lacked the traditional British fox. In this image, a bobbery pack opens chase on a jackal (possibly released by the Indian holding a basket), with a field that includes at least one woman riding sidesaddle. The sport was established by the 1840s, when Walter Campbell mentioned hunting jackals in his chapter on the Ooty Hunt in *The Old Forest Ranger*.
Credit: Collection of the author.

lightly, to an inch, on to the narrow bank, and so on over the whole seven."[117] One of the male hunt servants tried to follow her performance, but failed. He crashed at the third obstacle, and his horse ended upside down at the bottom of a dyke.[118] Though such feats may have seemed extraordinary to sporting enthusiasts at home in Britain, they were merely an ordinary day's work for imperial equestrians in India.

As this example illustrates, hunting in India was a challenge, though there were fewer high fences and fearsome hedges than in Britain. Even preparation for it was demanding, especially rising so early in the morning to beat the heat. After heading to bed after 11 pm, Savory and her party were awoken at 4:30 am for a 6:00 am hunt, having dressed in their habits and sun-helmets (solar topis).[119] But, in many ways, hunting the Indian jackal was very similar to hunting the British fox. The jackal also hunted by night and slept during the day, although did not often "go to earth" as did foxes. His stamina and cunning behavior resulted in longer chases in India; a full hunt might start at half past seven in the morning and only end at 11 am, with intense bursts of galloping over many miles that could last over an hour.[120] Wherever the action ended, hunters then faced a long jog home in the hot morning sun.

Savory was not the only British woman to enthuse about hunting in India, or to encourage other women to participate. Many female writers also recorded their hunting experiences. Lady Greville was especially enamored of hunting in India, writing:

> In northern India, on a real cold, nipping morning before sunrise, you gather at the accustomed trysting-place and hear the welcome sound of the hounds' voices. A scratch pack, they are, perhaps, even a "Bobbery" pack, as the name goes in India; but the old excitement is on you, the rush for a start, and the sense of triumphant exhilaration, as the hounds settle to their work, and the wretched little jackal, or better still, the wolf, takes his unchecked course over the sandy hillocks and the short grass. A twenty-minutes' run covers the horses with lather, and sets your pulses tingling. Presently the sun is high in the horizon, and its rays are beginning to make themselves felt. A few friendly good-byes, some parting words of mutual congratulation, and you turn to ride gently home, with a feeling of self-righteousness in your heart, as you greet the lazy sister, or wife, or brother, who stands in the verandah looking for your coming.[121]

Greville spoke to many important issues in her description of hunting. Although hunting was a healthy and enjoyable pastime, it was much more than that. Hunting was a public activity that demonstrated the power of the "imagined community" of the British and enforced their sense of social and political stability as well as their collective identity. Greville's opinions echoed those of Alfred Lyall in 1864, who wrote that his posting to Agra was "excellent" because he "could ride across country after a jackal with a station pack in the morning," a way of making India British, of making it feel like home.[122]

Gymkhanas: Games on Horseback

Although the going was rougher than in Britain, with paddy fields, rocky paths, and cactus hedges, women had made enough headway in riding to be among the best riders in the field, and many did so by riding astride.[123] They had been encouraged to do so not only by the rigorous demands of hunting, but also by the needs of other imperial activities such as gymkhanas and polo. Gymkhanas were popular mounted games and contests held across India. They were outdoor social gatherings *par excellence*, better than stuffy teas or indoor dances, and they were also an opportunity for physical activity. These mounted games spread from hill stations to the major cities of Calcutta and Bombay, and outward to Dibrugarh, Shillong, Lucknow, Rawal Pindi, Poona, Secunderabad, and Madras.[124] Gulmurg, the summer capital of Kashmir, was renowned for its mounted events, as *The Ladies' Field* noted in 1900: "The gymkhanas are the great fortnightly events of the season. Tilting at the ring, for ladies, and cutting a lime (as a rule it is the common or garden potato up here), or tent-pegging, for men, are the favourite pastimes. The ladies' trotting race, as a rule, produces a large number of entries, and some good horsemanship is always seen."[125] Such imperial events rivalled equestrian sports at home in Britain, both in level of skill and social value.

Female equestrians were welcome participants in these games and were not excluded from trying their hand at various contests, even those which had previously been reserved for male riders. For example, tent-pegging (or spearing tent pegs plugged into the ground at regular intervals with a sharpened spear at a racing gallop) had clear military applications and descended from drill or cavalry training. Other events such as tilting (or ring-spearing with a lance from horseback) were no less demanding (Figure 4.5). These competitions instilled a games ethic among female participants, all in a spirit of competition that encouraged skilled horsemanship. They were not viewed as unfeminine activities; rather, they were public demonstrations of skill by the ruling class.

One of the foremost enthusiasts of mounted games was Lady Dufferin, who wrote about her experiences in *Our Viceregal Life in India*, published in 1890. According to her writings, women frequently participated in tilting at Simla and other imperial locations. The competition, however, was not an easy one:

> for it is not simple to ride forth alone and with assurance to run a lance through four successive brass rings, delicately swung from poles, and all too easily missed, and then crown the deed by running the point of the lance through a recumbent bun in such a way that the bun acts as stop to the rings, and carrying these and the bun on the lance in triumph to the post.[126]

Annandale, one of the few large pieces of flat ground near Simla, was the most popular location for such sports and was purposely developed for these pursuits. One of the earliest attractions of the locale was horse-racing, though the

Figure 4.5 "Ladies Tilting at the Ring, India," from *The Graphic* (February 9, 1889), 148–149: The word "gymkhana" was adopted by Anglo-Indians from the Hindustani word for "ball court," denoting a specific place for public sport. They were mounted games and horseback competitions held across British India. One popular event was tilting, or ring-spearing, which had descended from medieval jousting. As the hard-contact sport of jousting fell from favor, riders turned instead to using their horses and lances to spear small rings suspended from arches. Though such activities were derived from military contests and were a development of masculine warfare and equestrianism, British women, even riding sidesaddle, were not barred from participating. These games developed keen equestrian expertise and were a public demonstration of skills needed by the ruling class in India.
Credit: Collection of the author.

surrounding area was improved for other sports by 1847.[127] Initially there was a 1.5 mile track around the dell, but this pathway was soon improved, probably because seldom were there meetings without people or horses falling off the sharp edges of the precipice and into the valley below.[128] The popularity of horse sports demanded upkeep and modernization of the Annandale area so that more people could participate. By the 1880s, gymkhanas were regularly held, and, despite the ferocity of competition among women, these activities were seen as perfectly normal. As Lady Dufferin recalled, the ladies "rode wildly by me on ponies, stick in hand, looking very fierce and determined as they passed; they were all very much pleased with themselves, and thought they had made very good play."[129]

By the end of the Dufferins' stay in 1887, these mounted games had spread widely, from Simla in the north to Calcutta in the east and beyond. Lady Dufferin remarked that tilting and tent-pegging had never been tried before at Calcutta, but with some ingenuity suitable grounds were found and soon fourteen members of her party were engaged in the sport.[130] In Dehra Dun, at the foothills of the Himalayas, Lady Dufferin remarked that the mounted activities were also a huge success, for there was "tent-pegging and tilting, and everybody seemed amused, and all the ladies wondered why they had not tilted before."[131]

In Ootacamund, gymkhana events were held "all through the season," and many places had also instituted "paper chasing."[132] Paper chasing, sometimes called "Hare and Hounds," was generally a combination of hunting and the mounted games of gymkhanas. One or more persons were designated as "hares" which left a paper trail (literally of shredded papers) to mark the "scent" of the hare. The rest of the participants were the "hounds," whose object was to catch the hare. Following a staggered release, to give the "hares" a head start, the "hounds" had to carefully track their "prey" with the goal being to catch the "hares" before they reached the marked end of the race. The "chase" usually evolved into an outright race against time over a cross-country environment that called for spectacular horsemanship, and excellent tracking, as the paper "scent" could blow away or be left at scarce intervals, making the pursuit a difficult one.

The game was popular at least by the 1880s, when it was mentioned by Lady Dufferin[133], and David Fraser recalled in 1902 that "I have met lots of people in India, of both sexes, who have hunted paper on horse-back, as regularly as the opportunity permitted, during the last five-and-twenty years" – thus, from the late 1870s onward.[134] Fraser prominently noted the success of women, who all went "at a ripping pace."[135] While local competitions might draw 30 or so riders, larger ones could bring together fields of 60 or 70, with crowds of spectators.[136]

Lady Greville was particularly enthusiastic about paper chasing, writing:

> Then on Sunday, the day voted to sport in India, merry paper chases fill an idle hour or two just before sunset. Any old screw, country-bred pony or short-shouldered Arab may be brought out on these occasions. The hard ground resounds with a noise like the distant roll of thunder, as the line of horsemen clatter along, raising a cloud of dust behind them. Falls abound, for the pace is good, and the leader of the chase well mounted. The sugar canes rattle crisply like peas on a drum, as you push your way quickly through the tall grass crops, which, forced violently asunder by your horse's progress, fall together again, and leave no trace of your passage. Down a soft, sandy lane, you canter, while your horse sinks in up to his fetlocks, past a dirty little native village, swarming with black children, where women in picturesque attitudes lean and chatter by the shady well; then over a rough, stony plain, intersected by cracks and crevices in the hard gaping earth, where you must pick your way carefully, and hold your horse together lest he break his leg and your neck, for (drawback of all in India) the ground is

Figure 4.6 "Indian Paper-Chase," from *The Illustrated Sporting and Dramatic News* (April 19, 1879), page 101: In India, paperchases proved a popular substitute for English fox hunting. "Paper-chases are generally very popular amongst the ladies, who often show the astonished and admiring natives what Englishwomen are up to in the sporting line." The sketch shows two sidesaddle riders clearing a mud bank at speed, to the "astonishment" of two Indian men. It highlights the difference between imperial rulers (male or female, white, and mounted), with the native ruled (colored and unmounted).
Credit: Collection of the author.

dreadfully hard, and falls do hurt. At last the chase is over, and your wearied beast stands with legs apart and nostrils heaving, trying to get his wind. The sun has gone down in the sudden fashion peculiar to tropical climes. Gloaming there is none, but a lovely starlight, and the clear rays of the moon to guide you safely on your way home.[137]

It was a rough and wild sport, and one which also highlighted the differences between imperial rulers (male or female, white, and mounted), with the native ruled (colored and unmounted) (Figure 4.6). Sex did not matter in this imperial classification as British women consciously accommodated themselves into the ruling imperial ideology via horse sports.

Pig Sticking or Hog Hunting

Beyond hunting and mounted games, British women in India also pursued the most dangerous of equestrian sports, pig sticking (also called hog hunting). Made famous by Robert Baden-Powell, Army officer and later founder of the

Boy Scouts, the sport involved chasing a wild boar at top speed and spearing him to death from horseback.[138] Indian boars, commonly called pigs or hogs, were volatile and vicious animals, standing three feet high and five feet long, and weighing up to 300 pounds.[139] Boars were also fast and powerful, armed with sharp tusks and thick hides. When chased, boars often "jinked" or pivoted suddenly, sometimes into the path of horse and rider, causing them to collide and somersault.[140] An enraged boar often turned and charged horse and rider; injured horses were common, and a man on the ground was all but defenseless against the angry beast.

Killing a boar with a spear was no easy feat. As Mrs. Alan Gardner related, the first difficulty was finding the boar in dense grasslands: "the grass being very thick and high, it was rather difficult to keep the boar in sight. Sometimes as we raced along we had nothing to guide us but the ripple of grass at the top, as the boar galloped through it beneath."[141] Once flushed, the chase was on. "Go at the boar, at a smart gallop," advised Walter Campbell in 1853, "and, as he meets you, you strike straight down, while he is under your right stirrup."[142] Hunters rode out in small parties and split up until a boar broke cover.[143] Then all riders galloped out to meet him. The ultimate goal was death of the boar, but the real honor was achieving the "first spear" (or first blood) from the individual who reached and wounded the boar first.[144]

Unlike the modern pursuit of fox hunting, boar hunting had an ancient heritage. Ovid described a boar hunt in 1400 B.C., but the sport was only revitalized in British India around 1800. The planters of Behar in eastern India used dogs to chase sloth bear from the thick cane fields into the open, grass country.[145] The bears soon tired of this treatment and moved further upcountry where they could not be pursued, which inspired the idea of hunting boar instead.[146] As a result, pig sticking quickly spread from Calcutta to Bombay and beyond, depending on the necessary conditions and availability of pigs.

Most British officers (as well as their wives or female relatives) who came to India had a background in equestrian sports and especially in fox hunting, which was at its peak of popularity in Britain after the mid-nineteenth century. Arriving with considerable skill on horseback and an interest in hunting, they found plentiful game in India for all types of pursuit, from big game for shooting to small game for chasing. Just as the jackal was substituted for the fox, so was the boar, which was considered a "more formidable opponent than the fox, but just as plentiful as rabbits in the English countryside they had left behind them."[147]

In 1860, Henry Shakespear, a Victorian explorer who served with the Bengal Lancers, wrote that he considered pig sticking "the very first sport in the world," but as Captain J.T. Newall wrote seven years later, initially there was little literature available on the sport. By the 1880s, many more works had appeared on the subject, including the Old Shikarri's [G.A.R. Dawson] *Nilgiri Sporting Reminiscences* and Newall's own *Scottish Moors and Indian Jungles: Scenes of Sport in the Lews and India*.

The increase in the sport's popularity led to interested sportsmen banding together in "tent clubs," which were pig sticking's organizational mainstay. The first such club in India was at Poona, said to have been founded in 1817,[148] though other clubs formed in Delhi, Cawnpore, and Meerut by the 1840s.[149] Tent clubs were crucial to the success of pig sticking because they helped turn an impromptu activity into an organized sport and brought together a like-minded community of participants based on a mutual interest in horse sports. Pig sticking grew so popular that a "national" tournament was held every year to recognize the best hunter. This was the fabled Kadir Cup competition, sponsored by the Meerut Tent Club from 1871. Selecting a single winner was no easy task; in a single season, 400 spears (participants) from over 30 clubs hunted pigs from Calcutta to Hyderabad.[150] In the British military, participation was considered so important that the work week was even shifted to make way for the sport – weekends were extended from Wednesday to Sunday evening to allow extra time for hunting.[151]

Spears for boar-hunting were sharp, uncompromising, and dangerous weapons. According to Campbell, the "light elastic spear" was "a faultless male bamboo from the jungles of the Concan, about ten feet long, tough as whalebone, and tapering away beautifully to the smaller end, where it terminated in a keen glittering blade, about the size and shape of a laurel-leaf" – similar to, but more lethal than, the lances used for tilting and tent-pegging.[152] The equipment required skilled handling, unlike the blunted lances used for tilting at the ring, although that was certainly good practice for developing the necessary eye-hand coordination.

Originally ten-foot spears had been thrown like javelins at the running boars, but this was abandoned around 1830 in favor of overhand stabbing at closer quarters, which was far more successful.[153] Around the same time, spears were shortened (6' 6"), and made of bamboo with a diamond head (rather than triangular), which was balanced by a lead weight in the butt. This method was used in Calcutta until 1938 and was effective in thick jungle when the hog turned and charged and the spear could be driven home through heart or backbone. The method was less effective with hogs that "jinked" or dodged, especially in open territory. This led to the adoption of the "long spear" (8–9 feet), also narrow in the head and weighted in the butt, but used underhand. This method became prevalent in India (except in Calcutta), being more effective because of the spear's extra length.[154]

How spears and spearing methods changed was especially important for female participants, who would have been at a disadvantage in throwing the spear like a javelin, but who could exert a great deal of stabbing pressure downwards from their locked-in seats riding sidesaddle. Shorter, lighter spears were easier for them to manage, as well as an overhand style that allowed them to stab downwards rather than thrust forward. As sporting enthusiast J.W. Best noted, it was not human strength that necessarily skewered a boar – it was the power of the horse's forward motion which was conducted through the grip and spear. As he wrote, "It is the weight and pace of a horse behind a sharp spear that sends it through a pig like a needle into butter, so 'sit down in your saddle and ride like hell!'"[155] All of these changes enabled women's participation.

Many argued that women should be allowed to participate in such sports. "Frank Forester," the pen name for sporting author William Henry Herbert, confirmed his support in his introduction to *The Old Forest Ranger* in 1853, writing "no race, no class, no age, *no sex* of the human family seems to be exempt from this pervading, passionate, self-originated, frenzy for pursuit."[156] One reason for this acceptance was likely women's excellent participation in fox hunting fields across Britain. As they joined in increasing numbers from the 1850s onward, many noted their skilled horsemanship, nerve, and clear thinking. These were skills needed by any participant in pig sticking. Women could also participate in pig sticking without taking a spear, or aiming for a kill. In this way, the sport did compare with fox hunting in providing thrilling runs and fast gallops, but without requiring a woman to personally kill the prey at the end.

Thus, British women in India took part in pig sticking, though the sport was also popular in other places in the British Empire as well. In an article on "African Pig-sticking," *Baily's Magazine* noted that at Tangier, Minister Sir John Hay's camp "was graced by the presence of ladies of his Excellency's family, who, as they next day fearlessly rode over the rough ground, seemed as if they would not have been very sorry to have exchanged riding-whips for boar spears."[157] Mrs. Alan Gardner recorded her participation in India during the early 1890s in *Rifle and Spear with the Rajpoots*. Gardner was quite knowledgeable about the sport, not only due to her husband's avid participation, but also her own. Her involvement was not regarded as unusual, writing "we all went out," meaning everyone, men, and women, British and Indian.[158] She joined the mounted chase with her husband, Alan. Though they were picked up at 3 am to get to the "principal Jeypore meet," they had at least four runs. She and her husband enjoyed several "capital gallops" together in which he finally killed a boar.[159]

It was the final pursuit that proved most dangerous, when Gardner's husband provoked a reticent boar from cover which charged directly at her (Figure 4.7). Gardner recalled:

> I had no spear, and should not have known how to use it if I had, so rode all I knew, and fled at the top speed I could get out of my old hunter [horse], who, I feel certain, had the meanest opinion of me for not showing fight.[160]

Though Gardner saw to her own safety and her husband killed the boar, her disappointment in herself was evident. She wanted to do more than spectate and wished for the ability to participate fully as a hunter.

Years later, Lt.-Col. Jack Hance's wife accompanied a pig-sticking party, "riding side-saddle without a spear."[161] Though women could ride in the chase after boar, without a spear, they could not protect or defend themselves except by running away. Such actions made them poor sportsmen by demonstrating a lack of courage and will. It also set a bad example for imperial rulers to show cowardice in the face of native Indians, who were usually present as well. These reasons may have been why women took up the spear.

Horse Sports and Imperial Ideology 207

Figure 4.7 Pig sticking from Mrs. Alan Gardner's *Rifle and Spear with the Rajpoots: Being the Narrative of a Winter's Travel and Sport in Northern India* (London: Chatto and Windus, 1895), page 269: Gardner participated in many "capital gallops," although she did not carry a spear, and, in this instance, when a boar charged her, it was left to her weapon-wielding husband to kill the animal. Gardner regretted her inability to participate fully in this sport, but especially her lack of skill and ability to defend herself. Later, British women took up the spear and successfully participated in the sport.
Credit: Collection of the author.

Isabel Savory was one woman who did take a spear, recording her adventures in *A Sportswoman in India*. She and her friend "M." were given mounts by the Maharajah, accoutered with Champion and Wilton sidesaddles which belonged to his newest wife.[162] Savory described pig sticking, including the company, the procedures, and the type of horse needed. M. was an "old hand" at the game, and Savory herself was also knowledgeable and experienced. M. was bold, "taking her own line more or less between the two" other hunters, and charging the boar directly.[163] However, her horse blundered over "a big prickly pear hedge" and fell down, which "unnecessarily ventilated M.'s skirt, and exposed a large amount of boot."[164] Once remounted, M. was poised for first spear but missed, so the boar catapulted her off her horse and tore at her as she played dead on the ground.[165] Unhurt, she gamely remounted once more and then the "first spear did actually fall to M.'s proud lot. The boar went straight for her; for the second time that day she leaned well down, and this time drove it home in triumph."[166]

Despite the physical demands of pig sticking, Savory argued that women should carry spears and participate directly,[167] even if the press at home in Britain sometimes raised an eyebrow at this unfamiliar and unorthodox sport. *The Ladies' Field* magazine was unusually critical in a review of Savory's adventures, writing: "We are not quite sure that all her experiences are suitable even for a modern woman to seek."[168] Certainly the sport was dangerous, as injury to both participants and horses illustrated, but was it more dangerous than the massive fences one faced at a gallop in the fox hunting fields of the Shires? Or was *The Ladies' Field* commenting on the problematic style of riding sidesaddle in such rough conditions?

The sidesaddle did give women a strong platform from which to spear, in that the pommels locked a woman into place. However, this stationary position was also problematic, especially in a fall, which was common. The momentum of spearing would also have been more jarring to a sidesaddle rider who could not adjust to the shock and recoil of stabbing. Finally, the sidesaddle restricted freedom of action to one side only, as Savory noted, which was also problematic for polo. These limitations spurred women to abandon the sidesaddle for a more utilitarian, comfortable, and safer alternative. This was the man's cross-saddle, which was becoming ever more popular for ladies in India because it enabled more freedom and authority when riding, whether in hunting boar or playing polo.

Polo: Playing the Imperial Game

Polo was one of the most important equestrian sports in India, fondly represented in popular culture by Rudyard Kipling's story, "The Maltese Cat," in which the ferocity of game and play is narrated by the pony.[169] As Winston Churchill related about his Indian service, "the serious purpose of life ... was expressed in one word: Polo."[170] Although, like boar hunting, the game had an ancient heritage, the modern mounted contest was not "invented" until the 1850s by British military officers who had witnessed natives playing on ponies.

By 1854, Lieutenant Joseph Ford Sherer and Captain Robert Stewart joined tea planters in playing the game in Manipur, near the district of Cachar in Assam near Myanmar.[171] They formed a club in 1859, the Silchar Kangjai Club, from the native words "*sagol*" for horse and "*kangjai*" for hockey stick. By the 1860s, the game had come to Calcutta where it was often played at Ballygunge, a military encampment in the suburbs.[172] The first formal match was between the Barrackpore Club and the Calcutta Club in 1863.[173] By the 1870s, polo had become so popular that it was typically played at stations on Mondays, Wednesdays, and Fridays, and became a central part of daily routine.[174]

Polo became the horse sport of choice for military men in India. As T.F. Dale noted:

> Pig sticking is not to be had everywhere nor indeed to any good purpose in many places, cricket and football are not well suited to the climate, big game shooting is scarce, and leave is often scarcer still at the best seasons of the year, but polo is always possible and can be played all the year round.[175]

Modern polo developed in India (after 1857 and the Indian Rebellion), and later in England (1872), so women were already hunting and developing equestrian skills that enabled them to play a brisk and effective game.

Polo was a demanding sport, requiring both mental and physical prowess. Polo games were fast and furious affairs, as J.N.P. Watson described:

> Fundamentally, [polo] consists of driving a ball three and a half inches in diameter with a long and strangely balanced bamboo mallet from the back of a galloping horse. Your opponents, meanwhile, are constantly trying to obstruct your endeavors in the hope of keeping the ball to themselves. The result is that the play twists and turns relentlessly in a dizzying flurry of sticks and a stampede of ponies' feet.[176]

Polo was divided into periods of play called *chukkers*, during which members of two teams vied to score points by driving a small ball through goal posts at opposite ends of the field.[177] As Dale wrote, "A [polo] team in fact is something like an English political party whose object is to govern the country if possible, but if not, to hinder their opponents from doing so" – usually by whatever means necessary.[178] Initially the game had been centered on slower and more polite play until about 1880, as "An Elderly Gentleman" wrote in the *Civil and Military Gazette*: "We did not have any foolishness, such as hustling, and riding off and galloping about like maniacs. Not at all; we took our pleasures calmly."[179] This milder play was conducive to ladies' participation, but as the game developed and was taken up by British officers, the sport became more competitive and the play was rougher.

Polo was a game based on warfare, at least in its traditional roots. Mr. Jorrocks could claim that hunting was "the sport of kings, the image of war without its guilt, and only five-and-twenty per cent of its danger," but the same claim, and perhaps a stronger one, could be made for polo.[180] As Dale wrote,

> Polo is a sport which is suitable to a warlike people and is, in itself, almost a military exercise. The qualities which make a man a good cavalry soldier are exactly those which are needed in a good polo player – quickness, dash, decision, and pluck.[181]

Dale pointed out that the military and warlike characteristics of polo, and the qualities it developed ("quickness, dash, decision, and pluck"), applied to women as well as men. There were only two things necessary to become a good polo player: ponies and practice.[182] Women as well as men could become skilled players by practice, and they could train ponies. The rest was natural: a "good eye," "good horsemanship," and good aim were all that was needed.[183] Dale admitted that polo was a great aid in learning to ride well, as it developed seat and control – necessary for both male and female equestrians.[184] Many gymkhana games like tilting also contributed to developing these qualities.

Women were needed for polo in a way that they were not for other horse sports. As station and tournament polo increased in popularity during the late 1800s, specially trained ponies (and lots of them) were needed for the high level of play. At least 6–12 ponies were needed per player.[185] Working men did not have the time to train and ride so many ponies due to their career responsibilities and professional commitments, but their wives or female relatives did, and could. In India, it was also common for British wives to train and condition polo ponies for their husbands who did not have time to do so themselves, given constraints of their imperial roles in the Indian Civil Service, but for whom competition in military polo matches was a high priority. As riding was the predominant social activity in India, it was easy to use equestrian skills and activities to train the quick, agile, and clever ponies for competition. In fact, this was a rewarding occupation for women.[186]

Women who trained polo ponies became better riders, but also better sportswomen, and even better representatives of their sex.[187] In stark contrast to earlier stereotypes, these women were literally "pretty horsebreakers," and there was not believed to be anything wrong with such activities. In India, their training and visual display of expertise was both useful and necessary. It was not considered unfeminine to be valuable.

By the 1880s, the popularity of polo had caused a sharp increase in the price of polo ponies. Single ponies might cost thousands of pounds. In 1899, the author of an article in *The Ladies' Field* wondered whether ordinary Britons could afford to play the game: "Whether husbands will appreciate their wives' latest craze [for polo] remains to be seen, as polo ponies in India are fast becoming a luxury, even to men of means, and to have to provide ponies for one's wife, and perhaps daughters, is no light matter."[188] The author completely missed the point: women could train cheaper, unbroken ponies for their husbands' use, while also participating in the game themselves.

More than that, because polo was a game that required an even number of players per side, it was often necessary to recruit women to complete full teams of players. As Dale noted about station polo in 1879,

> It was difficult to get together eight players for a team with anything like regularity, and when I first played men were collected from all the services represented in a large station. A civilian, a barrister, a parson, a veterinary surgeon, two gunners, and a policeman were among the most regular players we had.[189]

Women were therefore important and often regular participants in training games and informal competitions – and many probably rode and played far better than off-duty lawyers or parsons.

Sidesaddles were not much use for polo, however, especially if the ponies were intended for a man's use. Thus, women switched to riding astride to train for and play the game. As equestrian and author Ivy Maddison noted, "Playing polo [aside] is practically impossible since the rider cannot do much twisting around in her saddle."[190] Therefore, for both travel and sport, women abandoned the sidesaddle – and its clothing – to ride astride like men. As Anna Chitty explained, "My future husband, the adjutant, Captain Arthur Chitty, was horse mad too, and taught me to ride, and then school horses for polo."[191] She and other women frequently played polo in Calcutta or at the Tollygunhe Country Club, just south of the city, where "a pleasant outing was to send the ponies to one club and ride cross country to the other."[192]

By the 1890s, commentators wrote about women playing polo in India. "[W]e see polo played by ladies on clever blood ponies," W.A. Kerr noted in 1891, and others agreed.[193] "Ladies have begun at last to play genuine polo," *The Ladies' Field* noted, "They have been playing regularly for some time past at Gulmurg, the hot weather resort of Cashmir ... After much practice and perseverance, they play a very fair, if not altogether fast, game."[194] A special ladies' tournament was even held, with three to side. Ladies' participation in Gulmurg was even stronger by 1900.[195] "When one looks back, or rather reads accounts of the sort of existence passed by Anglo-Indians of the gentler sex some years ago," concluded *The Ladies' Field* magazine, "one cannot but feel proud of the way in which women have improved and developed."[196]

Female players increased during the early twentieth century, as illustrated by the example of Noëla Whiting (later Mrs. James Brander-Dunbar) (Figure 4.8). Whiting is important not only because she was handicapped two goals, denoting her expertise, but because she learned to play polo in Burma, then a province of British India.[197] She regularly participated in station games and tournaments, and was on winning teams.[198] *The Polo Monthly* wrote:

Figure 4.8 "Miss Noëla Whiting, who plays polo regularly at the Taunton Vale Club. She learnt the game in Burma, and is handicapped at two points," from *The Polo Monthly* (July 1920), page 301: Whiting learned to play polo in Burma and became a member of the Taunton Polo Club in Somerset when she returned to England in 1921, playing the full 56-minute game with men. The reason for her success was evident: in Burma, she had "been accustomed to ride astride from her youth up, has obtained a mastery of this method of horsemanship, and adopts it even when riding to hounds in preference to the most usual sidesaddle." Competing and riding publicly in the astride style was yet another gender-neutral form of public mastery and imperial power, showing the superiority of both British men and women in the Empire.

There is in this country, for some reason or other, a prejudice against women playing polo, possibly because it is thought that they are not equal to the strenuous happening of the game – the riding-off, etc. But as Miss Whiting is concerned, no such prejudice can exist, as she is a strong horsewoman and can ride out as well as most men. She is very quick on the ball, hits well on both sides of the pony, is a very certain goal hitter, and last, but certainly not least, not only knows the game thoroughly, but plays it. She is well mounted on quick, handy ponies. To those who do not believe in a woman being able to play polo all I can say is: come and see her play.[199]

The Polo Monthly also drew out the benefits of this imperial experience for the sport of polo in Britain

> Until Miss Whiting arrived in Burma in October 1915 there had been no thought of a 2/5 Somerset polo team. Miss Whiting for several years had ample opportunity of watching good polo and schooling her step-father's [Maj. Claude Ward Jackson] ponies. Within a month, slow chukkers were in full swing, and gradually as the fever developed, polo became the sole topic of conversation. The fact stands that had it not been for Miss Whiting's energy and organizing capacity there would have been no team.[200]

After her sojourn in Burma, Whiting returned to England. By 1921, she was a member of the Taunton Polo Club in Somerset, and played the full 56-minute game with men.[201] The reason for her success was evident: in Burma, she had "been accustomed to ride astride from her youth up, has obtained a mastery of this method of horsemanship, and adopts it even when riding to hounds in preference to the most usual sidesaddle."[202] Whiting brought her imperial experience back to Britain, serving as the Master of the Taunton Vale Harriers and continuing to ride astride.[203]

In India, therefore, polo served three interrelated purposes for British women: it made them better riders by improving their horsemanship; it encouraged healthy, outdoor social gatherings; and it added purpose and value to the lives of female riders as they trained their husbands' polo ponies. Competing and riding publicly in the astride style was yet another gender-neutral form of public mastery and imperial power, showing the superiority of both British men and women.

Riding Astride in British India

In tandem with the pursuit of other equestrian sports like pig sticking, polo showed why women needed to ride astride rather than sidesaddle. Given the demanding nature of riding and hunting in India, a majority of British women had abandoned the sidesaddle for the cross-saddle well before the First World War. By 1909, riding astride was declared "a time-honoured custom" for "women of all ages abroad in the Colonies."[204] The Ladies Field confirmed:

> riding astride is a safer, more rational, and more comfortable method than that now in vogue. A woman's command over a horse is admittedly greater when she is riding astride, while concerning the additional freedom and ease of the astride position for rough riding and long distances there can be no question.[205]

This was the issue for British women riding throughout India: rough conditions demanded that female riders exercise more control over their mounts than a traditional sidesaddle would allow. As W.A. Kerr admitted by 1890, "There is no doubt that the Duchess de Berri mode of sitting on a horse [astride] is much less fatiguing to the rider [and] gives her more power over the half-broken animals that in foreign countries do duty for ladies' horses."[206]

Because sidesaddles were custom-fitted, women often traveled with them wherever they went. But sidesaddles were problematic to ship due to their weight and the awkward but delicate construction of the pommels. If the pommels or the saddle tree (the wooden backbone beneath the seat) broke in transit, the expensive sidesaddle was useless.[207] In addition, imperial horses were narrower; therefore, they were less suited to large and heavy sidesaddles and more suited for women to ride astride. Men's saddles fit these horses, were more easily available around the Empire, and could be purchased without undue difficulty or expense. Cross-saddles were also easier to travel with because they weighed less than ten pounds, while sidesaddles were much bulkier and heavier – at least double the weight.[208]

Mrs. R.H. Tyacke also endorsed the practice of riding astride for travelling in the 1890s. She recorded her two years' adventuring in Kullu and Lahoul, in today's Himachal Pradesh in the western Himalayas of northern India. "Directly we left civilization and began camp life," she wrote,

> I discarded promptly my Champion and Wilton saddle and my Busvine habit, and took to riding cross-legged in my shooting-dress, after the manner of the Kullu ladies. There is no doubt that the cross seat, in my Thibetan saddle, greatly added to my comfort on the bad roads, and was far less fatiguing on the rough and tiny ponies of the country, and with the perpetual up and down hill.[209]

Tyacke considered riding astride "far preferable" to riding sidesaddle. She cautioned that conditions in India were much rougher than could be imagined in Britain, and that a certain amount of social leeway was necessary for not only comfort, but for safety and survival.[210]

Traveling from Dalhousie to Mahmool via horseback around 1900, Isabel Savory wrote: "The last thing a woman ought to have ridden on was a sidesaddle, which is invariably uncomfortable for herself and her horse uphill. Mine slipped on the Arab pony continually, until at last, from sheer discomfort, I rode on it crossways."[211] Mrs. Alan Gardner endured similar circumstances: she was presented with a pony for riding – "of course no side-saddle."[212] Mrs. Stuart Menzies echoed the sentiment, falling off a donkey in front of a large crowd due to her unstable position on a sidesaddle: she vowed, "I should certainly ride astride now and so prevent a repetition of my ignominy. This I proceeded to do, and confess it was not graceful, but nobody seemed the least surprised or shocked."[213] Other women did the same, and found that praise, rather than censure, followed.[214] These women were celebrated for their ingenuity as well as for their strength, skill, and – especially important – authority and power. There was little shock or surprise because other women were openly riding astride in India. Mrs. Marc Clementson ("Marky") was "the first lady to hunt astride at Ootacamund in 1904 in a divided skirt."[215] Miss Ursula Lawley and her sister Celia, fine riders to hounds, followed her lead by also riding astride.[216]

Indian Army officer Charles Chenevix-Trench affirmed that both his mother and grandmother switched from riding sidesaddle to riding cross-saddle based on their experiences abroad, including India, in the early 1900s. As he wrote, "their saddles seldom fitted local horses, who never understood these lop-sided contraptions. So they took to riding astride."[217] This change was virtually required: in Jodhpur, the Maharajah forbid sidesaddles to be used on any of his horses. Hanut Singh, who would become an international polo star, initially criticized Chenevix-Trench's mother's cross-saddle riding and refused to allow her to go pig sticking until she improved. After intensive training at the Jodhpur riding school, in which she was taught to ride astride without stirrups or reins, she was permitted to ride on the polo field, "galloping down the side-lines, still without stirrups, while the two brothers, one on each side, tried to ride her off down the line."[218] After she had proved her skill, she was finally invited to go pig sticking. Thus, women not only found it more practical and comfortable to ride astride, but they were also prohibited from participating in equestrian sports in India unless they did so, which was a motivation to change.

Clothes for Riding in the Empire

To ride astride effectively, women needed appropriate riding clothing. As Chenevix-Trench hinted, Jodhpur, a town in northwest India, was especially important in this transition, as imperial experience led to the adoption of "jodhpurs," or riding trousers, and still called so today.[219] By the 1890s, G. W. Steevens remarked, "The Jodhpur riding-breeches – breeches and gaiters all in one piece, as full as you like above the knee, fitting tight below it, without a single button or strap ... are on the way to be world-famous."[220] This new trend was more significant for women, who had been limited to wearing divided skirts or trousers, while men already had breeches.

The development of masculine riding clothes for women was also significant because women expressed new identities through dress and fashion. Fashion is "a response to women's changing values about themselves," and nowhere were such values evolving more quickly and advantageously than in the British Empire.[221] As one author wrote in 1891, "In the backwoods and jungles a wide latitude in dress may be permitted without assailing the strictest modesty."[222] In Britain, the early Rational Dress movement had urged women to abandon corsets and petticoats, but was not popular, did not gain widespread approval, and did not instigate a widespread transformation in dress.[223]

Riding habits threatened the gendered social order by making men and women appear alike. In India, it created a single, white, gender-neutral ruling class. Although Victorian fashion had become more restrictive over the course of the nineteenth century – from the simple Grecian lines of the 1800s to the "imprisoning carapace" of late Victorianism – female riders around the Empire fought such constraints by donning clothes that allowed free movement for new activities.[224] Increased movement led to an increase in status and control, as women redefined their public roles and appearances. As the sidesaddle itself had created friction with technology and the ideology of separate spheres, by enabling women to break out of their domestic cages, so too did riding clothes spark conflict between fashion and gendered respectability.

But choosing exactly what to wear and how to wear it was no easy matter, as Guterbock's, a famous habit-maker, pointed out:

> What is the best kind of feminine riding kit for tropical countries, and in what respects must it differ from that worn in England? Here is a matter on which prospective Anglo-Indian mem-sahibs and Colonials frequently find it hard to gain correct information. Now please note "what is worn" by the woman experienced in Indian and Colonial riding. The smart, cool-looking habit, with its perfected astride skirt and open-fronted coat, is of Guterbock's own special rainproof and sunproof tropical material as cool and light as linen, but with the texture and smart appearance of cloth.[225]

By 1903, an advertisement for Guterbock's enthused that astride riding:

> is a subject of which we are likely to hear more in time to come, especially where the case of the Colonial comes in. Riding miles and miles over prairie land, the good horsewoman who occupied a man's saddle would, in Mr. Guterbock's estimation, possess a decided pull over her more conventional sisters.[226]

A year later, in 1904, *The Ladies' Field* admitted "there are certain conditions under which the ride-astride habit is absolutely necessary and most advisable, notably abroad, in the Bush, or on the prairies, where long stretches of country are covered and entire freedom of action is necessary."[227] By 1907, it was noted "that the popularity of riding astride waxes there can be no doubt."[228]

The fashion of imperial habits went through many changes from the late 1800s, from knock-off copies of masculine breeches and jackets to trendy and elegant ride-astride designs by the most popular habit-makers in Britain. Just as the sidesaddle habit had gone through many iterations before settling into the apron safety skirt in Britain, so too did the astride habit evolve before it became the modern boots, breeches, and jacket. The astride habit began as a long, divided skirt, which fell to the foot on either side of the horse, thus resembling a skirt on either side.[229] This created a neat outline and appearance, whether on or off the horse, and it doubled as a regular or walking outfit. As many designers pointed out, this versatility was a great benefit to British women around the Empire who might be in the saddle a great deal during the day, but also required a smart, proper outfit for visiting or other duties when dismounted.[230]

Most designers emphatically associated astride riding with the "modern" woman, an independent female who was fashionable, energetic, and by no means improper because of her sporting choices. For British women around the Empire, the ride-astride skirt was an "indispensable possession," part of an outfit that enabled her to complete her duties in rough conditions.[231] By 1906, the ride-astride habit had been "adopted by every sensible woman who realizes that an orthodox habit skirt is out of place on the veldt, and in the wilds of Mexico and the East."[232] Two years later, the ride-astride habit was deemed "one of the smartest garments" in the style and fashion column of *The Ladies' Field* magazine, by which time it had evolved so that a "long coat is cut full so that it forms the skirt, with nothing worn beneath the riding breeches and long top-boots."[233] By 1908, Guterbock's claimed that their habits were "immaculate both from the point of view of Mrs. Grundy and the wearer."[234] By 1909, "the ever-increasing band of horsewomen who adopt riding astride" could choose from Guterbock's "every imaginable innovation in the way of special coats, breeches, skirts, leggings and puttees," including many designs of women's breeches "modelled on the regulation Army pattern."[235] Form and function had merged, and women – in terms of riding dress, at least – were finally made equal with men, and indeed the most masculine of military men, all without jeopardizing their feminine qualities or appearance.

It was true that riding clothes for diverse parts of the Empire needed to be made differently than those riding habits for use in Britain. The heat of the tropics was a major concern, as traditional wool fabrics like heavy Melton cloth could not be used abroad. In the 1860s, Charlotte Canning complained how stifling her habit was – "oh, how hot a habit is!" – and surely many more women felt the same.[236] This was also part of the impetus for women to switch to riding astride, simply because the clothes were much lighter and cooler. In 1878, *The European in India; or, Anglo-Indian's Vade-Mecum* recommended "lighter material" such as "brown holland, grey linsey, or drab pique riding-habits [as] preferable to the stereotyped black cloth garment."[237] In 1878, the authors of *Tropical Trials: A Handbook for Women in the Tropics* urged women to "select cloth of a lighter make than that used in England: a good description is that known as 'The Oriental Cloth'," and to choose serge for rougher riding.[238] By the 1880s, habits were being made of "very light stuffs."[239] By the early 1900s, many habit-makers advertised special lightweight fabric for imperial riding habits, often under the general name of "Indian Whipcord."[240] These ride-astride garments were "much in vogue" in lightweight fabrics like whipcords (rather than wool) and in clever shades of grey that did not show the dust or dirt.[241] By 1915, Montague Smyth marketed "khaki drill" as "ideal for India and the Colonies."[242] A year later, the firm boasted, "For tropical countries – Anglo-Indian horsewomen please note – they have a special water-proofed linen, in 'covert-coating' shade [of greens or browns]; it is excellent for hot climate riding kit, as it has all the nice appearance of covert-coating allied with the coolness of linen."[243]

Another reason that so many women could so easily make the switch to riding astride was that it was easy for a *durzi*, or a local tailor in India, to copy these designs. In 1860, Henry Shakespear advised male hunters to have all clothing made in England if possible, but admitted that durable and presentable copies could be made on-site.[244] By the early 1900s, this practice of using local tailors for astride habits had been in full swing for years. An article from *The Ladies' Field* in 1903 included instructions for those "removed from the metropolis": "Everyone, for instance, knows and accepts the copying capabilities of the Dhurzies of India, and riding there is only comparable to walking here."[245] In fact, these copying skills were often put to work at turning out astride habits for women.[246] Even young girls proudly sported "miniature jodhpores made by a durzi."[247] Through their sporting and sartorial choices, British women looked – and often acted – exactly like men in India, thus publicly exercising and demonstrating the same kind of equality they were expected to exercise on horseback.

An Empire of Equestrians

Horse sport in India enabled British women to transform their social, cultural, and gendered sporting roles. Riding was a way to be British, to show power and authority publicly. Faced with rough conditions and uncertain and sometimes unstable rule, British women became part of a single, white, gender-neutral ruling class. This meant that Britons in India, whether male or female, acted as rulers with power, authority, and command. For women, this included abandoning the sidesaddle, as a marker of difference, and riding like men. Objections were few in this transition, for riding astride enabled women to take part in more adventurous equestrian sports like hunting and polo, to say nothing of pig sticking. Riding astride also enabled women to aid their husbands and menfolk by training horses.

Riding, whether astride or aside, helped develop a woman's personal authority, confidence, and "self-possession," as many riding manuals advocated. Riding throughout British India also helped instill these values and qualities, even more so than at home within Britain. "The more or less isolated position people occupy in the tropics, tends to the development of a greater amount of interdependence than exists in the old country," wrote the authors of *Tropical Trials*, "and society in such countries is made up of a community of interests rather than of a mere contiguity of persons."[248] Horses brought people together, whether for a game of polo, a day's hunting, or an evening ride. These "communities of interest" were horse-based, and the sport further developed physical, mental, and public strength for Britons around the Empire. As H.J.A. Hervey wrote in *The European in India*, imperial life was not for the faint of heart, for "the poor creature ... who faints at the sight of a cut finger, shrieks if a mouse runs by; who becomes 'muddled' at a crisis, who whines and whimpers when anything dreadful happens."[249] This descriptive caveat paralleled almost exactly Samuel Sidney's warning about women riding: "A girl who is afraid of the common objects of the farm and the field, who screams on the slightest possible excuse, who flies from a peaceful milch cow, and trembles at a mouse, is not fit to mount a horse, that is, if her terrors are real."[250] Such parallels were not coincidental: riders made the best imperialists and vice versa.

From a physical point of view, by the early 1900s there was little that female equestrians could not and did not do – from riding and hunting, to polo and gymkhanas, and even to pig sticking.[251] Such pursuits did not make a lady unfeminine or improper. "Women who prefer exercise and liberty ... who are afraid neither of a little fatigue nor of a little exertion, are the better, the truer, and the healthier, and can yet remain essentially feminine in their thoughts and manners," wrote Lady Greville.[252] This was true for women in Britain and in places around the Empire such as India, where Isabel Savory argued that, "The *mem-sahib* of the nineteenth century is an energetic, tennis, Badminton, calling and riding – sometimes sporting – creation."[253] Sports, and especially equestrian sports, made Britons "British": "the moral qualities necessary to make a good rider are precisely those which have given England her superiority in the rank of nations."[254]

Women no longer traveled to India only to dutifully follow their husbands, if they already had one, or ensnare a match if they did not. By the late 1800s, the possibilities – indeed, the very horizons – of women's worlds had broadened. What women learned and did around the Empire mattered very much to the constructions of their personal identity, as well as to that of gendered, imperial, and national identity. Robert Baden-Powell wrote, "If polo and pig sticking have not altered the history of British India, they have at any rate altered the lives and careers of many young officers," and indeed these horse sports changed the lives of many British women as well.[255] If, by riding astride in India, women were considered – and considered themselves – no less feminine or proper, why should they be considered any differently for doing the same thing, or for riding the same way, at home in Britain?

Notes

1 John M. MacKenzie, *The Empire of Nature: Hunting, Conservation and British Imperialism* (Manchester: Manchester University Press, 1988), 168.
2 The "Indian fox" (*Vulpes bengalensis*) is native to the subcontinent, but the wily and tenacious golden jackal (*Canis aureus*) was preferred for the chase.
3 John M. MacKenzie, "The Imperial Pioneer and Hunter and the British Masculine Stereotype in Late Victorian and Edwardian Times," in *Manliness and Morality: Middle-class Masculinity in Britain and America, 1800-1914*, J.A. Mangan and James Walvin (eds.), (New York: St. Martin's Press, 1987), 179.
4 Ronald Hyam, *Empire and Sexuality: The British Experience* (Manchester: Manchester University Press, 1990), 141.

5. Mary A. Procida, "Good Sports and Right Sorts: Guns, Gender, and Imperialism in British India," *The Journal of British Studies*, 40.4 (October 2001), 461.
6. G.R. Searle, *A New England? Peace and War, 1886-1918* (Oxford: Clarendon Press, 2004), 44.
7. Albert Spencer, ed., *Memoirs of William Hickey, Volume III (1782-1790)* (London: Hurst and Blackett, Ltd., [1913–1925?]), 377.
8. Allen Guttmann, *Games and Empires: Modern Sports and Cultural Imperialism* (New York: Columbia University Press, 1994).
9. Frederick Watson, *Robert Smith Surtees: A Critical Survey* (Norwood, PA: Norwood Editions, 1978), 53.
10. M.S.S. Pandian, "Gendered Negotiations: Hunting and Colonialism in the Late 19th Century Nilgiris," in Patricia Uberoi (ed.), *Social Reform, Sexuality, and the State* (London: Sage Publications, 1996), 245.
11. Scott Bennett, "Shikar and the Raj," *South Asia*, 7.2 (1984), 72–88.
12. Joseph Sramek, "'Face Him like a Briton': Tiger Hunting, Imperialism, and British Masculinity in Colonial India, 1800-1875," *Victorian Studies*, 48.4 (Summer 2006), 659–680.
13. Mrs. C. [Kate] Martelli, "Tigers I Have Shot," in Lady Violet Beatrice Greville (ed.), *Ladies in the Field: Sketches of Sport* (New York: D. Appleton and Company, 1894), 145. The book was also published in London the same year.
14. Kenneth P. Czech, *With Rifle and Petticoat: Women as Big Game Hunters, 1880-1940* (New York: The Derrydale Press, 2002), and for comparison, Angela Thompsell, "Nimrods and Amazons: The Gendering of Big Game Hunting in Africa, 1880-1914," in Maryann Gialanella Valiulis (ed.), *Gender and Power in Irish History* (Dublin: Irish Academic Press, 2009).
15. William K. Storey, "Big Cats and Imperialism: Lion and Tiger Hunting in Kenya and Northern India, 1898-1930," *Journal of World History*, 2.2 (Fall 1991), 154–155.
16. Brian Stoddart and Keith A.P. Sandiford, eds., *The Imperial Game: Cricket, Culture, and Society* (Manchester: Manchester University Press, 1998).
17. "Snaffles" [Charles Payne], *My Sketch Book in the Shiny* (London: Gale & Polden, 1930).
18. Ramachandra Guha, "Cricket and Politics in Colonial India," *Past & Present*, 161 (November 1998), 164, 182.
19. Rachael Heyhoe Flint and Netta Rheinberg, *Fair Play: The Story of Women's Cricket* (London: Angus and Robertson Publishers, 1976), 111.
20. Dane Kennedy, *The Magic Mountains: Hill Stations and the British Raj* (Berkeley: University of California Press, 1996).
21. William Dalrymple, *White Mughals: Love and Betrayal in the Eighteenth-Century India* (New York: Viking, 2003).
22. Major Walter Campbell, *The Old Forest Ranger; or, Wild Sports of India* (New York: Stringer and Townsend, 1853), 16–17.
23. Captain Pennell Elmhirst, "Jackal Hunting on the Neilgherries, 1876," *Fox-hound, Forest, and Prairie* (London: George Routledge and Sons, 1892), 127. Underlined italics mine.
24. Pandian, 239. See also Mrinalini Sinha, *Colonial Masculinity: The 'Manly Englishman' and the 'Effeminate Bengali' in the Late Nineteenth Century* (Manchester: Manchester University Press, 1995).
25. Procida (2001), 470.
26. Sir Humphrey F. De Trafford, Bart., *The Horses of the British Empire* (London: Walter Southwood and Co., Limited, 1907).
27. Anna Chitty, *Musings of a Memsahib, 1921-1933* (Lymington: Belhaven, 1988), 37. Horace Hayes, prolific author and husband of Alice, also references "syces" in his

many texts. See M. Horace Hayes, *Training and Horse Management in India* (Calcutta: Thacker, Spink, and Co., 1885), 97–99.
28 Captain G.J. Younghusband, *The Queen's Commission* (London: John Murray, 1891), 116. See also Chitty, 3.
29 Younghusband (1891), 116.
30 Sandra Swart, "Riding High – Horses, Power and Settler Society, c.1654-1840," *Kronos*, 29 (November 2003), 47–63. See also Greg Bankoff and Sandra Swart, eds., *Breeds of Empire: The 'Invention' of the Horse in Southeast Asia and Southern Africa, 1500-1950* (Copenhagen: NIAS, 2007); and James L.A. Webb, Jr., "The Horse and Slave Trade between the Western Sahara and Senegambia," *The Journal of African History*, 34.2 (1993), 221–246.
31 John Singleton, "Britain's Military Use of Horses, 1914–1918," *Past & Present*, 139 (May 1993), 199.
32 Greville, 25.
33 Mrs. Alan Gardner, *Rifle and Spear with the Rajpoots: Being the Narrative of a Winter's Travel and Sport in Northern India* (London: Chatto and Windus, 1895), 175.
34 Violet Dickinson, ed., *Miss Eden's Letters* (London: Macmillan and Co., Ltd., 1919), "Miss Eden to Mr. C. Greville, Simla, November 1, 1838," specifically Roopur, November 13, 1838, 305–306.
35 Samuel Sidney, *The Book of the Horse* (London: Cassell, Petter & Galpin, Limited, 1875), 353.
36 "Vieille Moustache" [Robert Henderson], *The Barb and the Bridle: A Handbook of Equitation for Ladies* (London: The "Queen" Newspaper Office, 1874), 119.
37 Leonora Starr, *Colonel's Lady* (London: G. Bell & Sons, 1937), 41. "Starr" was actually a pseudonym; the author was Leonora Dorothy Rivers Mackesy.
38 Augustus J.C. Hare, *The Story of Two Noble Lives, Being Memorials of Charlotte, Countess Canning, and Louisa, Marchioness of Waterford*, 3 Volumes (London: George Allen, 1893). See Volume 2, the entry for Barrackpore, October 22, page 100.
39 Chitty, 3.
40 "Vieille Moustache," 3.
41 "Sketches in Bengal," *Baily's Magazine of Sports and Pastimes*, Volume 75 (December 1829), 105.
42 Dickinson, ix.
43 Dickinson, "Miss Eden to Mr. C. Greville, Simla, November 1, 1838," specifically Roopur, November 13, 1838, 305.
44 Dickinson, "Miss Eden to Mr. C. Greville, Simla, November 1, 1838," specifically Roopur, November 13, 1838, 305–306.
45 Edward J. Buck, *Simla, Past and Present* (Bombay: The Times Press, 1925), 204. This was the second edition, the first having been published in 1904.
46 Buck, 210, citing an article "London Society" from April 1872.
47 "The Wild Sports of the Neilgherry Mountains," *Baily's Magazine of Sports and Pastimes*, Volume 2 (February 1861), 249.
48 C.T. Buckland, *Sketches of Social Life in India* (London: W.H. Allen and Co., 1884), 87. See also "Sketches in Bengal," *Baily's Magazine of Sports and Pastimes*, Volume 75 (December 1829), 105.
49 Dr. W. Hoffmeister, *Travels to Ceylon and Continental India* (Edinburgh: William P. Kennedy, 1848), 422. His Twelfth Letter, dated 23 September 1845, concerned his visit to Simla, having arrived there 4 September.
50 Hoffmeister, 476.
51 Hoffmeister, 475 and 480.
52 George Francklin Atkinson, *"Curry and Rice," on Forty Plates; Or, The Ingredients of Social Life at "Our Station" in India* (London: Day and Son, 1859), title page.

53 Atkinson, unpaginated. A riding habit jacket (circa 1760–1770) of white fustian lined with linen that might have seen imperial service is preserved at the Victoria and Albert Museum (T.57-2009): http://collections.vam.ac.uk/item/O251137/riding-habit-jacket-unknown/.
54 Atkinson, unpaginated.
55 "Vieille Moustache," 144.
56 Atkinson, unpaginated.
57 Hare, 59, for Calcutta, March 11, 1856.
58 Hare, 65, for Calcutta, May 3, 1856 and Calcutta, April 1, 1856.
59 Hare, 72–73.
60 Hare, 52 and 58.
61 Hare, 62–63, for Barrackpore, March 19, 1856.
62 Hare, 132, for Calcutta, December 18, 1856.
63 Hare, 89, for Calcutta, June 17, 1856.
64 Sir Mortimer Durand, *Life of the Right Hon. Sir Alfred Comyn Lyall, P.C., K.C.B., G.C.I.E., D.C.L., LL.D.* (London/Edinburgh: William Blackwood and Sons, 1913), 112.
65 Durand, 114.
66 Durand, 116.
67 Durand, 109–110.
68 Durand, 134.
69 "Vieille Moustache," 161.
70 Durand, 162.
71 Augustus Frederick Oakes, *The Young Lady's Equestrian Assistant, Dedicated to My First Pupil, and Printed for the Benefit of Those Ladies Residing in India* (Madras: R. Twigg, 1850), 2–3.
72 Sidney (1875), 343.
73 "Vieille Moustache," 161.
74 Professor Furbor, *The Lady's Equestrian Companion; or, Golden Key to Equitation* (London: Saunders and Otley, 1847), v, 86.
75 T.A. Jenkins, *The Lady and her Horse; being Hints Selected from Various Sources and Compiled into a System of Equitation* (Madras: Pharoah and Co., 1857). For example, compare Jenkins' pages 38–69 with *The Young Lady's Equestrian Manual* (1838), 84.
76 Oakes, 29.
77 Victoria Condie, "Thacker, Spink and Company: Bookselling and Publishing in Mid-Nineteenth-Century Calcutta," in R. Fraser and M. Hammond (eds.), *Books Without Borders*, Volume 2: Perspectives from South Asia (London: Palgrave Macmillan, 2008), 112–124.
78 Mrs. Power O'Donoghue, *(The Common Sense of Riding) Riding for Ladies, with Hints on the Stable* (Calcutta: Thacker, Spink and Co., 1887 and Bombay: Thacker and Co., Ltd., 1887). It was also published in 1905 in Calcutta and Simla by Thacker, Spink and Co.
79 Alice Hayes, *The Horsewoman* (Calcutta: Thacker, Spink & Co., 1893 and Bombay: Thacker & Co., 1893).
80 See Buckland, advertisements following the end of the book.
81 Marchioness of Dufferin and Ava, *Our Viceregal Life in India*, 2 volumes (London: John Murray, 1890), see Volume 2, the entry for Dehra Dun, 1887, 153.
82 Marchioness of Dufferin and Ava, see Volume 1, the entry for Simla, 1885, 138.
83 Marchioness of Dufferin and Ava, see Volume 1, the entry for Simla, 1885, 138.
84 Marchioness of Dufferin and Ava, see Volume 1, the entry for Simla, 1885, 184.
85 Marchioness of Dufferin and Ava, see Volume 1, the entry for Simla, 1885, 139.
86 Greville, 19–20.

87 "Chota Mem," *The English Bride in India* (London: Luzac, 1909), 2–3.
88 Greville, 19–20.
89 Greville, iv–v.
90 "Sports and Pastimes in Kashmir: Gulmurg, as summer capital of Kashmir," *The Ladies' Field* (November 10, 1900), Supplement: Sports and Pastimes, unpaginated.
91 "Old Shikarri" [G.A.R. Dawson], *Nilgiri Sporting Reminiscences* (Madras: Higginbotham and Co., 1880), 126.
92 J.K. Stanford, *Ladies in the Sun: The Memsahibs' India, 1790-1860* (London: The Gallery Press, 1962), 10.
93 "Old Shikarri," 128.
94 J.F. Smail, *A Centenary Chronicle of the Ootacamund Hunt, 1845-1945* (Madras: Associated Printers, 1945).
95 "Fox-hounds in India," *The Sporting Magazine*, Volume 82, First Series/Volume 7, Second Series (May 1833), 53.
96 "Fox-hounds in India," *The Sporting Magazine*, Volume 82, First Series/Volume 7, Second Series (May 1833), 56.
97 "Stonehenge" [John Henry Walsh], *Manual of British Rural Sports* (London: G. Routledge and Co., 1856), 118–119.
98 C. J. Apperley, *Nimrod Abroad*, Volume 2 (London: Henry Colburn, 1842), 86. See also Dawson, 126–127.
99 Hon. J.W. Best, *Indian Shikar Notes* (Lahore: The Pioneer Press, 1931), 147.
100 Campbell (1853), 27.
101 Atkinson, unpaginated.
102 Isabel Savory, *A Sportswoman in India* (London: Hutchinson and Co., 1900), 47.
103 Campbell, 47 [1853]; 393–394 [1842].
104 *The Call of the Nilgiris: Ootacamund, Coonoor, Kotagiri* (Ootacamund: Nilgiri Information Bureau, 1911), 11.
105 "The Wild Sports of the Neilgherry Mountains," *Baily's Magazine of Sports and Pastimes*, Volume 2 (February 1861), 249.
106 Frederick Price, *Ootacamund: A History* (Madras: Government Press, 1908).
107 Smail, 10.
108 "Old Shikarri," 137.
109 "Old Shikarri," 136.
110 Savory, 47.
111 *The Call of the Nilgiris*, 11.
112 "Old Shikarri," 146.
113 "Old Shikarri," 49–50.
114 "Old Shikarri," 50.
115 "Old Shikarri," 50.
116 Savory, 17.
117 Savory, 52.
118 Savory, 53.
119 Savory, 45.
120 Thomas F. Dale, *The Fox* (London: Longmans, Green, and Co., 1906), 180–201. The book was also published in Bombay the same year. See also Savory, 53.
121 Greville, 21–22.
122 Durand, 115, citing Lyall letter from Hoshungabad, 1864.
123 "The Bombay Hounds," *The Ladies' Field*, Volume 81 (March 23, 1918), 105.
124 "A Woman of No Importance" [Amy Charlotte Bewicke Menzies], *Memories Discreet and Indiscreet* (London: Herbert Jenkins Limited, 1917), 86. See also David Fraser, "Paper-chasing in India," *The Badminton Magazine of Sports and Pastimes*, Volume 15 (July 1902), 50.

125 "Sports and Pastimes in Kashmir: Gulmurg, as summer capital of Kashmir," *The Ladies' Field* (November 10, 1900), Supplement: Sports and Pastimes.
126 "Ladies' Gymkhana at Wimbledon," *The Ladies' Field*, Volume 6 (August 5, 1899), unpaginated.
127 Buck, 146, 149, 152.
128 A good photograph illustrating the yet-unimproved area is in the British Library's India Office Photographs Collections, Bailey Collection (Album of Indian and European views compiled by Frederick Bailey), photo 1083/3 (6), c. 1864.
129 Marchioness of Dufferin and Ava, Volume 2, Simla, 1886, 25–6. See also Buck, 153, for illustration of a gymkhana (no date) with a lady sidesaddle clearly visible and ready to tilt at the ring.
130 Marchioness of Dufferin and Ava, Volume 2, Calcutta, 1886–7, 104.
131 Marchioness of Dufferin and Ava, Volume 2, Dehra Dun, 1887, 167–8.
132 *The Call of the Nilgiris*, 9.
133 Marchioness of Dufferin and Ava, Volume 2, Calcutta, 1887, 112.
134 Fraser, 49.
135 Fraser, 51, 55, 60.
136 Fraser, 51, 58.
137 Greville, 23–24.
138 Campbell (1853), 369.
139 "Maori" [James Inglis], *Sport and Work on the Nepal Frontier* (London: Macmillan and Co., 1878), 85. Captain R.S.S. Baden-Powell, *Pigsticking or Hoghunting* (London: Harrison and Sons, 1889), 26–31.
140 See illustration "Triumph!" in Baden-Powell, frontispiece.
141 Gardner, 268.
142 Campbell (1853), 369.
143 Captain J.T. Newall, *Hog Hunting in the East and Other Sports* (London: Tinsley Brothers, 1867), 9.
144 Campbell (1853), 369.
145 Major-General J.G. Elliott, *Field Sports in India, 1800-1947* (London: Gentry Books, 1973), 61.
146 Elliott, 23.
147 Elliott, 36–37.
148 Elliott, 61. See also the British Library's India Office Photograph Collections, Forbes Collection (Miscellaneous Portraits and Views), 816/59-110 (Box 42).
149 Elliott, 70.
150 Elliott, 74 and 76.
151 Elliott, 70.
152 Elliott, 208.
153 Elliott, 62.
154 Elliott, 64.
155 Best, 191.
156 Elliott, 7. Italics mine.
157 "African Pig-sticking," *Baily's Magazine of Sports and Pastimes*, Volume 35 (May 1880), 282.
158 Gardner, 211.
159 Gardner, 268.
160 Gardner, 171.
161 Lt.-Col. Jack Hance, *Riding Master* (London: Robert Hale Limited, 1960), quote on page 66 and background on page 63.
162 Savory, 16.
163 Savory, 19.

164 Savory, 21.
165 Savory, 24.
166 Savory, 27.
167 Savory, 16.
168 "Books of the Day: A *Sportswoman in India* by Isabel Savory," *The Ladies' Field*, Volume 11 (October 13, 1900), 197.
169 Rudyard Kipling, "The Maltese Cat," *The Day's Work* (London: Macmillan and Co., Limited, 1948).
170 Winston Churchill, *My Early Life: A Roving Commission* (London: Odhams Press Limited, 1948), 104. This text was originally published in 1930.
171 Horace A. Laffaye, *The Evolution of Polo* (Jefferson, NC: McFarland and Company, Inc., 2009), 10 and 73.
172 Laffaye, 11 and 73.
173 Laffaye, 11.
174 Laffaye, 56–57.
175 T.F. Dale, *The Game of Polo* (Westminster: Archibald Constable and Company, 1897), 17.
176 J.N.P. Watson, *The World of Polo: Past and Present* (Topsfield, MA: Salem House, 1986), 1.
177 Current polo rules call for seven-minute chukkers, or periods of play, with three- to five-minute breaks in between, and four to six chukkers per club match or eight chukkers per full game. See "Polo Rules," *Hurlingham Polo Magazine*, at http://www.hurlinghammedia.com/polo_rules.php.
178 Dale, 90.
179 Cited in G.J. Younghusband, *Polo in India* (London: W.H. Allen & Co., 1890), 4.
180 Robert Smith Surtees, *Handley Cross; or, Mr. Jorrocks's Hunt* (London, 1854), 130.
181 Dale, 1.
182 Dale, 19.
183 Dale, 25.
184 Dale, 29.
185 Younghusband (1890), 60.
186 Dale, 33–34.
187 Greville, iv–v.
188 "Ladies' Polo in Cashmir," *The Ladies' Field*, Volume 7 (October 14, 1899), 224.
189 Dale, 207.
190 Ivy Maddison, *Riding Astride for Girls* (London: Hutchinson, 1924), 8.
191 Chitty, 3.
192 Chitty, 5. The Tollygunge Club is still in existence: http://www.tollygungeclub.org/.
193 W.A. [William Alexander] Kerr, *Riding for Ladies* (New York: Frederick A. Stokes Company, 1891), 77.
194 "Ladies' Polo in Cashmir," *The Ladies' Field*, Volume 7 (October 14, 1899), 224.
195 "Sports and Pastimes in Kashmir," *The Ladies' Field* (November 10, 1900), Supplement, unpaginated.
196 "Ladies' Polo in Cashmir," *The Ladies' Field*, Volume 7 (October 14, 1899), 224.
197 "Polo: What to Watch and How," *The Sketch: A Journal of Art and Actuality*, Volume 114 (May 11, 1921), 202.
198 "A Lady Polo Player," *The Polo Monthly* (July 1920), 295.
199 *The Polo Monthly* (July 1920), 321, with photo on 301, cited in Laffaye, *The Evolution of Polo*, 235–236.
200 The letter was by "The Cantonment Coper" (likely Col. Thomas Townley Macan (T.T.M.)) in *The Polo Monthly*. See Laffaye, *The Evolution of Polo*, 236, from "Miss Noela Whiting," *The Polo Monthly* (September 1920), 522–524.

201 *The Sketch: A Journal of Art and Actuality*, Volume 116 (December 7, 1921), 365.
202 "Should Women Play Polo?" *The Press* (Christchurch, New Zealand), Tuesday, June 26, 1923, 2.
203 *The Sketch: A Journal of Art and Actuality*, Volume 116 (December 7, 1921), 365.
204 "Saunters through the Shops, At Hart and Sons'," *The Ladies' Field*, Volume 47 (October 30, 1909), unpaginated.
205 "Saunters through the Shops, At Guterbock's," *The Ladies' Field*, Volume 31 (October 21, 1905), unpaginated.
206 Kerr, 87.
207 Shelley Leigh Hunt and Alexander S. Kenny, *Tropical Trials: A Hand-book for Women in the Tropics* (London: W. H. Allen & Co., 1883), "Saddlery," 49–50.
208 Alice M. Hayes, *The Horsewoman: A Practical Guide to Side-Saddle Riding* (New York: Charles Scribner's Sons, 1903), 54–55.
209 Mrs. R.H Tyacke, *How I Shot My Bears; or, Two Years' Tent Life in Kullu and Lahoul* (London: Sampson Low, Marston and Company, 1893), 48–49.
210 Tyacke, 49–50.
211 Savory, 80.
212 Gardner, 59.
213 "A Woman of No Importance," 189.
214 "A Woman of No Importance," 189.
215 Smail, 63.
216 Smail, 65.
217 Charles Pocklington Chenevix-Trench, *A History of Horsemanship* (New York: Doubleday and Company, 1970), 289.
218 Chenevix-Trench, 289.
219 "Jodhpurs, n.," *Oxford English Dictionary* (Oxford University Press, 1933 edition).
220 G.W. Steevens, *In India* (New York: Dodd, Mead and Company, 1899), 28.
221 Patricia Marks, *Bicycles, Bangs, and Bloomers: The New Woman in the Popular Press* (Lexington: The University Press of Kentucky, 1990), 172.
222 Kerr, 79.
223 Don Chapman, *Wearing the Trousers: Fashion, Freedom and the Rise of the Modern Woman* (The Hill, Stroud: Amberley Publishing, 2017), 144.
224 Marks, 149.
225 "Correct Riding Habits for Home and Tropical Wear at Guterbock's, advertisement," *The Ladies' Field*, Volume 60 (December 21, 1912), 197.
226 "Saunters Through the Shops: Guterbock, ride-astride habit," *The Ladies' Field*, Volume 23 (October 21, 1903), 296.
227 "Saunters thro' the Shops, At Guterbock's," *The Ladies' Field*, Volume 27 (December 3, 1904), 560.
228 "Saunters Through the Shops, at Thomas and Sons", *The Ladies' Field*, Volume 37 (March 23, 1907), 138. See also "The Thomas Convertible Ride-Astride Habit at Thomas and Sons', advertisement," *The Ladies' Field*, Volume 37 (March 23, 1907), 117.
229 "Saunters thro' the Shops, At Guterbock's," *The Ladies' Field*, Volume 27 (December 3, 1904), 560.
230 "Guterbock's, ride-astride habit," *The Ladies' Field*, Volume 28 (February 4, 1905), 384.
231 "Saunters through the Shops, At Guterbock's," *The Ladies' Field*, Volume 32 (February 10, 1906), unpaginated.
232 "Saunters through the Shops, At Guterbock's," *The Ladies' Field*, Volume 34 (September 1, 1906), 511.

233 "Vanity's Visions: Riding Habits," *The Ladies' Field*, Volume 43 (November 7, 1908), 376.
234 "Saunters through the Shops, At Guterbock's," *The Ladies' Field*, Volume 43 (September 26, 1908), unpaginated.
235 "Saunter through the Shops, At Guterbock's," *The Ladies' Field*, Volume 44 (February 27, 1909), unpaginated.
236 Hare, 43, see entry for Madras, February 22, 1856.
237 Edmund C.P. Hull, *The European in India; or, Anglo-Indian's Vade-Mecum* (London: C. Kegan Paul and Co., 1878), 14.
238 Hunt and Kenny, 12–13.
239 "Theo. Stephenson Browne" [Miss G. Hamlin], *In the Riding-School: Chats with Esmeralda* (Boston: D. Lothrop Company, 1890), 190.
240 "Saunter thro' the Shops: E. Tautz and Sons'," *The Ladies' Field*, Volume 19 (November 22, 1902), unpaginated. See also "Saunters through the Shops, At Montague Smyth's," *The Ladies' Field*, Volume 43 (December 11, 1909), unpaginated.
241 "Vanity's Visions: Riding Habits," *The Ladies' Field*, Volume 43 (November 7, 1908), 376.
242 "Up-to-date Riding Kit, at Montague Smyth's: Ride astride coats," *The Ladies' Field*, Volume 71 (October 23, 1915), 396.
243 "These are the New Season's Correct Designs from Montague Smyth, advertisement," *The Ladies' Field*, Volume 75 (October 21, 1916), 292.
244 Captain Henry Shakespear, *The Wild Sports of India* (Boston: Ticknor and Fields, 1860), 6–7.
245 "Wrinkles: Practical Riding Habit, and How to Make It," *The Ladies' Field*, Volume 23 (October 10, 1903), 178.
246 Starr, 41.
247 Starr, 161.
248 Hunt and Kenny, 448.
249 H.J.A. Hervey, *The European in India* (London: Stanley Paul and Co., 1913), 201.
250 Sidney (1875), 343.
251 "The Athletic Woman," *The Ladies' Field*, Volume 15 (October 12, 1901), 183.
252 Greville, iv–v.
253 Savory, 338.
254 Greville, 16.
255 Lieutenant-General Sir Robert Baden-Powell, *Memories of India: Recollections of Soldiering and Sport* (Philadelphia: David McKay, 1915), 31.

Chapter 5

Femininity, Sporting Equality, and Riding Astride in Britain Before and After the First World War, 1894–1932

While riding astride was acceptable for British women in India, the respectability of the style was still being debated in Britain. The few brave women who had pursued the style prior to 1900 were often crucified as unfeminine or even unnatural. After riding cross-saddle in Jodhpur to pursue polo and pig sticking, Charles Chenevix-Trench's mother returned to Britain and hunted astride, where she was initially deemed "eccentric."[1] Polo player Noëla Whiting returned from Burma and became Master of the Taunton Vale Harriers, where she too rode astride.[2] But, at the turn of the century, there was more criticism than praise for women riding astride in Britain. In May 1890, "a lady, wife of an English baronet, appeared in the Row, attended by her groom, and mounted cross-legged," wearing a long, divided skirt.[3] Or, as *The Times* reported, "the wife of a well-known R.A. electrified Exmoor by appearing astride at a meet of the Devon and Somerset Staghounds, an innovation which furnished the illustrated papers with material for many criticisms and witticisms."[4] William Fawcett, *The Field*'s editor for hunting and racing, listed many reasons why women should only ride sidesaddle: they "were said to be endangering their health; horses did not like it; no woman could grip like a man; and the leading shows resolutely set their faces against the new style."[5]

But with so many British women riding this way around the Empire, their sisters at home were quickly drawn by these examples to the comfort, effectiveness, and safety of the cross-saddle seat. Thus, this chapter spans from the publication of Lady Greville's *Ladies in the Field: Sketches of Sport* in 1894, acknowledging the importance of imperial experience in transforming equestrian sports, to Eva (E.V.A.) Christy's *Cross-Saddle and Side-Saddle: Modern Riding for Men and Women* in 1932, by which point the astride style had long been the preferred choice of female riders. As early as 1894, Caspar Whitney, an American visitor to Britain, noted the "very general feeling among thinking and reasoning people that riding astride was far and away the safer and more hygienic, and certain to become recognized as such at no distant time."[6]

The wider emancipation of the First World War was important in advancing the women's movement as a whole, but a sporting revolution for women had occurred much earlier. Scholars have consistently credited the First World War with instigating the change to riding astride for women, as do many contemporary sources. But archival research shows that British women were already riding astride in Britain and around the Empire well before 1914. The cross-saddle seat was popularly adopted in Britain during what Captain Pennell Elmhirst called "these equality days" of the early 1900s, and the style gained widespread acceptance before 1914.[7] It was this seat that enabled British women to so effectively aid the war effort, from teaching male recruits how to ride and retraining cavalry remount horses, to spearheading horse-breeding efforts and leading hunts as Masters of Hounds in the absence of menfolk.[8]

The war may have strengthened the idea of domesticity, of women as homemakers on a "home" front, but it also provided them with new prospects. After 1918, female participation in activities and sports increased, as had been the case after 1815.[9] In the post-Great War years, modern amenities provided women of all social classes with more time for leisure, while there was a rise in real wages that enabled women to afford to take part in other activities such as riding and hunting.[10] By the end of Victoria's reign, there were approximately four million horses in Great Britain, with 300,000 in London alone.[11] F.M.L. Thompson estimated that there were more private/pleasure horses in Britain in 1924 than in 1911.[12] While the total horse population might have declined (new mechanization meant fewer draft and carriage horses were needed), riding horses increased, leading to a post-war boom in equestrianism.

This boom owed much to domestic horse breeding efforts as well as the surplus of military horses after the First World War. After 1918, the British government was left in possession of thousands of military horses it did not need. The government decided to sell the surplus to French slaughterhouses, but the scheme, exposed by Dorothy Brooke, was met with massive public outcry and measures were instituted to ensure that horses were sold for labor.[13] A year after the end of the war, 250,000 horses had been sold for £8 million, or roughly £32 per horse. Approximately 100,000 of these horses were sold at auction in Britain alone, and prices dropped sharply for non-draft horses, allowing the purchase of affordable riding horses by people new to the sport.[14]

Following the war, the revival of the riding horse brought sport to a wider cross-section of the population. Whereas riding and hunting had been a pastime for upper and upper middle-class women before the war, participation declined in these groups after the war as they pursued new hobbies like motor yachting and automobiling. The rise in women's status, corresponding to better education and wages, with shorter working hours and more opportunities for leisure, meant that more middle-class women could now pursue new sports.[15] Riding cross-saddle was less expensive than riding sidesaddle, which boosted participation among these women and brought horse sports to a much wider audience. After the Great War, hunting fields abounded with female participants, most of whom were riding astride.[16]

In sporting author Edith Somerville's opinion, no sport "broadened down" faster to include new participants than fox hunting.[17] As Lady Randolph

Churchill pointed out, women's war work had blurred class distinctions by encouraging women of many social levels to join together for "a common platform"; afterward, many sporting women continued this association.[18] Given the new affordability of horses and horse sports, wider social levels could take part, for "out hunting there is no class distinction."[19] Even those who possessed only two horses could see as many as 40–50 days of sport during the hunting season, which meant going out once every three days.[20] To fully partake in these opportunities, women justified their involvement based on their natural feminine qualities and their practical skills such as riding and stable management, gained not only through participation in late Victorian hunting fields and in the Great War, but also across the British Empire.

Ladies' Cross-Saddle Riding in Britain

Ladies riding cross-saddle debuted in Britain well before 1900. In 1887, equestrian author Fox Russell argued against the sidesaddle for women because it deprived a rider of the requisite "touch" (contact) with her horse, which is the foundation of good equitation. Having ridden in a sidesaddle himself, he found it "uncomfortable," said that trotting was "agony," and admitted he would never jump in one. But he thought it was pointless to argue the matter because opinion was so dead set on women riding in that fashion. The debate did not affect him personally – he did not have to ride sidesaddle other than out of curiosity.

In 1891, W. A. Kerr, who described himself as "formerly second in command of the 2nd regiment, Southern Maharatta Horse," published two books on riding: *Practical Horsemanship* and *Riding for Ladies*. Designed to be read in tandem, Kerr said instructions "should be studied by all, of either sex, who aim at perfection in the accomplishment of Equitation."[21] He continued, "What I have said on the excellence of horse-exercise for boys and men, applies equally to girls and women, if, indeed, it does not recommend itself more especially in the case of the latter."[22] Kerr heartily recommended the cross-saddle seat for female riders in Britain. As he argued,

> In spite of preconceived prejudices, I think that if ladies will kindly peruse my short chapter on this common sense method, they will come to the conclusion that Anne of Luxembourg, who introduced the side-saddle, did not confer an unmixed benefit on the subjects of Richard the Second, and that riding astride is no more indelicate than the modern short habit in the hunting field. We are too apt to prostrate ourselves before the Juggernaut of fashion, and to hug our own conservative ideals.[23]

Kerr's view was influenced by his imperial experience, and his views were echoed by others in Britain, including sporting illustrator Georgina Bowers who depicted a woman riding cross-saddle in her book, *Mr. Crop's Harriers* in 1891 (Figure 5.1).[24] Kerr even went so far as to publicly lambast equestrian author

Figure 5.1 "The Ladies' Race: Miss Matchem appears in boots and breeches on a man's saddle!!!" from G. Bowers, *Mr. Crop's Harriers* (London: Day and Son, 1891), 39: Miss Matchem, riding cross-saddle, is declared the co-winner after two challenging rounds of a ladies' race, in which other lady participants (riding sidesaddle) bowed out or suffered falls. Bowers highlighted the safety and utility of the cross-saddle for ladies, especially for demanding events like hunting or racing.
Credit: Collection of the author.

Nannie Power O'Donoghue for her strict refusal to contemplate the cross-saddle seat for women. "Mrs. Power O'Donoghue runs a tilt with all her might against the idea of any of her sex riding like men," he lamented, "But there are so many manly maidens about now who excel in all open-air pastimes requiring pluck, energy, physical activity, and strength, and who attire themselves suitably in a sort of semi-masculine style, that is not asking too much of them to try the virtues of the cross-saddle."[25]

Many contemporary authors noted the increasing number of people – especially women – who rode and participated in horse sports such as fox hunting before the turn of the century. Books were designed to educate:

> a growing number of riders who had no background of horses, who did not associate in any way with the horse world, and whose only connection with the horse was a burning desire to ride and to acquire the distinguished and

somewhat glamorous title of "horseman"; most of them, by the way, hoped to be called "horsewomen," which of course is just as coveted.[26]

To satisfy the demand for information on such topics, more books were published and directed to new reading audiences. One of these was T.F. Dale's *Riding, Driving and Kindred Sports* (1899), which was intended as "a kind of cheap Badminton Library to the thousands of sportsmen who cannot command the price of that series."[27] Begun in 1885, the Badminton Library was conceived by the Duke of Beaufort as a modern encyclopedia of British sport.[28] Though these were excellent volumes, they were intended for a predominantly upper class reading audience. This market was already familiar with equestrian activities and was not concerned about the costs of participation. These new equestrian manuals were not directed at advanced riders, but rather at novice and aspiring equestrians. By the early 1900s, the horse trade was thriving, new stables had opened across the country, and fox hunting was flourishing. As a result, "all sorts and conditions of men and women take their pleasure on a horse who would never have thought of such an adventure not so very long ago."[29]

Dale's text was important because he linked these new riders with imperial experiences. He included chapters on polo, pig sticking, and jackal hunting, and in his introduction to the ladies' riding chapter, he noted that his directions on riding were suitable for both sexes.[30] He tacitly approved the modern astride fashion for ladies, though he wrote explicitly only about the sidesaddle.[31] Women, he noted, were making the most of this riding revolution as equestrians, and he personally thought they were "infinitely superior to most of us."[32] He concluded, "Nor can it be said of the majority of ladies that they are in the way. They seldom jump on us because, to tell the truth, they are generally in front."[33]

Nonetheless, it had become evident to many that the real problem was the sidesaddle, which hindered equestrian advancement for women. "Safety skirts, safety bars, and straight-seated saddles have done much to render the danger less than it used to be," Dale admitted in 1899, "but still the one-sided seat and the pommels always remain."[34] In 1906, a correspondent wrote to *The Ladies' Field* about this dilemma, noting that "the cavalier fashion [of riding astride] is suitable for short purses, and suggests that while those women who can afford a [side] saddle for each horse they may own may escape, yet for their poorer sisters the disadvantages of the side-saddle are very great."[35]

By 1906, authors directed riding manuals at both sexes because directions for riding cross-saddle, now the preferred style for women, were equally applicable to both men and women. Charles Richardson addressed his instructions to both sexes in *Practical Hints for Hunting Novices*,[36] and Major Noel Birch noted in his revised volume of *Modern Riding and Horse Education* that the instructions within were meant not only for male riders, but would "prove useful to the lady who wishes to adopt the cross-legged seat."[37] Richardson wrote:

> But, personally, I strongly favour the man's saddle and the man's seat for all girls, say, until they are sixteen years old. Where I mostly hunt all the little girls have ridden astride for the last eight or ten years, and now some of them who are grown up and "out" have taken to the side saddle. Yet these one and all declare that riding astride is the most comfortable, and that in a man's saddle they have more command of their horse. There I leave it.[38]

By 1908, even "Harby," the conservative hunting correspondent for *The Ladies' Field* and a staunch supporter of the sidesaddle, had been converted to the benefits of the cross-saddle for ladies and published her support in print.[39] In 1913, hunting journalist and author William Scarth Dixon first featured an image of a ladies' cross-saddle in his book, *The Complete Horseman*.[40] In the same year, Mrs. Stuart Menzies advanced opinion by urging women to ride astride in her book, *Women in the Hunting Field*.

Like Dale, Menzies specifically cited her imperial experiences in encouraging the practice of riding astride, illustrating the process of imperial "bounce-back."[41] She had traveled to India with her husband, Capt. Stuart Alexander Menzies, and, in her book, she recalled her times of "hunting in hot climates"[42] and riding at Lucknow.[43] Menzies supported her case for riding astride in both India and Britain by comparing the rough terrain of both locations, and how riding astride was far easier and safer for horse and rider. She urged women to ride astride because the style was "much the safest" compared to riding sidesaddle.[44] She admitted that while "apron skirts, safety bars, straight-seated saddles, etc." had improved sidesaddle riding for women, in any trouble (which inevitably occurred when riding), a woman riding sidesaddle stupidly placed herself in a far more life-endangering position compared to the safer cross-saddle.[45] She dismissed social criticism of the astride style:

> When I hear people criticizing astride with "so indelicate," "such bad form," "what *would* our great-grandmothers have said," I always long to tell them what I think they would have said, but remembering discretion is the greater part of valour I refrain. Perhaps they do not know as much about the histories of some of their great-grandmothers as they might do.[46]

Menzies pointed out that women were already riding cross-saddle in Britain for safety, practicality, and comfort, and she estimated that by 1913 at least 30% of women were riding like men to hunts such as the Devon and Somerset Staghounds.[47] Women had been riding astride in this region since at least 1900, as *The Queen* magazine confirmed.[48] In 1908, *The Times* wrote that "a good many ladies" had adopted the style,[49] while two years later, *The Queen* added, "ladies are taking very kindly to cross-saddle riding."[50]

Not everyone supported this shift. *The Times* admitted that riding astride might be popular around the Empire and in provincial areas of Britain, but it was unlikely to make headway in traditional hunting country of the conservative Midlands.

Alice Hayes, author of *The Horsewoman*, had initially encouraged cross-saddle riding in her early manuals, albeit in a limited fashion and only for travel in rough and uncivilized areas.[51] She reversed this position, however, in the third edition of her manual in 1910. Having returned to Britain and taken up hunting in the Midlands, she disparaged riding astride as "incompetent and totally unsuitable" and "a sadly retrograde move." Furthermore, she labeled those who did so "a new breed of woman, of a more or less violent and desperate type."[52] Yet reviewers of her book, not to mention readers, found her opinions reactionary and increasingly obsolete.[53]

In fact, the cross-saddle style became so popular that the first decades of the twentieth century actually witnessed the publication of *fewer* equestrian books for women than normal. Excluding Menzies' work, between 1899 and 1932, no entirely new riding guidebooks by British authors were published for women in Britain. 1907 did see the publication of Eva Christy's *Modern Side-Saddle Riding: A Practical Handbook for Horsewomen*, although this was largely a substantial revision of her 1899 work, *Side-Saddle Riding: A Practical Handbook for Horsewomen*. American horsewoman Belle Beach's *Riding and Driving for Women* was published in London in 1913, a year after it appeared in America, but was printed in such limited numbers that only a few still exist.[54] It was not until 1932 that two new riding handbooks appeared for female riders: Eva Christy's *Cross-Saddle and Side-Saddle: Modern Riding for Men and Women* and Lady Diana Maude Shedden's and Lady Apsley's, *"To Whom the Goddess ...": Hunting and Riding for Women*. Female equestrians seeking information on riding astride could simply turn to any general book on horsemanship, while the women still riding sidesaddle already had plenty of options through continually revised editions of O'Donoghue and Hayes dating back to the Victorian era.

Thus, the popularity and acceptance of cross-saddle riding for women was established well before the First World War. This prominence was recognized by a series of articles printed in *The Ladies' Field* magazine between October 4, 1913 and November 22, 1913.[55] In six separate columns, female equestrians, medical doctors, and riding instructors sent in letters and testimonials arguing in favor of their preferred style. In the end, 22 (42%) preferred the sidesaddle seat only, while 30 (58%) preferred the cross-saddle or whatever style best suited the rider. Those in favor of the sidesaddle included the Duchess of Newcastle, the Marchioness of Downshire, and Lady Willoughby de Broke. These were all expert horsewomen, members of the upper class, and followers of prestigious Midlands hunts such as Belvoir and Quorn. They had been trained sidesaddle and had come of age and experience in the late Victorian era in Britain, when nothing but the sidesaddle had been socially acceptable for female riders. On the other hand, supporters of the cross-saddle included Lady Castlereagh (a devoted disciple of the style, see Figure 5.2), doctors and medical practitioners who believed it was physically better for women, owners and instructors of riding academies, and the principals of several gymnasiums who found it superior for growing girls. The cross-saddle style of riding was also praised by two correspondents from the Empire who declared the style was the best.[56]

Figure 5.2 "For Safety and Common Sense," featuring Lady Castlereagh from *The Bystander* (October 24, 1906), 183: Lady Castlereagh was praised as "a charming exponent" of riding astride for ladies, "with no absence of dignity and grace." By the turn of the twentieth century, female equestrians were publicly praised for their elegant adoption of the cross-saddle seat.
Credit: Collection of the author.

The Empire Rides Back

So, how did imperial experience come home to influence Britain, and specifically British horse sports, before 1914? The impact is seen in three areas of equestrianism: the publication of riding books in Britain with an enhanced focus on imperial sports and/or by authors with imperial experience; the adoption of imperial horse sports like gymkhanas and polo; and the transition to astride saddles and riding clothes. Imperial sports such as hunting, polo, and pig sticking were increasingly included in riding manuals and guidebooks published for a British audience. As T.F. Dale noted in 1899,

> In addition to the usual English sports, I have added sections on Indian polo, pig-sticking and jackal-hunting, because India is still a paradise for the sportsman of moderate means with some leisure, and offers a far from exhausted field for the traveler, or to those whom the search for daily bread may lead thither in one capacity or another.[57]

Dale's book was intended for both male and female riders, not only those at home in Britain, but for those heading to or already abroad within the Empire. Colonel R.F. Meysey-Thompson similarly published *A Hunting Catechism* in 1907, arguing "in favour of ladies riding on a cross-saddle."[58] The volume, which covered hunting in Britain, was based on his imperial experience. Meysey-Thompson had joined the Rifle Brigade at age 19 in 1866, and served in the Anglo-Ashanti war of 1873.[59] Captain J.E. Hance, author of many riding books and father to successful show-rider Jackie, also cited his imperial experiences as a riding instructor in India and encouraged his daughter (and other female equestrians) to ride astride.[60] Thus, imperial influence was closely linked to, and even inseparable from, equestrian sports in Britain.

Besides the shift to ladies' riding astride, as first made popular in the Empire and subsequently reflected and encouraged in riding manuals published in Britain, imperial influence was also seen in the uptick of "gymkhanas," or mounted games. The word "gymkhana" was adopted by Anglo-Indians from the Hindustani word for "ball court," denoting a specific place for public sport.[61] These informal competitions consisted of activities like tent-pegging and tilting at the ring (ring-spearing) (Figure 5.3). Women had competed in such events throughout India, and soon the games spread across Britain. These mounted contests were popular not only for recreational entertainment, but as valuable learning tools. As Captain Hance wrote, "if gymkhanas are treated as a test of accurate riding and for training ponies, there is no limit to what the riders may teach themselves in the process."[62]

By the late 1890s, gymkhanas took place at Wimbledon and Ranelagh, which were home to prestigious polo clubs, another imperial sporting competition that had come home to Britain.[63] As in India, gymkhanas often featured creative and eccentric competitions to test competitors' horsemanship skills. Eva Christy

Femininity and Sporting Equality 237

Figure 5.3 "Tilting at the Ring at Ranelagh," by Sidney Paget, cover page from *The Sphere* (June 22, 1901): In British India, gymkhanas were valuable training tools and amusement for both the British military as well as civilians. Such activities were imported back to England and enthusiastically embraced at prestigious equestrian facilities like polo paradise Ranelagh. These mounted contests involved both sexes, usually competing together on equal terms.
Credit: Collection of the author.

included a picture and description of one such race: "The rider had to jump several fences, dismount, eat a bun, open a bottle of lemonade, drink it, put on pajamas, light a cigarette and keep it burning to the finish, open a sunshade, then mount again and jump the same fences back."[64]

In 1899, a Ladies' Gymkhana was held at Wimbledon, consisting of tilting at the ring, tent-pegging, polo ball, needle threading,[65] a bending race,[66] and "pig-sticking."[67] Although England had no wild boars as in India, a viable substitute was found: "Lord Harrington and two other gentlemen trailed the air balloons (officially recognized as 'pigs') at full gallop across the polo ground, and the ladies followed at top speed. A pig of this description is an impossible quarry to spear" (Figure 5.4).[68] Another kind of pig-sticking competition was like a

Figure 5.4 "A Gymkhana," issued by John Player & Sons (Player's Cigarettes), No. 11 in a series of 25 cards on "Country Sports" (1930): Pig sticking as practiced in India was amended for play in England as a popular gymkhana event. Without live boars, "dummies" like stuffed balloons were used instead. As the card states, "In dummy pigsticking, the 'pigstickers,' about three in each heat, are armed with long, chalked sticks; the dummy pig is a stuffed bag towed over the ground by a rider. In his gallop to avoid the 'stickers,' the 'pig's' keeper must take great care not to get the towline round his horse's legs." In this image, two lady "stickers" riding astride stalk the "pig"; one is about to make a successful "spear."
Credit: Collection of the author.

pin-the-tail-on-the-donkey contest: the outline of a pig was drawn on a moving board, and contestants had to try to "spear" him with chalked lances like billiards' cues.[69] The competitor who scored the most points over three runs won.

These events showed clear imperial influence and demonstrated how women around the Empire had become such strong riders. As *The Ladies' Field* reported, there were some "pretty attempts" but more importantly there was much "splendid riding." One contestant, Miss A.O. Turner, was singled out: "the admirable way in which she managed a fine but rebellious mount at the hurdles in the Needle-threading Competition, aroused the admiration of all beholders."[70] She was also a first-class rider to hounds in Yorkshire, thus illustrating the direct connection between British horsemanship learned through hunting and the pay-off in terms of success in imperial sport. Turner showed how imperial activities, such as gymkhanas and pig sticking, were brought home and enthusiastically embraced partly because these female riders already had a strong foundation of equitation gained through fox hunting.

Such programs continued to be popular throughout the early 1900s. A 1905 gymkhana at Ranelagh featured aunt sally races,[71] bending races, a ladies' polo ball race, potato races, and a rescue race.[72] The polo ball race was considered the "most interesting," as ladies had to hit a polo ball from one end of the field to the goal at the other.[73] Even those most masculine of imperial equestrian sports – polo and pig sticking – were brought home to Britain and gender equalized so that women could and did join in. Pig sticking was an especially dangerous sport, and one in which women's participation had initially been questioned. Yet when the pursuit was brought back to England and amended in its practice, men and women were equally able to participate. Mounted contests based on horsemanship were therefore becoming less and less segregated by sex, due in large part to the imperial conditions that had fostered and encouraged women to ride, engage in equestrian sports, and eventually transition to riding astride.

Polo Post Futurum

From its modern beginnings in India during the mid-nineteenth century, polo spread quickly to Britain, being first played there in 1869 by the officers of the 10th Hussars at Aldershot.[74] Unlike other imperial equestrian sports, polo did not initially transition to Britain very well for women's play. Even *Baily's Magazine* was cautious about encouraging women's participation. In 1873, the sporting periodical referenced a cartoon from *Punch* that showed a full field of women at boisterous play: "We don't know if *Punch's* charming sketch of "*Polo Post Futurum*" will be quite realized. We must wait for another decade before our fairest and dearest take part in those manly exercises" (Figure 5.5).[75] Despite British women's achievements abroad, *The Ladies' Field* noted, "there will be many who would hardly hail with enthusiasm a report that proceedings at Hurlingham and Ranelagh were to commence early in the season with a Ladies' Day."[76]

Figure 5.5 "Polo Post Futurum," from *Punch's Almanack for 1873* (Vol. 64), December 17, 1862: Playing on the Latin phrase *"paulo post futurum"* for "sometime in the future," this *Punch* cartoon shows a bevy of keen British women and girls skirmishing for the polo ball while Mr. Punch (in the center foreground) serves as referee. Polo was initially deemed too rough and physical for female play, but British women were playing polo in India by the late nineteenth century and doing very well. Although female equestrians were initially limited to riding sidesaddle, authors like Ivy Maddison rightly pointed out: "Playing polo [aside] is practically impossible since the rider cannot do much twisting around in her saddle. She can hit the ball when it comes to her right [the off-side] but it is very difficult to swing a mallet well on her left [due to the pommels]." The ability to play polo well and competitively was yet another reason many women switched from riding sidesaddle to cross-saddle.
Credit: Collection of the author.

Female participation in polo was singled out for criticism by many social commentators of the time, being somewhat of a scapegoat for other activities. In 1891, Eliza Lynn Linton, famous for her essays on "The Girl of Period," wrote in the article, "The Wild Women as Social Insurgents,"

> We have not yet heard of women polo-players; but that will come. In the absurd endeavour to be like men, these modern homasses[77] will leave nothing untried; and polo-playing, tent-pegging, and tilting at the quintain are all sure to come in time.[78]

Blackwood's Magazine had printed an almost identical passage a year earlier:

> May our Cynthias of the future rest content with the side-saddle and riding-whip, nor ever be persuaded by radical reformers to adopt mannish modes of sitting a horse, whether with the aid of the divided skirt, or otherwise. Nor, again, let them aspire to tent-pegging, polo, or suchlike rougher diversions, which should be left to their husbands and brothers![79]

The idea of ladies' polo was initially met with "universal ridicule," with male polo players at Hurlingham and Ranelagh at the forefront of the criticism. George Underhill noted, when he was on the staff of *Polo Magazine* in 1898, his editor "laughed at [him] for suggesting ladies' polo."[80] This initial ridicule did not stick, however, especially since British women were already playing polo by this time, if not openly in Britain, then certainly in India.

The first reference to ladies' play came from Captain G.J. Younghusband's *Polo in India* published in 1890.[81] The game, as Younghusband concluded, was "a very fast and good one" with "stern and businesslike play."[82] The main problem was that the ladies' sidesaddle clothes got in the way of play; veils and gloves handicapped the female riders. Once the offending garments had been removed, "some really good runs were made," and Younghusband admitted that the game "was really astonishingly good considering the inexperience of the players."[83] In fact, he concluded that women riding sidesaddle actually had one advantage compared to men playing polo: "Having the off-side of the pony quite clear, they could get a clean hit on that side, and those on handy, well-trained ponies appeared to be very nearly as active after the ball as men would be."[84] Though Younghusband was not sold on mixed play, he saw no reason to prohibit ladies' polo: "As long as ladies play only in a ladies' game, and ride handy, well-trained ponies, there is no reason why polo should not, like hunting, become a pastime for our sisters and cousins and aunts as well as for ourselves."[85]

Therefore, it was not horsemanship that was the issue (women's prowess in fox hunting had long ago proved that point), but rather the rough play of scrimmages that was considered unsuitable for ladies, both socially and physically. *Fores's Sporting Notes and Sketches* included articles and stories about women's polo at least by the 1890s, especially Cuthbert Bradley's work with accompanying illustrations of women riding sidesaddle and skillfully handling mallets.[86] George Underhill drew up amended regulations for ladies' play printed in *The Ladies' Field*.[87] Underhill encouraged polo because it made women better riders by increasing their steadiness of balance and the firmness of seat. He also encouraged play during the slow summer months, when most hunting people did not ride consistently, in order to keep up muscle strength and vigor for the coming season. In 1905, a ladies' polo match was even played for the Queen. In this game, the Rainbows and Whites battled out an hour and a half of play, ending only when the Whites had gained eight goals and the Rainbows none.[88]

Still polo remained less popular than other horseback activities for women in Britain. It was not for lack of trying, as women did promote the sport as much as possible, especially as a means to increase general riding ability and horsemanship, which had been proven in the Empire. The main obstacle was that women in Britain played polo riding sidesaddle. As *The Ladies' Field* magazine noted in 1907, "Men have a great advantage over women in having polo for the summer. Until someone invents a good game for women on horseback, or till women ride cavalier fashion, men will start the hunting season much fitter to ride a hard run than women can do."[89]

Riding astride eliminated these concerns, and by 1903, huntsman and author J. Otho Paget encouraged parents to form a "boy and girl polo club" to encourage the young to learn horsemanship.[90] As long as ponies stood under 13 hands, the ball soft rubber, and the sticks very lightweight, Paget concluded, "You might have lots of fun in this way, and it would improve your riding more than anything."[91] Paget explicitly stated that his directions were equally applicable for both boys and girls, because girls, he said, should ride astride. "The unnatural position in which a side-saddle puts a woman must be bad for the adult," he concluded, "but it must be positively injurious to the health of a growing girl."[92]

As girls grew up and more women shifted to riding astride before 1914, polo did become more prominent, though for female riders it continued to be less popular than other horse sports such as hunting, showing, and jumping because it required deep pockets for a string of ponies (Figure 5.6). Still, imperial influence clearly had an impact on women's riding at home, and it was estimated that polo in Britain was at its most popular in 1914, with 16 polo grounds in London alone.[93]

Straddle-Skirts and Riding Habits Before the Great War

Female pioneers of the cross-saddle faced social pressures not only over their sporting choices but their sartorial ones as well. In fact, they often faced far more criticism over what they wore than how they rode. As Mary Howarth pointed out in the *Badminton Magazine* in 1902:

> Yet I have often thought that if prejudice [against riding astride] were to be overcome completely, and those women who liked to do so, and felt they looked "nice" in the clothes men wear, were permitted to ride in breeches, either on horseback or their bicycles, without inn-doors being shut in their faces, and column lengths of angry dismay and condemnation in the papers, matters would be happier and much more fair.[94]

Nonetheless, given the sporting and practical advantages of such clothing, not to mention comfort, women persevered and the astride style flourished.

Thus, another consequence of imperial experience was the transformation of riding clothes for women in Britain. As Hart and Sons' tailors noted, "Now that riding astride is becoming quite a time-honoured custom for girls at home and women of all ages abroad in the Colonies, the special advantages of the

Femininity and Sporting Equality 243

Figure 5.6 Advertisement for the National School of Equitation near Richmond Park, London, featuring "Ladies Playing Indoor Polo at the School," from *Colour* (April 1931), page 23: Ladies' polo increased in the early twentieth century, including public competitions at Ranelagh, Hurlingham, Brighton, Southwick, and Melton Mowbray during the 1920s and 1930s. The National School of Equitation invented the mounted game of "polocrosse," a hybrid of polo and lacrosse, to develop riding skills, which today is a global sport (culminating with a World Cup) and an official Pony Club activity.
Credit: Collection of the author.

exclusive Hart coat are well worth considering."[95] By 1902, Ross was making an astride hunting coat and skirt that looked almost identical to a regular side-saddle skirt, except that it was divided so a woman could have a leg on each side of her saddle.[96] However, this skirt was criticized for being neither masculine nor feminine enough – it was neither breeches nor skirt. Therefore, the divided skirt did not last long in fashion, possibly also because some were marketed under the unappealing label of "straddle-skirts."[97] British women quickly transitioned, as their imperial sisters had done before them, to the standard outfit of breeches, jacket, and tall boots. By 1904, Tautz was advertising "a very neat and workmanlike ride-astride habit for ladies, the long-skirted coat reaching to the knees, and consequently showing very little of the riding breeches below."[98]

By 1908, the style had taken over the equestrian fashion world. As riding habit makers undoubtedly noticed in their orders,

> Each season finds more converts to cross-saddle riding, not only in the Colonies and such countries as Mexico, but also in Ireland, in Wales, and in many parts of England. And, as a result, each season finds experts ready with designs for suitable coats and breeches.[99]

"What could be smarter or more sensible," asked Guterbock's,

> Not only the Colonial, but her sister-woman who hunts at home over the rough country found in many of the Shires, would instantly realise that additional pleasure – to say nothing of the safety – derivable from such apparel, which, in allowing the less fatiguing and freer cross-saddle posture to be assumed, gives a rider increased command over her mount.[100]

Riding astride for women in Britain was thus well developed and popular before the First World War began in 1914. This style, accompanying activities, and clothes had been transformed by imperial experiences brought home. The development of sporting clothing was the catalyst for women's emancipation; being more liberating to action, they were more liberating socially. New clothing broke down traditional gender roles, because it allowed new mobility. New clothes equaled new power, and sartorial and sporting mobility indicated new social and political mobility.[101] Though the Great War undoubtedly contributed to more women beginning to ride in this style to aid in the war efforts, it was not the war itself which made the astride style acceptable at home. That had occurred before the twentieth century when imperial experience helped contribute to the widespread adoption of cross-saddle riding for women. What the war did, then, was validate this method of riding for a world that was much changed after 1918.

Women's War Work at Remount Depots

The outbreak of war spurred additional advances in equestrianism. Women made many contributions to the war effort. Part of their job was "taming the savage Horse," a purpose which years of equestrian training in the hunting fields of Britain and around the Empire had well prepared them.[102] From teaching recruits how to ride and retraining cavalry remount horses, to spearheading horse-breeding efforts and leading hunts as Masters, British women contributed significantly to the war effort and the eventual victory. Women's war-time equestrian contributions demonstrate that imperial experience played an important role in enabling female war work and that women continued to make advances after 1918, rather than retreating into the home and post-war ideas of domesticity.

The first way that equestrian women aided the war effort was by training the men and horses who would serve in battle. Sportswomen like Eva Christy, author of several popular sidesaddle books in the late 1800s and early 1900s, was an officially appointed Riding Instructor during the First World War.[103] As Christy herself noted, "I had a number of officers and others wearing uniform to train."[104] This was a gender-bending shift as women were now teaching male soldiers the finer points of horsemanship. They had to be knowledgeable in the astride style to do so.

However, training men was not the only service women provided; they also trained the horses the men rode. Remount depots were intended to provide fresh, healthy, well-trained horses, donkeys, and mules for army use. The Army's Remount section had been established in 1887.[105] In 1914, the Army had less than 25,000 horses; by 1917, it possessed over half a million, having spent £67.5 million to acquire them.[106] When the war began, the Remount Department consisted of only four squadrons in the Army Service Corps, with each unit of 200 men responsible for 500 horses.[107] At least one million horses served with British forces in the First World War: many were injured, wounded, or killed during the conflict, thus requiring either recuperation or replacement. In fact, only 60,000 horses came home to Britain after the war.[108]

The Army Remount Corps located, trained, and recuperated over 340,000 horses during the course of the war. Remount depots were set up around the country and acted as collecting points for horses from farms, businesses, hunts, and riding stables. As the war continued, however, the remount depots became about more than just accumulating horses and shipping them out; they were transformed into "convalescent" homes where sick or injured army horses were sent to be made fit again for service. Some depots even specialized in healing horses that had been suspended from duty because they were deemed "incurably vicious."[109]

Acquiring and training horses for the Boer War had been a disaster. 75% of horses sent to South Africa had been labeled as bad or unfit. As Captain T.T.

246 Femininity and Sporting Equality

Pitman remarked, "Never before have such a collection of inferior horses been gathered together in any portion of the globe."[110] This failure had to be remedied, as the *Remount Manual* for 1913 stated plainly, "The function of the depots is to feed units of the army with animals ... and similarly to relieve one another of inefficients." "Inefficients" were "horses not sufficiently fit or conditioned for work apart from those actually sick."[111]

By caring for sick horses and returning them to active service, women's work in remount depots was critical to the war effort (Figure 5.7). As sporting author Edith Somerville stated, "cavalry remounts must not fail. Thus it came about that 'the woman's place,' as often as not, was, necessarily the stables, and lady-masters and lady-grooms laid the axe to the root of a long-cherished monopoly."[112] Many British women eagerly sought remount work, and so were employed throughout the course of the war.[113] As Lady Randolph Churchill pointed out, it was perfectly acceptable and even admirable to pursue such work: "That one [girl] has no talent at all for clerical work, but she knows the points of

Figure 5.7 "Women Staffing an Army Remount Depot: Former-Day Lady Riders to Hounds who Release Soldiers," from *The Illustrated War News* (June 7, 1916), page 30: This illustrated spread shows women riding, training, and caring for horses destined for war service with the British Army. Sidesaddles were forbidden at these depots; women rode cross-saddle like men, "breeched and booted and spurred."
Credit: Collection of the author.

a horse. She had found her war vocation in the Remount Department."[114] As one "girl groom" recalled,

> Depots, all recognized by and under the control of the War Office, are now already in existence or being started all over the country. The hazardous experiment of 'war horses trained by women' has certainly justified itself, both in its success with regard to the actual work and efficiency and in the number of men released thereby for service.[115]

Women remount workers took over masculine jobs at home and thus freed men to fight on their behalf in the war abroad.

Queries in periodical columns about joining up and providing equestrian assistance were numerous. In response to "Inez" in 1916, *The Ladies' Field* replied, "Yours is one of many inquiries we have been receiving lately concerning remount depots which are wholly or partly run by women."[116] According to records in the Imperial War Museum, over 200 women were officially employed by at least 23 remount depots, including major centers at Worcester, Rugby, Strengham, Russley Park, Stansted, Elsenham, Pluckley, Chester, Shrewsbury, Monmouth, Wembley, Arborfield Cross, and Melton Mowbray.[117] These figures do not include the numerous other women employed or volunteering at private remount depots.[118] So many women were involved in this work that contemporaries claimed was "impossible" to list all remount depots where women were employed.[119]

These remount depots were "unique": "for the first time in the history of the British Army, not one man is on any of the staffs, and ... all the work is done by gentlewomen."[120] As a proud remount worker stated, "not a single man is employed upon the premises in any capacity whatever."[121] One of the major figures involved in remount organization was Cecil Aldin, the renowned sporting artist and Master of the South Berks Hunt, who was then the District Remount Officer for Berkshire. Aldin initially became a Remount Purchasing Officer, but found there were real problems recruiting the men left at home to help with horses. When he tried to recruit local infantry men they knew almost nothing about horses and were not young and fit enough anyway. What Aldin realized, however, was that there were many women around who were expert horsewomen. He was the first to employ women at remount depots in 1915 with successful results.

Female horsewomen were natural leaders for these equestrian encampments. Remount Depot (No. 1) was set up by Miss E.G. Bather near Chester, while a further Remount Depot (No. 2) was set up by Miss Dorothy Ravenscroft. Another depot was established at Bradfield by Miss Jenny, with a much larger farm managed by Miss Horrocks at Holyport near Maidenhead.[122] Private depots were also organized by civilian women, including additional posts organized by Mrs. Rigby near Chester. Russley Park, between Baydon and Bishopstone in North Wiltshire, was established in 1916 and run by Lady Mabel Birkbeck, the wife of Major General Sir William Henry Birkbeck, who was Director of Remounts from 1912 to 1920. The Russley Park contingent concentrated on horses belonging to officers; once re-trained, these horses were quickly sent back to the front.

Female workers reconditioned horses (from heavy draft animals to officer's chargers, as well as mules) and to train them into fitness, so that these mounts could then be issued to troops by the Remount Department.[123] At any one time depots could house hundreds of horses, all of which had to be fed and exercised, while the stables and equipment also had to be cleaned and managed. Being a remount worker not only required riding well, but more importantly "real hard work, requiring strength, courage, infinite patience and firmness."[124] Workers might be called "Smiling Dianas," but remount depots were not picnics, and the work was often dangerous.[125] Some injuries might be minor, like being stepped on or kicked, but there were also major injuries like being thrown from a high-strung mount. The Queen's Lady-in-Waiting, the Countess of Airlie, lost her daughter to an accident that occurred doing remount work.[126] Still this did not deter women nor lessen the popularity of the work: "we go on doing work which must be done, and if we were not doing it an equal number of men would have to replace us. As it is we have the satisfaction of actively helping our country to 'carry on' – and a great satisfaction it is."[127]

Depots were managed by a Headwoman, who was responsible for the organization as a whole, with her "riding lady" as second-in-command. To assist with these duties, headwomen oversaw staffs ranging from small (around 12, for Miss Bather, for 40 horses) to large (around 50, for Miss Horrocks, for 100 horses). The depot near Worcester run by Mrs. Bullock and Miss Logan routinely managed 300–400 horses,[128] while by the end of Miss Bather's first year in 1916, her depot alone had rehabilitated around 500 horses.[129] Horses had to pass a high standard of muster, for they were inspected constantly by the Director of Remounts, Sir William Birkbeck, as well as any number of subinspectors. The praise for the women's efforts was unstinting: as *The Times* confirmed, "The inspectors of remounts who periodically visit the depots say they have never known horses to be so well attended to by men."[130]

"I am a great believer, and always have been, in this work for women," Cecil Aldin stated, "As regards their work, I have nothing but good to say about it. They were more thorough than the men, started work at 7 a.m., and did not finish until everything was done whatever the hour."[131] Not only were women doing the work, thus freeing more men to join the fighting, but they were doing the work better than men usually did. As S.R. Church noted in the *Daily Mail*, "We are doing men's work, as much of it as men could do and considerably more than men would have done in those dim, distant days before the war had taught most of us to put our backs into a job of work and keep them there."[132]

Importantly, contemporaries noted that this success was due to women's pre-war involvement in equestrian sports such as hunting, which had fitted them for the arduous task. What made this work so significant, however, was that all women workers rode astride: "No side saddles are allowed, and no men are employed."[133] Cecil Aldin praised the women as "infinitely better" riders than men, and supported riding astride completely.[134] Horsemanship and riding skills – not only riding well but being able to train fractious and difficult horses – were taken for granted among the workers who were required to ride and train cross-saddle in the style that male soldiers would use. Women took "complete and entire charge" of the horses and their roles in producing them. In making and training horses, these women were also making themselves. In this line of work, women faced many challenges – physical and mental – but they also realized their own strength and power, and that they could overcome obstacles. As government records concluded, "no man ever did it better or with sounder judgment."[135]

The imperial origins of riding astride were clearly illustrated in the ease of transition from women's riding astride in civilian life to training military remounts in Britain. The style made major headway before the war; now the war effort confirmed it. *The Times* noted that a few female remount workers had imperial connections, having been raised on ranches in Australia and Canada, for example, but the vast majority of the employees were local hunting women.[136] Therefore, the astride style was not made popular by the war, but was already being popularly pursued and encouraged before the war made the style more necessary.

This was also seen in the clothes women wore for remount work. Work at remount depots was physically challenging, which meant that clothing had to be tough enough to withstand both mounted and unmounted demands, whether riding or performing stable chores. Fabric had to be durable yet comfortable, while also light enough for hot, sweaty work. Imperial riding habits provided the perfect template, and experienced habit makers turned from exporting such products around the Empire to making garments for use at home in wartime Britain. In 1916, an advertisement in *The Ladies' Field* magazine made the point: "For those patriotic women who are helping to train remounts Montague Smyth has designed some completely perfect riding kit. ... With his long experience in making ride-astride clothes for Colonial women, he is naturally just the man to know what the remount trainer needs" (Figure 5.8).[137]

Queries in the advice columns of ladies' fashion magazines repeatedly asked where to purchase the best garments for such work, and the answers were unanimous: the habit makers who had previously made ladies' astride habits for imperial wear. In *The Ladies' Field*, Mrs. Jack May urged correspondents to select Montague Smyth's "khaki drill ride-astride habit," which had previously been advertised for wear in the Empire. In response to another query about a "Ride-Astride Habit for War-Worker," she wrote, "Why not go to some well known reliable man, like Mr. Montague Smyth ... He will make you a beautifully cut and finished khaki drill ride-astride habit from 3 guineas ... The riding breeches start at 25s. 6d., and, like the habits, these are in every way satisfactory."[138]

Riding clothes for remount work drew on imperial models for their lighter weight yet also durable fabrics. This was especially important during the war

Figure 5.8 Advertisement for Montague Smyth, *The Ladies' Field* (March 25, 1916), page 163: The script of this advertisement links imperial experience with wartime service: "For those patriotic women who are helping to train remounts Montague Smyth has designed some completely perfect riding kit … With his long experience in making ride-astride clothes for Colonial women, he is naturally just the man to know what the remount trainer needs." Though the Great War undoubtedly contributed to more women beginning to ride astride to aid in the war effort, it was not the war that made the style acceptable in Britain. That occurred before the twentieth century when imperial experience helped contribute to the widespread adoption of cross-saddle riding for women. What the war did, then, was validate this method of riding for a world that was much changed after 1918.

Credit: Collection of the author.

years, when heavy cloth such as hunting woolens was at a premium for military uniforms. As advertised in 1915, "Montague Smyth would also like to remind his clients that he has a good selection of both light and medium weight cloths in hand for his riding habits, a fact which should be noted with interest, since considerable difficulties are being experienced in some quarters in securing woolen weaves of any description."[139] In these ways, imperial experience in horse sports contributed to the adoption of the cross-saddle before 1914 and further enabled war work for female riders. A government report by the end of the war cited women's superb remount work as "one of the revelations of the times," but women had been riding and training horses much earlier, especially for work in the hunting fields around the Empire.[140]

Horses and Hunting During the First World War

Remount work was not the only way for women to contribute to the war effort through equestrianism. Hunting was sanctioned and even encouraged during the war years, partly because it stimulated horse breeding programs across the country, and partly for normalcy and morale. As "Harby," the hunting correspondent for *The Ladies' Field*, noted in 1916: "The generous appreciation of the head of the Army Remount Department and of Lord Derby of the services of the Hunts to the country must have been very welcome to the hunting women who have done so much to keep the sport going and to help to supply horses to the country at a time of need."[141] Here too imperial experience and women's wholehearted participation in field sports during the late nineteenth century were crucial. Almost single-handedly from the first days of the Great War, it was British women who saved fox hunting in Britain. While men were fighting at the front, women filled their empty positions and cared for horses, hounds, and sport in their absence. As "Harby" asked in 1914,

> What is to be done about keeping up the hunts? ... We in the country know that it would be a blow to horse breeding ... we shall be able to carry on the various hunts. For this women can do a great deal, both by money and influence. The sight and sounds of the hunt will help to keep people's spirits up; and ... when our defenders come back to their homes they may be able to take part once more in the sports that have made them what they are.[142]

As "Harby" pointed out, hunting served many uses. First, it trained and conditioned mature horses for military purposes. Second, it aided horse-breeding programs, as women sought to create a new kind of "blood horse" for multipurpose use. Third, it helped raise morale and preserve a distinctly British tradition and way of life, which provided a sense of normalcy not only for those at home, but for soldiers serving abroad who hoped to return home after the conflict.

Fox hunting provided an ideal training ground for horses to be sent to the front. As "Harby" argued, "Women of note and influence in the country have seen that hunting must go on for the sake of the men and the horses it produces."[143] The hunting correspondent continued:

> When a horse goes on service you can teach him quickly all that is necessary, but you cannot give him condition and that gift of taking care of his rider on rough ground on which the rider's life may depend – there is nothing like the hunting field for that. To this end it is not necessary that we should take part in fast runs, but that we should go out often.[144]

This kind of preparation could save lives in the strenuous conditions of the battlefield. "Hunting is at once the school and test of the highest class of war-horse of the day in England,"[145] which was confirmed by a cavalry soldier who wrote to *The Ladies' Field* in 1915. He had initially been skeptical of the hunting horses sent to the front, but having tried them, he praised them highly: "I have no doubt now these hunter bred and conditioned horses have a reserve of fitness which makes them invaluable, while their power of taking care of themselves in rough ground cannot be overpraised."[146]

Women also preserved hunting in Britain for those who would return when the war ended. As "Harby" noted in 1915,

> I feel, too, that the longer the war goes on the more necessary it is for us to keep life at home going. It does not seem to occur to people how necessary, how vital to a healthy state of things after the war it is that our soldiers should settle down after it is all over, or how difficult it will be for some of them to do so. I have not forgotten the last war and the restlessness that followed.[147]

When military men returned home on leave, often one of the first things they longed to do was join a hunt, and fields swelled to double or triple their normal numbers when this occurred.[148] Many of these soldiers had not been regular riders before the war; even sailors who had never been on a horse before came home and rode out. Indeed it was for these new recruits to the sport as well as its old devotees – indeed, to the British way of life and the countryside – that hunting had to be preserved, not only as an homage but to solidify its place in the future. "We call to mind the splendid memory of the dead," wrote one commentator, "but we do not forget the living and the longing, so strong in them, that when they come back, they may find the old country life ready for them. How many people have realised and sympathised with this desire to offer the best to those who return."[149]

This is not to say that it was hunting as usual. By 1917 it was estimated that there were approximately 164 fewer meets of foxhounds per week than before the war, and only about 25 percent of hunting hounds.[150] Many of the usual hunting hotspots like Melton Mowbray and Market Harborough were practically empty. Regular fields consisted only of women, a few old men, and children home for the holidays. A premier hunt like the Quorn might only have 15 to 20 out, whereas pre-war fields regularly numbered 400 or more—yet the sport continued.[151]

Masters – or Mistresses – of Hounds

As the numbers in hunting fields declined and men were called to the front, it was left to hunting women to fill the leadership positions they left vacant, especially as Masters and Hunt Servants. Well before 1914, British women had been contributing to hunting in these ways. The Marchioness of Salisbury, who took over her husband's pack in 1775, is generally recognized as the first female Master of Hounds.[152] The first "modern" female Master of Hounds was Mrs. Cheape (née Maud Mary Hemming) who formed the Bentley Harriers in 1891.[153] In 1894, both Mrs. Pryse-Rice and Lady Gifford took over the Masterships of harrier packs.[154] Other women took over these leadership roles as well, including Lady Portal (Vine Foxhounds), Miss Somerville (West Carbery Foxhounds), Miss McClintock (Tynan and Armagh Harriers), and Mrs. Hughes (Neuadd Fawr Foxhounds). McClintock had been offered her Mastership in 1899, and she was re-elected with popular acclaim to the position by the members of the Hunt every year (Figure 5.9).[155] Lady Greenall acted as Field Master for the prestigious Belvoir pack by the early 1900s.[156]

The presence and aid of the wives of Masters had been indispensable for years, but many women had moved beyond this aid and assistance into leadership positions by the 1890s. After 1914, some women filled in when their male family members went to the western front, while others filled empty positions in subscription packs that were in need of management. These women took over nearly every position of Hunt leadership across the country, from Masters of Foxhounds, Staghounds, and Harriers, to acting as Hunt Servants and Whippers-In, to acting as earth-stoppers and Hunt Secretaries.[157]

A Master of Hounds was the ultimate authority in any hunting district. As G.F. Underhill noted, "The Master of Hounds is the sporting Prime Minister of the country which he hunts."[158] The Master had to oversee all aspects of hunting in a particular and defined area (a hunt country), including training, upkeep, and breeding of hounds; mounting and upkeep of hunt servants; and ensuring the preservation of a healthy fox population in the district by working with farmers and owners. It was a difficult and time-consuming job, requiring no small amounts of stamina, diplomacy, and passion for the sport.

It was due to these examples that women were able to fill such positions in 1914 when men were called to war.[159] "We owe a debt to those older women who were pioneers and who first assumed the responsibility and the labours as well as the pleasures of hunting hounds," "Harby" acknowledged in *The Ladies' Field*, "They showed that women were able to carry on a Hunt and prepared the way for what might have seemed an impossible task."[160] In the hunting season

Figure 5.9 "British Votaries of Diana: Lady Masters of the Hounds," from *The Illustrated London News* (January 25, 1908), page 132: The Marchioness of Salisbury, who took over her husband's pack in 1775, is generally recognized as the first female Master of Hounds, but the first "modern" female Master of Hounds was Mrs. Cheape who formed the Bentley Harriers in 1891. Others soon followed, and, in the hunting season before the war (fall 1913–winter 1914), there were 22 female Masters listed in *Baily's Hunting Directory*.
Credit: Collection of the author.

before the war (fall 1913–winter 1914), there were 22 female Masters listed in *Baily's Hunting Directory*. During the war years, the number peaked at 33 female Masters, and 14 Masters of Foxhounds, though there were fewer total hunts due to war shortages, though *Baily's Magazine* did not keep totals in these years. This increase was paralleled by female Hunt Staff, such as Huntsmen or Whippers-In, also listed in *Baily's Magazine*. In the year before the war (1913–1914), there were 15 women listed as serving in such positions; during the war, the number peaked at 31.[161] The number of women taking these positions was by no means small, nor were their actions unusual or insignificant.

Women who took up the roles of Masters were also important in confirming and publicizing astride riding for women. Also among those who advocated for the cross-saddle in Britain was Mrs. T.H.R. Hughes, Master of the Neuadd Fawr Hunt in Wales, who had taken to the style years earlier and declared she never looked back (Figure 5.10).[162] The main reason for this switch was that riding astride helped Mrs. Hughes manage her hunting duties better than riding sidesaddle, a fact also demonstrated by other female Masters such as Miss Aston of the Quarme Harriers.[163] As Master of the Taunton Vale Harriers, polo player Noëla Whiting also continued riding astride.[164] Mrs. Cheape, Master of the

Figure 5.10 "Meet of the Neuadd Fawr Foxhounds at Moyddin, January 20, 1910," with Master Mrs. T.H.R. Hughes riding astride: Hughes started riding astride in 1908 to better pursue her hunting duties as Master. She declared, "[I] have not ridden *once* on a side-saddle since," and "I never knew what the joys of riding really were till I took to riding astride."
Credit: © Amgueddfa Ceredigion Museum.

Bentley Harriers, also insisted that her daughters ride astride, being much respected for encouraging her children and establishing a public precedent.[165]

Not only did women fill these positions, but they also did so extremely well. Contemporaries acknowledged their efforts with widespread praise. At the same time, however, some opinions on hunting as an essential sport had begun to change. The problem was that many people did not consider fox hunting necessary during the war, and questioned any justification for its continuance under the circumstances, whether the sport was led by men or women. Not surprisingly, these years saw increased challenges to hunting – both the challenge of keeping it going, and the challenge posed by those trying to shut it down. Horses were sent to the front, feed was scarce, and many packs went under. That hunting survived at all was popularly attributed to women's efforts. The continuation of horse racing during the war also came under criticism, leading to an unexpected decision by the War Cabinet to suspend racing until the war was over. This racing ban was met with such opposition that Prime Minister David Lloyd George approved the resumption of a limited amount of racing.[166] Such decisions reflected a widespread feeling of how important horse sports were to a national identity that was now under threat.

This hostility grew from earlier humanitarian and anti-hunting campaigns, and those at home struggled to convince detractors. As "Harby" wrote in 1915:

> It is a witness to the greatness of the struggle in which we are engaged that this war has interfered with hunting in many ways, whereas the struggle against Napoleon's power occasioned no disturbance of the ordinary routine of country life at all. The principal difficulty to-day is one from within. There are many people who are doubtful as to whether hunting is justified under the circumstances, and there are others who are not doubtful at all, but who think that any interest that distracts our minds from the critical situation of the country is undesirable and not to be justified … To deal with this distaste for seeing the Hunt crossing a country, we can only show as well as we can that it is not so much a sport as a business. This point should be obtained to objectors, and we cannot too often recite the enormous source of strength that the business of hunting has been to the country.[167]

The detractors were vocal in their opposition. For example, Sir Ian Heathcoat-Amory sent a letter to the press, in which he wrote: "All forms of sport, including hunting, seem to me to be out of tune with this new spirit which the call of our country has aroused; and I mean, accordingly, to stop hunting at once."[168] What was most surprising about this particular opposition was that Sir Ian, as Master of the Tiverton Foxhounds, had hunted for 36 years (and later died as a result of a hunting accident), though more general opposition came from those who had never hunted and opposed hunting on moral or ethical grounds.[169]

The hunting community – now largely female – responded accordingly. As "Harby" wrote in 1917,

The question of the continuance of fox-hunting has been raised, and, I think, in the tone of those who write on the side of hunting being given up, we recognise those who would be equally ready to do away with hunting in peace or war. ... The sport had been kept going in direct obedience to the wishes of the Government, and those who have supported the hunts have done so at the cost of much trouble and self-denial. It is, perhaps, worth while to consider what the result will be if fox-hunting is prohibited. If once a hunt is given up, the pack dispersed, and the foxes killed, the sport might, but probably would not, revive in that country. There will be no more light horse breeding, for the market will be closed. The country, then, if horses are necessary, will have to shoulder the cost of keeping up Government studs. By far the larger number of horses are bred in twos and threes by men and women who wish to breed horses for their own use with the hunt. These studs will cease to exist. The £20,000 expended on King's premium[170] and other horses will be wasted. There will be a considerable exodus from country places, whose sole attraction is the hunting. A very large number of men ineligible for service will be thrown out of their unemployment.[171]

Women were encouraged to keep up their important and valuable work: "it is a mistake to take up too apologetic an attitude as to carrying on our Hunts. We are doing a real national service under great difficulties and are entitled to claim the credit for it."[172] But while the Great War may have encouraged more women to take on such positions of leadership, many women had already served as successful examples of Masters in the three decades prior to 1914 and continued their service afterward.

Equestrian Sports After the Great War

After the hard-earned victory in 1918, praise was due – and given – to the women who had saved hunting and horse sports for Britain. Not only had they nearly single-handedly carried on a national sport and countryside necessity without men, but also defended the pursuit against criticism. "As for the services of women hunting in these hard times, the Hunts could not have existed without them," *The Ladies' Field* noted, "There are no Hunts which have not benefited by the support and presence of their lady members."[173] By December 1918, hunting notes and columns reappeared in sporting magazines like *The Ladies' Field*, well before other sporting columns returned.[174] This corresponded to the resurgence of hunting. Fields ballooned to pre-war proportions, and with the post-war social shifts, many equestrian enthusiasts correctly predicted the massive increase in riding and hunting.[175]

In the hunting season of 1918–1919, male leadership as Masters and other Hunt roles did not return to pre-war levels.[176] Some women did graciously surrender their positions to returning men, like Lady Portal, who had taken over the Vine Hunt since 1913, and who offered the Mastership to Colonel Croft.[177] Lady Lowther also gave up the prestigious Pytchley Hunt to Colonel Faber.[178] However, many women continued in the positions which they had filled so well from 1914. Mrs. Fernie continued hunting her husband's pack, while others such as Mrs. Hall (Carlow), Lady Masham (Bedale), Mrs. Pryse-Rice (Wales), and Miss Isa McClintock (Tynan and Armagh) continued their leadership.[179] Often daughters riding cross-saddle became more involved after the war, building on the positions they had held during it, such as Mrs. Pryse-Rice's daughter who acted as whipper-in.[180]

Much of this involvement continued because of the high standard of leadership and success under the ladies' tenure. Some stemmed from the necessity of the returning men being required to work when they came home, thus only being able to devote a single day of the week to hunting, whereas women could ride far more often. In fact, women far outnumbered the men in post-war hunting fields. While some traditionalists still grumbled that women hunting hounds themselves was to be "deprecated," others like Lord Dorchester saw the positive in these new roles: "nor are we surprised when in each recurrent season we see a male M.F.H. [Master of Foxhounds] replaced by a lady."[181]

Though equestrian sports did not continue unchanged from the pre-war years, the post-war transformations were less dramatic than was sometimes proclaimed. Imperial experience had bounced back to affect Britain before 1914, and because of this, the women who "saved" hunting or trained remount horses were able to do so by riding astride. Changes had certainly come, and none were more visually evident than the shift from ladies riding sidesaddle to riding cross-saddle. Women had avidly been riding in this style well before 1914. It was only because cross-saddle riding had been made so acceptable before the war that many women were able to aid the war effort as they did. As Lord Dorchester reported,

> The pre-War hunting men went to the War in a body, and such of their hunters as were not requisitioned for the War were at the disposal of their wives and daughters, who hunted them as a matter of duty, to keep the horses fit and to keep hunting alive against the return of their lords; possibly, too, there were one or two young horses coming on, which had to be handled and schooled. These ladies thus acquired an intimate knowledge of and interest in hunting, and whereas in former years they had ridden only well-mannered horses and had looked to a pilot, *they now had to think and act for themselves*.[182]

This was the logical conclusion of the decades of developing "self-possession" that had been encouraged in riding manuals throughout the Victorian era. Through riding and hunting, female riders self-fashioned strong and independent identities through sport that contributed to Britain's victory in the Great War.

As Lieutenant-Colonel F.C. Hitchcock acknowledged, women had so admirably served in remount service by riding cross-saddle and continued "to do so afterwards in the hunting-field to influence those about to commence riding to learn the astride method."[183] Even women who had not served in Remount Service were thus influenced by those female examples who acted as role models.

Post-War Riding Manuals

As hunting and riding blossomed in popularity after the First World War, it was no surprise that the mid to late 1920s witnessed another boom in equestrian guidebooks. What was different about these manuals, as compared to late Victorian instruction books, was that they were no longer differentiated by sex. Women no longer needed separate books devoted only to ladies' riding. What was applicable for a male rider was equally applicable for a female rider, as it was assumed both would be riding astride.

In his 1927 manual entitled *Mount and Man: A Key to Better Horsemanship*, Lieutenant-Colonel M.F. McTaggart enthusiastically supported cross-saddle riding for women. He argued that it was better for both equine and equestrian. He believed it was women's natural "feminine attributes" which made them such strong and effective riders, including a "delicacy of touch" and sympathy with their mount. He rebutted the claim that women were physically unable to ride astride. True horsemanship did not require brute muscular power but rather a combination of strength, grip, and balance that women often achieved naturally. This was not to say that beginners could simply become expert riders overnight. He advised, "I trust ladies will take courage. Let them go to good tailors and good riding instructors, and then they will be able to show the men the way a stiff country should be crossed both attractively and efficiently."[184] In conclusion, he wrote, "Personally, I hope that the time is not far distant when the side saddle will look as absurd as the crinoline, and that the only place to find one will be in the museums."[185]

Others took this position as well. By 1929, Captain J.L.M. Barrett seconded this opinion in his classic work, *Practical Horsemanship*, in which he plainly stated: "To put it brutally when real horsemanship is required the rider must be astride."[186] Lieutenant-Colonel S.G. Goldschmidt agreed in his 1930 riding manual, *The Fellowship of the Horse*. Like other authors before him, Goldschmidt gave a litany of reasons why women should not ride sidesaddle. One fact was that young girls brought up to ride astride as children were forced into an abrupt shift to the sidesaddle when they "came out." There was little incentive to make this switch, and much inconvenience as a whole new method of riding had to be learned. Therefore, few girls apparently transitioned as they were supposed to.[187] This was a far cry from the early Victorian era when little girls were brought up riding sidesaddle.

Besides the inconvenience, the cost of such a transition was immense. A horse trained for a sidesaddle cost far more than one that could be ridden astride, and Goldschmidt estimated that a sidesaddle habit was twice the cost of an astride habit, while the sidesaddle was at least three times the cost of a utilitarian cross-saddle.[188] Furthermore, sidesaddles and the habits to ride in them were tailored individually to mount and rider so they had little value on the second-hand market, although it was easy and inexpensive to buy breeches, boots, and a cross-saddle this way, making the option much more appealing to beginners and Saturday riders. It also helped, Goldschmidt continued, that riding astride was more convenient for learning, more comfortable in practice, and safer in a fall.[189]

Goldschmidt's primary argument against the sidesaddle, however, was that it was a "limitation" to true fellowship with the horse: it allowed only "incomplete contact," thus "incomplete mutual understanding."[190] Therefore, he concluded tartly:

> I personally prefer astride for all – old, young, stout or thin. It is entirely a matter of turn-out and a graceful seat, and in both cases a good tailor, bootmaker, and hatter, combined with good taste, are necessary, no less than a course of lessons under a good teacher. To listen to all the enemies of the cross-saddle one would imagine that all side-saddle riders were graceful swans, and their astride sisters ungainly geese. And are all men paragons of elegance and accomplished horsemen?[191]

His answer was an unspoken but obvious and resounding "no."

By 1932, Captain J.E. Hance in *School for Horse and Rider* went even further and stated outright: "riding is really the same for both sexes."[192] As he continued,

> we must entirely ignore the question of sex. Granted that certain fundamentals are necessary for successful astride riding, these must remain the same for women as for men; again, if men rode side-saddle, the laws governing that form of riding would apply to them as well as to women.[193]

He aimed all directions in his book equally at male and female riders: "I have not differentiated between the sexes in my remarks about teaching riding, so it is not necessary to give ladies any special instruction."[194] He argued that any woman who devoted the same time and effort to riding as a man would develop the same independent seat.[195] In terms of lady beginners, "I am sure that the chances of being able to ride astride are equal to those of a man starting at the same time" – women were no longer considered the weaker vessels.[196] Interestingly, Hance mentioned that he had had a terrible accident that had maimed his right leg, so he rode the way a sidesaddle rider would. He was thus one of the very few men who could offer informed opinions on the two methods of riding and decide which was more effective.[197]

1932 was a watershed year in the development of horsemanship in Britain. Not only did Hance's volume appear, but so did two of the most significant interwar works on equestrianism for women. The first was Eva (E.V.A.) Christy's *Cross-Saddle and Side-Saddle: Modern Riding for Men and Women*. Christy had been a prominent author on ladies' horsemanship before the First World War, having published sidesaddle manuals and revised editions during the late 1890s and early 1900s.[198] During the war, however, she had served as a riding instructor for the military, and afterward she recognized the utility and effectiveness of riding astride, which she had taught and also practiced. In the end, she concluded that women must choose the style of riding that best suited them, as either style was an acceptable choice. As Christy argued, "I fail to find any reason why each individual – irrespective of sex – should not ride in the style which he or she finds more advantageous."[199]

Christy favored the cross-saddle seat for women, for its ease in riding and its effectiveness in advanced horsemanship, especially for rough or demanding activities like hunting or jumping.[200] The cross-saddle seat was the only effective way to train horses, which more women were successfully doing.[201] As she pointed out, however, the sidesaddle seat did have some benefits too, including the ease of staying on (largely because there was only one side to fall off from) and the resulting security which aided a non-interfering and passive horsemanship. For Christy, equality in horsemanship did not mean that women must choose to ride cross-saddle like men, but rather that they had a choice in deciding whether to ride aside or astride. This choice was based on personal preference rather than social dictates. In fact, in her later book, *If Wishes Were Horses*, Christy advocated the sidesaddle for disabled riders who could not ride cross-saddle, specifically the officers and men from the Great War who had suffered major amputations.[202]

As Christy pointed out, riding was not merely about muscular strength or physically controlling a horse. If it had been, women would never have been able to ride sidesaddle as well as they did. Instead, riding was a delicate combination of skills (balance and grip), knowledge (of horsemanship), and the mental qualities necessary to pursue and excel at a sport. Following the Great War, there was a new impetus to understanding the mental aspects of riding for both horse and rider – what we today call sports psychology. Instructors and equestrian authors had long recited the requisite attributes for riding (nerve, patience, compassion), and this new focus was both the evolution and culmination of that trend. As Christy noted, "It is very truly said that a horseman rides with his brain more than with his muscles."[203] Horsemanship was not only about self-control but also about self-reliance in developing both authority and command. As Christy's work demonstrated, by this time riding had indeed become an equal sport for all, for she specifically noted that her book was intended "not only for the man and woman rider, but for the child as well."[204]

While Christy's work was important in advancing an equality of choice in riding for female equestrians, the other major work on ladies' horsemanship, published in 1932, focused on equality in the hunting field. This was Lady Diana Shedden's and Lady Viola Apsley's *"To whom the goddess...": Hunting and Riding for Women*. The interwar period saw a massive surge in the number of riders and those interested in equestrian sports, but it also saw fewer riding publications specifically for women than were produced in the Victorian era. To educate these newcomers – of whom fully half were women – Shedden and Apsley, both of them distinguished and experienced riders, wrote their volume for ladies.[205] Like Christy and the majority of post-Victorian equestrian authors, the duo believed that riders were made, not born, hence their directions and instructions for achieving skilled and efficient horsemanship.

Although lessons and expert instruction were the first and foremost requirements on the path to advanced horsemanship, the co-authors also highlighted the personal qualities a good horsewoman needed. In their view, a woman must possess three qualities: "Judgment to decide what ought to be done, Coolness in carrying out the intention, and Nerve to throw the heart boldly over the obstacle."[206] Novices could learn all about balance and grip, hands, legs, and aids, but one also needed the virtues of sympathy and harmony to be a strong rider – qualities which had long been associated with femininity.[207]

Of course, muscular fitness (for endurance strength, not peak exertion) and cardiovascular stamina remained important, as it did in any physical activity, but the additional (and more stereotypically masculine) qualities of confidence, anticipation, and resolution were equally necessary. As Shedden and Apsley stated, "The first requisite towards a firm seat is CONFIDENCE in yourself based on certain knowledge," which summed up what female riders had been cultivating since the 1830s.[208] In addition, one of the most important qualities was anticipation: "The best way is to *cultivate a sense of looking ahead*, of preparedness for whatever betides."[209] Resolution was particularly important:

> The spineless sort of rider who does not know her own mind, has no idea of her own, or has two minds about everything, invariably communicates her indecisions to her horse, till the pair are a danger to themselves and a nuisance to other people. It is better to make up your mind wrong than to have no mind at all or try to do several things at the same moment.[210]

They added, "self-control is the highest attribute of character."[211] Finally, they concluded that women must "cultivate a clear-cut mind" and added the strict injunction: do not follow the example of others, but rather "think for yourself, see if you can use your own brains."[212] This mental strength contributed to the determination necessary to be a good rider, for as the authors noted, "If it comes to a tussle with a horse or pony, remember you must win or else part with him. He will never forget and your prestige and influence will be gone forever."[213] In these ways, the authors encouraged many strong and independent qualities in female riders which naturally carried over into other areas of their lives.

These qualities were ones that they believed increased a woman's natural femininity and added to her independence. "The qualities required in a horsewoman are much those natural to the sex," they concluded, "sympathy with your horse; keenness to persevere; quickness of mind, to look ahead, to anticipate, to be ready; a stoutish heart, gentle hands, a firm seat and good fellowship – to which might be added good health."[214] A woman's essential femininity was at the heart of what made her not only an effective – but also a successful – rider.[215]

In line with Christy's assertion, Shedden and Apsley concluded, "At the present time it is a moot point whether a woman should ride side-saddle or astride. ... Today a woman may please herself entirely as to which seat she adopts without upsetting anyone."[216] In their view, the object should always be to find what style suited each person best: "the ideal is to be proficient in both saddles."[217]

Both methods of riding – cross-saddle and sidesaddle – had pros and cons. According to the authors, however, the advantages of the cross-saddle outweighed the benefits of the sidesaddle. They listed ten advantages that cross-saddle riders had over their sisters riding sidesaddle. First, cross-saddle riders could ride smaller horses, while sidesaddle riders needed a larger, stronger horse, capable of carrying and balancing the heavier (and lop-sided) weight of sidesaddle and rider. Second, cross-saddle horses were cheaper as they required less specialized training, and therefore purchasers could select from a wider variety of horses. Third, a cross-saddle rider did not require a groom experienced in dealing with sidesaddles, nor did she need a saddle fitter to constantly look after her sidesaddles and keep them in good working order. Fourth, clothes for riding astride were far cheaper, about one-sixth the cost of a sidesaddle habit, and fifth, a cross-saddle was far less costly than a sidesaddle, £10 compared to £25. Sixth, cross-saddle riding did not tire horses as quickly and a female rider rode about 1.5 stone (or 21 pounds) lighter. Seventh, it was easier for the cross-saddle rider to mount and dismount when hunting, and eighth, it was far easier to exchange horses with men if needed. Ninth, a woman was less likely to be badly injured if she fell when riding astride, and tenth, riding astride was simply more comfortable. As Shedden and Apsley concluded, "In every way astride is cheaper and less trouble."[218]

They did concede that riding sidesaddle had some advantages. First, many beginning riders felt safer riding sidesaddle, being locked into the saddle and forced into an artificial sense of safety. Second, many felt more comfortable riding in this way. Third, sidesaddle riders looked nicer in the opinions of some, and fourth, they could ride bigger horses. Still, by this count, riding astride for women won hands down by a count of ten positives to four.

If there were fewer positives about riding sidesaddle, there were also more negatives as well. The heavy sidesaddle (to say nothing of the weight being carried only on one side) frequently gave horses sore backs, which in turn required an experienced groom and a limitless pocket for veterinary bills. Another downside was that saddles, habits, grooms, and horses cost more for one to ride sidesaddle. Costs were an important factor when considering both medical bills (from injury) and repairs (for equipment). One novice rider estimated that she had at least 250 falls in her first two seasons of hunting.[219] As she continued, "... my numerous accidents were rather expensive, as I got one saddle broken four times" and the "crutch [was] straightened out like a poker."[220] After being thrown badly against the crutches and doubled in two, Lillian Bland concluded,

> Certainly side saddles are cruel inventions, both for the horse and rider, and I hope in some enlightened age they will be consigned to museums. It is, after all, merely a matter of fashion, and if the right set of ladies would show their common sense by adopting men's saddles it would become the rule and not the exception to see ladies riding astride.[221]

These experiences convinced Bland of the necessity of riding astride for women as early as 1906. Finally, even Shedden and Apsley admitted that even the best sidesaddle rider would forever be "handicapped" at riding because she rode only on one side and therefore did not have the strength of leg on both sides to guide her mount.[222] By riding astride, women were equal with men, and this equality was what had drawn the large numbers of converts to the style.[223]

Perhaps it was Lord Dorchester who best described the changes in hunting. Having begun hunting at the age of eight in 1884, he had witnessed the glories of the late Victorian and Edwardian eras and compared them to the war and interwar years. In his book *Sport, Foxhunting and Shooting* from 1935, Dorchester expressed that female equestrians had become even more numerous by the early twentieth century than they had been in the late nineteenth century. He attributed this increase to riding astride.[224] Based on six years of calculating, he estimated that, on a "fashionable day," women made up about 65% of the field, while on the other three days 70%–80%. Not only were women turning out in higher numbers, but they were also riding better. As Dorchester concluded:

> I think it will be conceded that their average performance, their horsemanship and courage have improved in proportion to their numbers, and out of all knowledge during the past twenty years [1915-1935]. Much of the improvement is attributable to more sensible clothes and a different outlook from that possessed by their mothers.[225]

As *The Ladies' Field* concluded in 1920, "Now women who hunt can be numbered in their hundreds, losing in the world of sport not one whit of their feminine charm."[226]

The reason for this surge of participation in equestrian sports, especially by women, corresponded with the rise of the automobile after the First World War. Major-General Geoffrey Brooke saw the rise in equestrian sports as a "very definite reaction to this cycle of mechanization. More than ever the horse is considered *an essential means of recreation*, bringing an ever-increasing number of recruits to the hunting-field."[227] By the early 1930s, the London Post Office Directory listed nine riding schools near Hyde Park, two near Regents Park, and many livery stables. Just one of those schools – the Cadogan Riding School –

kept 260 horses and ponies at Cadogan Lane, Belgrave Square.[228] Horses were no longer required for labor, and so could be used for leisure.

After the war, there were 80% fewer draft-type horses in England, but the number of riding horses boomed because fewer were needed for everyday tasks such as transportation and light labor.[229] The price of these horses decreased as well, as they flooded the market domestically and war horses returned, resulting in increased opportunities for ownership. Although renting horses for riding and hunting had been popular during the Victorian era, the practice took off after 1918 as "hirelings" made possible the participation of even the most cash-conscious novices who could not afford to buy and keep their own mounts. As Major-General Geoffrey Brooke pointed out, the trade in hirelings was both necessary and desirable:

> It is necessary because a large number of would-be participants in the sport could not take part in it without [hired horses], and desirable since however much masters, huntsmen, and reactionaries may deplore, and even endeavor in some cases to cut down, the large fields to be found in some countries, and admitting their disadvantages, the more people who indulge the better it is for foxhunting in the long run.[230]

Captain Lionel Dawson even went so far as to oppose the label "hireling" and to christen them "hunters in transit from one owner to another."[231]

To satisfy the voracious interest in hunting by the reading and riding public, a plethora of books on the subject appeared during the interwar years. They differed from the products of previous booms in hunting literature as they were meant for a new audience of riders with a background of economic thrift and frugality. C.R. Acton's *Hunting for All* stated the matter plainly in the title, which he directed at male and female riders equally under the assumption that the majority of the latter were riding astride, as did Captain Lionel Dawson's *Hunting without Tears*.[232]

Horse Girls

Although adult women had joined fox-hunting fields and equestrian activities since the early Victorian era, the widespread involvement of children in horse sports did not pick up until the early 1900s. Some medical opinions continued to criticize female equestrianism, but, by and large, these were outliers. The mental and physical benefits of riding had long been recognized, and many parents realized the advantages of children's participation. Major Geoffrey Brooke, the husband of Dorothy who had campaigned to save the horses of the Great War, wrote: "Modern parents appreciate the moral and physical advantages attached to riding and are at pains and expense to have their children taught to ride and encourage them in every way."[233] Typically young girls had ridden cross-saddle until they were old enough to "come out," with the expectation that they would then switch to the more proper sidesaddle.[234] This strategy had initially been instituted to prevent any curvature of the spine in growing bodies, due to the twisted nature of riding sidesaddle, though there were other factors at play.

By the early 1900s, however, few girls followed through on switching riding styles (Figure 5.11). It was expensive to transition to sidesaddle riding, which demanded a new saddle, new clothing, and possibly even a new horse.[235] Many girls refused to make the switch from one style to the other – not wanting to learn to ride all over again. As one equestrian correspondent noted in 1902, "I know several girls, who, though riding capitally astride, found themselves so helpless and awkward when made to ride sideways, and hampered with a habit, that they declared they would rather not ride at all than continue so, and entreated to be allowed to go back to the cross saddle."[236] Even before the war, Mrs. Stuart Menzies proclaimed that "the coming generation will doubtless be astriders."[237] The emphasis on riding lessons and specialized instruction for

Figure 5.11 A determined young horsewoman by esteemed photographer John Hawke (8 George Street, Plymouth): By the late Victorian era, young girls often learned to ride cross-saddle, with the expectation that they would transition to the more ladylike style of riding sidesaddle when they became teenagers. This strategy backfired, however, as "hampered with a habit, they declared they would rather not ride at all than continue so," and thus a new generation of "astriders" was born.

Credit: Collection of the author.

children – rather than being taught by the family coachman or groom – created a wave of better and more effective young equestrians than ever before, who joined pre-war fox hunting fields in ever-increasing numbers.[238]

During the First World War, children contributed to the war effort through horse sports, often going out with hunts and providing support where they could. Unlike adults whose mounts were usually sent to the front, children's ponies were not considered war horses and remained available for riding throughout the war. By 1918, youth participation was seen as necessary for horse sports to continue. As *The Ladies' Field* directed,

> we should pay especial attention to the training of the young sportsmen and their sisters who are coming on. With them rests the future of hunting. We have seen what splendid results have come from the training given by the hunting-field both to men and women in the particular crisis. We should therefore pay particular attention to the education in the field of our young people. They should be encouraged to go out and be taught to take an intelligent interest in the handling and work of the hounds. To them the war will be a memory. They will be able to read the complete and detailed story as we can never do. But on them will rest the duty of keeping up our invaluable sports and games and the spirits these represent.[239]

Only by encouraging children in equestrian sports would Britain's national pastimes survive and thrive.

Many, like Shedden and Apsley, concluded that female riders, young and old, had much to gain from and give to horse sports:

> The majority of the good horsewomen of our day prove conclusively that the best feminine charm is not lost but rather enhanced by the subtle distinction of riding … one is inclined to think that the rising Dianas, thanks to better riding-lessons and good ponies, will be even more attractive to look at than the past and present generations.[240]

Many authors published books on children's riding, including Audrey Blewitt in 1933, with *Ponies and Children*. These books encouraged the equestrian equality of both sexes, not only by assuming that they rode the same way, but also by giving the same instructions to boys and girls. She advised the same dress and encouraged participation in the same mounted games and activities under the same rules.[241] Blewitt argued, "it is more comfortable and convenient for horse and rider to ride astride," and specified "girl astriders are advised to dress exactly as boys."[242] Young girls had traditionally been taught to ride astride, but now they could ride that way for the rest of their lives.

Blewitt also recognized how the influence of imperial experience had transformed British riding. She acknowledged the great changes in female riding clothes, especially the jodhpur pant.[243] She noted how many imperial games such as paper chases and gymkhanas had become exceedingly popular in Britain, especially through the Pony Club, which fostered the education of horsemanship for children across Britain. Shirley Faulkner-Horne also described this impact in her 1936 book, *Riding for Children*. The author was a teenage member of the Pony Club, and she aimed her volume at the estimated 10,000 other Pony Club members across Britain, so that they could better participate in activities such as show jumping, gymkhanas, cubbing, and hunting.[244] She never mentioned sidesaddle riding in her book, and she assumed (and depicted in illustrations) that girls would be riding astride. Such books also illustrated the close association of the Pony Club, begun in 1929, with hunting and activities like gymkhanas, but also the new sport of show jumping.

The focus on girls' riding was not entirely new, although a modern wave of "horse-craziness" spread through the younger generation of girls in the early twentieth century. Girls were widely recognized to be more interested in horses and riding than their male counterparts, and they were superior pupils.[245] Many attributed this passion and sustained interest to the astride style in which girls were educated and continued riding (Figure 5.12). Sir Edward Durand in *Ponies' Progress* directed his comments to young riders (as well as old) of both sexes, and his photos showed women only riding astride. Having spent time in India before being invalided home, Durand's opinions reflected the continued imperial influence in terms of female equestrianism.[246]

Figure 5.12 Riding astride in 1908, from "Cross v. Side Saddle," by Maud V. Wynter, *The Badminton Magazine of Sports and Pastimes* (June 1908), pages 634 and 637: Riding astride had become a popular choice for female riders before 1914. Many young girls and women rode this way, to hunt, compete, or train horses. Notably two of these photos show the wife and daughter of Masters of Hounds riding astride. Appearing astride normalized the practice for others, especially in conservative areas like the Midlands.
Credit: Collection of the author.

Eight years after he argued that women should ride astride in his book *Mount and Man*, Lieutenant-Colonel M.F. McTaggart followed up with *Horsemanship for Boys and Girls* in 1935. McTaggart directed his instructions to both sexes, and all images showed girls riding astride. He objected to sidesaddle riding as it was injurious for both horse and rider:

> Physically, both for horse and rider, it is a wrong method of riding. The rider is so screwed round that muscles on only one side are used, and the horse inevitably becomes one-sided both in the canter and the trot. The rider has much less control than on the cross-saddle, so that special "ladies'" hunters have to be purchased for them.[247]

He rebutted the argument that girls should grow up riding sidesaddle because ladies looked smarter that way. "Well do they?" he asked his readers, "What is smart about sitting askew like this? 'Oh,' is the reply, 'the habit looks so smart.' This is tantamount to saying that it is the habit that is smart and not the lady inside it."[248] It was a woman's inner qualities that made her feminine, not whether she rode aside or astride.

The Eternal Feminine in Riding Habits

Clothing was especially important in gendered constructions of equestrian sports. As early as 1915, Mrs. Jack May had predicted in *The Queen* magazine the forthcoming changes in female clothes: "Although the war leaves us little or nothing to be thankful for at present, when the end comes – the right, and only, end for us – we shall realise what an extraordinary influence it has had upon women's dress."[249] Riding clothes were certainly no exception, though women wearing breeches had been accepted well before 1914.

Post-war sartorial shifts were important in gaining a wider acceptance of astride riding for women. Equestrians were not the only ones wearing trousers for war efforts: munitionettes, ambulance drivers, and miners, among others, also wore similar clothing, and fashion and behaviors changed accordingly in the interwar years.[250] By 1920, magazines were already claiming that "The up-to-date horsewoman now rides astride as a matter of course."[251] A neat appearance was necessary to the style's acceptance, for against "the cynosure of many eyes [the female rider] must be certain that she is as perfectly turned out as it is possible to be."[252] Astride kits were offered by myriad designers and firms that sold riding clothes, but although astride clothes (breeches, boots, and jacket) had been *accepted* for female riders before the First World War – and indeed, even earlier around the British Empire – the female cross-saddle habit only became *standardized* afterward.[253]

In fact, it was this lack of a standardized costume for lady astride riders, that was the main obstacle to the style gaining widespread acceptance. As W.A. Kerr had noted in 1891, "It is not so much the prudery about sitting like men that excites the wrathful indignation of the opponents of cross-saddle riding as the apparent difficulty of deciding upon the thoroughly neat and workwoman-like costume."[254] Four decades later, Lieutenant-Colonel S.G. Goldschmidt continued, "that there are still so many absurd-looking astride riders is due to the absence of a conventional, established and accepted uniform, such as there is for the [sidesaddle] riding-habit, and the result is a greater scope for the display of bad taste."[255]

Without clear and understandable standards of what was (and was not) acceptable clothing for riding, women tended to wear a variety of different combinations when hacking, hunting, or showing. As hunting author C.R. Acton implored,

> Let me beg of a lady-beginner *not* to go out cub-hunting in a beret, tweed jacket and scarf, and jodhpurs, attractive in the extreme as such an outfit may be for early morning exercise, or, say, for watching work on Newmarket Heath. I am quite aware that many ladies do it, but I am also mindful of some of the comments I have heard from Masters of Hounds, condemning the practice. Remember, it is far more difficult for an M.F.H. to expostulate with a lady on her personal attire than it is for him to deal with a mere man.[256]

The Queen magazine also admitted the skyrocketing popularity of astride clothing but cautioned "it calls emphatically for kit which is just right. This is essentially a matter for a man's tailor" rather than the usual female dressmaker.[257]

Although making specialty riding clothes had traditionally been a male-dominated profession, it was not difficult for women to take the lead and influence widespread sartorial change for their sex. Male tailors dominated the business of making sporting clothing, which was fine for women who wanted masculine breeches and jacket for riding astride, but not as valuable if a woman wanted a sidesadddle outfit. Thus, many women invented and innovated advances in feminine riding clothing. Alice Hayes, author of *The Horsewoman*, designed and patented her own riding habit. However, as Hayes pointed out,

> Other experienced horsewomen besides myself have recognized [the need for better riding garments], and have invented safety skirts which they have failed to get taken up by tailors, and which, therefore, however excellent they may be, have not been placed on the market.[258]

At least two other women designed their own safety skirts – Mrs. Cuthbert Bradley (wife of the sporting artist) and Lady Hilda McNeil – but they did not publicly patent or sell their innovations.[259] Thus, while a few women publicized their inventions, it is impossible to know how many women were behind so many other patents and advances which were lodged in men's names and sold by their brands, or simply used privately and shared among a chosen few. Given the close community of female riders, the latter were probably far more numerous than we know. Women took the lead in ultimately abandoning the riding skirt altogether and switching to the masculine breeches and jacket.

Riding astride called for clothes that were virtually the same for both men and women. What many had taken issue with in the early 1900s was the "hermaphrodite" quality of much women's riding apparel.[260] Rather than trying to feminize astride clothing (which could not be done), women were encouraged to embrace what had been exclusively male attire as femininity came from inner qualities and actions rather than apparel. As Goldschmidt noted,

> The divided skirt, or any other attempt to feminize the astride costume is objectionable, because it is trying to disguise the fact that the wearer is riding astride, and is a suggestion that she is too self-conscious to wear, without embarrassment, what has, up to now, been considered exclusively male attire.[261]

For propriety, effectiveness, and comfort, women were advised "to wear clothes of as similar a cut to a well-dressed man's as possible."[262] In a 1920 article on "Kit for the Hunting Woman," *The Ladies' Field* advised, "Breeches are cut on strictly masculine lines and achieve the same degree of perfection as their male prototypes."[263]

In 1921, the famous maker Tautz advertised astride habits for ladies under the heading, "The Eternal Feminine," boasting that their women's coats were made on exactly the same principles and patterns as a man's.[264] Another ad from the same year proclaimed that "Trimness and Smartness Characterize both the 'Hunting Woman' and the 'Woman Who Hunts'," conceding that while cross-saddle outfits were "frankly masculine" in appearance, the fashion had its glamour and sex appeal because "short coats mean, needless to say, perfectly cut breeches."[265] Astride riding, and by association the clothing needed for it, had become so popular among women that many makers stopped offering sidesaddle outfits. By 1922, T.W. Winter was among the first of these, proclaiming in advertisements throughout *The Ladies' Field* that the firm would only construct clothes for riding astride.[266]

Wearing the Breeches

So women wore the breeches during the Great War, just as they had before, and they kept doing so afterward. The effects of the First World War are often credited for causing this shift in riding styles as part of a larger program of social and political emancipation for women. But women in Britain were riding astride years before the war, so the war itself cannot be solely credited with encouraging women to do so. What the war did, then, was further encourage riding astride as a means to accomplish these wartime duties more fully. Indeed, riding astride before the war made it possible for women to contribute so greatly during the conflict.

The changes in riding for women in Britain in just a few decades should not be understated. Not only did more people ride, but female riders had conclusively adopted the cross-saddle. Shedden and Apsley could claim in 1932 that "the modern young horsewoman is a miles better performer than the pioneers of the astride seat, who in addition were hampered with divided skirts and had every man's word against them!"[267] Riding astride for women had been accepted before the First World War, and it continued afterward in all but the most conservative areas, such as the hunting heartland of the Shires where many continued riding sidesaddle to demonstrate their high-class status in a fast-changing world where social divisions were no longer so visible.

The experiences of British women in horse sports around the Empire, especially in British India, transformed the social, sporting, and cultural worlds of Britain before the First World War. While the most significant impact was the transition to riding cross-saddle rather than sidesaddle, the influence of imperial equestrian activities like gymkhanas and polo was also important in confirming these changes. This imperial experience laid the solid foundations of equestrianism for women that would prove so necessary and influential in aiding the war effort. Cross-saddle riding for women had been accepted before 1914, but it was endorsed after 1918 when more women began riding, hunting, and competing in horse shows (against male competitors). Due to the more exacting and strenuous nature of these activities, women needed to ride astride to be successful – which they did and were. As author Edith Somerville wrote in 1920,

Figure 5.13 "Happy Days," postcard by James E. Pitts (c. 1920s): In this postcard from the early twentieth century, a woman riding cross-saddle in a divided skirt easily clears a fence while hunting. "These equality days" of riding astride for women were "happy days" indeed, and they laid the groundwork for a not-distant future when men and women competed equally on horseback.
Credit: Collection of the author.

"Improvement in these matters was gradual, but it came. The modern sidesaddle did much; the introduction of safety-aprons did more, riding astride will probably do most of all."[268] As she would see, living until 1949, it certainly did.

The cross-saddle seat was popularly adopted in Britain during what Captain Pennell Elmhirst called "these equality days" of the early 1900s, though the style had gained widespread acceptance before 1914.[269] Choosing to ride in this way and wear these garments indicated ways in which women re-imagined their public images and gender roles (Figure 5.13). While war experiences helped normalize new constructions of gender and class for equestrians and non-equestrians alike, it was imperial Amazons who first helped catalyze this sporting and sartorial revolution. After all, they were the ones who first wore the breeches.

Notes

1 Charles Pocklington Chenevix-Trench, *A History of Horsemanship* (New York: Doubleday and Company, 1970), 289.
2 *The Sketch: A Journal of Art and Actuality*, Volume 116 (December 7, 1921), 365.
3 "When did ladies first commence to ride sideways on horseback?" *Saddlery and Harness: A Monthly Trade Journal*, 2.2 (August 1892), 24.
4 See "Stag-hunting in Somerset," *The Times* (London) (August 5, 1919), 4 (Issue 42170). The incident was also mentioned by Maud V. Wynter, "Cross v. Side Saddle," *The Badminton Magazine of Sports and Pastimes* (June 1908), 634.
5 William Fawcett, *Riding and Horsemanship* (New York: Charles Scribner's Sons, 1935), 156.
6 Caspar A. Whitney, *A Sporting Pilgrimage* (New York: Harper and Brothers, 1895), 41.
7 Captain Pennell Elmhirst, *The Best of the Fun, 1891–1897* (London: Chatto and Windus, 1903), 439.
8 G.R. Searle, *A New England? Peace and War, 1886–1918* (Oxford: Clarendon Press, 2004), 3.
9 Deirdre Beddoe, *Back to Home and Duty: Women Between the Wars, 1918-1939* (London: Pandora, 1989).
10 Fiona Skillen, "'Woman and the Sport Fetish': Modernity, Consumerism and Sports Participation in Inter-War Britain," *The International Journal of the History of Sport.*, 29.5 (2012), 750–765.
11 Anthony Dent, *The Horse Through Fifty Centuries of Civilization* (New York: Holt Rinehart and Winston, 1974). One "knacker," Harrison Barber, estimated that he killed 26,000 a year at an average age of 11 (243).
12 F.M.L. Thompson, "Nineteenth-Century Horse Sense," *The Economic History Review*, 29.1 (February 1976), 60–81.
13 Grant Hayter-Menzies, *The Lost War Horses of Cairo: The Passion of Dorothy Brooke* (London: Allen & Unwin, 2017). See also John Singleton, "Britain's Military Use of Horses, 1914–1918," *Past & Present*, 139 (May 1993), 200–201.
14 Simon Butler, *The War Horses* (Wellington, Somerset: Halsgrove, 2011), 139–140.
15 Fiona Skillen, *Women, Sport and Modernity in Interwar Britain* (Oxford: Peter Lang, 2013).
16 "Hunting Notes," *The Ladies' Field*, Volume 84 (December 21, 1918), 35.
17 E. Œ. Somerville and Martin Ross, *Stray-Aways* (London: Longman, Green and Co., 1920), 230.

18 Lady Randolph Churchill, ed., *Women's War Work* (London: C. Arthur Pearson, Ltd., 1916), 24.
19 Major-General Geoffrey Brooke, *Horsemen All: For Parents of the Rising Generation and Young Aspiring Horsemen* (New York: Charles Scribner's Sons, 1938), 136.
20 Anthony Gibbs, "A Chapter of Small Accidents," *Badminton Magazine of Sports and Pastimes*, Volume 5 (August 1897), 214.
21 W.A. [William Alexander] Kerr, *Riding for Ladies* (New York: Frederick A. Stokes Company, 1891), preface. The book was originally published in London the same year.
22 Kerr, 1.
23 Kerr, 4.
24 G. Bowers, *Mr. Crop's Harriers* (London: Day and Son, 1891), unpaginated.
25 Kerr, 77.
26 R.S. Summerhays, *Elements of Riding* (Brattleboro, VT: The Stephen Greene Press, 1963), 1.
27 T.F. Dale, *Riding, Driving and Kindred Sports* (London: T. Fisher Unwin, 1899), xi–xii.
28 The full title of the series was *The Badminton Library of Sports and Pastimes*. Of the 33 eventual volumes, 4 focused on equestrian sports: *Hunting* (Volume 1, 1885); *Racing & Steeple-Chasing* (Volume 4, 1886); *Driving* (Volume 11, 1889); and *Riding and Polo* (Volume 15, 1891).
29 Captain Lionel Dawson, *Hunting without Tears* (London: Country Life, Ltd., 1938), 9.
30 Dawson, 12.
31 Dawson, xi–xii.
32 Dawson, 37.
33 Dawson, 37.
34 Dawson, 38.
35 "Hunting Notes," *The Ladies' Field*, Volume 32 (January 6, 1906), 189.
36 Charles Richardson, *Practical Hints for Hunting Novices* (London: Horace Cox, 1906), 23.
37 Major Noel Birch, *Modern Riding and Horse Education* (New York: William R. Jenkins and Co., 1912), 7.
38 Richardson, 30–31.
39 "Hunting Notes," *The Ladies' Field* (July 25, 1908), 295.
40 William Scarth Dixon, *The Complete Horseman* (London: Methuen and Co., Ltd., 1913), 232.
41 Mrs. Stuart Menzies, *Women in the Hunting Field* (London: Vinton and Company, 1913). She mentions her imperial experiences in no less than eight separate references. See pages 16–17, 69, 95, 105, 144, 159, 178.
42 Menzies, 95 and 144, and 16.
43 Menzies, 69.
44 Menzies, 42 and 144.
45 Menzies, 26–27.
46 Menzies, 37.
47 Menzies, 143.
48 "The Hunting Field," *The Queen: The Ladies Newspaper and Court Chronicle* (September 8, 1900), 371.
49 "The Coming Hunting Season (from a Correspondent)," *The Times* (London), (November 3, 1908) (Issue 38794), page 13.
50 *The Queen: The Ladies Newspaper and Court Chronicle* (August 13, 1910), 317.

51 Alice M. Hayes, *The Horsewoman: A Practical Guide to Side-Saddle Riding* (London: W. Thacker & Co., 1893), 179–181.
52 Alice M. Hayes, *The Horsewoman: A Practical Guide to Side-Saddle Riding and Hunting* (London: Hurst and Blackett Limited, 1910), 265 and 266.
53 "The Varied Shelf," *The Queen: The Ladies Newspaper and Court Chronicle* (December 3, 1910), 1029.
54 Belle Beach, *Riding and Driving for Women* (London: T. Werner Laurie, 1913).
55 The six articles from 1913 are:
 1) October 4: "Ladies' Field Hunting Supplement, the Cross and Sidesaddles Compared," pages 7–10.
 2) October 11: "The Cross and Side Saddles Compared, The Opinions of Some Noted Sportswomen and Others," pages 280–282.
 3) October 18: "The Cross and Side Saddles Compared," page 409.
 4) October 25: "Some Colonial Views on the Cross-Saddle Question," pages 473–474.
 5) November 1: "Cross saddle and Sidesaddle Compared," pages 529–531.
 6) November 22: "The Cross and Side Saddle Compared," pages 723–724.
56 "Some Colonial Views on the Cross-Saddle Question," *The Ladies' Field* (October 25, 1913), 473–474. Despite being a man, Mr. B. Hickman even claimed that he had ridden sidesaddle.
57 Dale, 4.
58 Colonel R.F. Meysey-Thompson, *A Hunting Catechism* (London: Edward Arnold, 1907), 239.
59 Meysey-Thompson, v.
60 Captain J.E. [John Edward] Hance, *Riders of Tomorrow* (London: Country Life, Ltd., 1935), xv. When her father was posted to India, Jackie, age four, went with him and her mother, though her brother did not. See Lt.-Col. Jack Hance, *Riding Master* (London: Robert Hale Limited, 1960), 62–63.
61 "Gymkhana, n.," *OED Online* (Oxford University Press, March 2020), www.oed.com/view/Entry/82814.
62 Hance (1935), 42.
63 A special ladies' gymkhana was held at Wimbledon in 1899. See "Ladies' Gymkhana at Wimbledon," *The Ladies' Field* (August 5, 1899), 389.
64 E.V.A. Christy, *If Wishes Were Horses Beggars Could Ride* (London: Nicholson and Watson, 1947), illustration #1, following page 48.
65 "The Needle-threading Competition, aroused the admiration of all beholders." For this race, "Each lady, after selecting her partner, who stood at the other end of the course, had to jump a pair of hurdles, needle and thread in hand. Arrived at the spot where her partner stood, she handed him the needle and a button. He threaded the needle, sewed the button on her habit, and she galloped back to the starting point, taking the two hurdles once more en route. … The gentlemen fumbled, and the riders pleaded for dispatch, and needles broke and thread knotted, all in wild haste." "Ladies' Gymkhana at Wimbledon," *The Ladies' Field* (August 5, 1899), 389.
66 The Affinity Bending Race consisted of "A lady and a gentleman, each holding one end of a handkerchief, had to race through a line of six posts, winding in and out in absolute unison, and returning the same way to the starting point." "Ladies' Gymkhana at Wimbledon," *The Ladies' Field* (August 5, 1899), 389. *The Graphic* depicted "A Novel Competition in a Gymkhana: An Affinity Race" on January 23, 1897, 105.
67 *The Sphere* depicted "Pig-Sticking as Practiced at Ranelagh" on July 6, 1901, 5, noting the event was part of the Ranelegh Club program.
68 "Ladies' Gymkhana at Wimbledon," *The Ladies' Field* (August 5, 1899), 389.

69 *The Graphic* depicted "A Novel Event in a Gymkhana: A Pig-Sticking Competition" on March 16, 1901 on page 400. "The competitors, who rode in turns, armed with lances chalked at the top, had to jump a hurdle and then try to make a mark on the pig as near the center of the target as possible."
70 "Ladies' Gymkhana at Wimbledon," *The Ladies' Field* (August 5, 1899), 389.
71 "A dozen competitors rode to a table at a given point, through a row of bending staves, picked up sticks, dismantled one of the aunt sallies and galloped back through the staves to the winning post, and this amid much excitement." "Ladies' Sports at Ranelagh," *The Queen: The Ladies Newspaper and Court Chronicle* (June 10, 1905), 907.
72 "Ladies' Sports at Ranelagh," *The Queen: The Ladies Newspaper and Court Chronicle* (June 10, 1905), 907.
73 "Ladies' Sports at Ranelagh," *The Queen: The Ladies Newspaper and Court Chronicle* (June 10, 1905), 907.
74 Horace A. Laffaye, *The Evolution of Polo* (Jefferson, NC: McFarland and Company, Inc., 2009), 20.
75 "Our Van," *Baily's Magazine of Sports and Pastimes*, Volume 23 (February 1873), 124.
76 "Ladies' Polo in Cashmir," *The Ladies' Field* (October 14, 1899), 224.
77 "Homasses" came from the eighteenth century French expression for sexual deviance. Linton likely used it to represent overly masculine women. See footnote 2 on page 420 in Eliza Lynn Linton, *The Rebel of the Family*, Deborah T. Meem (ed.) (Orchard Park, NY: Broadview Press, 2002).
78 Eliza Lynn Linton, "The Wild Women as Social Insurgents," in Deborah T. Meem (ed.), *The Rebel of the Family*, (Orchard Park, NY: Broadview Press, 2002), 420. Originally published in *The Nineteenth Century*, Volume XXX, no. 176 (October 1891), 596–605.
79 "Modern Mannish Maidens," *Blackwood's Edinburgh Magazine*, Volume 147 (February 1890), 252–264.
80 George F. Underhill, *A Century of English Fox-Hunting* (London: R.A. Everett and Co., 1900), 298.
81 Captain G.J. Younghusband, *Polo in India* (London and Calcutta: W.H. Allen, 1890), 70–73.
82 Younghusband, 71.
83 Younghusband, 72.
84 Younghusband, 72.
85 Younghusband, 72–73.
86 See Cuthbert Bradley, "Polo Bewitched," *Fores's Sporting Notes and Sketches*, Volume 15 (1898), 174–181.
87 Underhill, 295. Underhill amended rules 7, 8, and 17 – for duration of play, changing ponies, and crooking of sticks.
88 "Doings of the Week in Society," *The Queen: The Ladies Newspaper and Court Chronicle* (July 22, 1905), 133–134.
89 "Hunting and Polo Notes," *The Ladies' Field* (May 11, 1907), 379.
90 J. Otho Paget, George A.B. Dewar, A.B. Portman, and A. Innes Shand, *Horses, Guns, and Dogs* (London: J. George Allen, 1903), 104.
91 Paget et al, 105.
92 Paget et al, 104.
93 Lieutenant-Colonel E.D. Miller, *Fifty Years of Sport* (New York: E.P. Dutton and Company, 1925), 155.
94 Mary Howarth, "Sportswomen and Their Attire," *The Badminton Magazine of Sports and Pastimes*, Volume 14 (June 1902), 601–602.

95 "Saunters through the Shops, at Hart and Sons'," *The Ladies' Field* (October 30, 1909), unpaginated.
96 "Ross's Astride Exmoor Hunting Coat/Skirt, Advertisement," *The Ladies' Field* (October 4, 1902), unpaginated. See also "The Evolution of the Riding Habit," *The Ladies' Field* (January 2, 1909), 217.
97 "John Simmons, Straddle-Skirts, Advertisement," *The Ladies' Field* (October 7, 1905), unpaginated. The advertisement listed "hunting and hacking habits, safety skirt, straddle skirts." See also "Hart and Sons' Advertisement," *The Ladies' Field* (October 21, 1905), Liii. This advertisement listed "hunting and riding habits, Improved Apron, Patent Safety, All-around and Astride Skirts" and "school habits a specialty."
98 "Saunter thro' the Shops: At Tautz's," *The Ladies' Field* (October 1, 1904), 145.
99 "The Latest Improvements in Riding Kit," *The Ladies' Field* (October 3, 1908), 159.
100 "Saunters through the Shops, at Guterbock's," *The Ladies' Field* (July 24, 1909), 319–320.
101 Tracy J.R. Collins, "Athletic Fashion, 'Punch', and the Creation of the New Woman," *Victorian Periodicals Review*, 43.3 (Fall 2010), 309–335.
102 *The Ladies' Field* (October 21, 1916), The Ladies' Field Supplement, Women and Empire, 2.
103 E.V.A. Christy, *Cross-Saddle and Side-Saddle: Modern Riding for Men and Women* (London: Seeley, Service and Co., Ltd., 1932), title page. See also E.V.A. Christy, *If Wishes Were Horses, Beggars Could Ride* (London: Nicholson and Watson, 1947), title page.
104 Christy (1947), 175.
105 Butler, 42.
106 Singleton, 178. Major-General Sir W.H. Birkbeck estimated that at the beginning of the war in August 1914, the British Army possessed only 19,000 horses. See Colonel Sir H.M. Jessel, *The Story of the Romsey Remount Depot* (London: The Abbey Press, 1920), 112.
107 Butler, 44.
108 Butler, 11.
109 "Sick Army Horses: Useful Work by Hunting Women," *The Times* (London) (December 6, 1915) (Issue 41030), 3.
110 Captain T.T. Pitman, "Horses and the War," *The Badminton Magazine of Sports and Pastimes*, Volume 14 (January 1902), 82.
111 *Remount Manual (War)* (London: His Majesty's Stationary Office, 1913), 6.
112 Somerville and Ross, 233.
113 Cecil Aldin, "Account of Women's Work in Army Remount Depots under Cecil Aldin," *Women at War Work Collection*, Microfilm, Army 5, see 1/2, page 2 (London: The Imperial War Museum, 1984).
114 Churchill, 155.
115 "Army Remounts by a Girl Groom," *The Ladies' Field* (May 20, 1916), 420–421.
116 Answers to Correspondents: "Concerning Remount Depots Employing Women (Inez)," *The Ladies' Field* (October 28, 1916), 326.
117 "Statistics Re: Remount Depots" and "Wages Paid at Remount Depots," *Women at War Work Collection*, Microfilm, Army 5, see 3/12 and 3/13 (London: The Imperial War Museum, 1984).
118 "Correspondence Re: Work at Russley Park, Wilts., 10. IV 1919," *Women at War Work Collection*, Microfilm, Army 5, see 3/6 (London: The Imperial War Museum, 1984). See also "Correspondence re: a report," *Women at War Work Collection*, Microfilm, Army 5, see 3/10, page 1 (London: The Imperial War Museum, 1984).

119 "Report of Work at Ladies' Remount Depot," *Women at War Work Collection*, Microfilm, Army 5, see 3/11, page 3 (London: The Imperial War Museum, 1984).
120 "Sick Army Horses: Useful Work by Hunting Women," *The Times* (London) (December 6, 1915) (Issue 41030), 3. Also, "Hints about Remount Work I," *The Ladies' Field* (July 22, 1916), 272; "Hints about Remount Work," (October 14, 1916), 250.
121 "Army Remounts by a Girl Groom," *The Ladies' Field* (May 20, 1916), 420.
122 "Report of work at ladies' Remount Depot," *Women at War Work Collection*, Microfilm, Army 5, see 3/11, page 1 (London: The Imperial War Museum, 1984).
123 "What Hunting Women Are Doing for the War: Our Pictures Show Women at Work in the Convalescent Remount Depot in Berkshire," *The Ladies' Field* (December 18, 1915), 154.
124 Barbara McLaren, *Women of the War* (New York: George H. Doran Company, 1918), 49.
125 "Women Grooms," *Hawera and Normanby Star*, Volume LXXI (February 22, 1916).
126 Diana Condell and Jean Liddiard, *Working for Victory? Images of Women in the First World War, 1914–1918* (London: Routledge and Kegan Paul, 1987), 144.
127 "Army Remounts by a Girl Groom," *The Ladies' Field* (May 20, 1916), 421.
128 "Report of Work at Ladies' Remount Depot," *Women at War Work Collection*, Microfilm, Army 5, see 3/11, page 2 (London: The Imperial War Museum, 1984).
129 McLaren, 49.
130 "Sick Army Horses: Useful Work by Hunting Women," *The Times* (London) (December 6, 1915) (Issue 41030), 3. See "What Hunting Women are Doing for the War: Our Pictures Show Women at Work in the Convalescent Remount Depot in Berkshire," *The Ladies' Field* (December 18, 1915), 155.
131 Cecil Aldin, "Account of Women's Work in Army Remount Depots under Cecil Aldin," *Women at War Work Collection*, Microfilm, Army 5, see 1/2, page 2 (London: The Imperial War Museum, 1984).
132 "Women Grooms," *Hawera and Normanby Star*, Volume LXXI (February 22, 1916), 3.
133 "What Hunting Women are Doing for the War: Our Pictures Show Women at Work in the Convalescent Remount Depot in Berkshire," *The Ladies' Field* (December 18, 1915), 154. See also McLaren, 49.
134 Cecil Aldin, "Account of Women's Work in Army Remount Depots under Cecil Aldin," *Women at War Work Collection*, Microfilm, Army 5, see 1/2, page 2 (London: The Imperial War Museum, 1984).
135 "Report of work at ladies' Remount Depot," *Women at War Work Collection*, Microfilm, Army 5, see 3/11, page 2 (London: The Imperial War Museum, 1984).
136 "Sick Army Horses: Useful Work by Hunting Women," *The Times* (London) (December 6, 1915) (Issue 41030), 3.
137 *The Ladies' Field* (March 25, 1916), 163.
138 *The Ladies' Field* (February 2, 1918), Answers to Correspondents (Mrs. Jack May): "Ride-Astride Habit for War-Worker (Mountain Maid)," 355.
139 "Early Spring Survey of the Shops," *The Queen: The Ladies Newspaper and Court Chronicle* (March 6, 1915), 411.
140 "Report of work at ladies' Remount Depot," *Women at War Work Collection*, Microfilm, Army 5, see 3/11, page 1 (London: The Imperial War Museum, 1984).
141 "Harby's Notes, Hunting and the War," *The Ladies' Field* (January 8, 1916), 242.
142 "Harby's Notes," *The Ladies' Field* (August 15, 1914).
143 "Harby's Notes, Baily's Hunting Directory," *The Ladies' Field* (November 27, 1915), 4. For a traditional argument on the value of hunting to the military, see Edwin

Alfred Hervey Alderson, *Pink and Scarlet; or, Hunting as a School for Soldiering* (London: William Heinemann, 1900).
144 "Harby's Notes," *The Ladies' Field* (July 31, 1915), 379. These were the first notes of the new hunting season.
145 "The Irish Hunting Season: Some Lady Masters and Prominent Followers," *The Ladies' Field* (November 12, 1915), 506.
146 "Harby's Notes, The Hunting Season, 1915-16," *The Ladies' Field* (August 7, 1915), 445.
147 "Harby's Notes, Melton," *The Ladies' Field* (January 9, 1915), 275. These were specifically titled "Harby's Notes," not "Hunting Notes."
148 "Harby's Notes, Melton," *The Ladies' Field* (January 9, 1915), 275. These were specifically titled "Harby's Notes," not "Hunting Notes."
149 "Harby's Notes, Baily's Hunting Directory," *The Ladies' Field* (November 27, 1915), 4.
150 "The Present State of Fox-Hunting: Facts and Figures," *The Ladies' Field* (December 15, 1917), 142.
151 "Hunting Notes, with the Quorn and Lord Harrington's Hounds," *The Ladies' Field* (January 23, 1915), 356.
152 E.H. Chalus, "Cecil, Mary Amelia, Marchioness of Salisbury (1750–1835)", *Oxford Dictionary of National Biography*.
153 Maudie Ellis, *The Squire of Bentley (Mrs. Cheape): Memory's Milestones in the Life of a Great Sportswoman* (Edinburgh and London: William Blackwood and Sons Ltd., 1926), xiii, 74, 106, 126. See also "The Bentley Harriers," *The Ladies' Field* (October 28, 1899), 2, in *The Ladies' Field* Sports Supplement.
154 H.A. Bryden, *Hare Hunting and Harriers* (London: Grant Richards, 1903), 158 and 143.
155 "Our Lady Masters of Hounds: Famous Packs of Foxhounds and Harriers," *The Ladies' Field* (December 18, 1920), 34–35.
156 "Notable Foxhunters, III: Sir Gilbert Greenall, Bart., M.F.H.," *The Polo Monthly*, 2.4 (December 1909), 312–314.
157 Erica Munkwitz, "'The Master is the Mistress': Women and Fox Hunting as Sports Coaching in Britain," *Sport in History*, 37.4 (2017), 395–422.
158 G.F. Underhill, *The Master of Hounds* (London: Grant Richards, 1903), 142.
159 *The Ladies' Field* (October 28, 1911), 348.
160 "The Hunting Season, 1916, by Harby," *The Ladies' Field* (November 25, 1916), 4.
161 Erica Munkwitz, "'The Master is the Mistress': Women and Fox Hunting as Sports Coaching in Britain," *Sport in History*, 37.4 (2017), 395–422.
162 "The Cross and Sidesaddles Compared," *The Ladies' Field* (October 4, 1913), 7–10.
163 "The Staghunting Season," *The Ladies' Field* (August 12, 1916), 360.
164 *The Sketch: A Journal of Art and Actuality*, Volume 116 (December 7, 1921), 365.
165 Ellis, 143.
166 "The Racing Ban and Its Removal," *The Polo Monthly*, 17.3 (May–June 1917), 172–174.
167 "Harby's Notes, The Hunting Season, 1915-16," *The Ladies' Field* (August 7, 1915), 445.
168 "Hunting Notes, War and Sport," *The Ladies' Field* (January 20, 1917), 355.
169 For more on this subject, see Michael Tichelar, *The History of Opposition to Blood Sports in Twentieth Century England: Hunting at Bay* (London: Routledge, 2017).
170 The "King's Premium" was an award and cash subsidy given by the Royal Commission on Horse-Breeding to the best horses for breeding purposes. See Charles Richardson, *The New Book of the Horse* (London: Cassell and Co., 1911), 16.

280 Femininity and Sporting Equality

171 "The Hunting Question," *The Ladies' Field* (February 10, 1917), 439.
172 "The Cheshire," *The Ladies' Field* (October 27, 1917), 291.
173 "Hunting Notes: The Coming Season," *The Ladies' Field* (November 23, 1918), 332.
174 See *The Ladies' Field* (December 21, 1918) for when Hunting Notes reappears on its own again, for first time since the war. See March 8, 1919 for when Golf and Tennis Notes reappear. See March 15, 1919 for when the Sports and Pastimes section appears for the first time since the war.
175 "Hunting Notes," *The Ladies' Field* (December 21, 1918), 35. See also "The Future of Hunting," *The Ladies' Field* (March 23, 1918), 105.
176 "Women Masters," *The Polo Monthly*, 22.2 (November 1920), 152.
177 "Hunting Notes, The Vine," *The Ladies' Field* (October 9, 1915), 286–287. See also "Hunting Notes: The Coming Season," *The Ladies' Field* (November 23, 1918), 332.
178 "Hunting Notes: The Coming Season," *The Ladies' Field* (November 23, 1918), 332.
179 "Our Lady Masters of Hounds: Famous Packs of Foxhounds and Harriers," *The Ladies' Field* (December 18, 1920), 34–35.
180 "Our Lady Masters of Hounds: Famous Packs of Foxhounds and Harriers," *The Ladies' Field* (December 18, 1920), 34–35.
181 Lord Dorchester [Dudley Massey Pigott Carleton], *Sport, Foxhunting and Shooting* (London: Rich and Cowan, 1935), 37.
182 Dorchester, 74–75. Italics mine.
183 Lieutenant-Colonel F.C. Hitchcock, *Saddle Up: A Guide to Equitation and Stable Management Including Hints to Instructors* (New York: Arco Publishing Company, 1959), 101.
184 Lieutenant-Colonel M.F. McTaggart, *Mount and Man: A Key to Better Horsemanship* (London: Country Life, Ltd., 1927), 87.
185 McTaggart (1927), 87.
186 Captain J.L.M. Barrett, *Practical Horsemanship: A Book for the Novice of All Ages, with Chapters on Advanced Work and Practical Hints on Horse and Pony Buying* (London: H.F. & G. Witherby, 1929), 140.
187 Barrett, 132.
188 Barrett, 142.
189 Barrett, 143.
190 Barrett, 131.
191 Barrett, 142–143.
192 Captain J.E. Hance, *School for Horse and Rider* (London: Country Life, Ltd., 1932), 33.
193 Hance, 28.
194 Hance, 31.
195 Hance, 28.
196 Hance, 29.
197 Hance, 33.
198 Christy's *Side-Saddle Riding* first appeared in 1899, received a second edition in 1901, and went into a third revised edition under the new title, *Modern Side-saddle Riding*, in 1907. Additional titles *The Rule of the Road* and *If Wishes Were Horses* appeared in 1925 and 1947, respectively.
199 E.V.A. Christy, *Cross-Saddle and Side-Saddle: Modern Riding for Men and Women* (London: Seeley, Service and Co., Ltd., 1932), 210.
200 Christy (1932), 207.
201 Christy (1932), 204–205.
202 Christy (1947), 27–32.
203 Christy (1932), 22.
204 Christy (1932), 8. The cross-saddle seat is described before the sidesaddle seat

(Chapter 4 vs. Chapter 6) and there is a chapter comparing the two (Chapter 15). In fact, sketches of black horseshoes appear in the text to demarcate passages that are only applicable to sidesaddle riders – as Christy notes, these sections can be "more easily omitted by the cross-saddle rider" (16).
205 Lady Diana Shedden and Lady Viola Apsley, *"To whom the goddess ..."*: *Hunting and Riding for Women* (London: Hutchinson and Co., 1932), 7, 15, 20.
206 Shedden and Apsley, 167–168.
207 Shedden and Apsley, 45.
208 Shedden and Apsley, 52.
209 Shedden and Apsley, 51.
210 Shedden and Apsley, 65.
211 Shedden and Apsley, 64.
212 Shedden and Apsley, 208.
213 Shedden and Apsley, 208.
214 Shedden and Apsley, 203.
215 Shedden and Apsley, 204.
216 Shedden and Apsley, 91–92.
217 Shedden and Apsley, 94.
218 Shedden and Apsley, 93.
219 Lilian E. Bland, "The Art of Falling," *The Badminton Magazine of Sports and Pastimes*, Volume 22 (April 1906), 447.
220 Bland, 451.
221 Bland, 453.
222 Shedden and Apsley, 80 and 230.
223 Shedden and Apsley, 40, 91–93, 204.
224 Dorchester, 75–76.
225 Dorchester, 39.
226 "Kit for the Hunting Woman," *The Ladies' Field* (October 9, 1920), 143.
227 Major-General Geoffrey Brooke, *The Foxhunter's England* (Philadelphia: J.B. Lippincott, 1937), 20. Italics mine.
228 Bellamy, 95.
229 Brooke (1937), 23.
230 Captain Lionel Dawson, *Hunting without Tears* (London: Country Life, Ltd., 1938), 55.
231 Dawson, 57.
232 C.R. Acton, *Hunting for All* (London: H.F. & G. Witherby, Ltd., 1937), 9, 27.
233 Quote from Brooke (1937), 23. See also Sir Edward Durand, *Ponies' Progress* (New York: Charles Scribner's Sons, 1935), 179, and Patricia A. Vertinsky, *The Eternally Wounded Woman: Women, Doctors, and Exercise in the Late Nineteenth Century* (Urbana: University of Illinois Press, 1994).
234 Fawcett, 157.
235 Fawcett, 157.
236 "Juvenile Sportswomen," *The Ladies' Field* (January 25, 1902), 277.
237 Mrs. Stuart Menzies, "'Thrusters' in the Hunting Field," *The Queen: The Ladies Newspaper and Court Chronicle*, Volume 63 (September 6, 1913), 54–55.
238 "Children in the Hunting Field," *The Ladies' Field* (January 27, 1912), 356–357. See also "'Thrusters' in the Hunting Field,' by Mrs. Stuart Menzies," *The Queen: The Ladies Newspaper and Court Chronicle* (September 6, 1913), 54.
239 "Hunting Notes," *The Ladies' Field* (January 12, 1918), 253.
240 Shedden and Apsley, 204.
241 Audrey Blewitt, *Ponies and Children* (London: Country Life, Ltd., 1933), 40.
242 Blewitt, 52 and 40.
243 Blewitt, 40.

244 Shirley Faulkner-Horne, *Riding for Children* (London: Country Life, Ltd., 1936). The author was described as a 15- to 16-year-old member, thus being born around 1920.
245 Durand, 173. This title was published in London by G. Allen & Unwin in 1934.
246 Durand 164, 166.
247 Lieutenant-Colonel M.F. McTaggart, *Horsemanship for Boys and Girls* (New York: Charles Scribner's Sons, 1935), 122.
248 McTaggart (1935), 119–120.
249 "Fashion's Forecast by Mrs. Jack May," *The Queen: The Ladies Newspaper and Court Chronicle* (June 12, 1915), 1015.
250 Nina Edwards, *Dressed for War: Uniform, Civilian Clothing & Trappings, 1914 to 1918* (London: I.B. Tauris, 2014).
251 "Perfection of Cut Is Beloved of the Modern Diana," *The Ladies' Field* (April 17, 1920), 174. "And very workmanlike she looks …" (174).
252 "The Best Tonic in the World," Henry Hall advertisement, *The Ladies' Field* (April 23, 1921), XV.
253 See, for example, "Perfection in Ride-Astride Kit," Montague Smyth advertisement, *The Ladies' Field* (February 23, 1918), 13. See also Harrod's advertisement, ride-astride habits, *The Ladies' Field* (March 29, 1919); and Montague Smyth advertisement, for girls' ride-astride costumes, *The Ladies' Field* (September 6, 1919).
254 W.A. [William Alexander] Kerr, *Riding for Ladies* (New York: Frederick A. Stokes Company, 1891), 77.
255 Lieutenant-Colonel S.G. Goldschmidt, *The Fellowship of the Horse* (London: Country Life, Ltd., 1930 134.
256 Acton, 67–68.
257 *The Queen: The Ladies Newspaper and Court Chronicle* (October 2, 1920), 404.
258 Alice M. Hayes, *The Horsewoman: A Practical Guide to Side-Saddle Riding* (London: Hurst and Blackett, 1910), 118.
259 Erica Munkwitz, "Designing Diana: Female Sports Entrepreneurs and Equestrian Innovation," *The International Journal of the History of Sport*, 35:7-8 (2018), 745–766.
260 Shedden and Apsley, 140.
261 Goldschmidt, 133.
262 Acton, 67.
263 "Kit for the Hunting Woman," *The Ladies' Field* (October 9, 1920), 143.
264 "The Eternal Feminine in Different Aspects," advertisement for Tautz, *The Ladies' Field* (March 19, 1921), 64.
265 *The Ladies' Field* (October 8, 1921), 44–45.
266 T.W. Winter advertisement, *The Ladies' Field* (February 18, 1922), vi.
267 Shedden and Apsley, 49.
268 Somerville and Ross, 231.
269 Captain Pennell Elmhirst, *The Best of the Fun, 1891-1897* (London: Chatto and Windus, 1903), 439.

Conclusion
Equestrianism, Feminism, and the Olympic Games, 1932–1956

In 1957, sidesaddle makers *par excellence* Champion and Wilton shuttered their Oxford Street store, first opened in 1786, upon the death of namesake saddler, Major Wilton.[1] When they closed, "sidesaddles were thrown, one after the other, into the municipal refuse lorry!"[2] Other sidesaddle makers in Britain did not even last this long, as the great Victorian firms of Owen and Co. and Mayhew and Co. had gone out of business before the Second World War.[3] The reign of the sidesaddle was over.

Having adopted the sidesaddle in the fourteenth century, British women abandoned it by the late nineteenth. Although the transition did not happen all once, some wondered why the sidesaddle had not been jettisoned sooner. Lady Mary Wortley Montagu, writing in 1748, was well ahead of her time when she criticized the stubbornness of British women in clinging to the sidesaddle. Having switched to the cross-saddle, she wrote, "[I] am a better horsewoman than ever I was in my life ... I cannot help being amazed at the obstinate folly by which the English ladies venture every day their lives and limbs." She was then 61 years old and declared that only "constant riding" had preserved her health.[4]

Yet the practice of riding sidesaddle in Britain continued until imperial experience led to a refashioning of sporting and gender ideals, in which women finally rejected the sidesaddle for the man's cross-saddle. Before the First World War transformed British life, women were already riding astride, and afterward this practice only increased.[5] Women's equestrianism transformed ideas about femininity by encouraging and enabling a freedom, agency, and independence for women that was far different, though no less valuable, than the vote. As sporting author Edith Somerville concluded, "The playing-fields of Eton did not as surely win Waterloo as the hunting-fields ... won the vote for women."[6]

It was on the basis of this imperial influence and the acceptance of the astride riding style that the next generation of female equestrians in Britain had made such remarkable accomplishments, not only politically and culturally but at the highest level of sporting accomplishment: the Olympic Games. This conclusion spans from 1932 and the publication of Lady Diana Shedden's and Lady

Viola Apsley's *"To whom the goddess ..."*: *Hunting and Riding for Women*, which encouraged riding astride but lamented the decline of the sidesaddle, to 1956, when British rider Patricia "Pat" Smythe won a bronze medal in show jumping at the Olympic Games in the first year the event was opened to female competitors. During this time, female riders unquestionably "won their spurs" with success.[7] As horse sports like show jumping increased in difficulty and competitiveness, women were able to rival – and beat – male contenders because they had adopted this more balanced and effective way of riding. British women had gained true equality with men in riding, and they had done so by making cross-saddle riding respectable and admirable.

Sidesaddle Redux?

As early as 1920, some called for a return to the traditional style of sidesaddle riding. The painter Alfred Munnings visually captured some of these elegant riders in his portraits, but the only area of the country where women continued to ride sidesaddle consistently was in the Shires, the conservative heart of hunting country. As *The Field's* hunting and racing editor William Fawcett noted, "The sidesaddle, as I have seen it, is the most popular way of riding in the Shires; but in other places practically everyone rides on a man's saddle."[8] Munnings himself confirmed the change: "I wish I had painted more women riding sidesaddle before the fashion died out." Yet even he admitted the advantages of riding astride: "But there must have been considerable discomfort in so riding [and] how much better the astride seat must be for a horse!"[9] Even in the Shires, women were advised to ride and condition their horses by riding astride, to carry an extra stirrup when hunting so they could ride astride at the end of the day, and to eschew the full habit and skirt for breeches when not hunting.[10] Lord Annaly, the Master of the Pytchley Hunt from 1902 to 1914, had refused to give the hunt colors to any woman who rode astride, but the world of the interwar years was a very different place.[11]

The sidesaddle had been in use since the fourteenth century, so it did have its defenders. The first and foremost of these advocates was trainer and sidesaddle expert Doreen Archer Houblon, who published her book, *Sidesaddle*, in 1938. The book became a classic text on a "lost art" and was reprinted in several editions from 1951 onward.[12] Although Houblon spoke to a continued interest in riding aside, this was because sidesaddle riding and its practitioners continued to be visible markers of social distinction for an upper class and a way of life that had largely disappeared. Shedden and Apsley's *"To whom the goddess ..."*: *Hunting and Riding for Women* was an earlier paean to this ideal, in which they, as representatives of the upper class, admitted the benefits of riding astride for women, while continuing to ride sidesaddle themselves. As many noted, everything associated with sidesaddle riding was more expensive, from saddle to horse to clothes.[13] Those who continued riding in this style had to be well-off (especially after 1918) to furnish this equestrian lifestyle. For upper class women, riding sidesaddle enabled them to visually distinguish themselves in a world where class lines had been blurred, if not sometimes made invisible, and where ability (and the cross-saddle) had leveled the sporting and social field.

Houblon's book implied a possible sidesaddle renaissance in Britain, beginning with her star pupil, the woman who was crowned Queen Elizabeth II. This implication could not have been further from the truth, for, as royal biographer Judith Campbell states, the Queen with her passion for all things equestrian was brought up to ride astride and preferred this style of riding. At the age of four, Princess Elizabeth was given her first pony by her father, and she rode with the Pytchley Hunt the next year.[14] She and her sister Margaret were taught to ride by Owen the groom, and, during World War II, by teaching themselves in Scotland and at Windsor.[15] In fact, it was not until after 1943 that Horace Smith, instructor at the Holyport stables, remarked to the future Queen, "I should love to see your Royal Highness mounted sidesaddle."[16] This suggestion evolved into lessons that culminated in her riding sidesaddle alongside her father, King George VI, in Trooping the Colour in 1947 (coincidentally, this was the year Pat Smythe was first selected to the British Show Jumping Team riding astride). For this occasion, and for other ceremonial events that followed, the Princess (and later Queen) rode sidesaddle, having received painstaking lessons from Mrs. Archer Houblon, who also supplied Tommy, the mount she rode.[17]

Queen Elizabeth, as she became, did not ride sidesaddle exclusively. As Campbell noted,

> Some people seem to imagine that on the morning of her official birthday the Queen puts on a becoming uniform, mounts the horse chosen for the day, rides out to Horse Guards Parade and back again, and that that is all there is to the ceremony. In fact, and as always, the Queen takes infinite pains to ensure that her part in the proceedings shall be as correct as she can make it, and since this is the only time in the year when she rides sidesaddle, she practices for an hour or more on most days for a month beforehand.[18]

Every May, Mrs. Archer Houblon began preparing the Queen's horses (a primary mount and an alternate), schooling them both sidesaddle, "to which they must be re-introduced each year."[19] Sidesaddle riding – even for the most prominent public practitioner in the country – was the exception, not the rule.

Although it might have seemed that there could be a resurgence of sidesaddle riding before the mid-twentieth century, based on the Queen's example and Houblon's book, the reality was rather different. As R.S. Summerhays, venerable horse show judge for four decades, opined, "I have heard it said on a number of occasions that women are going back to the sidesaddle, but I do not believe this. I believe that, in proportion to the number of women riding, so the number of women who ride sidesaddle tends to decrease."[20] Riding sidesaddle had been relegated to its original function as imported by Anne of Bohemia: it was for ceremonial functions only. For practicality, safety, and more, British women chose to ride astride.

High Hurdles

One reason for the continued decrease in sidesaddle riding was increased female participation in horse shows and jumping. Descended from agricultural competitions, horse shows were ostensibly introduced as public incentives to improve breeding standards. Competitions offered public acclaim, prizes, and sometimes cash. Initially competitions (divided into separate classes) for park hacks and riding horses received the most interest, as urban riders entered in droves. But the improvement and breeding of hunting horses became prominent in the 1880s, so contests in which horses and riders could prove their hunting skills grew in popularity. Show jumping descended as a stylized demonstration of leaping skills used when hunting, based on the horse's natural athletic ability to clear fences cleanly (without any knock-downs) within a specific time allowed. These jumping competitions provided entertainment and excitement and were often the largest draw for spectators. At the Royal Dublin Society Horse Show in 1868, so many spectators crowded onto "rickety" viewing stands that the entire structure collapsed, depositing them all into the Irish mud.[21]

The new popularity of horse shows was credited to the influx of female competitors after the First World War.[22] Women entered equestrian competitions and horse shows during the Victorian era, but throughout the early 1900s, their numbers – riding sidesaddle – blossomed. As early as 1900, Mrs. Blockley gained fame for her jumping successes, clearing obstacles over 5'8" seven times in one competition and winning over £2000 in prizes during a single year.[23] Initially, show jumping was viewed as an exhibition or spectacle rather than a competition, and it was not taken seriously in Britain until the 1907 International Horse Show at Olympia.[24] One reason that few British women entered these early competitions is that they were initially forbidden to ride astride at the most prestigious competitions like the historic Olympia show, thanks to a ban by King George IV against ladies riding astride.[25]

But the king was outnumbered by proponents – both male and female – championing the astride style for women. Veteran judge and rider Sam Marsh encouraged female show jumpers to ride astride, as did author and rider William Fawcett, who promoted the style because women were less likely to be hung up by their habits or come to injury.[26] He also encouraged competitions to hold separate classes for women who rode aside versus astride, as comparing the two styles was unfair because cross-saddle riders had so many advantages.[27] One compelling reason for women to ride astride was that, in show classes, the judges also rode the best competitors' horses to fully evaluate their performances. For the overwhelmingly male judges, requiring the horse to be stripped of a sidesaddle and re-tacked with a man's cross-saddle was tiresome and time consuming. As *The Ladies' Field* pointed out, "The cross-saddle is an advantage to a lady who shows, for I am sure that judges are often rather shy of riding ladies' exhibits because of the trouble and delay of changing from one sort of saddle to another."[28] Female competitors thus faced the possibility that they might not win or even do well if they rode sidesaddle.

Women were not the only ones taking advantage of these equestrian possibilities. Much of the interwar showing impetus came from a new equestrian audience: young girls. Children were not only riding more in these years, but they were also showing competitively as well, laying the foundation for the successful British equestrian community of today. Jill Farmiloe was a key example, and *Country Life* published her "memoirs" of showing between 1934 and 1938 in *Clear Round: Four Years in the Show-Ring*.[29] Although she did not come from a rich or "horsey" family, Farmiloe was an enthusiastic pupil as well as a member of the British Pony Club, which had been formed in 1929. Though she enjoyed hunting and it played an important role in the development of her horsemanship, the focus of the book was her showing and jumping career. In just a few years, she won 310 rosettes (about 200 first place ribbons), 56 silver cups, and assorted other prizes from competing in over 100 horse shows.[30]

What was so extraordinary about Farmiloe's story is that when she began showing in 1934 she was only 11 years old.[31] Born in inter-war Britain, Farmiloe was representative of an entire generation of female riders who built on the successes and experience of the women who had competed in Victorian and Edwardian contests. Nor was Farmiloe by any means an exception, as she mentioned countless other talented and dedicated girl riders, all of whom rode astride to compete in the difficult and demanding children's jumping classes.[32] These contests were so competitive that it was not unusual for the fence height in jump-offs to be well over five feet. Such challenging obstacles required that female equestrians ride cross-saddle, for as Lieutenant-Colonel M.F. McTaggart had pointed out in 1927, "To clear a five-foot gate and other fences of similar size, with any degree of certainty, denotes a high standard of efficiency, and nullifies all argument on the incapacity of ladies on the cross saddle."[33]

Young girls made big waves in the showjumping ring because their figurative (and, in some cases, actual) mothers and sisters had been paving the way for them through participation in point-to-point competitions. These events, like steeplechasing, are horse races over set fences, though point-to-point racing usually must be done by amateurs (rather than professional jockeys) with certified membership in a Hunt. In 1899 Mrs. C. Bayly was awarded the first prize in the Hampshire Ladies' Steeplechase; she also won several other smaller races the same day and came in third in the competitive jumping event.[34] By the early 1900s, point-to-point races had become extremely popular for women, and Ladies' Races were the most anticipated event in the program.[35]

The practice had made significant headway in Ireland, where women were actually allowed to compete against men in the races, but in Britain, they initially competed in women-only events, such as those depicted by Georgina Bowers (see Figure 5.1 in Chapter 5 of this volume).[36] In the beginning women competed sidesaddle, but as horse show judge Sam Marsh noted, "they were at a great disadvantage as compared with those who rode astride."[37] These contests were too demanding and dangerous for riding aside, and Lord Dorchester campaigned to have sidesaddles banned from such races: "I hope that local Hunts will pass an additional rule, and that is sidesaddles are not permitted in Ladies' Races."[38] As Shedden and Apsley admitted, this was only to be expected, as the sidesaddle was not an advantage – indeed, it was a disadvantage – in such sports: "[astride] gives a horse a better chance, as it is difficult to ride a good finish in a sidesaddle."[39] By the mid-twentieth century, British women had entered – and won – horse show competitions, point-to-point races, and high-jumping contests. But there was still one arena they could not enter – the Olympic Games. That was soon to change.

Equestrianism and the Olympic Games

Patricia "Pat" Smythe rose to sporting prominence at age 11 – like Farmiloe – when she won her class at the Richmond Horse Show.[40] Smythe's mother was an avid horsewoman, riding hunters and competing in point-to-point races.[41] Her daughter shared the same interests, and, growing up close to the Roehampton Club, she also helped her mother break and train polo ponies. Smythe actually gained much of her experience in local gymkhanas during the Second World War, demonstrating continuing imperial "bounce-back." She and Jill Farmiloe could have been twins, sisters to the countless other British girls who were following in their footsteps. As equine historian Susanna Forrest wrote, "Pat Smythe had two backbones and a heart that did not know what it could not do."[42] In Smythe's case, this was literally true, as later in life she was diagnosed with a heart condition that, if it had been known earlier, would likely have prevented her from riding at all. Her determination was legendary, and her daughter Lucy simply concluded, "She wanted to prove herself as a woman in a man's world."[43]

From the very beginning, Smythe was a determined horsewoman, paying her own way in entry fees and transport for horse shows from her own winnings. She did this from the age of 11 onward; if she failed to win, she could not afford to continue competing. In 1947, at the age of 18, she competed at the White City international show, winning her class on Finality, a mare whose dam had drawn a milk cart. Based on this performance, she received an invitation to join the British Equestrian Team, with legendary teammates Colonel Harry Llewellyn, Ruby Holland-Martin, Peter Robeson, and Brian Butler. By 1948, she was competing internationally, both in Europe and America,[44] and, in 1949, at the age of 21, she was named Showjumper of the Year.[45]

Based on her impressive successes, Smythe was selected for the British Olympic Team in 1952 but could not compete because the International Olympic Committee (IOC) prohibited female competitors in show jumping. Numerous works of fiction explored this setback, including Alice L. O'Connell's

Figure 6.1 "Olympic Games Equestrian Team In Training: The Women Members": In March 1956, selection trials for the British Equestrian show jumping team that would compete at the XVI Olympiad were held at the Queen's Windsor Forest Stud. Among the hopefuls were a deep bench of successful female show jumpers (left to right): Dawn Palethorpe, Mary Marshall, Pat Smythe, and Susan Whitehead. The final team included Smythe and two men, Wilf White and Peter Robeson, the latter riding Scorchin, a horse that Smythe had trained and shown to many victories. Dawn Palethorpe was selected as an alternate.
Credit: Keystone Press/Alamy Stock Photo.

The Blue Mare in the Olympic Trials (1955) and Dorothy Lyon's *Smoke Rings* (1960),[46] but, prior to 1952, no woman was allowed to compete in Olympic equestrian events.[47] Women finally competed in dressage (no jumping) in 1952; in show jumping in 1956; and in three-day eventing (a combination of dressage, cross-country, and show jumping) in 1964. Though Smythe had been a member of the British Equestrian Team for nine years, since 1947, she was not allowed to compete in the Olympic Games until 1956 (Figure 6.1). In that year she finally got her chance, and she and Brigitte Schockaert from Belgium were the first women to compete in Olympic show jumping. Though Schockaert received a startling 59 faults, Smythe received only eight in the first round and thirteen in the second, individually placing tenth out of 66 competitors.[48] In the team competition, it was her superb performances that propelled the team to their bronze medal finish; thus, Smythe became the first British female equestrian to win an Olympic medal. It is arguable (and likely) that Smythe could have easily won the individual gold medal had she been allowed to use her best horse, Prince Hal, rather than her second choice, Flanagan. The team coach had forbidden her to ride Prince Hal, based on his personal dislike of the high-strung mount. Flanagan, being a smaller horse, had more trouble with the larger jumps requiring a longer stride. As Smythe admitted, "I think he [Prince Hal] could have won the gold medal, given the chance."[49] And soon he did: at an international show jumping competition held in Stockholm after the Olympic Games – over the same fences – Prince Hal won.[50]

Farmiloe and Smythe's examples helped popularize equestrian sports for a larger, mass-viewing audience. Smythe became a sports celebrity, receiving the OBE from the Queen for her efforts, and competing in the 1960 Olympics with Flanagan, finishing eleventh individually.[51] Women's involvement and success helped transform show jumping from an exclusively male and military sport into a more open and competitive event with riders from a wider range of social backgrounds. Following these brilliant triumphs in the 1950s, equestrian events became a media "darling," broadcast on the new medium of television. These successes did not end there, as other female equestrians quickly took the baton. The Queen's daughter, HRH Princess Anne, popularized the sport of three-day eventing in the 1970s, and the Queen's granddaughter, Zara Phillips, aided the British team in winning the silver medal at the 2012 London Olympics. This female success had been a long time coming.

Equestrianism and the Women's Movement

Women's participation in equestrianism has been especially important in advancing female liberation. But what was the relationship between horse sport and the women's movement? The 1860s, when women's involvement in riding and hunting was peaking, have been called "the key decade of development in nineteenth-century feminist consciousness."[52] As historian June Purvis has pointed out, "the suffragette struggle for women's enfranchisement was never a single-issue campaign but part of a wider reform movement to end women's subordinate role in British society," and horse sports played an important but so far uncredited role in this revolution.[53]

One should not assume, however, that equestrianism and political feminism were directly linked. Suffragists did play sports, as Joyce Kay has shown, but activists did not believe that sport was a priority in their challenge.[54] As Mike Huggins has argued, "Although the growth of sports played among women can be conceptualized as a form of women's liberation, sport did not figure prominently in feminist discourse in the 1920s and 1930s."[55] Female equestrians had attained equality in sport and did not work to achieve it elsewhere, though they did contribute to new ideas about femininity and opportunities for female freedom via sports and athleticism. Sporting femininity, after all, was very different from political femininity. As Shedden and Apsley noted, there was a model for an ideal female equestrian:

Conclusion   291

> "She goes like a bird – the best lady in our Hunt." And how does a bird go? Why, without apparent effort, or thrust, silently, serenely, neatly, perfectly, gaily, and graciously – a thing of beauty and joy, without troubling its fellows, without knocking things down and without rooting things up. This should be the type for every woman out hunting to aim at ...[56]

By contrast, suffragettes were guilty of many sins: "troubling [their] fellows," "knocking things down," and "rooting things up." Their efforts were public, but in all the wrong ways, as compared to female equestrians who embodied different qualities and characteristics than their campaigning sisters. These traits were based on the needs and requirements of equestrianism: courage, coolness, confidence, and, above all, self-possession. The process of possessing one's self resulted in self-fashioning a personal identity, becoming a recognized and accepted individual. After that, what else was left to achieve? Sport was part of a larger movement for women's rights, but this political activism was not common among equestrians.[57]

In 1913, militant suffragette Emily Davison linked horse sports and the women's rights movement in a fatal way: she was killed after throwing herself at King George V's horse during the Derby at Epsom. Davison may not have intended to commit suicide; she may have been reaching for the horse's reins, onto which she wanted to thread a suffragette flag.[58] But Anmer, the horse, was travelling at a racing gallop of about 35 miles per hour, and Davison's skull was fatally fractured when the two collided. Davison became a martyr to the suffragette cause, and this tragic incident was seen as a heroic sacrifice by female activists. But female sportswomen had a very different view. Animal painter and devoted rider Lucy Kemp-Welch was more concerned for the horse and jockey than the activist.[59] In fact, jockey Herbert Jones was tormented by the event and later committed suicide. For horsewomen, this event was not only terrible but pointless, as equality was achieved by the quiet and sober act of riding horses, not by such a garish and public spectacle.

Having achieved sporting equality, the majority of female equestrians did not push for political equality, inclining toward conservative anti-suffrage leanings. These female equestrians did not endorse militant action for political reform. Instead, the paradox is that many sportswomen felt that issues of formal political suffrage and liberation were irrelevant because they had so many other opportunities. Suffragists might be committed sportswomen, but sportswomen were not necessarily committed feminists.[60] When one hunting heroine was asked why she did not "become an exponent of women's rights," she responded, "I don't approve of that sort of thing. ... A woman's real strength lies elsewhere, in my opinion."[61] Her strengths lay in equestrianism, as women had been making their mark across the British countryside and around the British Empire through their riding abilities.[62] This level of freedom and choice led to a radical conservatism, or conservative radicalism, centered on sport and gender. Female equestrians advocated and competed for a revolutionary change: they rode astride like men, attaining complete equality on horseback if not elsewhere. Women chose to ride astride – that choice *was* radical in equestrianism terms, but conservative in that they did not use that choice to campaign for further rights or representation. Many female riders did not believe that they needed more independence or freedom than they had gained already through horse sport. Equality by vote was secondary to equality in the field.[63]

Although suffragettes and suffragists are traditionally recognized for breaking down gender divisions in Britain and achieving social and political equality for women, that credit may better belong to sportswomen for catalyzing and confirming these changes. As Pat Thane has argued, "the difference the vote made was to enable women to feel that their presence in public life was legitimate."[64] But female equestrians had legitimated their public presence almost a century earlier, on urban avenues like Rotten Row, in fox-hunting fields throughout Britain, and on horseback across the Empire. Thus, even those sportswomen who did not support the suffrage campaign aided changing ideas about gender construction and proper femininity through their public presence and example. In fact, when the women's movement faltered after the First World War, it was "sporting women [who] were, less obviously, advancing the feminist cause."[65] As Edith Somerville concluded,

> Probably when the history is written of how The Woman's place in the world came to include "All out-doors" (as they say in America), as well as what has been called in Ireland, "the work that is within," it will be acknowledged that sport, Lawn Tennis, Bicycling, and Hunting, played quite as potent a part as education in the emancipation that has culminated in the Representation of the People Bill.[66]

Somerville was one of the few female equestrians who was actively involved in the women's movement; she became the first President of the Munster Women's Franchise League.[67] But even if other sporting women did not actively campaign for the vote, they and their examples were nonetheless crucial to obtaining greater public recognition and political rights. Their power was not limited to how they saw themselves, but how others saw them; they were the focal point of an engaged – and engaging – female gaze.

So, were female equestrians anti-feminists? As Rosamund Owen contended, "there is nothing 'Women's Lib' about we sidesaddle riders."[68] Few, if any, well-known equestrians supported the anti-feminist cause, and few except Somerville publicly supported the suffrage and suffragette campaigns.[69] Sporting periodicals such as *The Ladies' Field* published supplements on the suffrage campaign, but did not necessarily champion the cause.[70] Feminism was alive and well in the 1920s, though admittedly weaker than in the pre-war era.[71] By that time, and in the decades that followed, more women from a much wider social background were riding, hunting, and competing in equestrian sports and had made remarkable gains, as witnessed by the popular successes of Jill Farmiloe and Pat Smythe. Women achieved much without the vote, and continued to do so afterward, hinting that women's equality might not have so much to do with political representation as previously thought.

Many, if not most, female equestrians believed in essential feminism. Women riders did view themselves as naturally different from men; their sex – as well as their sidesaddles – defined them. But it defined them in extraordinarily positive and successful ways. Because they were different from men and possessed special feminine qualities – like sympathy, empathy, and compassion – women were the better equestrians, far and away surpassing male riders. Once they shifted to riding astride, they believed that these fixed feminine attributes and characteristics gave women a huge advantage over male riders. Female riders acted on a public equestrian stage; although they believed in an unchangeable and essential femininity, they also consciously performed gendered roles based on the power they achieved via horse sport.[72] The external trappings of sport – like saddle and clothing, and arguably even the female form – were ephemeral and superficial; far more important were the internal qualities of essential womanhood. Paradoxically, by being the weaker sex, they were the stronger – and better – riders.

Female equestrians were not anti-feminists, though they have may have been anti-liberal in today's sense of the term. In a prevailing liberal view of history, everything is political. Many twentieth century contemporaries and historians have understood feminism, as well as the suffrage movement and the struggle for women's rights, as necessarily or inherently political. Politics is viewed as the highest and most important form of activity, and the only meaningful measure of equality. But for female equestrians, politics was far less important than sport. Having achieved not only egality but true equality on horseback, they saw little reason to ask for, or desire, any more.

The example of female Masters of Hounds illustrates this equestrian equality. Female Masters – whether intentionally or not – furthered the movement for women's rights as a whole. During the First World War, over 30 women acted as Masters of Foxhounds (M.F.H.s) for hunts across Britain, and their leadership continued after 1918.[73] By 1938, Cecil Pelham, in his tally of Masters in Britain, listed over 113 female Masters.[74] Riding for women had opened the way for sporting emancipation, to being considered equal on horseback; being a Master naturally extended that authority even further through genuine leadership positions and a public place of power in the community.[75] These female Masters were featured in magazines, bringing their roles to a non-riding but reading public (Figure 5.9, in the previous chapter). Thus, they gave hunting and riding a public profile. They made the work respectable for women, and, as a result, they provided positive examples to encourage others to follow in their footsteps, especially as they were consistently portrayed as important exemplars in print. *The Ladies' Field* devoted an illustrated spread to their achievements almost every year of its publication.[76] Even if these female Masters did not consciously set out to expand women's rights, they did so simply by living their day-to-day lives.

At least by the time some women achieved the vote in 1918 – and certainly by the time all women did in 1928 – the sidesaddle was widely considered "an amusing relic of a bygone folly." Looking back, Lieutenant-Colonel McTaggart compared the battle of acceptance over the cross-saddle to that of women gaining the vote – at first, the very thought had been revolutionary, but it was soon accepted and people wondered what the fuss had been all about.[77] As *The Field*'s editor William Fawcett noted, "nothing very dreadful happened after all."[78] By the 1930s, the opinion that women should not ride astride was a minority view; most women rode astride as a matter of course. Just as the forward-thinking suffragists had helped achieve political representation for their British sisters, so too did the imperial cross-saddle riders who helped make the style of riding popular and respectable in Britain.

"Straight Ahead and Over Everything"

British women had opportunities and advantages via equestrianism that they did not have elsewhere, and, through their public participation, they advanced social and cultural (even, arguably, political) changes. In contrast to ball games and other sports, equestrian activities were viewed as compatible with respectable femininity, and it was this public sporting participation, rather than private domesticity, that became a defining characteristic of women's lives in the upper and aspiring classes. Well before women began participating in other sports, female equestrians in Britain had challenged (and continued to challenge) prevailing gender ideals of submissive femininity via riding and hunting. In the field, horse sports like riding and hunting – as well as imperial sports like polo and pig sticking – did not increase gender segregation, but rather promoted a mixing of the sexes because all participated together. Riding astride rather than sidesaddle confirmed this point, as both men and women rode and competed equally. As Raymond Carr contended, "Women's emancipation, it could be argued, to the horror of modern liberators, began in the hunting field."[79]

Despite continuing political, economic, and social inequalities, female riders achieved a large measure of independence and equality in horse sports. They were not limited by domestic ideals or separate spheres, and thus, after achieving that radical end of riding astride, their behaviors and reactions were largely conservative. As M. Jeanne Paterson has argued:

> the issues of suffrage and emancipation in any broader sense were meaningless; to women who had so many choices open to them, who did not need to struggle to open any door that attracted them, the women's movement must simply have been irrelevant. Closed doors, anomalous status, ideological commitment – these made women activists. But liberties and comforts enjoyed by most women of the upper-middle class left them with no time or need for movements. *Contentment rarely makes rebels*.[80]

Had the strict dictates of domesticity been enforced on all women, an army of rebels would likely have been created. This revolt was largely averted because sporting women had made other opportunities for themselves and opened

Conclusion 295

Figure 6.2 Cover image for "Beauty and Style," in *McCall's* (September 1933), page 69: Today's equestrians are indebted to the pioneers of the past. Having adopted the sidesaddle in the fourteenth century, British women abandoned it by the late nineteenth. Today, horsewomen "wear the breeches," but they owe it to generations of female riders before them who, as this image shows, transformed riding aside into riding astride.
Credit: Collection of the author.

other spaces for their participation. Horsewomen were not rebels because they were, by all appearances, content. Their power was not necessarily political, nor they did actively agitate for it. Their achievements and successes were quite different. They aided the larger women's movement via their examples, whether they intended to or not. Augusta Fane credited "those brave pioneers in the Victorian times" for achieving equality, writing in 1926, "It is not the modern girl who fought the battle. She is only the lucky recipient of the fruits of victory won by the courage and perseverance of the valiant and clever women of the past century," including the generations of Amazons on horseback following in the footsteps and hoofbeats of their ancient Scythian forebears.[81]

Through their equestrian involvement and excellence, female riders forced a redefinition of gender, class, and sport in Britain over the long nineteenth century and beyond (Figure 6.2). They forged new visions about femininity, Empire, and the British nation. These triumphs were not unexpected, for as *The Ladies' Field* noted in 1905:

> There are few sports in which late years ladies have both literally and metaphorically come so much to the front as hunting, for though, of course, it is only in comparatively recent decades that they have become, as it were, like the sands of the sea that cannot be numbered for multitude. The artist, poet, and the novelist have long pressed the hunting woman into their service, and to-day there are lady masters of hounds who have their sisters to whip in to them; hunting ladies who write novels, and very good ones too; hunting ladies who instruct their sisters how to ride; and though it may be that the hunting lady historian is still to come, it is very probable that she will not be long in making her appearance.[82]

As this hunting and equestrian historian argues, women popularized fox hunting in Britain and spread horse sports around the Empire; they won Olympic medals and made equestrianism the sport it is today. The skills they gained in riding gave them the ability and confidence to conquer new worlds, both at home in Britain and around the Empire. In going "straight ahead and over everything," they helped make a modern Britain.

Notes

1 Rosamund Owen, *The Art of Sidesaddle: History, Etiquette, Showing* (Saltash, Cornwall: Trematon Press, 1986), 17.
2 Owen, 29.
3 Owen, 31.
4 Letter to the Countess of Bute, from October 1, 1748, in *The Letters and Works of Lady Mary Wortley Montagu, Volume II* (London: Richard Bentley, 1837), 400–401.
5 Joyce M. Bellamy, *Hyde Park for Horsemanship* (London: J.A. Allen, 1975), 95.

Conclusion 297

6 E. Œ. Somerville and Martin Ross, *Stray-Aways* (London: Longman, Green and Co., 1920), 230.
7 Hylton Cleaver, *They've Won Their Spurs* (London: Robert Hale, Limited, 1956).
8 William Fawcett, *Riding and Horsemanship* (New York: Charles Scribner's Sons, 1935), 156.
9 Sir Alfred Munnings, K.C.V.O., *The Finish* (London: Museum Press Limited, 1952), 27.
10 T. [Theresa] Howe, *The Owner Groom: Guide to Horse Management by Amateurs* (London: Country Life, Ltd., 1938), 133–134; Doreen Archer Houblon, *Sidesaddle* (London: Country Life, Ltd., 1938), 5; "The Sidesaddle: Modern Version," *The Ladies' Field*, Volume 92 (December 18, 1920), 57.
11 Guy Paget, *The History of the Althorp and Pytchley Hunt, 1634–1920* (London: William Collins Sons & Co., 1938), 228.
12 Houblon's book was initially published in 1938 (in both London and New York) and subsequently appeared in revised editions in 1951, 1973, and 1977. In 1986, it was revised and reissued by Sylvia Stanier as *Mrs. Houblon's Sidesaddle* (London: J.A. Allen).
13 Lady Diana Shedden and Lady Viola Apsley, *"To whom the goddess …": Hunting and Riding for Women* (London: Hutchinson and Co., 1932), 76; Lieutenant-Colonel S.G. Goldschmidt, *The Fellowship of the Horse* (London: Country Life, Ltd., 1930), 143.
14 Judith Campbell, *The Queen Rides* (New York: The Viking Press, 1965), 5, 7.
15 Campbell, 7–10.
16 Campbell, 12.
17 Campbell, 12.
18 Campbell, 74.
19 Campbell, 71, 75.
20 R.S. Summerhays, *Elements of Riding* (Brattleboro, VT: The Stephen Greene Press, 1963), 46.
21 Sherra Murphy, "Victorian Horse Shows: Spectacle, Leisure, Commodity," *Journal of Victorian Culture Online* (June 18, 2020), http://jvc.oup.com/2020/06/18/victorian-horse-shows/#_ednref9.
22 Sam Marsh, *Hunting, Showing and 'Chasing: With Chapters on Hunter Trials and Breaking and Making a Hunter Colt* (London: Jarrolds Publishers, 1932), 178.
23 "A Famous Rider and her Horses," *The Ladies' Field*, Volume 11 (November 11, 1900), 364–345.
24 Marsh, 177.
25 "Woman In The Saddle," *The Times* (London), (March 17, 1914), 11.
26 Fawcett, 157.
27 Fawcett, 159–160.
28 "Cross-Saddle Riding in the Hunting Field: Hints for Beginners, I," *The Ladies' Field*, Volume 87 (October 18, 1919), 197.
29 Jill Farmiloe, *Clear Round: Four Years in the Show-Ring* (London: Country Life, Ltd., 1939).
30 Farmiloe, 68.
31 Farmiloe, 11, 12, 67.
32 Farmiloe, 15, 20, 53–58.
33 Lieutenant-Colonel M.F. McTaggart, *Mount and Man: A Key to Better Horsemanship* (London: Country Life, Ltd., 1927), 86.
34 "Hunting Notes: Hampshire Ladies' Steeplechase," *The Ladies' Field*, Volume 5 (April 22, 1899), 290.
35 Shedden and Apsley, 253–254; Captain Lionel Dawson, *Hunting without Tears* (London: Country Life, Ltd., 1938), 103.

36 Lord Dorchester [Dudley Massey Pigott Carleton], *Sport, Foxhunting and Shooting* (London: Rich and Cowan, 1935), 78.
37 Marsh, 216.
38 Dorchester, 81.
39 Shedden and Apsley, 260–261.
40 Smythe published several autobiographical books including *Jump for Joy, One Jump Ahead*, and *Jumping Round the World*.
41 Jean Williams, "The Immediate Legacy of Pat Smythe: The Pony-mad Teenager in 1950s and 1960s Britain," in *Sporting Lives*, Dave Day (ed.), (Manchester: MMU Institute for Performance, 2011).
42 Susanna Forrest, *If Wishes Were Horses: A Memoir of Equine Obsession* (London: Atlantic Books, 2012), 127.
43 Forrest, 140.
44 Jackie C. Burke, *Equal to the Challenge: Pioneering Women of Horse Sports* (New York: Howell Book House, 1997), 76–78.
45 Forrest, 131.
46 Alice L. O'Connell, *The Blue Mare in the Olympic Trials* (Boston: Little, Brown, 1955); Dorothy Lyon, *Smoke Rings* (New York: Harcourt, Brace and Company, 1960).
47 Stephanie Daniels and Anita Tedder, *A Proper Spectacle: Women Olympians, 1900–1936* (Houghton Conquest, Bedfordshire: ZeNaNA Press, 2000), 16–25. Though there were no female competitors at the first modern Olympics held in Athens in 1896, they did receive (somewhat) official sanction in Paris in 1900, mainly because the World Exhibition was also held in Paris that year; thus, events were controlled more by those rules than the International Olympic Committee (IOC). Tradition holds that women competed in only tennis and golf in 1900, but according to Daniels and Tedder, "Old programmes of the Paris Exhibition show that women participated in ballooning, croquet, equestrianism, golf, tennis and yachting." They argue that Frenchwoman Elvira Guerra competed on her horse Libertin in "Chevaux de Salle" (Hacks and Hunters Combined) on May 31, 1900, but did not place in the medals/ribbons. They claim that she was "the second woman to compete as an individual in a mixed Olympic event," following yachtswoman Helen de Pourtales, but before tennis player Charlotte Cooper, balloonist Madame Maison, and several female croquet players. See also Bill Mallon, *The 1900 Olympic Games* (Jefferson, NC: McFarland Publishing Company, Inc., 1998); and Burke, 6.
48 Burke, 5, 79, 80.
49 Burke, 81.
50 Forrest, 140.
51 Burke, 81–82.
52 Hilary Fraser, Judith Johnston, Stephanie Green, eds., *Gender and the Victorian Periodical* (Cambridge: Cambridge University Press, 2003).
53 June Purvis, "Gendering the Historiography of the Women's Suffragette Movement in Edwardian Britain: Some Reflections," *Women's History Review*, 22.4 (2013), 582.
54 Joyce Kay, "'No Time for Recreations Till the Vote Is Won'? Suffrage Activists and Leisure in Edwardian Britain," *Women's History Review*, 16.4 (September 2007), 535–553.
55 Mike Huggins, "'And Now, Something for the Ladies': Representations of Women's Sport in Cinema Newsreels, 1918-1939," *Women's History Review*, 16.5 (November 2007), 69.
56 Lady Diana Shedden and Lady Viola Apsley, *"To whom the goddess ...": Hunting and Riding for Women* (London: Hutchinson and Co., 1932), 204.
57 Kay, 535–553.

58 Michael Tanner, *The Suffragette Derby* (London: The Robson Press, 2013).
59 Laura Wortley, *Lucy Kemp-Welch, 1869-1958: The Spirit of the Horse* (Woodbridge: Antique Collectors' Club, 1996), 114.
60 Kay, 535–553.
61 Mrs. Edward Kennard, *The Right Sort, A Romance of the Shires* (London: Ward, Lock, and Co., 1886), 65. The novel was first published in 1883.
62 Mrs. Edward Kennard, *The Right Sort, A Romance of the Shires* (London: Ward, Lock, and Co., 1886), 68.
63 For another take on such conservatism, see Alison Light, *Forever England: Femininity, Literature, and Conservatism Between the Wars* (London: Routledge, 1991).
64 Patricia M. Thane, "What Difference Did the Vote Make? Women in Public and Private Life in Britain Since 1918," *Historical Research*, 76.192 (May 2003), 285.
65 Catriona Parratt, "'Athletic "Womanhood': Exploring Sources for Female Sport in Victorian and Edwardian England," *Journal of Sport History*, 16.2 (Summer 1989), 156.
66 Somerville and Ross, 229–230.
67 Maurice Collis, *Somerville and Ross: A Biography* (London: Faber and Faber, 1968), 136.
68 Owen, 103.
69 Julia Bush, *Women Against the Vote: Female Anti-Suffrage in Britain* (Oxford: Oxford University Press, 2007).
70 *The Ladies' Field*, Volume 77 (May 12, 1917), 400.
71 Deirdre Beddoe, *Back to Home and Duty: Women Between the Wars, 1918–1939* (London: Pandora, 1989), 6; Susan Kingsley Kent, "The Politics of Sexual Difference: World War I and the Demise of British Feminism," *Journal of British Studies*, 27.3 (July 1988), 232–253.
72 Joy S. Ritchie, "Confronting the 'Essential' Problem: Reconnecting Feminist Theory and Pedagogy," *Journal of Advanced Composition*, 10.2, (Fall 1990), 249-273; Valerie Walkerdine, "Femininity as Performance," *Oxford Review of Education*, 15.3 (1989), 267–279.
73 Erica Munkwitz, "'The Master is the Mistress': Women and Fox Hunting as Sports Coaching in Britain," *Sport in History*, 37.4 (2017), 395–422.
74 Cecil A. Pelham, *Past and Present Masters of Foxhounds* (London: Masters of Foxhounds Association, 1938).
75 Maude Ellis, *The Squire of Bentley (Mrs. Cheape)* (Edinburgh: William Blackwood and Sons, 1926), xi.
76 See *The Ladies' Field*: "The Bentley Harriers," October 28, 1899; "The Clumber Harriers: Master: Her Grace the Duchess of Newcastle," March 18, 1899; "Our Lady Masters of Hounds," November 16, 1901; "The Bentley Harriers," November 15, 1902; "Lady Masters of Hounds in 1903," November 11, 1903; "The Bentley Harriers," January 12, 1907; "Some Lady Masters and Their Views," December 21, 1907; "Mrs. Hughes, M.F.H., Neuadd Fawr," March 21, 1908; "Lady Masters of 1911," October 28, 1911; "Our Lady Masters: Mrs. Proctor, Master of the Biggleswade Harriers," December 28, 1912; "Lady Masters of Hounds: Mrs. T.H.R. Hughes – The Neuadd Fawr," February 15, 1912; "Lady Masters and the Hunting Season," March 28, 1914; "Our Lady Masters," October 23, 1915; "Irish Hunting Season: Lady Masters and Prominent Followers," November 13, 1915; "The Lady Masters," October 27, 1917; "Our Lady Masters of Hounds: Famous Packs of Foxhounds and Harriers," December 18, 1920.
77 Lieutenant-Colonel M.F. McTaggart, *Two Horseman and Mabel* (London: Country Life Limited, 1933), 160. This was a revised and enlarged edition of *From Colonel to Subaltern* (London: Country Life, Ltd., 1928).

78 Fawcett, 156.
79 Raymond Carr, *English Fox Hunting* (London: Weidenfeld and Nicholson, 1986), 243.
80 M. Jeanne Peterson, "No Angels in the House: The Victorian Myth and the Paget Women," *The American Historical Review*, 89.3 (June 1984), 708. Italics mine.
81 Augusta Fane, *Chit-chat* (London: Thornton, Butterworth, Limited, 1926), 284.
82 "Ladies in the Field," *The Queen* (April 1, 1905), 521.

Index

Note: Page numbers followed by *f* indicate figures.

Accomplishment, riding as 94–97
Ackermann, Rudolph 105
Ackermann's Repository 105
Acton, C. R. 265, 270
Adams, John 58, 91, 93, 98–99, 106, 116
Adelman, Miriam 26
Aeneid (Virgil) 74*f*
Africa 21, 185; pig sticking in 206
African horse sickness 185
Airlie, Countess of 248
Albert (Prince) 96, 100
Aldin, Cecil 247–249
Alken, Henry 72*f*
Allbutt, Mrs. Harry 148, 164
Allen, Fred 159
Allen, John 46, 50, 98, 106, 116, 127
Almond, Richard 14, 25
Amazones 12
Amazons 74*f*; British women as 13, 149; as equestrians 1–3; female Scythians as 1
Amelia (Princess) 7, 55
America, manuals printed in 101
Analysis of Horsemanship, An (Adams) 58, 91, 97–98
Anglicanism, and hunting 14
"Anglo-Indian Life: The Morning Ride" (Woodville) 191*f*
Animal conservation 67
Animal studies 24
Annaly, Lord 284
Annandale (India) 200
Anne (Queen) 15, 75
Anne (Princess), and three-day eventing 290
Anne of Bohemia 3, 285
Anne of Denmark 6
Anonyma 136

Anstruther-Thomson, John 155
Anti-feminists 292–293
Apperley, Charles James ("Nimrod") 11, 67–68, 71, 72*f*, 75, 80, 92–93, 121, 125
Apron skirt 165–167, 166*f*, 171
Apsley, Lady Viola 161, 234, 261–263, 267, 271, 284, 288, 290
Archery 75, 96, 107
Arden, Catharine 121
Aristocracy 10, 14, 18, 47, 53–54, 59, 102; and equestrianism 60–63; and female hunters 59–61; in France 12–13; *see also* Class; Social hierarchy
Artemis 1, 14
Arthur, Mrs. 165
Art of Riding, The (English) 149
Art of Sidesaddle, The: History, Etiquette, Showing (Owen) 26
Ascot races 75
Aspirational recreational riding 91
Astley, Philip 10, 56, 58, 110
Astley's Amphitheatre 10
Astley's System of Equestrian Education (Astley) 58
Aston, Miss 255
Astor, Miss 161
Athleticism: female 22; male 23
Atkinson, George 187, 188*f*, 195
Aubert, P. A. 113
Aunt sally races 239
Aurora Floyd (Braddon) 151
Austin, Alfred 136
Australia 185, 249
Automobiles 264

Baden-Powell, Robert 203, 219
Badminton Library 232
Badminton Magazine 242

Baily's Magazine of Sports and Pastimes 111, 139, 141, 156, 162, 167, 169, 171, 196, 206, 239
Baily's Hunting Directory 254f, 255
Bakewell, Robert 66
Balance strap 116, 141
Barbed-wire fencing 144
Barker, Hannah 78
Barking deer. *See* Muntjac hunting
Barrett, J.L.M. 259
Bather, (Miss) E. G. 247–248
Baucher, François 14, 111, 113
"Bay Hunter tethered to a Tree, A" (Gilpin) 48
Bayly, Mrs. C. 287
Bazalgette, Louis 53
Beach, Belle 234
Bear, Mytton's pet 71, 72f
Beaufort, Duke of 232
Beauty, horsewomen and 93–94
Beckford, Louisa 54
Beckford, Peter 13, 54, 126
Bedi, Rahul 21
Beeton, Samuel 150–151
Bellerophon 1
Belvoir Hunt 71, 234, 253
Bending race 238–239
Bentley Harriers 253, 254f, 256
Berenger, Richard 13, 50
Berkeley, Earl of 111
Berners, Juliana 10
Best, J. W. 205
Bicycling 6, 15, 23, 27, 140, 242, 292
Big game hunting 21, 182–183, 204, 209
Bingham, Adrian 23
Birch, Noel 232
Birkbeck, Lady Mabel 247
Birkbeck, Sir William Henry 248
Blackwood's Magazine 240
Bland, Lillian 264
Blank days 67
Blewitt, Audrey 267
Blockley, Mrs. 286
Bloodgood, Lida Fleitmann 26, 114f, 127
Blood-Smyth, Annie; *see* Allbutt, Mrs. Harry
Blood Sport: Hunting in Britain since 1066 (Griffin) 25
Blood sports, opposition to 25, 256–257
Blue Mare in the Olympic Trials, The (O'Connell) 289

Blyth, Henry 138
Boar hunting, in India; *see* Pig sticking, in India
Bobbery pack 195, 198f, 199
Body posture: leaping head and 113–114, 142f; for riding 93; saddle and 48–49, 49f, 51f; sidesaddle and 160
Boer War, horses for 245
Book of Sports and Mirror of Life (Egan) 76
Book of St. Albans, The (Berners) 10
Book of the Horse, The (Sidney) 147–148
Books/publications: on children's riding 267–269; cross-saddle and 230, 234; on equestrianism, after First World War 258–265; on female equestrianism 13; on fox hunting 13, 53–54; on horsemanship 10, 12–13; on hunting, in interwar years 265; and imperial ideology 182–183; on imperial sports 236; instructional, and riding astride 230–232; published in India 193; on sidesaddle riding 26; *see also* Horse history(ies); Hunting handbooks; Riding manuals; Sports history(ies)
Boots 163, 231f, 244
Bowers, Georgina 167, 168f, 230, 231f, 287
Boydston, Jeanne 16
Braddon, Mary Elizabeth 1, 151
Bradley, Cuthbert 241
Bradley, Mrs. Cuthbert 270
Brailsford, Dennis 27
Breastplate 50
Breeches: "better a live lady in..." 167, 168f; female 164, 216–217; masculine 164; women's wearing of 15, 21, 79, 108, 108f, 167, 169, 231f, 242, 244, 269–273, 284, 295f
Bridle 48; double 48, 64, 104; history of 47–48; as invented by Athena 1
Brighton 100; ladies' polo at 243f
Bristow, Mrs. 181–182
Britain's Experience of Empire in the Twentieth Century 21
British East India Company 184
British Empire 181–185; equestrians and 20–22; gender ideology and 20; and masculinity 181; pig-sticking in 206; rulers vs. native ruled in 202, 203f; women and 20; *see also* Imperial ideology; India (British); Social hierarchy

British Equestrian Team 288–289, 289f
British Manly Exercises (Walker) 94
British Manly Sports (Walker) 126
British Riding Academy 55
Bromford, Mr. 76
Brooke, Dorothy 229, 265
Brooke, Geoffrey 264–265
Brush, as reward, presentation of 69, 120
Buckle, Frank 75
Bullock, Mrs. 248
Bullfinches (Bullock Fences) 144
Bunbury, Mrs. John 161
Burma, polo in 211–212, 212f
Burn, Mrs. R. M. 155
Butler, Brian 288
Butler, John 27, 164
Buxton, Meriel 26
Byle, Mrs. 187

Cadogan Riding School 264
Calcutta, Rotten Row in 187
Call of the Nilgiris 195
Camilla 74f
Campbell, Judith 285
Campbell, Walter 184, 195, 198f, 204–205
Canada 185, 249
Canning, Charlotte 186, 189–190, 217
Canterbury Tales, The 4
Capping 156
Captain M***** 99–100, 125
Carr, Raymond 25, 294
Carter, Captain (Charles' father) 57
Carter, Charles 48, 50–52, 56–57, 67
Castlereagh, Lady 234, 235f
Catch of the County, The (Kennard) 158
Catholic Church: and hunting 14; views on riding astride by women 4
Cattle 67, 144
Cavalry 8–9
Cavendish, Spencer Compton (Lord Hartington, eighth Duke of Devonshire) 138
Cavendish, William (Marquess and later Duke of Newcastle) 10
Cecil, Mary Amelia ("Emily Mary," first Marchioness of Salisbury) 44–45, 50, 60, 62, 62f, 73, 74f, 79–80, 252–253, 254f
"Cecil" (equestrian author) 141, 155
Chalus, Elaine 45, 78
Champion and Wilton 283

Chaperones, for women 154
Charles I (King) 6
Charles II (King) 10
Charlotte (Queen) 55
Charlton Hunt 52
Cheape, Mrs. (née Maud Mary Hemming) 253, 254f, 255
Cheltenham 99
Chenevix-Trench, Charles 215, 228
Chiarini, Angelica 11
Children and young girls: contributions to war effort in Great War 266–267; and equestrian pursuits 265–269; in jumping contests 287; polo clubs for 242; and riding astride 265–268, 266f, 268f; riding by, in interwar years 267, 287; and switching riding styles 265–266, 266f; *see also* Pony Club
Chimney-sweep, and Grafton Hunt 119f
Chitty, Anna 186, 211
Chitty, Arthur 211
Christy, Eva (E.V.A.) 141, 148–149, 151–152, 228, 234, 236–238, 245, 260
Church, S. R. 248
Churchill, Lady Mary 7
Churchill, Lady Randolph 229–230, 246
Churchill, Winston 208
Circus 10–12, 58, 112, 124, 158
Civilizing influence, of women 89, 120–123, 126, 169
Civilizing Process, The (Elias) 17
Civil Wars (Britain) 10
Clarke, Mrs. J. Stirling 91, 97, 100, 102, 107–109, 117, 125, 139, 147, 164
Class: British Empire and 184–185; equestrianism and 19, 54, 80; and equestrianism in England 13, 47; and equestrianism in France 11–12, 14; and fox hunting 18–19, 143; and horse sports 17–18; and hunting on horseback in England 14–15; hunting participation after First World War and 229–230; and imperial life 182; and sidesaddle vs. riding astride 284–285; women's equestrianism and 15–17; women's wartime work in First World War and 229–230; *see also* Aristocracy; Social hierarchy
Classical equitation; *see Haute école*
Clear Round: Four Years in the Show-Ring (Farmiloe) 287
Clee Hills 63

Clementson, Mrs. Marc ("Marky") 215
Cler, Albert 17
Cleveland, Duchess of 6
Cleveland, Marchioness of 68
Cleveland, Marquis of 67; daughters of, and equestrianism 80
Clothes/clothing 26, 52–53, 62f, 126; after Great War 269–271; of courtesans 136; of female hunters 61f; for girl riders 267; military styling of 52–53, 105; for remount work in First World War 249, 250f; and riding astride 269–271; for riding astride 242–244; for riding in India 215–217; safety concerns and 161–169; and women in horse sports 79, 89, 104–110 see also Breeches; Riding habit(s)
Clove, Bella 189
Cockayne, Thomas 59
Cockney sportsman 73, 79
Collars 50
Collett, John 61f, 73, 79
Colley, Linda 16, 91, 120
Colors: for riding clothes 107, 108f, 163; in India 188, 189f; for sporting garments 52
"Common Sense of Riding" (O'Donoghue) 148
Communication, human–horse 27
Compleat Horseman, The (Hughes) 13, 46, 55f
Complete Horseman, The (Dixon) 233
Conduct guides, Victorian 96, 99
Conigsby, Countess of (1759–1760) 52
Conolly, Lady Louisa 64
Conyngham, Lady 60–62
Cook, John 54
Copley, John Singleton 52
Corsets 163–164; for riding 109
Costs; see Economics
Cottesmore Hunt 70
Country Life 144
Country women, and hunting 60–62
Courage, and riding 151
"Coursers, Taking the Field at Hatfield Park" (Pollard) 62f
Coursing 59
Courtesans 64–65, 136–138, 192; and hunting 60–62
Covert hack 143
Coverts 67
Craige, Thomas 93, 107

Craven, Earl of 63
Craven, Lady 63, 118
Cremorne Gardens 138
Cricket 23, 24, 182; as imperial game 183
Croquet 23, 27, 96, 107, 298
Cross-saddle: acceptance of 185, 213, 228–229, 231f, 234, 271–273, 272f, 294; advantages of 213, 262–264, 286–287; advocacy for 234, 235f, 259–261; economic effect of 229; popularity of 234; use by ladies in Britain 230–235; use by ladies in India 208; women's adoption of 283–284; and women's war work 258; young girls and 265, 266f see also Riding astride (by women)
Cross-Saddle and Side-Saddle: Modern Riding for Men and Women (Christy) 228, 234, 260
"Cross v. Side Saddle" (Wynter) 268f
Cruppers 50
Crutch [Second Pommel] 7, 48–49, 117; hunting 163; off-side 114–115
Cult of the Huntress 3
Culture of the Horse, The: Status, Discipline, and Identity in the Early Modern World (Raber and Tucker) 25
Cummings, John 25
Cundee, James 98
Cuneo, Pia 12, 26
"*Curry and Rice*" (Atkinson) 187, 188f, 195

Dale, T. F. 154, 209–210, 232–233, 236
Dareall, Lady 94
Darlington, Earl of, foxhounds of 59
Davidoff, Leonore 19
Davison, Emily 291
Dawson, G.A.R. "The Old Shikarri" 184, 195–197, 196f, 204
Dawson, Lionel 265
Deaths: of écuyères 160–161; of horsewomen 160–161
"Deathtraps" 166, 166f
Declaration of Independence, horsewoman's; see Magna Carta, horsewoman's
Deer 59
Defauconpret, Auguste-Jean-Baptiste 89
Deformity(ies), female pursuits and 93, 160, 265

Index

De l'équitation et des haras (Lancosme-Brèves) 113
Demi-monde 136
Depression, exercise and 92
Devonshire, Duchess of (18th c.) 45; (early 19th c.) 71; *see also* Georgianna (Duchess of Devonshire)
Devonshire, Duke of (18th c.) 53
Diana (Roman goddess) 3, 14, 74f
"Diana Return'd from the Chace" (Gillray) 74f
Dianas of the Chase 3
Dictionnaire raisonné d'équitation (Baucher) 112
Dismount 106, 165
Dixon, William Searth 233
Dogs: in British India 195; family-based packs, decline of 156; hunting, keeping of 19; hunting with, ban on 25; Lady Salisbury's 44–45; subscription packs 19, 70, 155–156, 195; *see also* Bobbery pack; Foxhounds; Harriers; Hounds
Domesticity: female equestrians and 294; First World War and 229; separate spheres and 79; and sport 70; Victorian 16, 91–92, 150; *see also* Gender; Separate Spheres
Dorchester, Lord 258, 264, 288
Dorrien, John 64
Double oxers 144
Downshire, Marchioness of 234
Dragging by a horse 162
Drainage 144
Draper, Diana 63
Dressage, Olympic 289
Dufferin, Lady 193–194, 200–202
Dunbar, J. Rimmel 95, 117
Duncan, Ian 88
"Dun Horse with Its Groom, A" (Stringer) 9f
Dunning, Eric 17
Durand, Sir Edward 268
Durzi 218

Economics: cross-saddle and 230, 263; of horse sports 17–19, 22, 95; of hunting in British India 197; of riding lessons 101; of riding schools 57; sidesaddle riding and 259, 263, 284–285; of women's participation in hunting 155–156

Écuyères 11–12, 113, 157–158; deaths of 160–161
Eden, Anthony 187
Eden, Emily 109, 187
Edinburgh Magazine, The 88
Edwards, Peter 25
Egan, Pierce 76–77, 76f
Elastic loops 165
Elias, Norbert 17
Elizabeth, Duchess of Hamilton 52
Elizabeth, Empress of Austria 157–159
Elizabeth I (Queen) 1, 5
Elizabeth II (Queen) 285
Ellesmere Manuscript of Chaucer's *The Canterbury Tales* 4
Elliott, Grace Dalrymple 53, 64
Elliott, John 118
Ellis, Colin 140
Ellis, Sarah Stickney 91
Emancipation of women, via horse sports 23, 150, 171–172, 292–294; before the Great War 228; via riding clothes 244, 271; in India 181
Empathy, human–horse 28
Enclosure movement 66, 144
English, H. G. 149
English Fox Hunting (Carr) 25
English Matron, The 92
English national identity; *see* National identity
Epping Hunt 72
Equality: in sports, women's achievement of 21–22, 171, 217, 294–296; women's, sportswomen and 22–23, 154–156, 283–284, 291–296
"Equality days" 229, 272f, 273
Equestrian [term] 12–13
Equestrian, The (Captain M*****) 99
Equestrian history 24–25
Equestrianism: hazards/dangers of 26; qualities required by 27–28; and self-possession 27, 126, 150–157, 291; and sport 26–28; *see also* Horse Sports; Hunting; Polo; Pig Sticking; Olympic Games
Equestrian's Manual (Wayte) 100
Equestrienne 13
Equipment, riding: for ladies 47–52; safety 141 *see also* Bridle; Cross-saddle; Crutch; Sidesaddle

Équitation des dames (Aubert) 113
Eroticism, hunting associated with 3
Eskine, Mr. 77
European in India, The; or, Anglo-Indian's Vade-Mecum 217–218
Exercise: riding as 90f, 91–94; in India 187; for women 45–46
Exercises for Ladies (Walker) 93–94

Fabrics: for colonial riding habits 217; for remount work clothes 249, 250f; for riding clothes 107, 108f, 163; for sporting garments 52–53; *see also* Velvet; Wool
Falling off a horse 61f, 64, 122f, 160; and getting back on 26–27; in hunting in British India 197; injuries from 26, 49–50; sidesaddle and 49–50, 153; wire fences and 144
Fane, Augusta 60, 118, 136, 144, 165, 296
Farmiloe, Jill 287–288, 292
Fashion(s): in British Empire 215–216; definition of 215; Victorian 92, 215
Faulkner-Horne, Shirley 268
Fawcett, William 228, 284, 286, 294
Fellowship of the Horse, The (Goldschmidt) 259
Felton, W. Sidney 13
Female equestrians: and feminism 22, 290–292; numbers of, in Britain 169
"Female Fox Hunter, The" 61f
Femininity: British imperialism and 20–21, 271–273; elite, equestrianism and 19; equestrianism and 96; as female advantage 293; female equestrians and 294; French ideas of 12; horsemanship and 12; horsewomen and 93–94; and hunting, in early 19th c. 73, 74f; and public horse sports, in early 19th c. 75–77, 76f; riding habit and 269–271; and riding position 4; and sport, in early 19th c. 70; and sporting prowess 63; sportswomen and 80, 169, 283; 18th-c. 45–46; Victorian ideals and 16, 90, 96, 150–151; *see also* Emancipation; Gender; Liberation; Separate Spheres
Feminism, female equestrians and 22, 290–292
Fences 60, 67–68, 141, 143–144; Empress Elizabeth and 158; height for show jumping 144, 145f
Ferneley, John, Jr. 118

Fernie, Mrs. 258
Fernie hunt 139, 161
Field, The 147, 228
Fifty Years' Biographical Reminisces (Lennox) 76
Fifty Years of Fox-Hunting (Elliott) 118
Finch, Jonathan 144
First spear, in pig sticking 204, 208
First World War: children's contributions to war effort in 267; equestrian sports after 257–258; horses in 229; hunting in 251–257; modern femininity and 22–23, 228–229, 271–273; and women's war work 244–249
Fitzherbert, Mrs 53, 65
Flint, Mr. 77
Floyd, Mrs. 121
Football 23–24
Foot rest, with sidesaddle 4
Footwear 53, 105, 163
Fores's Sporting Notes and Sketches 241
Forester, Frank; *see* Herbert, William Henry
Forester, George ("Squire") 63
Forester, Lord 81
Forrest, Susanna 288
Forward-facing horsemanship 49, 49f
Foxhounds: in Great War 252; in India 195, 196f; Lady Salisbury's 44–45 *see also* Master of Foxhounds (M.F.H.s)
Fox hunting: as "democratic" sport 139; in First World War 251–257; gender ideals and 16–17; histories of 25; history of female participation in 44, 58–60; Hungarian 157; leaping head and 117–120; as mixed-class pursuit 18, 118f; as national sport 169, 170f; new participants after First World War 229–230; pace of, in 18th c 59–60; popularity of 231–232; publications on 13, 53–54; safety considerations in 60; as socially inclusive 18–19; starting times for 59–60, 70; in 18th c 58–60; transformation after mid-18th c 65–67, 80; Wilde on 198f; women's participation in 44, 58–65, 61f, 80; young equestrians and 266–267 *see also* Master of Foxhounds (M.F.H.s)
Fozard, Mr. 96–97, 101
France: circus riders in 11–12; equestrianism in 11–12, 14; hunting on horseback in 13–15; national identity,

horse and 26; women riding in 11–12, 14, 89, 112, 124–125; women's wearing of trousers in 15
Frances (first wife of second Marquess of Salisbury) 62*f*
Franz Joseph, Emperor 157
Fraser, David 202
Freedom: women's riding in India as 190; women's sporting participation and 24; *see also* Emancipation; Liberation
French Revolution 16, 46–47, 58
Furbor, Paul Henry 100, 193

Galloping 44, 68, 79, 89, 100, 112, 115, 117, 119, 124, 126, 159, 187–188, 198–199
Game Act of 1671 18
Game laws 18, 59, 79
Game Reform Act of 1831 18
Gardner, Alan 206, 207*f*
Gardner, Mrs. Alan 203–204, 206, 207*f*, 214
Gatayes, Léon 112
Gender [term], definition of 15
Gender and Empire 21
Gender and Equestrian Sport: Riding Around the World (Adelman and Knijnik) 26
Gender ideals: British Empire and 20, 181, 184–185; and British riding style 125; in early 19th c. 74*f*, 80; female equestrians and 294; horsewomen and 169, 170*f*; in late 18th c. 63; and riding position 4; separate spheres and 78; in 18th- to 19th-c. Britain 15–16; Victorian 96; and Victorian fox hunting 120–123; and women in sport 23–24; women's equestrianism and 15–17; *see also* Femininity; Masculinity; Separate Spheres
Gender inversions, sporting women and 79
Gender roles: sporting women and 79, 150–151, 271–273; in 18th-c. Britain 46; World War I and 271–273; *see also* Femininity; Masculinity
"Gentleman Riding Sidesaddle" (Grant) 103*f*
George II (King) 7, 108
George III (King) 16, 50, 55
George IV (King) 11, 16, 64, 286
George V (King) 291
George VI (King) 285

George, Lord Auckland 187
Georgianna (Duchess of Devonshire) 45, 53
Gerald of Wales 3
Germany: equestrianism in 11–12; *haute école* in 25
Ghyga, Fanny 161
Gifford, Lady 253
Gillray, James 74*f*
Gilpin, Sawrey 48
Gilroy, Amanda 91
Girls; *see* Children and young girls
Girth 50
"Give Me My Skirt" (Bowers) 168*f*
Glitters, Lucy (Surtees' fictional character) 120
Gloves 164
Goddess(es), hunting 1–2
"Goers" 115
Goldschmidt, S. G. 259–260, 270
Golf 23, 27, 280, 298
"Gone Away" (Turner) 122*f*
Goodwood hounds 64
Grafton, Duke of 119*f*
Grafton Hunt 60, 119*f*
Grande Vénerie, la 13
Grant, Sir Francis 103*f*; "The Hon. Mrs. J. Wortley on Horseback" 2*f*
Greaves, James 113
Greenall, Lady 253
Greenwood, George 100, 113, 115, 121, 125
Greville, Lady 150, 154, 185, 194, 199, 202, 219, 228
Greyhounds, Lady Salisbury's 44–45
Griffin, Emma 25
Guha, Ramachandra 183
Gulmurg, Kashmir 200
Guterbock's 216–217, 244
Gymkhana [term] 236
Gymkhanas 21, 181, 199–202, 237*f*, 268, 272, 288; adoption in Britain 236–239, 238*f*

Hacking 91, 140–141
Haines, Mr. 99
Hair arrangement, for female riders 110
Hall, Catherine 19
Hall, Mrs. 258
Hampshire Ladies' Steeplechase 287
Hance, Jack 142*f*, 206, 236, 260
Hance, Jackie 236

Handbook of Horsemanship, The (Captain M*****) 100
"Happy Days" (postcard) 272f
"Harby" 233, 251–253, 256
Hare, hunting for 59, 65
Hargreaves, Jennifer 24
Harley, Lady Henrietta 7
Harriers 66; Lady Salisbury's 44–45; packs, in London 71–72
Harrington, Lady 161
Harrington, Lord 238
Hart and Sons 242
Harvey, Adrian 81, 124
Harvey, Lady 197
Hat(s) 167; for female riders 109; pork-pie 136
Hatfield harriers 59
Hatfield hounds 156
Hatfield Hunt 62f
Haute école: Adams' condemnation of 98; Astley's preference for 58; British hunting style vs 55–57, 124, 169–170; and circus 10; decline in England 10; in Europe vs. England 9–10, 12, 55–58, 89, 123, 157–158; and Protestant Germany 25; saddles for 47
Hawke, John 266f
Hawkes, John 19, 119f
Hawking 59
Hay, Sir John 206
Hayes, Alice 118, 121, 141, 146, 148, 153–154, 156–157, 166f, 171, 193, 234, 270
Hayes, M. Horace 148
Hazard, Willis P. 101
H.D. Nicholl and Co. 164
Headgear, for female riders 110
Health, riding for 91–94
Heathcoat-Armory, Sir Ian 256
Hedges 67
Hédouville, Vicomte d' 12
Henderson, Robert 103f, 127, 143, 170, 186–188, 192–193
Henrietta Maria (Queen) 6
Henry VIII (King) 7–8
Herbert, William Henry 206
Herodotus 1
Herring, John Frederick 114f, 115, 121
Hertfordshire Hunt 44
Hervey, H.J.A. 218
Hickey, William 181–182

Higgs, Phoebe 63, 80, 89
Hints on Horsemanship, to a Nephew and Niece (Greenwood) 100, 113
Hints to Horsewomen (Allbutt) 148
Hippodrome 11
Hirelings 146, 265
History(ies); *see also* Horse history(ies); Sports history(ies)
History and Art of Horsemanship, The (Berenger) 13
History of Horse Foxhunting, The (Longrigg) 25
History of Horse Racing, The (Longrigg) 25
Hitchcock, F. C. 258
Hockey 23
Hodges, Anna Sophia 65
Hoffmeister, Dr. 187
Hog hunting; *see* Pig sticking
Höhne, Mr. 165
Holland-Martin, Ruby 288
Holmes, Nelly 118
Holmes, Sherlock 151, 182
Holt, Richard 18, 23
Horlock, Knightly William; *see* "Scrutator"
Horn, of saddle 5, 7; *see also* Pommel
Horrocks, Miss 247–248
Horse(s): Arabian, in India 186; bred for hunting 65–66, 144–146; British love for 1; costs of 95–96, 146, 159; covert hack 143; crossbred 66; in England, after Great War 264; hack 91; hired 146, 264–265; hunters 66; and imperial life 182; in India 185–186; number of, in Britain 229; ownership rates, in 19th c 140; prices of 146; as privileged species 24; role in history 24; specially trained for ladies 57; women's relationship with 1
Horse and Man in Early Modern England (Edwards) 25
Horse Bazaar (King Street, London) 90
Horse breeding 10, 65, 144–146, 229; in First World War 251; and riding styles 25
Horse-craziness, in early 20th c 268
Horse history(ies) 24–26
Horsemanship; Or, The Art of Riding and Managing a Horse (Richardson) 100
Horsemanship; *see also* Human–horse relationships; Equestrianism
Horsemanship for Boys and Girls (McTaggart) 269

Horse racing 75–77; in First World War 255–256; in India 200; scholarly studies of 24–25
Horse shows 286–288
Horse sports: after First World War 257–258; in British India 21, 181; female participation in, in 19th c 140–141; imperial, adoption in Britain 236–239; in interwar years 22; women and, in 20th c 264; *see also* Equestrianism
Horse training 186, 190–192, 259; in First World War 245; in gymkhanas 236; hunting and, in First World War 251–252; for jumping 67; for polo 209–210; in remount depot work 248; by women 209–210, 245, 248
Horse Training Upon New Principles (Wiseman) 100
Horsewoman, The: A Practical Guide to Side-Saddle Riding (Hayes) 148, 166f, 193, 234, 270
Horsewomen, requisite attributes for 24–28, 261–262; *see also* Equestrianism; Human–horse relationships
Houblon, Doreen Archer 284–285
Hounds: bred for hunting 65–66; breeding of 65; in Great War 252; hunting with 13, 59; overriding 147, 159 packs of 59; *see also* Dogs
Howard, Lady Mabel 172
Howarth, Mary 242
Huggins, Mike 25, 290
Hughes, Charles 13, 46, 54–55, 55f, 94
Hughes, Mrs. Charles (Miss Tomlinson) 55, 56f
Hughes, Mrs. T.H.R. 253–255, 255f
Human–horse relationships 1, 24–25, 27–28, 54; British and 125; female riders and 126, 151–152; in India 186
Hunt clubs 71
Hunter (horse); *see* Horse(s)
Hunter (person) 183
Hunter Improvement Society 146
Hunting: after First World War 257–258; British imperialism and 20–21; in British India 195–199; and equitation 10; in First World War 251–257; in France 13; game laws and 18; gender ideals and 16–17; golden age of, railway age and 141–143; history of 58–60; horsewomen and, in 19th c 140–141; as masculine sphere 79; opposition to, in Great War 256–257; pace of, in 18th c 59–60; in 19th c 65–66, 68–69; popularity of 123; professionalization of 155; in Victorian era 103–104; by women, in India 20–21; women and, in 20th c 264; women's exclusion from, in 19th c 67–74, 80–81; young equestrians and 266–267 *see also* Fox hunting
Hunting Catechism, A (Meysey-Thompson) 236
Hunting crutch 163; *see also* Leaping Head
Hunting for All (Acton) 265
Hunting handbooks 146–150
Hunting on horseback: in England 14–15; in France 13–15
"Hunting Party, A" (Wootton) 7
"Hunting Scenes: A Hunting Morn" (Herring) 113, 114f
Hunting skirts 163; *see also* Skirt(s)
Hunting without Tears (Dawson) 265
Huntsmen, female 255
Hunt Staff, female 255
Hurlingham: ladies' polo at 243f; polo at 239, 241
Hyam, Ronald 20, 181
Hyde Park 79, 89, 90f, 95, 136, 187
Hysteria 92

If Wishes Were Horses (Christy) 261
Illness, female, Victorian views on 91–92
Illustrated London News 147
Illustrated Sporting and Dramatic News, The 148
Imagined community, Britain as 10, 171, 182, 199
"Impecuniosus" 147
Imperial hunters, hierarchy of 183
Imperial ideology: equestrians and 218–219; and gender ideals 283; and hunting 20–21; and modern femininity 271–273; and sport 182, 236–239; and sporting ideals 283; women's equestrianism and 15–17 *see also* British Empire
Independence, women's, on horseback 105, 150–151, 154, 171; in India 194
India (British): books on female equestrians published in 193; climate of 109, 188–190, 195–196, 196f; female riders in 186–192; horses and horse ownership in 185–186; horse sport in, transformative effects of 218–219; horse sports in 21, 181; humidity in 109;

hunting in 195–199; learning to ride in 192–193; manuals printed in 100, 193; morning/evening rides in 188–190, 191f, 194; polo in 181, 185, 208–213, 240f; racial mixing in 183–184; riding astride in (by women) 181–182; rising clothes for 215–217; sport as an obsession in 181; women riding astride in 213–215; women's roles and importance in 20, 181
Indian elk, hunting of 195
"Indian Paper-Chase" 203f
Indian Rebellion 183–184, 188f, 190
Industrial Revolution 16, 18, 46–47, 54
Ingestre, Lady Sarah 121
Injury(ies): horseback riding and 26, 95, 160–162, 165; in remount depot work 248; sidesaddle and 113–114, 153; wire fences and 144
Instructions for Ladies in Riding (Carter) 56–57
International Horse Show at Olympia (1907) 286
Invalidism, female, Victorian views on 91–92
Ireland, point-to-point races in 24, 193, 244, 292; Bay Middleton's racing in 159; hunting injuries in 161
Itzkowitz, David 25, 124

"Jackal Hunting in India" 198f
Jackals: habits of 198; hunting of, in India 21, 181, 184, 195, 196f, 197–199, 236
Jacket: of riding habit 109, 270; *see also* Spencer jacket
Jackson, Claude Ward 213
Jacobs, Mrs. 153
Janin, Jules 12
Jenkins, T. A. 100, 107, 118, 191f, 193
Jenny, Miss 247
Jersey, Lady 60
Jodhpurs 215, 270
Jones, Herbert 291
Jorrocks, John (Surtees' fictional character) 73, 143, 209
Jousting 201f; decline of 7–8; women and 3f
Jumping (leaping): horse training for 67; instructions on 193; leaping head and 116, 126; sidesaddle and 68; from standstill 60; stirrup length for 104; women and 98–99, 104; *see also* Fox Hunting; Olympic Games; Show Jumping
Jumping powder 144
Jungle sheep, hunting of 195

Kadir Cup competition 205
Kay, Joyce 290
Kemble, Fanny 92–93, 101
Kemp-Welch, Lucy 291
Kennard, Mrs. Edward 144–146, 155, 158, 160, 162, 165
Kerr, W. A. 148, 211, 214, 230–231, 269
Kington saddle 6
Kipling, Rudyard 208
Klein, Lawrence 78
Knijnik, Jorge 26
Kwint, Marius 11

Lacing, of corsets 164
Lade, Sir John 64
Lade, Lady (Laetitia) 64–65, 68, 79–80, 89, 138
Ladies' Equestrian Guide, The; or, The Habit and the Horse: A Treatise on Female Equitation (Clarke) 91, 100, 102, 140
Ladies' Field, The 70, 71, 81, 121, 156, 165, 169, 199–200, 207–208, 210–211, 213, 216–217, 232–234, 238–239, 241–242, 247, 249, 250f, 251–253, 257, 264, 266, 271, 286; on female Masters of Hounds 293; on hunting ladies 296; supplement on suffrage campaign 292
"Ladies' Horse Race, A" (Nicholson) 76f
Ladies in Racing: Sixteenth Century to the Present Day (Ramsden) 26
Ladies in the Field (Lady Greville) 194, 228
Ladies of the Chase (Buxton) 26
Ladies on Horseback (O'Donoghue) 148
"Ladies Tilting at the Ring, India" 201f
Lady and her Horse, The (Jenkins) 100, 191f, 193
Lady's Equestrian Companion, The: or, The Golden Key to Equitation (Furbor) 100
Lady's Equestrian Manual, The (Hazard) 101
"Lady's Hack, A." (Ward) 49f
Lady's Magazine 78
Lady's Pictorial 148
Lady's Practical Guide to the Science of Horsemanship, The (Reeves) 99
Laffaye, Horace 21

Index   311

Lancosme-Brèves, Comte Savary de 113
Landry, Donna 25, 79
Landscape: as damned pewey-country 67;
   and horse sports in Britain 18, 25, 60,
   63, 65–68, 73, 79–80, 95, 140–143,
   152–154; and horse sports in India 197;
   Hungarian 157; in India 194, 197, 199;
   management of 67, 143–144
   see also Fences; Hedges; Railroads;
   Enclosure movement; Fox Hunting
Landseer, Sir Edwin 137
La selle et le costume de l'amazone (Pellier)
   112–113
Lawley, Celia 215
Lawley, Ursula 215
Lawn Tennis; see Tennis
Lawrence, John 94, 118, 121
Leaping: instructions on 99, 193;
   see also Jumping
Leaping head [Third Pommel] 89, 100,
   110–116, 114f, 120, 126, 141, 142f, 160,
   163, 193; as hunting pommel 117;
   origins of 110–111; and women as fox
   hunters 117–120; see also Crutch
   [Second Pommel]
Leather: equipment made of 48;
   saddles made of 47; sidesaddles
   made of 48
Le Clerc, Henrietta 64–65, 138
*Lectures on Horsemanship Wherein Is
   Explained Every Necessary Instruction for
   Both Ladies and Gentlemen* (T.S.) 57–58
Leicester, Earl of 6
Leicestershire, hunting in 66, 69–70
Leisure: after first World War 229;
   commercialization of 18; and horse
   sports 17–18, 54, 95–96; in interwar
   years 22; mixed-gender public spheres
   of 79
Lennox, Charles (third Duke of
   Richmond) 64
Lennox, Lord William Pitt 76
Le Siècle 112
Liberation [women's] 31, 290–292;
   see also Emancipation
Libraries, circulating 54
Liedtke, Walter 17
Linton, Eliza Lynn 240
Literacy, female, in Georgian
   England 54
Llewellyn, Harry 288
Lloyd George, David 256

Lockley, Olga 161
Logan, Miss 248
Loisset, Emilie 158, 161
London: and horse sports, in early 19th c.
   71–72; Victorian, riding in 97;
   see also Park Riding; Rotten Row
London Labour and London Poor
   (Mayhew) 140
Longrigg, Roger 25
Loraine Smith, Charles 118, 119f
"Loraine Smith Family, The"
   (Ferneley) 118
Loughborough 70
Lowther, Lady 257
Loyo, Caroline 11, 113
Ludford, Juliana 63
Lyall, Cora 190–192
Lyall, Sir Alfred Comyn 190, 199
Lyon, Dorothy 289
Lysias 1

MacKenzie, John 181
Maddison, Ivy 211, 240f
Madras Hounds 195
Madras Hunt 195
Magna Carta, horsewoman's 114f, 127
"Maltese Cat, The" (Kipling) 208
Man and the Natural World (Thomas) 24
Mangan, J. A. 21
Manners, Miss 121
Mansey, Lewis 92
Margaret (Princess) 285
Market Harborough 71; in Great War 253
Markham, Gervase 10
Marsh, Sam 286, 288
Marshall, Mary 289f
Martelli, Kate 183
Martineau, Harriet 88
Martineau, Mrs. Philip 146–147, 161
Masculinity: British imperialism and
   20–21, 184; deviant, in early 19th c. 78;
   horsemanship and 12, 26; and hunting,
   in early 19th c 70–74, 80, 123; imperial
   identity and 181; and imperial life
   182–183; martial 78; in 18th-c. Britain
   46; Victorian ideals and 16;
   see also Gender
Masham, Lady 258
Mason, James ("Jem") 138, 159
Mason, Mrs. 161
Master of Foxhounds (M.F.H.s): in British
   India 195; female 44–45, 252–257,

254f–255f, 258, 293; responsibilities of 253
Master of Game, The 59
Mattfield, Monica 26
Maxse, Mr. 68
May, Mrs. Jack 249, 269
Mayhew, Barry 140
Mayhew and Co 283
McCall's (magazine), cover image of female equestrian 295f
McClintock, Anne 20
McClintock, Isa 253, 257
McCrone, Kathleen 24
McKenzie, Callum 21
McNeil, Lady Hilda 270
McTaggart, M. F. 259, 268–269, 287, 294
Mechanical horse-exercise machines 160
Medici, Catherine de (French Queen) 5
Meerut Tent Club 205
Melancholy 92
Melbourne, Lord 96
Melton Mowbray 70–71, 78, 120–123, 143–144; in Great War 252; ladies' polo at 243f
"Memoirs of a Celebrated Sporting Lady" (Lady Dareall) 94
Men: dependence on, decried 150, 154; in horse sports, women's superiority to 76, 119–120, 171, 232, 248; in remount depot work; riding sidesaddle 102, 103f
Mental health, female, Victorian views on 92
Menzies, Mrs. Stuart 140, 149, 185, 214, 233
Menzies, Stuart Alexander 233
Meynell, Hugo 44, 54, 65–66, 69–71, 80, 120, 144
Meynellian Science, The (Meynell) 54
Meysey-Thompson, R. F. 236
Middle Ages, female equestrians in 3–4, 3f
Middleton, Captain "Bay" 159, 171
Milbanke, Lady Augusta 68, 92
Militarism, and masculine identity 21
Military, use of horses in 8–9
Military horses: after First World War 229; in First World War 245
see also Remount depots
Military revolution (17th c.) 7
Military styles, and women's riding clothes 52–53, 105
Modern Riding and Horse Education (Birch) 232

Modern Riding-Master, The: or, A Key to the Knowledge of the Horse, and Horsemanship: with Several Necessary rules for Young Horsemen (Astley) 58
Modern Side-Saddle Riding: A Practical Handbook for Horsewomen (Christy) 234
Molier, Ernest 12
Montagu, Lady Mary Wortley 15, 283
Montpellier Riding School 99
Montresor, Mrs. John 52
Moody, Tom 63
Morning ride, in India 188, 190, 191f, 194
Mount a horse, women's ability to 150
Mount and Man: A Key to Better Horsemanship (McTaggart) 259, 269
Mr. Crop's Harriers (Bowers) 230, 231f
"Mr. and Mrs. Thomas Coltman" (Wright) 51f
Mule, ridden by Lady Dufferin, in India 194
Munnings, Alfred 284
Muntjac hunting 195
Musgrave, Sir James 81
Musters, Mrs. John 52
Mytens, Daniel 6
Mytton, John 71, 72f

Napoleon Bonaparte 75
Napoleonic Wars 10–11, 46, 58, 105, 124
National identity: equestrians in India and 218–219; equitation and 11, 15, 25–26, 124; horsewomen and 15–17, 169, 170f; sport and 218–219; hunting 126, 170; during war 256
National School of Equitation 243f
National sport, hunting as 124–126
Neck or nothing 69
Needle threading 238–239
Nesbitt, Colonel 182
Neuadd-Fawr Foxhounds 253–255, 255f
Newall, J. T. 204
Newcastle, Duchess of 234
Newcastle Courant 75
"New Hunter, A —Tally ho! Tally ho!" (Alken) 72f
Nicholson, Thomas Henry 76f
Nilgiri Sporting Reminiscences (Dawson) 195, 196f, 204
Nimrod; see Apperley, Charles James ("Nimrod")
Nimrod's Yorkshire Tour 182

Nouveau manuel complet d'équitation à l'usage des deux sexes (Vergnaud) 113
Nouveau riche 18, 54

Oakes, Augustus Frederick 185, 191*f*, 192–193
Observations on Foxhunting (Cook) 54
O'Connell, Alice L. 288–289
O'Donoghue, Nannie Power 141, 143, 148–151, 153, 160–161, 163, 167–168, 168*f*, 193, 231, 234
Oldaker, Thomas Fitzhardinge 110–111
Old Forest Ranger, The (Campbell) 198*f*, 206
"Old Shikarri, The"; *see* Dawson, G.A.R.
Oldstock, Olivia 77
"Old Woman's Observation, An, on Reading the Account of Mrs. Thornton's recent Race at York" (Oldstock) 77
Olympic Games: British Equestrian Team (1952) 288–289; British female equestrians and 283–284, 288–290 *see also* Show jumping; Smythe, Patricia ("Pat")
Ootacamund; *see* Ooty (Ootacamund)
Ooty (Ootacamund): gymkhana events in 201; hunting in 195–196, 196*f*, 198*f*; promenade in 187; subscription pack in 196
"Ooty Hunt Meet" (Dawson) 196*f*
Orientalism 20; equine 25
Osbaldistone, Frank (Scott's fictional character) 88–89
Osborne, Carol 24
Our Viceregal life in India (Lady Dufferin) 200
Overriding the hounds 147, 159
"Over the Five Bars" (Sturgess) 145*f*
Ovid 204
Owen, Rosamund 26, 292
Owen and Co. 283
Oxers 144

Paget, Guy 161
Paget, J. Otho 242
Paget, Sidney 237*f*
Painting the town red 71
Palethorpe, Dawn 289*f*
Pandian, M.S.S. 183
Pantaloons 109

Paper chasing 20–21, 202, 203*f*, 267
Park riding 91, 95, 117, 140; decline of 141
Park Riding (Dunbar) 117
Parratt, Catriona 24
Paterson, M. Jeanne 294
Payne, Charles 183
Peculiar Privilege: A Social History of English Foxhunting, 1753–1885 (Itzkowitz) 25
Peel, Sir Robert 97
Pegasus 1
Pelham, Cecil 293
Pellier, Jules 14, 111–113
Pennell Elmhirst, Edward 155, 164, 171, 184, 229, 273
Peshawur Vale Hunt 197
Peters, J. G. 99
Petite Vénerie, la 13
Petticoats 106, 108*f*, 164
Phillips, Zara 290
Physical education 23
Physical health, female, Victorian views on 92,
Pig sticking: in Britain 238–239, 238*f*; in India 21, 185, 203–208, 207*f*, 218–219, 236; history of 204; popularity of 204–205; safety concerns with 206–208, 207*f*; sidesaddle and 208; spears and spearing methods for 204–205; women riding astride and 214–215
Pillion 4, 50, 77
Pilot(s) 138, 152–154; Empress Elizabeth and 158–159
Pitman, T. T. 246
Pitt, William, the Elder 91
Pitts, James E. 272*f*
Planchette 4
Plumb, J. H. 18, 25
Poacher 183
Point-to-point races 287–288
Pole, Mrs. 153
Politics 293; and female equestrianism 45; 18th-c., women and 45
Pollard, James 62*f*
Polo 21, 236, 272; adoption in Britain 236–242; in British India 181, 185, 208–213, 218–219; development of 208, 239; and imperial ideology 183; military and warlike characteristics of 209
Polo ball (ladies') 238–239
Polocrosse 243*f*
Polo in India (Younghusband) 241

314 Index

Polo Magazine 241
Polo Monthly, The 211, 212f
Polo players, female: in Britain 239–242, 243f; in British India 210–213, 212f, 240f
Polo pony(ies) 194, 209–210; prices for 210; retired, as riding horses 146; training and conditioning, by women 209–210
"Polo Post Futurum" 239, 240f
Pommel 5, 7; impalement on 160; second; *see* Crutch; third; *see* Leaping head; *see also* Sidesaddle
Ponies and Children (Blewitt) 267
Ponies' Progress (Durand) 268
Pony(ies): children's, in Great War 266; *see also* Polo pony(ies)
Pony Club 187, 243f, 268; British Pony Club 287
Portal, Lady 253, 257
Postcard, Victorian, showing fox hunting 170f
Potato race 239
Power, women's 16, 28, 126
Practical Hints for Hunting Novices (Richardson) 232
Practical Horsemanship (Kerr) 230
Practical Physician, The (Mansey) 92
Pretty horsebreakers 136, 149, 192; and polo ponies in India 210
Prince of Wales (18th c.) 59, 62f, 63
Prince of Wales (early 19th c.) 75
Principles of Modern Riding for Ladies (Allen) 46, 98
Procida, Mary 181
Propriety, French ideas of 12
Prostitutes, in Melton 71
Pryse-Rice, Mrs. 253, 258
Public behaviors: equestrianism and 95; gender ideals and 17; riding lessons and 57; *see also* Separate Spheres
Punch, "Polo Post Futurum" 239, 240f
Pur-sang 12
Purvis, June 290
Pytchley Hunt 70, 161, 257, 284–285

Quadra, Álvaro de la 6
Quarme Harriers 255
Queen, The 147, 233, 269–270
Queen Mary Psalter 3f
Quorndon Hall 70

Quorn Hunt 44, 65, 70, 138, 161, 234; in Great War 252

Raber, Karen 25
Raby hunt 156
Raby pack 67
Race, British Empire and 20, 183–184, 202, 206
Racehorses, retired, as riding horses 146
Raciana (Egan) 76
Railroads, and participation in horse sports 140–141, 153
Railway age, and golden age of hunting 141–143
Ramsden, Caroline 26
Ranelagh: gymkhanas at 236, 237f, 239; ladies' polo at 243f; polo at 239, 241
Ravenscroft, Dorothy 247
Records of the Chase ("Cecil") 156
Recreation, and equitation 10
Reeves, George 93, 99, 104
Regency era 16
Reins 48, 104
Reiters 7
Religion: and horse sport 14; *see also* Catholic Church
Remount depots: in First World War, women's work in 245–248, 246f, 258; staff 248
Renaissance, and equestrian practices 7
"Rendezvous of the Quor'n Hounds at Grooby Pool, The" (Loraine Smith) 119f
Renz, Elisa 158
Rescue race 239
Reynolds, Sir Joshua 52
Richard II (King) 4
Richardson, Charles 232–233
Richardson, Mary 117
Richardson, Mervyn 100, 105, 115, 118
Richmond, Duchess of (1760) 52
Richmond, Duke of (1739) 60
Richmond, Duke of (early 1800s) 63
Richmond Horse Show 288
Riding 94; gender ideals and 16–17; revival after first World War 229, 264
Riding, Driving and Kindred Sports (Dale) 232
Riding: On the Flat and Across Country (Hayes) 148

Riding and Driving for Women (Beach) 234
Riding aside; *see* Sidesaddle
Riding astride (by women) 295*f*; acceptance of 234, 268*f*; advantages of 213, 262–264, 284, 286–287; advocacy for 232–234, 235*f*, 260–261; ban on 286; in Britain 228–229; in British India 213–215, 218–219; Catholic views on 4; clothing for 215–217, 269–271; criticism of 233–234; and equality 171; and female advantages 293; female Masters and 253–255, 255*f*; First World War and 249, 250*f*, 258, 271–273; and genital stimulation 4; history of 271, 283–284, 286–288, 294; for hunting 212–213; imperial ideology and 21, 181–182, 236–239, 268; in India 199; in Middle Ages 3–4, 3*f*; for polo 210–213, 212*f*, 240*f*; in remount depot work 248–249; and women's war work 258; young girls and 265–268, 266*f*, 268*f see also* Cross-saddle
Riding for Children (Faulkner-Horne) 268
Riding for Ladies (Kerr) 148, 230
Riding for Ladies, with Hints on the Stable (O'Donoghue) 148, 193
Riding habit(s) 26, 52–53, 88–89, 108*f*; after Great War 269–271; costs of 259; designed by women 270; and femininity 269–271; in India 188, 189*f*; modern, evolution of 216; plain and functional 163; for riding astride 215–217; safety concerns and 161–169; second-hand 167–168; skirt of 105–107; before World War I 242–244 *see also* Clothes/clothing
Riding instructors, female, in First World War 245
Riding manuals 53–58, 91, 124; advice on colonial riding 185, 191*f*, 192–194; after First World War 258–265; published in India 185; and riding astride 234; for women 46–48, 50–52, 54–55, 56*f*, 57–58, 102–104, 141, 146, 182–183, 234, 261; 1805–1857 97; and women in horse sports 79
Riding masters 101–102
"Riding on Horseback Recommended" 92
Riding schools 46–47, 55–58, 95, 98–104, 149–150, 264; French 124; in India 192–193; and women in horse sports 79

Riding styles: development in Britain 7–10, 55–57, 124; horse breeds and 25
Rifle and Spear with the Rajpoots (Gardner) 206, 207*f*
Rigby, Mrs. 247
Ring-spearing; *see* Tilting
Ripon Ladies' Plate 75
"Rising Woman and the Falling Man, The" (Collett) 79
RMS *Franconia* 160
RMS *Titanic* 160
Robeson, Peter 288, 289*f*
Rob Roy (Scott) 88–89
Roche, Daniel 26
Roehampton Club 288
Roger, Alfred 7, 112
Rotten Row 89, 124, 136, 149, 192; in India 187
"Rotten-Row, Hyde Park" (*The Illustrated London News*) 90*f*
Royal Dublin Society Horse Show (1868) 286
Rugby 23
Russell, Fox 230
Russell, Mrs. 69, 94
Russley Park 247

Saddle: history of 47; hunting 60; for hunting 47; leather 47 *see also* Cross-saddle; Sidesaddle
Saddle flap 5
Saddle of Queens, The: The Story of the Side-Saddle (Bloodgood) 26
Saddle pad 7
Saddle skirt (cloth) 5, 6*f*
Safe (of saddle) 48
Safety concerns: balance strap and 115; clothes and 161–169; and clothing on horseback 105–106; equipment addressing 141; with horse sports 54, 64, 68–69; for horsewomen 159–161; leaping head and 113–114; with pig sticking 206–208, 207*f*; and riding astride 214; riding habits and 107; with riding in Victorian London 97; sidesaddle and 4, 54, 67–69, 113–114, 116, 153, 160, 162, 171, 233, 263; wire fences and 144
Safety habit 162
Safety skirts 164–165; designed by women 270; types of 165–167, 166*f*

Said, Edward 20
St. Eustace 14
St. Hubert 14
Salisbury, Marchioness of 68, 70, 76
Sambur hunting 195
Sartorius, John Nost 50
Savory, Isabel 197–199, 206–208, 214, 218
School for Horse and Rider (Hance) 142*f*, 260
Schooling ring(s), in India 192
Scott, Joan 15
Scott, Sir Walter 3, 88
Scottish Moors and Indian Jungles: Scenes of Sport in the Lews and India (Newall) 204
"Scrutator" 143
Season, The: A Satire (Austin) 136
Self-possession: of British women in India 192, 218–219; equestrianism and 27, 126, 150–157, 291
Separate spheres 30, 154, 216, 294; ideology of 47, 75, 78–79, 91; Victorian ideals and 16–17; *see also* Gender; Victorian era
Sex Discrimination Removal Act (1919) 22
Sexuality: female involvement in horse racing and 77; French ideas of 12; riding and 79; and riding position 4
Seymour, James 7, 8*f*
Seymour Place 98, 159
Shakespear, Henry 204, 218
Shedden, Lady Diana Maude 234, 261–263, 267, 271, 283–284, 288, 290–291
Sherer, Joseph Ford 209
Sherwood, Adam 119*f*
Shockaert, Brigitte 289
Shooter (person) 183
Short Treatise on Hunting, A (Cockayne) 59
Show jumping 286–288; fence height for 144, 145*f*; Olympic 144, 145*f*, 284, 289; Pony Club and 267; by young girls 287 *see also* Smythe, Patricia ("Pat")
"Shrew Tamed, the" (Landseer) 137
Sidesaddle: abandonment of 185, 208, 234; adjustable for either side of horse 94, 114, 160; advocacy for 228, 232, 234, 261, 263; books on 26; construction of 4–6, 6*f*; costs of 259; disabled riders and 261; disadvantages of 230, 240*f*,

259–260, 263–264, 268–269; Elizabeth II and 285; in France 112; history of 4–7, 47–48, 283–286, 293–294; and horse racing 75–76; horse training for 186, 259; and hunting 14–15; in India 188, 189*f*, 198*f*, 203*f*, 206, 208, 213–214; introduced to England 4; and jumping 68; leather 48; materials used for 5, 6*f*; men's use of 102, 103*f*, 260; and polo 240*f*, 241–242; safety concerns and 4, 49–50, 67–69, 113–114, 116, 153, 160, 162, 171, 233, 263; shipping, problems of 213; in Shires 284; single-pommel 5, 6*f*; stress caused by 93; two-pommel 2*f*, 7, 8*f*–9*f*, 48–52, 49*f*, 51*f*, 54, 56, 67–69, 79, 110, 112–114, 116; weight of 213, 263; and women's inequality in hunting field 171; young girls and 265, 266*f see also* Balance strap; Leaping head; Crutch; Pommel
Sidesaddle (Archer Houblon) 284–285
Side-Saddle Riding: A Practical Handbook for Horsewomen (Christy) 148–149, 234
Sidney, Samuel 13, 147–152, 162, 186, 192, 219
Simla, 187, 193, 200, 202
Singh, Hanut 215
Singleton, John 185
"Sisi"; *see* Elizabeth, Empress of Austria
"Sixteen String Jack" (highwayman) 64
Skillen, Fiona 24
Skirt(s): divided 214, 216, 228, 242–244, 270–271, 272*f*; elastic straps for 165; hunting 163; pinning of 105–106; of riding habits 105–107; safety concerns and 162–163; weighted with lead 107, 165 *see also* Apron skirt; Safety skirts
"Skittles"; *see* Walters, Catherine ("Skittles")
Slipper stirrup 9*f*, 50
Sloth bear, Indian, hunting of 204
Smith, Horace 285
Smith, Lindsay 113
Smith, Sir Sidney 6
Smith, Thomas Ashton 69
Smoke Rings (Lyon) 289
Smyth, Montague 217, 249, 250*f*
Smythe, Patricia ("Pat") 284–285, 288–290, 289*f*, 292; receives OBE 290
"Snaffles" [Charles Payne] 183

Index 317

Social hierarchy: equestrianism and 17–18, 57, 62, 146, 155–156; and fox hunting 18–19, 146; imperialism and 183–184, 202, 203f; and riding in India 187, 202, 203f see also Aristocracy; Class
Social mobility, equestrianism and 63–65, 95, 136–137, 137f, 138
"Soft tumble after a Hard Ride, A" (Collett) 79
Somerville, Edith 229, 246, 253, 272, 283, 292
Southwick, ladies' polo at 243f
Spear(s), for boar hunting in India 205
Spencer, Charles (third Duke of Marlborough) 7
Spencer, Elizabeth (wife of third Duke of Marlborough; Lady Charles Spencer) 7, 52
Spencer, Lady (18th c.) 6
Spencer jacket 53
Spinal injury(ies), in horsewomen 161
Splittercockation pace 68–69
Sport: British, imperialism and 21; and civilizing process 17; equestrianism and 26–28; as male domain 23; and women's liberation 290
Sport, Foxhunting and Shooting (Lord Dorchester) 264
Sport [term], definition of 26
Sport and the British (Holt) 23
Sporting and Dramatic News, The 161
Sporting ideals, British Empire and 184–185
Sporting Magazine, The 44–45, 50, 62, 64, 67–69, 73, 75, 80, 94, 117, 195
Sports history(ies) 23–24
Sports psychology 261
Sportswoman in India, A (Savory) 208
Stag hunting 59, 63, 65, 72
Stamford, Lady 138–139
Stamford, Lord 138
Stanford, J. K. 195
Stanhope, Lady Hester 118
Stanley, Edward 95, 98–99, 105–106, 110
Starr, Leonora 186
Statues, equestrian 17
Steeplechasing 287–288
Steevens, G. W. 215
Stewart, Robert 209
Stirrup(s) 49f, 50, 51f, 60; length of 104; safety 141, 162; with sidesaddle 4, 7; skirts and 106 see also Slipper stirrup

Stoddard, Mrs. 80
Stormont, Lord 121
Stow, John 3
Straddle position; see Riding astride (by women)
Straddle-skirts 244
Stringer, Thomas 9f, 50
Stubbs, George 7, 48, 52, 54, 64
Sturgess, J. 145f
Suffragettes 23, 291–292
Summerhays, R. S. 285
Surcingle 50
Surtees, Robert Smith 67, 73, 118–119, 125, 143
Sussex, hunting in 68
Swart, Sandra 185

Tailby, W. W. 139
Tailor(s): vs. female dressmaker 107, 270; in India 217; male 165, 270
"Tally-Ho!" (Turner) 123f
Taunton Polo Club (Somerset) 212f, 213
Taunton Vale Harriers 213, 228, 255
Tautz 244, 271
Taymouth Hours 3–4, 3f
Tent clubs 204
Tennis [Lawn Tennis] 23, 27, 96, 219, 280, 292, 298
Tent-pegging 200–201, 236, 238, 240–241; lances used for 205
Thacker, Spink and Co. 193
Thackeray, William 20
Thane, Pat 22, 292
The Field 284
Thirsk, Joan 17–18
Thomas, fourth Lord Leigh 6
Thomas, Keith 24
Thompson, F.M.L. 140, 229
Thornton, Alicia 75–77, 76f, 81
Thornton, Thomas 75, 77
Thoroughbred breed 13, 26, 66, 146
Thoughts on Hunting (Beckford) 54, 126
Three-day eventing: Olympic 289; Princess Anne and 290
Thynne, Lady Edward 121
Tiger hunting 183
"Tigers I Have Shot" (Martelli) 183
Tilting 21, 200–201, 201f, 209, 236, 237f, 238, 240–241; lances used for 205
"Tilting at the Ring at Ranelagh" (Paget) 237f
Times, The 233–234, 248–249

Tomlinson, Miss; see Hughes, Mrs. Charles (Miss Tomlinson)
Tournament 7
"To whom the goddess . . .": Hunting and Riding for Women (Shedden and Apsley) 234, 283–284
Transport, riding for, in India 187
Treatise on the Art of Horsemanship, A (Peters) 99
Trollope, Anthony 19, 120, 123, 140, 142
Trooping the Colour 285
Tropical Trials: A Handbook for Women in the Tropics 217–218
Trousers: riding 164, 215; women's wearing of 15, 108, 269–271
Trypanosomiasis 185
T.S. ("professor of horsemanship") 57–58
Tucker, Treva 25–26
Turf, The (Vamplew) 25
Turner, (Miss) A. O 239
Turner, Francis Calcraft 122f–123f
"Two of Peter Beckford's Hunters" (Stubbs) 54
Tyacke, Mrs. R. H. 214

Undergarments, for female riders 107–108, 108f
Underhill, George 146, 156–157, 159, 170, 241, 253
Unicorn(s), females' taming of 1
Urban riding 89–90, 90f, 91, 95, 140, 154; dangers of 97

Vamplew, Wray 25
Vane, Arabella 93
van Somer, Paul 6
Veblen, Thorstein 18
Veil(s), for female riders 109–110
Velvet, sidesaddle made of 5–6, 6f
Venery, in Europe 13
Vergnaud, A. D. 113
Vernon, Diana (Scott's fictional character) 3, 88–89
Vickery, Amanda 16, 91
Victoria (Queen) 91, 94, 102, 103f, 120; on Empress Elizabeth 158; equestrian pursuits of 96; Grant's equestrian painting of 2f; on riding as "good for the nerves" 92; riding lessons 101; sidesaddle use by 120

Victoria, Countess of Yarborough 116
Victorian era: femininity in 16, 90, 140; gendered spaces in 16; gender ideals in 96; women as frailer sex in 91–92; women's sporting participation in 24; see also Separate Spheres; Civilizing Influence
"Vielle Moustache" (pseudonym); see Henderson, Robert
Vindication of the Rights of Woman, A (Wollstonecraft) 45–46
Vine Hunt 257
Voting rights 22–23, 283, 292, 294

Waldemar of Prussia, Prince 187
Walers 185–186
Walker, Donald 93–94, 109, 125, 160
Walters, Catherine ("Skittles") 13, 136–139, 137f, 149, 152, 157–159, 163
War(s): in 18th century 46; see also Boer War; see also First World War; see also Napoleonic Wars
Ward, James 49f
War work, women's, in First World War 244–249, 258; see also Remount depots
Waterford, Marquis of 71
Watson, J.N.P. 209
Wayte, Samuel C. 100–101, 106–108, 115–116
Wealth, and horse sports 17–18, 47, 54, 95, 155–156
Wedgwood, Josiah and Sarah 48
Weil, Kari 12, 26
Wellington, Arthur Wellesley, Duke of 11, 44, 96
What-Not, The, or Ladies' Handy-Book 97, 109
Whippers-In, female 253, 255
Whipping 151
Whippy (Whippy Steggall & Co.) 50
White, John 69
White, Wilf 289f
Whitehead, Susan 289f
Whiting, Noëla 211–213, 212f, 228, 255; Brander-Dunbar, Mrs. James 211
Whitney, Caspar 169, 228
Whyte-Melville, George 152–153, 171
Wife of Bath 4
Wild boars, Indian: characteristics of 203; see also Pig sticking

Wilde, Oscar 21, 198f
"Wild Women as Social Insurgents, The" (Linton) 240
Wilkinson and Kidd 50
William III (King) 90f
William IV (King) 100
Willoughby de Broke, Lady 234
Willoughby de Broke, Lord 159
Willoughby de Eresby, Lady 161
Wilson, Harriette 70–71
Wilton, Countess of 118
Wilton, Major 283
Wimbledon, gymkhanas at 236, 238
Winter, T.W. 271
Wire fences 144
Wiseman, Nicholas 100, 109, 125
Wollstonecraft, Mary 45–46
"Woman Wearing a Round Hat, Riding to Right" (Seymour) 8f
Women in the Hunting Field (Menzies) 140, 185, 233
Women of England (Ellis) 91
Women's movement 294; equestrianism and 290–294

Woodville, R. Caton 191f
Wool: in First World War 249; for sporting garments 52–53, 163
Wootton, John 7
Worsley, Lady 52–53
Wortley, Hon. Mrs. J. (née Jane Lawley) 2f
Wright, Joseph 51f
Wycherley, George 116
Wyndham, Mrs. Colonel 118
Wynter, Maude V. 268f

Young Horsewoman's Compendium of the Modern Art of Riding (Stanley) 98–99
Younghusband, G. J. (Captain) 185, 241
Young Lady's Book, The 96, 99, 106
Young Lady's Equestrian Assistant, The (Oakes) 185, 191f, 193
Young Lady's Equestrian Manual, The 89, 99–100, 104, 107, 110, 193

Zweiniger-Bargielowska, Ina 22

Milton Keynes UK
Ingram Content Group UK Ltd.
UKHW031500071224
451979UK00015B/166